The ANC's War against Apartheid

The ANC's War against Apartheid

UMKHONTO WE SIZWE AND
THE LIBERATION OF SOUTH AFRICA

STEPHEN R. DAVIS

INDIANA UNIVERSITY PRESS

This book is a publication of

Indiana University Press
Office of Scholarly Publishing
Herman B Wells Library 350
1320 East 10th Street
Bloomington, Indiana 47405 USA

iupress.indiana.edu

© 2018 by Stephen Davis

All rights reserved

No part of this book may be reproduced or utilized in any form or by any means, electronic or mechanical, including photocopying and recording, or by any information storage and retrieval system, without permission in writing from the publisher.

The paper used in this publication meets the minimum requirements of the American National Standard for Information Sciences—Permanence of Paper for Printed Library Materials, ANSI Z39.48-1992.

Manufactured in the United States of America

Library of Congress Cataloging-in-Publication Data

Names: Davis, Stephen R., author.
Title: The ANC's war against apartheid: Umkhonto we Sizwe and the liberation of South Africa / Stephen R. Davis.
Description: Bloomington, Indiana : Indiana University Press, 2018. | Includes bibliographical references and index.
Identifiers: LCCN 2017053535 (print) | LCCN 2017051095 (ebook) | ISBN 9780253032300 (e-book) | ISBN 9780253032287 (hardback : alk. paper) | ISBN 9780253032294 (pbk. : alk. paper)
Subjects: LCSH: Umkhonto we Sizwe (South Africa)--History. | African National Congress--History. | Anti-apartheid movements--South Africa. | Government, Resistance to--South Africa. | South Africa--History--1961-1994.
Classification: LCC DT1953 (print) | LCC DT1953 .D38 2018 (ebook) | DDC 322.420968--dc23
LC record available at https://lccn.loc.gov/2017053535

1 2 3 4 5 23 22 21 20 19 18

CONTENTS

Acknowledgments		vii
List of Abbreviations		xi
Introduction		xiii
1	A Brief History of Umkhonto we Sizwe and the Armed Struggle	1
2	"I Am Not Prepared to Answer at This Stage": History, Evidence, and the Mamre Camp, December 26–30, 1962	26
3	The Sight of Battle: Visuality, History, and Representations of the Wankie Campaign, July 31–September 8, 1967	58
4	Losing the Plot: Mystery, Narrativity, and Investigation in Novo Catengue, May 1977–March 1979	85
5	Everyday Life during Wartime: Experience, Modes of Writing, and the Underground in Cape Town during the Long Decade of the 1980s	127
	Conclusion: Making the Struggle Concrete; Nationalist Historiography at Freedom Park	197
	Appendix A: Lists of ANC Members Killed in the Matola Raid	229
	Appendix B: ANC/MK Deaths in Angola by Category	230
	Appendix C: ANC/MK Combat Deaths by Country	231
	Appendix D: ANC/MK Combat Deaths by Country	232
	Bibliography	233
	Index	261

ACKNOWLEDGMENTS

MANY INDIVIDUALS CONTRIBUTED TO THE research, writing, and revision of this book in ways that extend beyond any neat categorization but warrant special foregrounding. This book would not have been possible without the advice, encouragement, and support given to me by Luise White. Luise has been a reliable adviser, a close confidante, and trusted friend to me during every stage of this project. Although I could thank her for any number of things, I may have benefited most from her vast personal archive of analogies, anecdotes, metaphors, and one-liners about this kind of work. Her knack for offering the right thing at the right time has gotten me out of any number of binds, intellectual and otherwise; kept me from taking myself too seriously; and got me to think about history in exciting ways. I am forever grateful to her for these things and for much more than I can describe here. Patricia Hayes offered indispensable guidance and generous support at critical moments during my fieldwork in South Africa. Her keen eye and attention to detail allowed me to notice far more about this history than I would have on my own. Additionally, her interventions during my fieldwork prevented me from making countless errors and saved me from expending time and energy on dead ends. David Hlongwane helped me negotiate a path into veteran communities in the Western Cape and beyond. I owe him a debt of gratitude for helping me to establish my bona fides among them and for arranging interviews with individuals who would otherwise have been inaccessible to me. I am grateful to Anne Mager for her kind hospitality and for opening a window onto the personal dimensions of political activism in South Africa. Liz Gunner graciously hosted me during several research trips to Johannesburg and offered her valuable thoughts about how to approach questions of interpretation and the complexities of performance. I am especially indebted to the late Malixoli Hadi and his family and comrades who opened my eyes to the predicaments faced by veterans. My awareness of these predicaments shaped my interpretations of this history in incalculable ways.

This book would not have been possible without the education and support I received as a graduate student at the University of Florida. Leo Villalón's ever enthusiastic efforts as director of the African Studies Center at the University of Florida greatly contributed to my intellectual development as a student of African history. Peter Malanchuk and Dan Reboussin went above and beyond their duties as Africana librarians in finding me obscure materials and in helping me think laterally about research. Mantoa Smouse clued me into the wonderfully rich and varied ways South Africans use language to construct meaning and express themselves. I hope that at least a fraction of the subtleties she pointed out to me over the years are represented in this book. The History Department consistently provided generous financial support during each of my seven years in Florida. Last but not least, Hunt and Jean Davis provided me with funds that allowed me to travel to South Africa to sketch out the contours of this project and try my hand at interviewing.

Several institutions and individuals provided essential resources that allowed me to continue to research, write, and revise this book. The Fulbright-Hayes DDRA fellowship program funded my fieldwork in South Africa in 2007–2008. I am also grateful to the US embassy staff in Pretoria and the Cape Town consulate for their kind support and careful guidance during that time. The University of Kentucky enabled me to complete the final stages of writing and revision. Mark Kornbluh, as the dean of the College of Arts and Sciences, provided me with funds for several additional research trips to South Africa and gave generous support for a number of initiatives that have made South Africa an enduring part of the curriculum and intellectual life at the University of Kentucky. Karen Petrone, as chair of the History Department, made good on her commitment to create an environment where junior scholars could flourish. I recognize that I am a direct beneficiary of her sincere effort to make funding and time available to me and my cohort while we finish our first books. I am grateful to my colleagues at the University Kentucky for providing thoughtful comments on several draft chapters and for being so welcoming and collegial over the past six years.

Several archives provided the sources and research experiences that form the basis of this book. The staff at the Mayibuye Centre Archive not only assisted me in finding material but also provided me with a revealing introduction into the politics of archives. This initiation of sorts tempered my reading of the materials that I collected there and elsewhere. Nicky van Driel provided me with material from her personal archive that reshaped my understanding of the Wankie Campaign. Derek du Bruyn at the National Museum in Bloemfontein directed my attention to the invaluable archive of interview transcripts that he and his colleagues recorded with veterans in the Free State. Joel Krieg assisted me in finding the trial records that formed the basis of my chapter on the underground in Cape Town. Kennedy Rampeng granted me unprecedented access to the materials that he collected before and after his participation in the Write Your Own History workshops at the University of the Western Cape.

The revision of this book was influenced greatly by incisive readings of drafts and engaged conversations about how to improve them. Nicky Rousseau and Gary Baines provided me with incredibly insightful comments on the penultimate draft of the manuscript, identifying weaknesses that had escaped my attention, confirming my doubts about others, and explaining what was going on in terms I could not articulate on my own. I could not have asked for better readings of my work at such a critically important time in the revision process. At very short notice, Albie Sachs read an entire draft of this manuscript and offered me valuable thoughts from his dual perspective as an active participant and an empathetic observer. At the eleventh hour, Chris Gifford identified problems in my chapter on the underground and suggested useful ways to clarify things. Stephen Ellis patiently answered my questions about his work over the years and applied his sharp intellect and ample experience to problems that I encountered in my own research and writing. Finally, I am grateful to Denis Goldberg for being such a welcoming, passionate, and opinionated interlocutor.

LIST OF ABBREVIATIONS

ANC	African National Congress
APC	Area Politico-Military Committee
APLA	African People's Liberation Army
BCM	Black Consciousness Movement
CIO	Central Intelligence Office (Rhodesia)
COSATU	Congress of South African Trade Unions
FOSATU	Federation of South African Trade Unions
FRELIMO	Mozambique Liberation Front/Frente de Libertação de Moçambique
MCW	Military and Combat Work
MK	Umkhonto we Sizwe
MKMVA	Umkhonto we Sizwe Military Veterans Association
MPLA	People's Movement for the Liberation of Angola
MWT	Marxist Workers' Tendency
NAT	Department of National Security
NEUM	Non-European Unity Movement
NP	National Party
NPA	National Prosecuting Authority
NSMS	National Security Management System

OAU	Organization of African Unity
PAC	Pan-Africanist Congress
PAFMESCA	Pan-African Freedom Movement for East, Central, and Southern Africa
RAR	Rhodesian African Rifles
RENAMO	Mozambican National Resistance/Resistência Nacional Moçambicana
SAAF	South African Air Force
SACP	South African Communist Party
SADET	South African Democracy Education Trust
SADF	South African Defense Force
SANDF	South African National Defense Force
SWAPO	South West Africa People's Organization
TANU	Tanganyika African National Union
UNITA	União Nacional para a Independência Total de Angola
ZAPU	Zimbabwe African People's Union
ZIPRA	Zimbabwean People's Revolutionary Army

INTRODUCTION

THIS BOOK EXAMINES FIVE EPISODES during the armed struggle fought by Umkhonto we Sizwe (MK), the army composed of and commanded by members of the African National Congress (ANC) and the South African Communist Party (SACP). This armed struggle began with the formation of MK during mid-1961 and ended with the decommissioning of MK and the integration of former cadres into the post-apartheid South African National Defense Force (SANDF) in the mid-1990s. The episodes explored in this book include the formation and dissolution of a training camp outside of Cape Town in 1962, a guerrilla campaign fought by MK and the Zimbabwe African People's Union (ZAPU) in Rhodesia in 1967–68, allegations of poisoning and espionage in a training camp in Angola in the late 1970s, a survey of underground structures in Cape Town during the high water mark of internal unrest in the mid- to late 1980s, and a close reading of the conceptualization of Freedom Park, the most significant memorialization of the liberation struggle and armed struggle erected since the Mandela presidency.

Many of these episodes have been examined at length in other narrative histories of the armed struggle. Two episodes in particular—the guerrilla campaign in Rhodesia (aka the Wankie Campaign) and the alleged poisoning of cadres in Angola (aka Black September)—are deployed as rhetorically useful turning points in a variety of forms of writing about this past.[1] Despite countless retellings, the deployment of these episodes in grand narratives has rarely been a topic of concern in conventional histories of the armed struggle. This book attempts to address that deficit in self-reflection, while also suggesting new ways to explain these episodes.

Episodes about the training camp and the underground in Cape Town have not received the same level of attention as the Wankie Campaign and Black September but are no less instructive. I selected these episodes for two reasons. First, they offer an opportunity to examine stories and situations that have not and do not sit easily within the prevailing explanatory frames that structure and limit the historiography on the armed struggle. Their incompatibility with presentist concerns, their destabilization of old Cold War narratives, and their inutility in terms of the construction of legitimizing statist histories make them useful foils for understanding how the current conditions within the historiography on armed struggle channel, limit, or redirect what can and cannot be known about this past.

I examine these episodes as episodes, rather than deploy them as chapters in a grand narrative about the armed struggle. Definitions of the word *episode* vary. An episode can be defined as an event or group of events occurring as part of a larger sequence, or as an incident or period considered in isolation, or as an event or short period that is important or unusual. These definitions are instructive in that they all emphasize that episodes are in varying degrees somehow distinct and bounded and may contain meanings that need to be considered separately from the broader chronologies that they appear within. In keeping with this, I present these episodes as objects of inquiry into events and evidence, rather than building blocks of a single historical narrative.

It is my contention that each of these five episodes is indeed important but not necessarily for the reasons assumed in conventional narrative histories of the armed struggle. Indeed, their placement within narrative histories have concealed a number of important but underacknowledged historiographical problems that limit our understanding of the armed struggle. Rather than examine these episodes as a way to construct a complete narrative of the armed struggle that supersedes previous efforts or to fulfill some empiricist quest for a more geographically or chronologically complete history, I have chosen to use these episodes as examples of the way that this history is constructed. The "constructedness" of this history is an important way to understand the production of historical knowledge in revisionist nationalist discourses in South Africa, which in this context are not about championing sovereignty as in nationalist movements elsewhere but about laying claim over the history of the entire liberation struggle and hitching it to a contemporary political project.

The intellectual inspiration for this book came from a desire to place the historiography of the liberation struggle in South Africa and the production of historical knowledge about that struggle in conversation with the theoretical literature on nations and nationalism.² My starting point for this conversation is Eric Hobsbawm's interpretation of the emergence of nationalism as a modern political phenomenon. Hobsbawm argued that one could understand nationalism as a process that took place in three phases: first, a romantic cultural revival with no political content; second, a militant political project; and third, the diffusion of nationalist sentiment from elites to ordinary people through printing, mass literacy, and schooling. He also maintained that a given nationalist ideology was never a finished product, that it was in constant state of becoming, and that multiple versions of the "national idea" remained in competition at the same time. In his view, social history was indispensable for understanding the transition of a nationalist project from a militant political project aspiring to assume control of a state, to a ruling elite attempting to inculcate a politically useful and ideologically uniform nationalist consciousness among the nation they purported to lead. This was not an instrumentalist top-down process where citizens passively received nationalist ideas from nationalist activists or a nationalist government; rather, it involved a complex conversation where official nationalist discourses were filtered, deflected, and refracted by the assumptions, hopes, needs, longings, and interests of ordinary people as well as elites. As Hobsbawm put it, nationalism was a dual phenomenon that was "constructed from above, but could only be understood from below."³

This book is an attempt to understand how the historiography of the armed struggle is deployed in the complex "dual phenomenon" of nationalism imposed from above but reconfigured from below. Like Hobsbawm, I believe that this writing cannot be deciphered without the methodologies and assumptions of classic Thompsonian social history but, at the same time, must consider how regimes of truth and hierarchies of evidence impact the production of knowledge about this past.⁴

What Is Wrong with the Historiography on the Armed Struggle

There are five characteristics that overlap all major forms of historical writing on the liberation struggle: history as a proxy for legitimating or delegitimating the ANC as a ruling party, polarization, presentism, history written from above, and the organization as historical actor.

The first characteristic is a preoccupation with using history as a way of legitimizing or delegitimizing the current ANC as a ruling party. A cursory review of book introductions and conclusions shows that many authors justify their work in terms of contemporary debates about the political economy of post-apartheid South Africa.[5] On the one hand, sympathetic writers enlist a useful history to defend the credentials of the ANC as the rightful inheritor of the post-apartheid state. On the other hand, writers who are critical of the ANC compose this history almost like the Kremlinology that typified much Cold War historiography on the Soviet Union. The conceit of this side of the literature is that contemporary palace intrigues today can best be understood by tracing the lineage of various factions, deciphering the old disputes that animate present-day conflict, and exposing a chronology of rampant corruption, authoritarianism, and ineptitude within the movement. There are very few books that do not justify themselves in terms of a comment on some aspect of contemporary politics. This justification may be explicit and specific. In this regard, explicitly critical accounts often attempt to trace the origins of present-day corruption or authoritarianism in the party to developments or events during the exile period, or through the career paths of certain individuals.[6] Likewise, explicitly sympathetic histories that attempt to show that the transformative projects today are rooted in longer heritage of protest and solidarity between the party and its constituencies.[7] This tendency may also be implicit and general, where critical and sympathetic historians attempt to use the past to contextualize the present, rather than trace the lineage of some specific trait or aspect of official ideology. The implicit tendency tends to be a manifestation of "reasonable" apologists and "loyal critics" who acknowledge that there are problems with the way post-apartheid South Africa is governed but point to history to provide a contextualization of those problems, which, in their view, are really just the lingering effects of the previous regime, or necessary contingencies taken to preserve the struggle but that are now outdated and perhaps harmful.[8]

The result of this emphasis on explaining the present through the recent past is that this history is flattened under the countervailing rhetorical burdens it is forced to support in a severely polarized literature. Stories without a particular contemporary political valence are discarded, despite the fact that they might lend an altogether different understanding of this history if taken on their own terms. To take one example presented in this book, the Wankie Campaign was a guerrilla campaign composed of joint MK and Zimbabwean People's Revolutionary Army (ZIPRA) detachments that was supposed to blaze a Ho Chi Minh trail through western Rhodesia, allowing the exiled ANC the ability to deploy men and move materiel into South Africa from its distant base in Zambia. This military campaign was a failure by any measure, but the significance of this failure has been one point of contentious debate within this polarized literature. On the one hand, sympathetic histories stress that while a strategic and tactical failure, the Wankie Campaign was nonetheless a symbolic victory that gave hope to ordinary South Africans during a period of severe repression in the late 1960s and early 1970s.[9] On the other hand, critical histories stress that the significance of the Wankie Campaign lay within a memorandum written by Wankie fighters after their imprisonment in Botswana, which nearly led to their execution but ultimately resulted in a conference that provided an opportunity for the Communist Party to assume leadership posts in the ANC.[10] In this mode of writing, Wankie opened the door to Stalinist tendencies that characterized the exile leadership that in many interpretations extended into the post-apartheid government.

Neither of these interpretations has the capacity to closely read the experiences of the fighters themselves, rendered either in oral testimony, contemporary reports, or subsequent histories of the campaign. This means that an entire spectrum of evidence is removed from consideration—namely, the seemingly prosaic but crucially important texture of everyday life on a battlefield in the middle of the Rhodesian bush in the late 1960s.[11] Reading the battlefield is a fairly conventional method used to understand warfare in other historiographies, but it is simply not possible if this episode is placed within a narrative that is ultimately intended to be a referendum on the legitimacy or illegitimacy of the ANC as a ruling party. The visual experience of fighting in dense grasslands and bush explained much about the nature of this fighting and the ultimate outcome of the battle, but perhaps more importantly, it reveals volumes about the way evidence of this experience was rendered in oral testimony and written accounts. The way this experience is subsequently selectively deployed and strategically read in sympathetic and critical histories does not allow for a full appreciation of how veterans themselves have debated the significance of this event using their own categories of evidence.

The ability of historians to explain and intervene into contemporary politics through explorations of the exile period and the armed struggle is severely limited by the fact that the ANC today is a vastly different organization than the ANC of the 1960s, 1970s, and 1980s. Recent research has shown that there is a distinct discontinuity between the organizational culture that existed during the exile period and during negotiations, and the organizational culture that has emerged since the ANC became a ruling party.[12] Whether examining the contemporary relationship between party, state, and society in structuralist terms such as fractions of capital, networks of patronage, the struggle for political hegemony, or reading these shifts in a dramatically revised vocabulary of legitimating terms and a new repertoire of political pageantry, the party that sought to seize power through armed struggle for thirty years, and ended up taking power through negotiation did not pass through the looking glass of the transition to electoral politics without undergoing fundamental transformations.[13] Although the current language of officialdom may still include terms such as *comrade*, *deployment*, and *National Democratic Revolution* in contemporary position papers and electioneering, these are largely nostalgic or ritualistic nods to a revolutionary heritage in an organization that opted for negotiated settlement, awkwardly embraced capitalism, and was transformed by the contradictions and compromises of electoral democracy and constitutional governance.[14]

The second characteristic is the high degree of polarization found within this literature. One of the unique features of this historiography is the degree to which it was written by the subjects of the history itself or by politically engaged activist scholars with a deep personal investment in their own involvement with various formations within the broader anti-apartheid movement.[15] This is not an entirely unusual feature of the historiography of other liberation movements in southern Africa or elsewhere for that matter, but the sheer volume of autobiographies produced by struggle heroes combined with the symbiotic relationship between activism and segments of the academy in South Africa and beyond gives this literature a fractious complexity unseen in the writing on liberation struggles elsewhere. This means that political debates that had occurred within the movement decades ago—between activist scholars themselves and between the movement and activist scholars—have often leaked into secondary literature. These old debates frame the "new" questions this generation of writers asks in their work. Further, these old debates to some degree set the historiographical agenda and can often be found at heart of polemics and controversies in the interpretation of this literature. In short, the reciprocal relationship between personal histories of activism and attempts to make sense of these individual pasts in a scholarly or at least dispassionate way has severely polarized this literature. This polarization often expresses itself in dichotomous terms, either as exiles versus internal activists or communist versus anticommunist antagonists of Cold War historiography, MK leadership versus rank-and-file cadres, Africanist versus communist factions within the ANC, the "inziles" versus the exiles, the military versus the political wings of the exile leadership, those who have and have not leveraged party patronage in the post-apartheid period, generational divides, apartheid security officials versus ANC military leaders and intelligence operatives, or human rights abuse victims versus perpetrators of those abuses.

This polarization is one consequence of the presentist orientation of this historiography. As David Fischer put it, presentism is "[pruning] away the dead branches of the past . . . to preserve the green buds and twigs that which have grown into the dark forest of our contemporary world."[16] Presentism goes by many other names, but it is essentially, as Frederick Cooper described, "doing history backward," meaning starting with a predefined contemporary end point in mind and then tracing all of the antecedents that led to it, while disregarding anything in the past that cannot be connected to the present.[17] In some regards, presentism is a necessary evil, especially among social historians attempting to illustrate how the present is a construction of the past. But in this historiography, the questions asked of the past are often limited to those of contemporary relevance.[18] There is little attempt to understand the past as another country and to translate how they do things differently there.[19] This approach invites anachronism but more troublingly excludes episodes that do not neatly fit into the linear narratives that trace a direct and uninterrupted line to some feature of contemporary South Africa.

Presentism manifests itself in three principle branches of this historiography. First are the classically Whiggish histories of the ANC.[20] These histories conflate the history of the anti-apartheid struggle with the history of the

ANC, only one party among many in what was a much broader and complex landscape of protest in twentieth-century South Africa. History written in this mode is about the unfolding of a predetermined path of a nationalist movement that gained constituency after constituency until it was able to plausibly claim to be the sole representative of the South African people. Most critiques of this history identify the "dead branches" cut off this linear trunk as other organizations such as the Non-European Unity Movement (NEUM) and its antecedents, the Marxist Workers' Tendency (MWT) of the ANC, Federation of South African Trade Unions (FOSATU), the Pan-Africanist Congress (PAC), and/or various groups that emerged from the Black Consciousness Movement (BCM). Important as the story of the displacement, exclusion, or co-option of these other organizations is, presentism also precludes other dimensions of history from being explored as well. Any discussion of experience, save for that found in biographies of struggle heroes and foot soldiers, is by definition not fit for discussion unless it illustrates some important milestone in the singular path to liberation mapped out by Whiggish histories of the ANC.

The other two manifestation of presentism can be found in critical histories of the ANC. There are two general variants to these critical histories: left critiques portray this history as the compromise of a revolutionary socialist project and right critiques that reduce the ANC to a front organization of the SACP.[21] The left critiques tend to focus most closely on the relationship between the protest movement that emerged within South Africa in the 1980s and the exiled leadership of the ANC, which sought to bring this internal movement under its influence. These critiques generally portray the exile leadership of the ANC as largely out of touch with developments within the country, having focused almost exclusively on the armed struggle as the primary vehicle for change since the early 1960s. These critiques revisit debates between workerist activists in the ANC and outside of it, who had tussled with nationalist leaders in the ANC and their allies in the SACP over the primacy of armed struggle and the relative independence of the trade union movement. Seeing truly independent trade unionism as having real revolutionary potential, these histories tend to portray the armed struggle as a distraction that prevented the aboveground and underground organization that, in their view, would have resulted in an insurrection and seizure of state power and the means of production by workers via a general strike, or at least a stronger role for trade unions during the negotiations and the post-apartheid government.[22] This body of scholarship may have its origins in polemics circulating within the ANC and the trade union movement in the 1980s, but its contemporary relevance to tensions between the ANC and COSATU and the turmoil within the present-day labor movement cannot be mistaken.

In right critiques, the focus is on instances that demonstrate the growing influence of the SACP over the ANC primarily during the exile period.[23] The emphasis here is on tracking the spread of communist discipline over the ANC by exposing the significance of shifts in the composition of leadership bodies, revealing the inner ideological beliefs of key leaders, and charting the consequences of the authoritarian culture that was a direct result of this creeping influence. These works attempt to build a chronology of infiltration, one that began in the mass campaigns of the 1950s, accelerated significantly after the start of the armed struggle, and reached its apex during the exile years, when the ANC became financially, ideologically, and organizationally dependent on the SACP for its very survival. Like the literature on the left critique, the scope of this historical inquiry is largely limited to retracing the progression of communist ideologues, understanding bureaucratic maneuverings as primarily ideological in nature, and presenting human rights abuses as proof of an increasingly intolerant and assertive Stalinism within the movement. As the specter of communism has waned, the right critique is increasingly concerned with issues of contemporary governance—namely, tracing the origins of present government corruption to the authoritarian culture of the exile period.[24]

The third characteristic is telling this history from the perspective of elites. Until relatively recently, most histories of the armed struggle have used documents and oral testimony produced by elites.[25] Elites in this context largely means urban-born or urban-raised, university-educated middle-class individuals, who write and speak about this history primarily in English. In early works, this bias was largely a consequence of circumstances.[26] These circumstances included a pervasive fear of outsiders within the movement and the difficulties outsiders faced in accessing rank-and-file cadres who were then part of an active liberation movement engaged in a precarious set of negotiations with the apartheid state.[27] This layer of bureaucracy was often justified as a security measure while the armed struggle was still on, but the continuation of these wartime restrictions is a crucial function of the party's careful stage management and public relations efforts. Whether genuinely felt or cynically deployed, this sustained siege mentality largely determines who can and cannot ask questions and who can and who cannot answer in return, and what sort of answers are disbursed from on high. To a greater degree, this organizational mentality limits historical inquiry to approved scholars, party insiders, or trusted fellow travelers.

The history of elites also impacts the methodological approaches to oral testimony. There have been a few studies that have identified the top-down approach taken in much of the literature and argued that oral history may offer a path toward a bottom-up history.[28] The assumption that oral history has the potential to reveal the perspectives of individuals left out of the written archive has been the topic of significant debate and critique in the broader historiography on southern Africa at large. To be sure, this potential does not automatically open the door to a subaltern view of the past without a rigorous consideration of interpretation and attention to the context of the interview.

Turning attention to interpretation and context opens a series of unasked questions. Foremost among them is what constitutes an elite, and how do we define "ordinary"?[29] Is someone who was a rank-and-file cadre in a training camp in the 1970s still an "ordinary person" if he successfully leveraged himself into a comfortable government position after the transition? What bearing does his subsequent elite status have on his interpretation and recollection of his past experiences as an "ordinary" cadre? Conversely, who counts as an "ordinary" cadre? There certainly were powerful people in the exile structures who did not leave much of a mark in the written archive. Alternately, although the written archive primarily reflects elite views, rank-and-file cadres did occasionally leave small but indelible marks. If these marks are insufficiently frequent or legible in the written archive, does the oral archive then necessarily play a supplemental role? My evidence shows that the oral archive does not automatically reflect nonelite perspectives, and when it does, those perspectives may not be rendered in a transparent way. Former rank-and-file cadres can and do change their stories, especially if they became elites after the transition to democracy. If their subsequent oral testimony contradicts their written words, or the archive at large, should we necessarily privilege their spoken words over their written ones only because of the perception that the very quality of orality naturally conveys the authentic voice of nonelites? Finally, are so-called ordinary people more transparent in their testimony than elites? The working assumption of many histories is that nonelite interviewees come with less of an agenda than interviewees who were or are in a position of power and thus have to protect their authority or privilege through a variety of narrative maneuvers, concealments, or fabrications. However, in my experience, it is difficult, if not impossible, to disentangle layers of claims-making in the oral testimonies of rank-and-file former cadres who are currently seeking compensation as aggrieved and impoverished veterans today. The fact that their testimony is shaped by claims-making, however, does not make it any more or less truthful, but it does impact the generic conventions, rhetorical stances, and repertoire of stories they are willing to offer.

The fifth characteristic is the pervasive assumption that this history should be told as a history of organizations, bureaucracies or collectives.[30] The focus on elites lends itself to a history that focuses on debates within the leadership, detailed explorations of shifts in strategy and tactics, and a somewhat mechanistic understanding of the tensions between different strata and factions within the liberation movement at large. This emphasis on organization as the primary optic into this past is partly the result of limitation in sources but can also be linked to the polarization and presentist focus outlined above. Present-day political analysis generally focuses on disputes between factions within the ANC as well as the balance of power within the tripartite alliance as the primary way to understand changes in policy.[31] If the questions historians ask are attempting to explain the present through a reconstruction of the past, then it follows that tracing the lineage of these factions should be the appropriate frame for ordering historical narratives. This in and of itself is not an inappropriate approach, but organizational history does foreclose the possibility of examining the experience of those within these organizations in any way that does not comment on these disputes and the relative balance of power between factions within the liberation movement.

Thompsonian Social History and the Wits History Workshop

The theoretical and methodological agenda of this book is to bring together the two prevailing schools of historiography in South Africa. The first school is social history, born primarily out of the History Workshop at the University of the Witwatersrand (Wits) in the late 1970s.[32] The second school is poststructuralist and postcolonial history, born out of the intellectual and political uncertainties facing the profession after the transition to democracy in 1994, and the reconnection of the South African academy with wider intellectual currents elsewhere in the world.[33] Briefly, I would like to chart out the basic concerns of both schools, summarize the vigorous debates carried out between proponents of either school, and discuss how an alternation between both approaches may permit a new sort of history of the liberation struggle to be written.

Social history began as both a critique of the structuralist Marxist historiography that preceded it as well as a new form of oppositional history that challenged the official historiography sponsored and endorsed by the apartheid state. Although building on earlier revisionist Marxist historiography, social historians embraced an empirical form of history based primarily on oral sources as the solution to what they saw as an overly theoretical, economistic, and self-referential structuralism. Their embrace was not a rejection of structuralist analyses of South African history per se but rather an elaboration of it, by bringing the experiences of "ordinary people" into view as both an end in itself but also as a means of testing the theoretical formulations of the structuralists. Oral testimony, rendered primarily in the form of life histories, would provide the raw material with which to evaluate the assumptions about class formation, the articulation of capital, and the relationship between capitalism and race in South African history. The quarry of social historians was experience, consciousness, and culture, all of which they claimed had been underexamined, oversimplified, or disregarded by the previous generation of more theoretically minded Marxian historians. In their view, an examination of subjective experience rendered in oral testimony would yield a more sophisticated understanding of agency, which not only would ultimately revise structuralist interpretations of South African history but also allow historians to ask new questions about the past.

Social history also had a contemporary political agenda. Many of the founding social historians had experience in worker education or were at least politically engaged with the rising tide of protests emerging after the 1973 strikes and escalating after the 1976 Soweto uprising.[34] The Soweto uprising also coincided with the arrival of British-trained academics who brought with them Thompsonian social history. There was also a thriving exchange of photocopied papers written outside the country circulating among graduate students and scholars at South African universities.[35] Concurrent with this new intellectual challenge was a more or less direct challenge to the presumed public hegemony of the propagandistic historiography offered by the National Party either in the form of state-funded public history primary and secondary school curricula, or conventional scholarship produced at primarily Afrikaans universities. This challenge was premised on the belief that social history held the potential to raise the consciousness of the masses and thereby offer intellectuals a role in the burgeoning protest movement. To this end, the History Workshop hosted "Open Days" where various popular and workerist opposition groups were invited to participate in conferences that showcased the latest scholarship produced in the academy, serve as an audience for popular history "commodities" intended for consumption by laypeople, and allow opposition groups to perform and present their own historical and cultural productions. This engagement between academic production and contemporary politics and the fusing of the historical and political agendas was one of the hallmarks of social history in South Africa and became a point of pride in defenses of their work.

The Poststructuralist and Postcolonial Challenge

One of the most notable contributions of social history is its steadfast defense of oral history as a legitimate and effective method for uncovering the "submerged agency" of ordinary people, vaguely defined as a nonliterate urban or rural underclass. However, it was precisely this contribution that drew the attention of poststructuralist and postcolonial scholars in the 1990s. The transition to democracy presented a number of challenges to the profession in South Africa. South Africa had been largely isolated from developments occurring within the academy in North America and Europe during the 1980s.[36] Historians trained abroad and those from within the History Workshop began to identify certain problems that became more apparent in the new political context after the transition to democracy. This critique did not question the value of recovering the experiences of those without access to the written archive but did challenge the methodological and theoretical assumptions that motivated this "rescue from the condescension of posterity."[37] First among these was the artificial dichotomy between oral sources and written sources. Isabel Hofmeyr critiqued the tendency to privilege oral sources as truer by virtue of their very orality.[38] Concurrent with this belief was the assumption that "purer" oral sources—meaning ones free from the distortions of memory or contamination by written sources—were more authentic representations of experience. Her solution was to embrace the hybridity of oral sources and begin to explore *how* people say things rather than exclusively focusing on *what* people say. When the traces of narrative convention, the seepage of written word into the spoken word, and the complex transformations of memory are filtered out of oral testimony to make a "purer" or more "authentic" form of evidence, we lose the ability to actually analyze what informants say because we cannot see the contextual processes that shaped their testimony.

Alongside Hofmeyr's critique came a new skepticism about the role of the professional historian in the production of historical knowledge and the subtle hierarchies that ordered evidence presented in their work. Despite the gestures toward the democratizing potential of oral history, in practice social historians saw oral testimony as a storehouse of facts and raw material rather than as a set of interpretations that constituted a form of knowledge production in its own right. As Ciraj Rassool put it, "Life histories were not seen as history.... They were regarded as prior to history."[39] In the social historian's conception of oral history, critics charged, evidence preceded interpretation, and the role of the professional historian as final arbiter was held above that of the informant as producer of evidence. Following this, critics also turned their attention to the question of voice. Although the project of social history was defined as "giving voice to the marginalized," by the 1990s critics scrutinized the layers of mediation of oral testimony through translation, paraphrasing, or editing.[40] This line of critique was most forcefully presented in a review of Charles van Onselen's *Kas Maine*, in many ways the quintessential work of South African social history.[41] Noting that a book intended to give voice to an ordinary sharecropper was almost entirely narrated by the historian and offered precious little space to Maine's unmediated words, critics posed the provocative question, whose voice was actually heard in histories that paraphrased oral testimonies of "the people"?[42]

Another line of critique came to the fore in debates about the changing role of the professional historian in the post-apartheid era. Given the close association between social history's political agenda and intellectual project, the demise of the apartheid regime and the ascendency of the ANC posed a dilemma for historians invested in transformation in South Africa. This dilemma hinged on whether the ANC was the vehicle for transformation that it purported to be. Although many social historians remained skeptical of the intentions of the ANC and other Charterist formations during the high water mark of popular protest in the 1980s and remained skeptical after 1994, others charged that it was the professional historian's duty to contribute to transformation by engaging with government efforts, regardless of their individual opinions about the ANC's commitment and ability to foster change as a ruling party.[43]

This existential crisis over the political relevance of the profession and the practical relevance of historical research in society at large dovetailed with the theoretical and methodological challenges posed by new critics of social history. These critics did not question the emancipatory potential of social history but suggested that potential was diminished by some of the practices and theoretical presumptions of the particular configuration of social history that became dominant in South Africa in the 1980s. If anything, these critics of social history were taking its core values seriously by offering a more direct route toward the appreciation of the often forgotten interior and exterior lives of individuals locked out of the written archive. This alternative intellectual project echoed many of the same concerns first articulated by social historians in the late 1970s but placed social history in conversation with theoretical and methodological developments occurring outside South Africa since the 1980s. Indeed, many critics of social history began their careers working with the History Workshop or similar efforts related to the collection and synthesis of oral testimonies, alternative education, and popular history.

In order to escape the "politics of atonement" that characterized social history in its most paternalistic mode, historians needed to embrace the various ways that their informants made sense of their world. For poststructuralist and postcolonial historians, this meant appreciating various forms of the production of knowledge and bringing those forms of production into conversation with the production of historical knowledge in the academy.

Rather than accepting the division of labor between academics and their informants as the natural order of things, historians needed to meet the interpretive challenges of their informants head-on and grapple with the implications those interventions had on their scholarship.

These critics also recognized and accepted that the academy had "ceased to be a major site for the production of history."[44] Public history, as opposed to the popular history offered by the History Workshop, was identified as the arena within which the implicit hierarchy of historical knowledge was best challenged. It was also meant to speak directly to the masses. From the mid-1990s until the present, history, broadly conceived, has expanded outside the academy as governmental and community-based projects embarked on a massive renovation and expansion of the existing museum infrastructure, the school curriculum underwent several rounds of reform and redesign, and public heritage became a major part of government nation-building initiatives and prioritization of the tourist economy. The rise of heritage was met with hostility by some academic historians and indifference by others, but postcolonial and poststructuralist historians saw this expansion less as a threat than as an opportunity. As ambivalent as many of these historians were about the impact of heritage on public discourse, it was nonetheless embraced as a laboratory for attempting the new sort of history first articulated in critiques of social history.

This new critical historiography offered a new set of theoretical concerns that had not been addressed by social history in a sustained way. First among these was a basic skepticism about the accessibility of the past and a suspicion of teleological narratives based on rote forms of empiricism. Empiricism had been the History Workshop's answer to the theoretical abstractions of structural Marxist historiography and the gross mythologizations offered in official histories authored by the apartheid state. However, by the 1990s, many began to wonder if the collection of evidence, particularly oral evidence, had become an end in itself rather than a means to test theory or to challenge a regime that had negotiated its way out of political power.

The most worrying aspect of the rise of heritage for poststructuralists, postcolonial, and social historians alike was the appropriation of methodologies from both schools in a new nationalist historiography on the apartheid state and the liberation struggle. The new heritage professionals that led state-funded projects agreed in principle with social historians about the value of oral history and shared social historians' predilection to elevate oral history above the written archive, even when read against the grain. However, as the halo of the negotiated settlement faded into the static pessimism of the post-apartheid period, the state became ever more willing to inject its heritage projects with a version of history intended to legitimate the ruling party, which was at variance with the critical distance maintained by both social historians and postcolonial and poststructuralist historians. As Jacob Dlamini noted, official histories conflated the ANC with the entire liberation movement, created a dichotomous moral landscape populated by unambiguous villains and heroes, and insinuated that the "faceless masses of our people . . . experienced apartheid the same way, suffered the same way, and fought the same way against [it]."[45] Nationalists effectively built a "usable past" by appropriating social history's concern for the underrepresented and commitment to popularization, while striking the posture of an oppositional revisionist narrative, despite the fact that their "oppositional" narrative became ironically the new official narrative whose reason for being was the defense of the ruling party. Social historians recognized the danger of this co-option during their interaction with the burgeoning protest movement in the 1980s and attempted to preserve a separation between their historical production and nationalist politics.[46] It was not until the challenge to the hegemony of social history, however, that its project was self-reflexively examined and shown susceptible to a nationalist co-option because of its unease with questioning the self-apparent truths and easily translated experience inherent in source material, primarily oral testimony.[47] Gary Minkley and Rassool suggested social historians' "unwillingness to engage with issues of power in the conversational narratives" led to the inscription of an authenticated historical narrative that reduced "ordinary people" to mere representative allegories of correct political (and historical) practice. These sorts of allegories proved to be eminently useful to nationalist historians.[48]

Post-Apartheid Nationalism and Struggle History

Jonathan Hyslop argued that the early 2000s represented a time when "an overtly African nationalist position began to be articulated by sectors of the ANC," which became "especially strong" during the Thabo Mbeki presidency.⁴⁹ In many ways, this nationalist position was an attempt to cordon off the history of the liberation struggle through claims of authority, authenticity, and ownership.⁵⁰ The nationalist challenge largely revolved around the question of who could and who could not write "our history."⁵¹ As Hyslop points out, these methodological challenges went hand in hand with a sociological critique of racial demographics within the academy itself and the Wits Social History Workshop in particular all articulated in the new vocabulary of transformation rendered in the deadened voice of officialdom.⁵²

The conceit of nationalist historiography relies heavily on the rhetorical power of its conception of "our history," which can be glossed as the oral traditions, living memories, and writings of oppressed peoples that are presumed to remain outside the bounds of previous generations of academic historiography.⁵³ This knowledge has been dutifully kept by participants themselves, their descendants, and other insiders. Nationalist historians charge that past and present generations of professional historians have either overlooked, ignored, or suppressed these archives and narratives.⁵⁴ "Our history" is likewise positioned to be intrinsically oppositional. As such, nationalist historians presume that accepted historical narratives are incomplete, faulty, or biased and constitute an illegitimate orthodoxy in the field. By extension, including "our history" into the canon of professionally accepted historical knowledge will, in their view, result in a necessary and overdue revision of existing narratives. Use of the possessive pronoun *our* is an indication of the proprietary impulse in nationalist historiography and an indication of its gatekeeping tendencies. One cannot write "our history" if one is not part of the insider community that has access to the archives and production sites that are presumed to exist outside the academy and beyond the reach of its untransformed faculty. This proprietary impulse is as much a part of critiques of the pace of transformation in the academy as it is a theoretical intervention that elevates the subject position of the historian as the primary determinant of the quality of his or her work.

Methodological and theoretical borrowing aside, post-apartheid nationalist historiography owes its rhetorical flourish and narrative conventions to the oppositional histories that began with works by left-wing anti-apartheid activists and scholars authored primarily in the 1950s. Works by Communist Party members (or former members) such as Eddie Roux, Jack and Ray

Simons, and Govan Mbeki and to a lesser extent Trotskyists such as Dora Taylor, Hosea Jaffe, and I. B. Tabata all shared the common goal of constructing a historical context for the nascent anti-apartheid struggle, albeit rendered from the ideological perspective of their respective organizations or personal political beliefs.[55] These activists posed their works as a corrective to textbooks based on settler histories, as well as tools for raising the political consciousness of readers who were either already involved in the anti-apartheid struggle or could be persuaded to join through the act of reading a truly oppositional history. In many ways, the either-or model of resistance that became central to post-apartheid nationalist historiography began in these early works that promised to trace the origins of national oppression and nationalist resistance across centuries of conquest and colonization. Each episode in these narratives built on a previous set of events, ultimately culminating into the sharpened point of resistance, which invariably pointed to each author's respective ideology and organization. In these works, history was historicist, linear, and heavily determinist. Although most of these works acknowledge the recent origins of national consciousness, its emergence appears as logical, overdue, and pregnant with possibility.[56] The telescoping narratives fostered in early nationalist history set the mold into which a post-apartheid nationalist historiography would later take shape.

The crucial difference that separates 1950s-vintage nationalist historiography from its post-apartheid descendent are their differing political objectives. Wherever 1950s writers happened to fall on the left wing of the political spectrum, their respective organizations aspired to build a mass movement that encompassed the majority of those opposed to apartheid. This meant smoothing over unresolved ideological differences within their alliances through the writing of history. Within the orbit of the Congress Alliance, this meant striking a delicate balance between historical interpretations that placed special emphasis on the explanatory power of race over class or vice versa. However, this balance was struck in individual works, history was understood to be a powerful vehicle for explaining the political logic and strategic superiority of a particular organization in an increasingly repressive environment and hitching that organization to a mass constituency.

The motive of nationalist historiography after 1994 was nation-building and transformation in an electoral democracy under a constitutional order. In practical terms, this meant cohering a political constituency and shoring up the legitimacy of the ruling ANC by giving historical depth to its claim to be the sole liberator of African people in South Africa. Until the late 1990s, official histories and heritage projects manifested the "rainbow nation" ethos ambivalently adopted by the ANC government.[57] However, by the late 1990s, the broad inclusiveness that characterized the first years of democracy gave way to an assertive and unapologetic African identity rooted in a rhetoric of autochthony rather than citizenship and liberal democracy. This identity was heralded by Thabo Mbeki's "I Am an African" speech, delivered at the adoption of the new constitution in 1996.[58] Indigeneity and birthright became a part of the vocabulary of a historically contingent politics of transformation, as an ascendant African middle class sought its place within society, the economy, and the state. After this turn, nationalist histories and heritage projects, like earlier iterations, located a triumphant and celebrated liberation struggle as the final stage of centuries of resistance.[59] In this formulation, the ANC was uniquely qualified to rule South Africa because of its self-evident accomplishments during the liberation struggle, which represented the apex of a hoary cascade of struggles that began, as the museum at Freedom Park suggests, with the origin of life itself. History became less a critical evaluation of the past and rigorous reading of evidence and more a litany of events populated by illustrious heroes. Like the national histories written about other African nation-states shortly after the first wave of independence, nationalist historians could now claim that South Africa finally had the past it needed and that it was indeed useful.[60]

What This Book Does Differently

This book is an assemblage of archival and historiographical knots that provide new ways of looking at the armed struggle and the liberation struggle at large. My purpose in presenting these knots is not to untie them but to explore old evidence in new ways, introduce new evidence to old narratives, and apply a different set of critical lenses to all this material. If there is a common finding that emerges from these readings, it is that the armed struggle remains an unstable concept, even to those who fought within it.

Chapter 2 examines the multiple ways a training camp organized outside Cape Town in the first months of the armed struggle has been framed in a variety of different layers of writing including published diaries, autobiography, semifictional accounts, and oral testimony. The history of this camp could be used to evaluate the success of the sabotage campaign, or to legitimate present-day claims to heritage resources by establishing it as a "first" in the armed struggle, or as a way to retry the trial that led to the imprisonment of its organizers. I chose a different pathway into the significance of this camp. These layers of writing reveal what could and could not be said about this episode at different points in time. Collapsing differing accounts of the camp into a single corroborated narrative with the goal of establishing once and for all whether it was a guerrilla camp or the first guerrilla camp misses all of the ways the conventions of genre and the context of the present tempers our understanding of the past.

Chapter 3 follows the same approach to evidence but asks different questions: what gets lost when the history of the Wankie Campaign is written in an either-or mode as a failure or a success, and what is possible when we place the literal and figurative perspectives of participants at the center of this history? Casting veterans of this campaign as either heroes or antiheroes, overlooks the fact that they were soldiers entering battle for the first time. Their memories of this experience reveal how their expectations and imaginings of guerrilla warfare ran aground on the realities of combat in the dense and tangled Rhodesian bush. From this perspective, the value of the Wankie Campaign lies not in what it tells us about the progress (or lack thereof) of the armed struggle at that point in time and more in what it can reveal about soldiers' perceptions of themselves and their war.

Chapter 4 is about Black September, the alleged mass poisoning of cadres at Novo Catengue, the largest MK training camp in Angola. For officials, Black September became an oft-cited example of what could happen if the ANC in exile failed to ruthlessly root out spies within its ranks. But diaries kept by Jack Simons, the head of political education, suggest a more mundane explanation for the mass illness: poor sanitation, careless food preparation, and a questionable water supply. Despite the plausibility of Simons's alternative explanation, the event was labeled an attempted poisoning by ANC investigators who attributed it to a constellation of spies hidden within its ranks. While I conduct a close reading of the events of that evening, my primary objective is to demonstrate how certainty about the causes of the event successively accrued within subsequent investigations into espionage within the movement. A poisoning became an irresistible plot device in narratives that attempted to paint the ANC as the victim of insidious and far-reaching networks of spies.

Chapter 5 examines the underground in Cape Town in the 1980s to explore two related questions: how do we access the authentic experiences of the underground given all of the self-fashioning evident in oral testimony and the imaginative poetics of written accounts of everyday life in the underground, and how is the turn to experience justified in the historiography as the bedrock of historical truth? The prerequisite of any history of the experience of underground cadres is a consideration of how those same cadres craft their oral testimony, as well as a critical view of how that evidence is deployed in the historiography. This chapter takes the poststructuralist and postcolonial challenge to social history head-on in a close reading of the written and oral archive of the underground, beginning with the assumption that interpretation precedes evidence.

As suggested above, each chapter is a set piece that addresses itself to a different question as well as to the methodological challenge of dealing with different sorts of materials. In order to provide the context and vocabulary necessary for nonspecialists to make sense of the armed struggle, chapter 1 is a "potted history" of MK written largely from the perspective of exile looking inward to events in South Africa. To many, the inclusion of this overview in a book critiquing "grand narratives" may seem to diminish the impact of my arguments about the value of understanding the history of the armed struggle through episodes as objects. In response, I maintain that the account of MK provided makes no claim to final authority, which is the central conceit of "grand narratives," and the conceit that animates much conventional history. My use of diametrically opposed sources, and my emphasis on polarization in the literature on MK, is a deliberate attempt to acknowledge the fact that dissensus largely reigns supreme in this historiography, despite its positivist intentions. In order for readers to gain a greater feel for this dissensus, I encourage them to read other accounts that span MK's entire history, including those that are most likely identified as "grand narratives."

This book does not end with the disbanding ceremony held in Orlando Stadium in 1993 or the integration of MK veterans into the SANDF in 1995, or the emergence of the Umkhonto we Sizwe Military Veterans Association as a political force in the 2010 elections. In other words, there is no epilogue that would accompany a linear historical narrative. Instead, the final chapter takes a detour away from episodes to examine the creation of Freedom Park, the largest, costliest, and most significant post-apartheid heritage project that encompasses a museum, monuments, and memorial dedicated to the liberation struggle. This detour is necessary to demonstrate the way that nationalist history attempts to smooth out the archival and historiographical knots represented in the episodes presented here and others like them. This chapter provides a brief discussion of the debates that arose during the conceptualization of Freedom Park but focuses most closely on a close reading of monuments, memorials, and museum exhibits as texts conveying the official narrative of the liberation struggle. My finding is that the history of armed struggle has an awkward and ephemeral presence at Freedom Park. Nationalist histories thrive on successful armed struggles fought in straightforward and easily defined ways, but the armed struggle in South Africa largely defies an easy deployment in the struggle history on display at Freedom Park. Where the armed struggle does appear at Freedom Park, it is domesticated and stripped of its most problematic elements. This domestication resulted in a flattening of episodes presented in exhibits in the museum, as well as problems with the conceptualization and execution of the Wall of Names.

Notes

1. Chris Hani, "The Wankie Campaign," *Dawn* (1986): 1–7. African National Congress, "Statement to the Truth and Reconciliation Commission, August 1996," accessed June 17, 2016 (http://www.justice.gov.za/trc/hrvtrans/submit/anctruth.htm. African National Congress), "ANC Submission to the TRC in Reply to the TRC's 'Findings on the ANC,'" accessed June 17, 2016 (http://www.anc.org.za/show.php?id=2667). Eleanor Morse, *White Dog Fell from the Sky* (London: Penguin, 2013). James Ngculu, *The Honour to Serve: Recollections of an Umkhonto Soldier* (Cape Town: David Philip, 2009). Wonga Welile Bottoman, *The Making of an MK Cadre* (Pretoria: LiNc Publishers, 2010). Stephen Ellis, *External Mission: The ANC in Exile, 1960–1990* (Oxford: Oxford University Press, 2013). Stephen Ellis and Tsepo Sechaba, *Comrades against Apartheid: The ANC and the South African Communist Party in Exile* (Bloomington: Indiana University Press, 1992). Hugh Macmillan, *The Lusaka Years: The ANC in Exile in Zambia, 1963 to 1994* (Johannesburg: Jacana, 2013). Heidi Holland, *The Struggle: A History of the African National Congress* (New York: George Braziller, 1990).

Janet Cherry, *Umkhonto we Sizwe* (Johannesburg: Jacana Media, 2011). Rendani Ralinala et al., "The Wankie and Sipolilo Campaigns," in *The Road to Democracy in South Africa: Volume 1 (1960–1970)*, ed. Bernard Magubane (Cape Town: Zebra Press, 2004), 479–540. Gregory Houston and Bernard Magubane, "The ANC's Armed Struggle in the 1970s," in *The Road to Democracy in South Africa: Volume 2 (1970–1980)*, ed. Bernard Magubane (Pretoria: University of South Africa Press, 2006), 453–530. Thomas Karis and Gail Gerhart, *From Protest to Challenge: A Documentary History of African Politics in South Africa, 1882–1990* (Bloomington: Indiana University Press, 1997).

2. Eric Hobsbawm, *Nations and Nationalism since 1780: Programme, Myth, Reality* (Cambridge: Cambridge University Press, 2012). Eric Hobsbawm and Terence Ranger, eds., *The Invention of Tradition* (Cambridge University Press, 2012). Ernest Gellner and John Breuilly, *Nations and Nationalism* (Ithaca, NY: Cornell University Press, 2008). Benedict Anderson, *Imagined Communities: Reflections on the Origin and Spread of Nationalism* (New York: Verso, 2006). Anthony Marx, *Making Race and Nation: A Comparison of South Africa, the United States, and Brazil* (Cambridge: Cambridge University Press, 1998). Anthony Smith, *Theories of Nationalism* (New York: Holmes & Meier, 1983).

3. Hobsbawm, *Nations and Nationalism since 1780*, 11–13.

4. Jonathan Hyslop, "E. P. Thompson in South Africa," accessed October 14, 2014 (https://www.academia.edu/4690108/E.P._THOMPSON_IN_SOUTH_AFRICA_REVISED_). Leslie Witz and Ciraj Rassool, "Making Histories," *Kronos* 34 (2008): 6–15.

5. Ellis and Sechaba, *Comrades against Apartheid*. Macmillan, *The Lusaka Years*, 277–92. Thabo Mbeki, "Foreword," in *The Road to Democracy in South Africa, Vol. 1 (1960–1970)*, ed. Bernard Magubane (Cape Town: Zebra Press, 2004), vii–xii. Vladimir Shubin, *ANC: A View from Moscow* (Auckland Park: Jacana, 2012), 316–18. This tendency extends into literature written or published before the negotiations. Francis Meli, *South Africa Belongs to Us* (Bloomington: Indiana University Press, 1988). Bernard Magubane, *South Africa: From Soweto to Uitenhage: The Political Economy of the South African Revolution* (Trenton, NJ: Africa World Press, 1989), 182.

6. Alex Boraine, *What's Gone Wrong: On the Brink of a Failed State* (Cape Town: Jonathan Ball, 2014). Mark Gevisser, *Thabo Mbeki: A Dream Deferred* (Johannesburg: Jonathan Ball, 2007). Jeremy Gordin, *Zuma: A Biography* (Johannesburg: Jonathan Ball, 2008).

7. Raymond Suttner, *The ANC Underground in South Africa, 1950–1976* (London: First Forum Press, 2009). Johannes Rantete, "Facing the Challenges of Transition: A Critical Analysis of the African National Congress in the 1990s" (MA thesis, University of the Witwatersrand, 1994).

8. Padraig O'Malley, *Shades of Difference: Mac Maharaj and the Struggle for South Africa* (New York: Viking, 2007). Thula Bopela and Daluxolo Luthuli, *Umkhonto we Sizwe: Fighting for a Divided People* (Alberton: Galago, 2005).

9. Archie Sibeko, *Freedom in Our Lifetime* (Bellville: University of the Western Cape, 2006). T. Mali, *Chris Hani: The Sun That Set before Dawn* (Johannesburg: SACHED, 1993). Michelle Berger, "Chris Hani," in *They Fought for Freedom*, ed. John Pampallis (Cape Town: Maskew Miller Longman, 1994). Ralinala et al., "The Wankie and Sipolilo Campaigns," 479–540. Shubin, *ANC*. Suttner, *The ANC Underground in South Africa*. Meli, *South Africa Belongs to Us*. Ronald Kasrils, *Armed and Dangerous: From Undercover Struggle to Freedom* (Auckland Park: Jacana, 2013). Ben Turok, *The ANC and the Turn to Armed Struggle, 1950–1970* (Auckland Park: Jacana, 2011). John Pampallis, *Foundations of the New South Africa* (Cape Town: Maskew Miller Longman, 1991).

10. Tom Lodge, *Black Politics in South Africa since 1945* (New York: Longman, 1983). Tom Lodge, "Spectres from the Camps: The ANC's Commission of Enquiry," *Southern Africa Report* 8 (1993): 19–30. Paul Trewhela, *Inside Quatro* (Auckland Park: Jacana, 2009). Ellis and Sechaba, *Comrades against Apartheid*, 52–60. Howard Barrell, "Conscripts to Their Age: African National Congress Operational Strategy, 1976–1986" (PhD diss., Oxford University, 1993). O'Malley, *Shades of Difference*, 186–87. Ellis, *External Mission*, 60–82.

11. This spectrum is partially revealed in veterans' memoirs. See Bopela and Luthuli, *Umkhonto we Sizwe: Fighting for a Divided People*. See also Fanele Mbali, *In Transit: Autobiography of a South African Freedom Fighter* (Observatory: South African History Online, 2012), 129.

12. Colin Bundy, *Short Changed?: South Africa since Apartheid* (Auckland Park: Jacana, 2014). Susan Booysen, "Regeneration of ANC Political Power, from the 1994 Electoral Victory to the 2012 Centenary," in *One Hundred Years of the ANC: Debating Liberation Histories Today*, ed. Arianna Lissoni et al. (Johannesburg: University of the Witwatersrand Press, 2012), 301–24. Roger Southall, "The ANC: Party Vanguard of the Black Middle Class?," in *One Hundred Years of the ANC: Debating Liberation Histories Today*, ed. Arianna Lissoni et al. (Johannesburg: University of the Witwatersrand Press, 2012), 325–46. Paul Holden, *The Arms Deal in Your Pocket* (Johannesburg: Jonathan Ball, 2009). Ben Turok, *My Head above the Parapet* (Auckland Park: Jacana, 2014). Clive Glaser, *The ANC Youth League* (Auckland Park: Jacana, 2012), 121–51, 153–57. Andrew Feinstein, *After the Party: A Personal and Political Journey inside the ANC* (Johannesburg: Jonathan Ball, 2007), 239–55. For opposing viewpoints that stress continuities between the pre- and post-1994 ANC, see Anthony Butler, *The Idea of the ANC* (Athens: Ohio University Press, 2013). Raymond Suttner, "The Culture(s) of the African National Congress of South Africa: Imprint of Exile Experiences," *Journal of Contemporary African Studies* 21 (2003): 303–19. Stephen Ellis, "Politics and Crime: Reviewing the ANC's Exile History," *South African Historical Journal* 64 (2012): 622–36.

13. Susan Booysen, *The African National Congress and the Regeneration of Political Power* (Johannesburg: University of the Witwatersrand Press, 2011). Bundy, *Short-Changed?*, 137–57. Turok, *With My Head above the Parapet*, 135–74, 195–96.

14. Turok, *With My Head above the Parapet*. Bundy, *Short-Changed?*

15. The list of struggle activists who were either academics at the time of their activism or later became activists during exile or after the transition is lengthy. The following list is not exhaustive by any means but highlights more prominent scholar-activists and their most significant work on some aspect of the anti-apartheid struggle. Fatima Meer, *Higher Than Hope: The Authorized Biography of Nelson Mandela* (New York: Harper & Row, 1988). Martin Legassick, *Armed Struggle and Democracy: The Case of South Africa* (Uppsala, Sweden: Nordiska Afrikainstitutet, 2002). H. J. Simons and R. E. Simons, *Class and Colour in South Africa, 1850–1950* (Harmondsworth, UK: Penguin, 1969). Macmillan, *The Lusaka Years*. Baruch Hirson, *Year of Fire, Year of Ash: The Soweto Revolt: Roots of a Revolution?* (London: Zed, 1979). Bernard Magubane, *The Political Economy of Race and Class in South Africa* (New York: Monthly Review Press, 1979). Jabulani Sithole, "Contestations Over Knowledge Production or Ideological Bullying?: A Response to Legassick on the Workers' Movement," *Kronos* 35 (2009): 222–41. Turok, *The ANC and the Turn to Armed Struggle*. Joel Joffe, *The State versus Nelson Mandela: The Trial That Changed South Africa* (Oxford: Oneworld, 2011). Harold Wolpe, *Race, Class and the Apartheid State* (Trenton, NJ: Africa World Press, 1990).

16. David Hackett Fischer, *The Historians' Fallacy: Toward a Logic of Historical Thought* (New York: Harper & Row, 1970), 135.

17. Frederick Cooper, *Colonialism in Question: Theory, Knowledge, History* (Berkeley: University of California Press, 2005), 105.

18. William Worger's review of Francis Meli's *South Africa Belongs to Us* is a good example of the desire for a history of the ANC that explains the present. Meli wrote from the perspective of a loyal and high-ranking member of the ANC, who experienced decades of exile. Worger perceptively points out where Meli's narrative reflects his subject position but faults him for not writing a history that would provide clues to the unbanned ANC's policy positions for a democratic South Africa. This was a reasonable critique in 1990 when the ANC entered a crucially important transitional period as a largely unknown quantity. However, this desire to use history as an explanatory tool for deciphering the ruling party's future direction remains a stubbornly durable desire that prevents this historiography from being delinked to presentist concerns. William H. Worger, "Review: *South Africa Belongs to Us*," *African Studies Review* 34 (1991): 145–46.

19. Allister Sparks, *Tomorrow Is Another Country: The Inside Story of South Africa's Road to Change* (Chicago: University of Chicago Press, 1996).

20. Meli, *South Africa Belongs to Us*. Holland, *The Struggle*. Bernard Magubane, ed., *The Road to Democracy in South Africa, Volume I* (Cape Town: Zebra, 2004). Mary Benson, *The African National Congress: The African Patriots* (London: Faber & Faber, 1963). Pampallis, *Foundations of a New South Africa*.

21. Anthea Jeffrey, *A People's War: New Light on the Struggle for South Africa* (Johannesburg: Jonathan Ball, 2009). Ellis, *The External Mission*. John Saul, "Cry for

the Beloved Country: The Post-Apartheid Denouement," *Monthly Review* 52 (2001): 1–51. Patrick Bond, *Elite Transition: From Apartheid to Neo-Liberalism in South Africa* (London: Pluto, 2000). Terry Bell, *Comrade Moss: A Political Journey* (Cape Town: Redworks 2009). Martin Legassick, *Armed Struggle and Democracy*. Trewhela, *Inside Quatro*.

22. Interpretations of the relationship between the ANC and the internal trade union movement are a serious flashpoint of disagreement and controversy in the historiography on the liberation struggle. See David Hemson, Martin Legassick, and Nicole Ulrich, "White Activists and the Revival of the Workers' Movement," in *The Road to Democracy in South Africa: Volume 2: 1970–1980*, ed. Bernard Magubane (Pretoria: University of South Africa Press, 2006), 243–316. Sifiso Ndlovu and Jabulani Sithole, "The Revival of the Labour Movement, 1970–1980," in *The Road to Democracy in South Africa: Volume 2: 1970–1980*, ed. Bernard Magubane (Pretoria: University of South Africa Press, 2006), 187–242. Martin Legassick, "Debating the Revival of the Workers' Movement in the 1970s: The South African Democracy Education Trust and Post-Apartheid Patriotic History," *Kronos* 34 (2008): 240–66. Sithole, "Contestations over Knowledge Production or Ideological Bullying?" Stephen Friedman, "Whose Liberation?: A Partly-Forgotten Left Critique of ANC Strategy and Its Contemporary Implications," *Journal of Asian and African Studies* 47 (2012): 18–32. Bernard Magubane, "Whose Memory—Whose History?: The Illusion of Liberal and Radical Historical Debates," in *History Making and Present Day Politics: The Meaning of Collective Memory in South Africa*, ed. Hans Erik Stolten (Uppsala, Sweden: Nordiska Afrikainstitutet, 2007), 251–79.

23. Ellis and Sechaba, *Comrades against Apartheid*. Mwezi Twala and Ed Benard, *Mbokodo: Inside MK: A Soldier's Story* (Johannesburg: Jonathan Ball, 1994). Anthea Jeffrey, *The Truth about the Truth Commission* (Johannesburg: SAIRR, 1999). In some ways, this literature has roots in an older genealogy of anticommunist writing and Cold War–era writing on the history of Soviet foreign policy in southern Africa. See Henry Pike, *A History of Communism in South Africa* (Johannesburg: Christian Mission International of South Africa, 1988). Heinrich De Villiers, *Rivonia: Operation Mayibuye: A Review of the Rivonia Trial* (Johannesburg: Afrikaanse Pers Boekhandel, 1966). Sheridan Johns, "The Comintern, South Africa and the Black Diaspora," *The Review of Politics* 37 (1975): 200–34. Edward Feit, *Urban Revolt in South Africa, 1960–1964: A Case Study* (Evanston, IL: Northwestern University Press, 1971). Plotting literature on a strictly left-right spectrum obscures the similarities between right-leaning Cold War literature and anti-Stalinist Trotskyite literature, often characterized by their critics within the ANC and SACP as "ultra-leftist." For this literature, see Trewhela, *Inside Quatro*. Baruch Hirson, *Revolutions in My Life* (Johannesburg: University of the Witwatersrand Press, 1995). I. B. Tabata, *The Awakening of a People* (Cape Town: All African Convention, 1950). Tariq Ali, "Southern Africa: A Betrayal," *The Black Dwarf* (1969). Neville Alexander, "100 Years of the African

National Congress," last modified November 6, 2014 (http://www.sahistory.org.za/archive/100-years-african-national-congress-neville-alexander).

24. Stephen Ellis, "Politics and Crime: Reviewing the ANC's Exile History," *South African Historical Journal*, 64 (2012): 622–36.

25. Howard Barrell explicitly acknowledges this problem in his dissertation. Barrell, "Conscripts to Their Age."

26. Ellis and Sechaba, *Comrades against Apartheid*. Barrell, "Conscripts to Their Age." Feit, *Urban Revolt in South Africa*.

27. The exception are the unpublished biographical files by the Carter-Karis-Gerhart project, which contain a wealth of information compiled from published sources, significant body of unpublished writings, as well as formal and informal interviews. Nevertheless, the volume of information on figures who have official and unofficial authorization to speak with outsiders is considerably larger than more shadowy or lower ranking individuals, whose biographical files are composed of fleeting excerpts from published works, news clippings, and hearsay from interviews with higher ranking individuals.

28. Suttner, *The ANC Underground in South Africa*.

29. The earliest discussion of elite versus nonelite interviewees emerged out of public opinion research in the 1950s, and the theoretical assumptions made in the field of oral history have directly or indirectly bore the stamp of those early influences in terms of a preoccupation with correcting bias rather than theorizing what constitutes an elite. David Riesman, "Orbits of Tolerance, Interviewers, and Elites," *The Public Opinion Quarterly* 20 (1956): 49–73. Raymond Hopkins and Robert C. Mitchell, "The Validity of Survey Research in Africa: Some Propositions," *African Studies Review* 17 (1974): 565–74. Early sociologies on Africa show a greater concern with defining elites versus nonelites but are heavily wedded to quantitative rather than qualitative data. Hugh Smythe and Mabel M. Smythe, *The New Nigerian Elite* (Palo Alto, CA: Stanford University Press, 1960).

30. Jeremy Seekings, *The UDF: A History of the United Democratic Front in South Africa 1983–1991* (Cape Town: David Philip, 2000). Sean Morrow et al., *Education in Exile: SOMAFCO: The ANC School in Tanzania, 1978 to 1992* (Cape Town: HSRC Press, 2004). Peter Limb, *The ANC's Early Years: Nation, Class and Place in South Africa before 1940* (Pretoria: University of South Africa Press, 2010), xiv. Macmillan, *The Lusaka Years*, 134–42. Meli, *South Africa Belongs to Us*, 21–62. Barrell, "Conscripts to Their Age."

31. Feinstein, *After the Party*. Booysen, *The African National Congress and the Regeneration of Political Power*. Turok, *My Head above the Parapet*. Glaser, *The ANC Youth League*, 121–51, 153–57.

32. Belinda Bozzoli, "Intellectuals, Audiences and Histories: South African Experiences, 1978–88," *Radical History Review* 46 (1990): 237–63. Hyslop, "E. P. Thompson in South Africa." Phil Bonner, "Keynote Address to the 'Life after Thirty' Colloquium,"

African Studies 69 (2010): 13–27. Steven Friedman, "From Classroom to Class Struggle: Radical Academics and the Rebirth of Trade Unionism in the 1970s," *Journal of Asian and African Studies* 49 (2014): 526–43. Steven Friedman, "Before and After: Reflections on Regime Change and Its Aftermath," *Transformation: Critical Perspectives on Southern Africa* 75 (2011): 4–12. Luli Callinicos, "The 'People's Past': Toward Transforming the Present," in *Class, Community and Conflict*, ed. Belinda Bozzoli (Johannesburg: Ravan, 1987), 44–60. Witz and Rassool, "Making Histories," 6–15.

33. Les Witz, "The Write Your Own History Project," *Radical History Review* 46 (1990): 377–87. Carolyn Hamilton, "'The Future of the Past': New Trajectories," *South African History Journal* 35 (1996): 146–48. Gary Minkley and Martin Legassick, "Recent Trends in the Production of South African History," *Alternation* 5 (1998): 98–129. Witz and Rassool, "Making Histories," 6–15.

34. Hyslop, "E. P. Thompson in South Africa."

35. Belinda Bozzoli and Peter Delius, "Radical History and South African History," in *History from South Africa: Alternative Visions and Practices*, ed. Joshua Brown (Philadelphia: Temple University Press, 1991), 4–25.

36. Bonner, "Keynote Address to the 'Life after Thirty' Colloquium." Paul Maylam, "Tensions within the Practice of History," *South African Historical Journal* 33 (1999): 3–12. Bozzoli and Delius, "Radical History and South African History." Witz and Rassool, "Making Histories," 6–15.

37. E. P. Thompson, *The Making of the English Working Class* (New York: Vintage, 1963), 12.

38. Isabel Hofmeyr, "'Wailing for Purity': Oral Studies in Southern African Studies," *African Studies* 54 (1995): 16–31.

39. Ciraj Rassool, "Power, Knowledge and the Politics of Public Pasts," accessed September 4, 2014 (http://www.nelsonmandela.org/images/uploads/PAPER_-_RASSOOL.pdf).

40. Luise White, "True Stories: Narrative, Event, History, and Blood in the Lake Victoria Basin," in *African Words, African Voices: Critical Practices in Oral History*, ed. Luise White and Stephen Miescher (Bloomington: Indiana University Press, 2001), 281–304.

41. Charles Van Onselen, *The Seed Is Mine: The Life of Kas Maine, a South African Sharecropper, 1894–1985* (Cape Town: David Philip, 1996).

42. Minkley and Legassick, "Recent Trends in the Production of South African History."

43. Steven Friedman traces this anxiety about the role of nationalist formations within the trade union movement. Friedman, "From Classroom to Class Struggle." Belinda Bozzoli anticipated these anxieties in her description of the relations between various parties participating in the Open Days in the late 1980s. Bozzoli, "Intellectuals, Audiences and Histories." Jeff Peires advocated that historians collaborate with the post-transition ANC government. Jeff Peires, "The Art of Writing History," *South*

African Review of Books 6 (1994): 24. Bill Freund's rejoinder to Peires marked out the independent path for politically engaged historians. Bill Freund, "The Art of Writing History," *Southern African Review of Books* 7 (1994): 24.

44. Rassool, "Power, Knowledge and the Politics of Public Pasts."

45. Jacob Dlamini, *Native Nostalgia* (Auckland Park: Jacana 2009), 18.

46. Bonner, "Keynote Address to 'Life after 30' Colloquium," 18. Bozzoli, "Intellectuals, Audiences and Histories."

47. Ciraj Rassool, "Writing, Authorship and I. B. Tabata's Biography: From Collective Leadership to Presidentialism," *Kronos* 34 (2008): 181–14. Minkley and Legassick, "Recent Trends in the Production of South African History." Gary Minkley and Ciraj Rassool, "Orality, Memory, and Social History in South Africa," in *Negotiating the Past: The Making of Memory in South Africa*, ed. Sarah Nuttall et al. (Oxford: Oxford University Press, 1998), 89–99. Witz and Rassool, "Making Histories," 6–15.

48. Minkley and Rassool, "Orality, Memory, and Social History in South Africa," 94.

49. Hyslop, "E. P. Thompson in South Africa."

50. Writing in 1996, Bill Freund suggested that the "real revolutionary road" that could be taken by post-apartheid historians was a path away from a struggle-centric history of South Africa. In other words, there should be a place for histories whose central purpose is something other than taking sides in a fight over whom struggle history belongs to and who has the right to write it. Freund argued the scope of historical inquiry needed widening in order to include topics not directly related to telling the story of the ruling party. I would add that historical inquiry could also be widened by telling the story of the ruling party in a different way: by calling attention to overlooked or displaced episodes of that story and pointing out the way they have been tidied up through misinterpretation of evidence. Freund, "The Art of Writing History," 24.

51. This sentiment is best expressed by Thabo Mbeki in his foreword to the South Africa Democratic Education Trust's The Road to Democracy series. Mbeki laments that "most unfortunately we allowed some of our greatest heroes and heroines, the patriots who personified our struggle in its complexity to pass away without recording one word about themselves, their role in our history, their views about their past, their lives and times, and what they saw of our future." Mbeki further praises the "patriots" led by Ben Magubane and wishes them "success in their supremely important work, and urge them to produce yet more volumes that will document our road to democracy.'" Mbeki, "Foreword," vii–xii.

52. Hyslop, "E. P. Thompson in South Africa."

53. "Our history" has an old pedigree despite its recent reemergence as a critical term in the intellectual lexicon of the post-apartheid nationalist historiography. Z. K. Matthews was an incredibly influential professor at Fort Hare who taught a generation of liberation movement leaders. His recollection of his own experiences with the history taught when he was a student at Fort Hare anticipate the way 'our history' was

deployed in post-apartheid nationalist historiography. Matthews wrote: "As African students in a land dominated by Europeans, we were in a particularly uncomfortable position. Our history, as we had absorbed it from the tales and talk of our elders, bore no resemblance to South African history as it has been written by European scholars, or as it has been taught in South African schools, and as it was taught to us at Fort Hare. The European insisted that we accept his version of the past and what is more, if we wanted to get ahead educationally, even to pass examinations in the subject as he presents it. It was one thing to accept willingly and even eagerly the white man's world of literature and science. It was quite another to accept his picture of how we all came to occupy the places in life now assigned to us." Z. K. Matthews, *Freedom for My People: The Autobiography of Z. K. Matthews: Southern Africa 1901 to 1968* (Cape Town: David Philip, 1981), 59. Quoted in Donovan Williams, *A History of the University College of Fort Hare, South Africa, the 1950s: The Waiting Years* (Lewiston, NY: Edwin Mellen, 2001), 215.

54. The quintessential statement of "our history" was articulated by Ben Magubane in a polemic written when he was then chief editor of the SADET project. Magubane, "Whose Memory—Whose History?," 251–79.

55. Edward Roux, *Time Longer Than Rope* (London: V. Gollancz, 1948). Tabata, *The Awakening of a People*. Nosipho Majeke (Dora Taylor), *The Role of Missionaries in Conquest* (Johannesburg: Society of Young Africa, 1952). Mnguni (Hosea Jaffe), *Three Hundred Years* (Cape Town: New Era Fellowship, 1952). Simons and Simons, *Class and Colour in South Africa*. Govan Mbeki, *The Peasants' Revolt* (Harmondsworth, UK: Penguin, 1965). A separate but related set of biographies of activists was an influential parallel literature. Brian Bunting, *Moses Kotan: South African Revolutionary* (London: Inkululeko, 1975). Edward Roux, *S. P. Bunting: A Political Biography* (Johannesburg: self-published, 1944).

56. Although it would be a misnomer to call 1950s-vintage historiography nationalist in orientation, communist authors did justify their alliance with their strategy of allying with "bourgeois" nationalists in the medium term in their histories. The theoretical prescription that allowed for this deviation from orthodox Marxist praxis came in the form of the colonialism of a special type theory (CST) developed by party members in the 1950s. This theory presumed that South Africa must undergo a two-stage revolution: first, national liberation and later, a class struggle leading to socialism. For a closer, albeit partisan, reading of how these theoretical bridges inform history, see Baruch Hirson, "The Struggle for a Post-Apartheid Society in South Africa," *Third World Quarterly* 12 (1990): 159–65.

57. This transition is most clear in Veronique Rioufol's examination of the Robben Island Museum and World Heritage Site. Veronique Rioufol, "Behind Telling: Post-Apartheid Representations of Robben Island's Past," *Kronos* 26 (2000): 22–41. Colin Bundy identifies an early critique of the rainbow nation concept in a position paper presented at the ANC National Consultative Conference in Mafeking in 1997

that suggests the turn to African nationalism was well afoot prior to Mbeki assuming the presidency. "Nation-Formation and Nation Building: The National Question in South Africa," accessed June 18, 2016 (http://www.anc.org.za/show.php?id=309).

58. Mbeki's inclusion of Malay slaves, reverence for Boer War graves, and acknowledgment of indentured Indian laborers seems to suggest that he accepts that the new South African nation possesses a more complicated genealogy than a stock-in-trade nativist interpretation would allow. But keep in mind the subtle but crucial difference in wording that reinforces an implicit hierarchy between those who can *say* they are Africans and those who can *claim* they are Africans. Colin Bundy, "New Nation, New History?: Constructing the Past in Post-Apartheid South Africa," in *History Making and Present Day Politics*, ed. Hans Erik Stolten (Uppsala, Sweden: Nordiska Afrikainstitutet, 2007), 73–97.

59. This chronological sleight of hand that belies the nationalist assumption that an advance to socialism after national liberation was not only unnecessary but also harmful to the body politic of the nation and perhaps even an "unnatural" misapplication of an "alien" ideology.

60. Eric Hobsbawm commented directly on the nation-building task the ANC had set for itself. Quoting Massimo d'Azeglio's famous declaration made after the political unification of Italy, "We have made Italy, now we have to make Italians." Hobsbawm suggests that this statement referred to the task of making a nation out of "the inhabitants of the peninsula who had all sorts of identities, but not one based on a language they did not speak, and a state that had come into existence over their heads." He then drew direct comparison between nationalist projects in late-nineteenth-century Italy and late-twentieth-century South Africa: "there was nothing primordial about Italianness, just as there is not about the South Africanness of the ANC." He argued that the hollowness of the history of new nations explained nationalists' appeal to ethnicity as a resource for nationalists to give a primordial aura to national identity. Eric Hobsbawm, "Ethnicity and Nationalism in Europe Today," *Anthropology Today* 8 (1992): 3–8.

The ANC's War against Apartheid

1. A Brief History of Umkhonto we Sizwe and the Armed Struggle

THIS CHAPTER PROVIDES A BASIC accounting of the events that occurred during the armed struggle in parallel with a discussion of the origins, transformations, and dissolution of Umkhonto we Sizwe (MK). The purpose of this chapter is to provide nonspecialist readers with the context necessary to make the episodes featured in subsequent chapters comprehensible, rather than provide a frame to make them into a grand narrative with MK cast as a central protagonist in a heroic or antiheroic struggle against the apartheid state. Toward this end, I flag points where this history has failed to cohere into a consensus interpretation, rather than use events to mark a discrete beginning, middle, and end. This chapter is less a composite account of "what actually happened" so much as an index of points of contestation in both written and oral accounts of this history, as well as a primer in the vocabulary deployed in chapters that focus closely on more discrete episodes.

Readers familiar with the history of armed struggle will immediately notice my emphasis on the experience of exile in this summary. Placing exile at the center of this history is crucial for contextualizing the following chapters because much of the dramatic action of the armed struggle was largely orchestrated from the backstage of exile. Although all history is comprised of multiple experiences and perspectives, the conditions of exile and nature of combat in the armed struggle exaggerated this tendency to a seemingly unworkable degree. As Mwezi Twala wrote of his experience in African National Congress (ANC) camps in the Angolan bush, "a cadre really only knew what was going on in his camp; he did not know what was going on in other camps except by word of mouth and news which was conveyed by truck drivers who brought supplies to the camps. It was frequently difficult to separate fact from fiction."[1] Although Twala is specifically referring to camps, his observation serves as a useful metaphor for illustrating how the armed struggle was always an unstable concept and that this instability is an important part of the experiences of the people who fought within it.

In spite of this inherent instability, memoirs and histories of the armed struggle commonly make claims to some degree of comprehensiveness, while more often than not presenting a segmented understanding of this supposedly unified experience. Furthermore, these works often employ the triple conceit of telling "nothing but the truth" by revealing the "undercover struggle" from an "insider's perspective."[2] Whether marketing strategy, narrative strategy, or a combination of both, the effect of these histories is to suggest that a bedrock of experience exists and that it can be contained within a single text written by a single author. Based on my reading of these often frustratingly contradictory accounts, I argue that arriving at any "comprehensive truth" of the armed struggle is, at best, problematic, at worst, pointless. Nevertheless, there is value in placing these disparate narrative strands together—not in an attempt to cobble together some patchwork account that achieves a probable accuracy, but rather to describe the myriad ways this history was written and rewritten. Placing the historical narrative of a dogged anticommunist against that of a party stalwart while aligning both against an account written by a dissident MK guerrilla presents not only an intellectual challenge but also reveals the spaces, concealments, and silences that run through each perspective.

Origins

The turn to violence that prefaced the creation of MK must be viewed in the context of the shifting political scene in late 1950s and early 1960s. During the 1950s, the ANC led a coalition of political parties, trade unions, and community organizations under the banner of the Congress Alliance. The aim of the alliance, as outlined in the Freedom Charter, was to achieve racial equality, democracy, and an ill-defined redistribution of wealth.[3] Their tactics included a combination of nonviolent passive resistance and mass protest, most often taking the form of labor protests, stay-at-home strikes, boycotts, and civil disobedience.[4] Although alliance members discussed the possibility of violence throughout this period, and in some instances laid the groundwork for later military activity, at this stage most believed exclusively nonviolent means could achieve political change.[5]

The broad alliances and mass protests of the 1950s should not suggest that members shared any consensus beyond the ultimate aims of the struggle and the immediate range of tactics. Instead, the political terrain between various components of the alliance was wide and varied—containing at any given time a motley assortment of Marxists, white liberals, Africanists, and black bourgeois interests, with members assuming multiple guises—sometimes simultaneously. Aside from the ANC leadership itself, communists stood as the most cohesive and disciplined faction within this fluid political environment. Outlawed as a political organization since 1950, key members of the then named Communist Party of South Africa (CPSA) secretly reconstituted their organization as the South African Communist Party (SACP), a tightly organized, underground version of its predecessor.[6] During the mass protests of the 1950s, SACP members joined a variety of organizations within the Congress Alliance, gaining a particularly disproportionate share of leadership posts within the left-leaning Congress of Democrats, as well as within the ANC itself.[7]

As the decade drew to a close, competition between various factions with the Congress Alliance intensified, as popular calls for change outstripped actual gains.[8] In the excited atmosphere of early decolonization, demands for racial equality and democracy in South Africa became ever more urgent, with some openly articulating a political vision markedly different from that enshrined in the Freedom Charter. By 1959, this plurality became untenable, as a faction of Africanists within the ANC split with the organization over the principle of nonracialism and formed a rival organization, the Pan-Africanist Congress (PAC).[9] The PAC quickly questioned the degree to which the ANC and the Congress Alliance could claim to be the sole representative of the oppressed masses. In a series of strikes and protests, the PAC and the ANC each attempted to discredit the populist credentials of their rival. This situation reached a climax on March 21, 1960, when the PAC staged a hastily arranged antipass campaign ten days ahead of a similar campaign scheduled by the ANC.[10] On that day, crowds gathered around a police station in Sharpeville to protest pass laws by returning their hated passbooks. Police fired on the protesters, killing sixty-nine and wounding countless others. In the wake of the Sharpeville massacre, an already-changing political environment accelerated beyond all expectations.

The government reacted to the Sharpeville massacre by outlawing the ANC as well as its rival, the PAC, trying the leaders of both organizations for treason, arbitrarily arresting and detaining some, while subjecting the remainder to intense surveillance and harassment. In the context of this severe disruption and violent government repression, many within the ANC began to seriously question its future as an exclusively nonviolent organization.[11] In the summer of 1961, the Working Committee of the ANC met to discuss the issue of violence. Leading the case for violence was Nelson Mandela, who gained notoriety as the youthful face of ANC passive resistance campaigns during the 1950s. As Mandela recalled in his autobiography, advocates of violence did not want to replace other tactics of passive resistance, so much as complement the range of possibilities available to ANC leaders. Those arguing against Mandela suggested that violence would only invite further government repression, opening the possibility of future massacres and ultimately undermining more conventional tactics. Although sources differ over which circles actually endorsed violence versus nonviolence, the executive committee eventually arrived at a compromise. The ANC itself would not accept violence as a new resolution but would create a "separate and independent organ, linked to the ANC and under the overall control of the ANC, but fundamentally autonomous."[12]

With this momentous decision, the ANC embarked on a thirty-year intermittent armed struggle against the apartheid government. This new organization, dubbed Umkhonto we Sizwe and abbreviated as MK, also established the first sustained administrative link between the SACP and the ANC, fostering a level of cooperation greater than previously enjoyed between the two organizations.[13] In these early years, this collaboration was far from equal. Black and white planners alike carefully managed perceptions of white communist involvement by staffing conspicuous MK positions with prominent black leaders. Behind the scenes, white communists—many veterans of the Springbok Legion that served in World War II—trained new recruits in clandestine operations and sabotage techniques.[14] In the final months of 1961, a regional structure emerged, with each group securing chemicals and explosives locally, through legal channels or by theft.[15]

Sabotage and Operation Mayibuye

Ronnie Kasrils, then a junior member of the Natal Regional Command, recalled that the ultimate aim of these preparations was far from apparent, especially to those on the inside. Kasrils writes of the confusion: "Were we aiming to simply put pressure on the government—to force it to change—or to overthrow it? If so, how? I perceived these questions only dimly at the time. In retrospect, from what Jack [Hodgson] and others told us, I came to realize that the strategy had not been clearly worked out."[16] Kasrils suggests that MK served a counterhegemonic function, by "demonstrate[ing] that apartheid rule could be challenged," rather than engaging in wholescale revolutionary warfare. This joint mobilization also provided new recruits with their first sustained exposure to Marxist theory, acquired as a consequence of learning the proper way to operate a clandestine military organization.

On December 16, 1961, during a public holiday commemorating the Voortrekker victory over Dingaan, bombs exploded near government offices and critical infrastructure in all major cities in South Africa. In conjunction with the bombings, leaflets and posters publicly announced the arrival of MK. This carefully orchestrated operation would be the first of dozens carried out over the next two years, all designed to minimize the possibility of "civilian" casualties, while maximizing damage to visible government symbols and disrupting economic prosperity.

Concurrent with the domestic sabotage campaign, the ANC accelerated existing plans to internationalize their organization by establishing relationships with sympathetic governments. Ghana was a likely choice, given Kwame Nkrumah's professed Pan-Africanist commitment to the decolonization of Africa.[17] Tennyson Makiwane, the first director of international affairs, established an office there as early as 1959, only to be expelled in 1961 when Nkrumah mercurially realigned himself with the PAC.[18] Fortunes changed in 1962, when the Pan-African Freedom Movement for Eastern, Central, and Southern Africa (PAFMECSA) sent Mandela on a whirlwind tour of recently decolonized African states.[19] Traveling to Egypt, Morocco, Algeria, Ghana, Tanganyika, and Ethiopia, among other African states, Mandela, later accompanied by Joe Matthews and Oliver Tambo, received assurances of limited funding as well as permission to establish guerilla training camps. In addition, Mandela visited ANC offices in London while meeting with parliamentary opposition leaders. Despite effusive promises, PAFMECSA member nations remained fair weather allies. Akin to its indirect descendent, the Organization of African Unity Liberation Committee, the commitment of member states to Pan-African struggles against colonialism waxed and waned as diplomatic pressures mounted and internal disputes divided African nations.[20]

Following Mandela's arrest on August 5, 1962, the tenor of MK operations shifted from sabotage to preparations for probable exile. In October, the ANC held its first annual conference in three years in Lobatse, across the border from the Transvaal in the Bechuanaland Protectorate. This unusual meeting consisted of only a handful of ANC leaders, accompanied by a significantly larger contingent of dual SACP/ANC members serving on the influential steering committee.[21] The Lobatse Conference, as historian Stephen Ellis points out, marked an important turning point in MK, as well as in the ever-changing relationship between the ANC and the SACP. At this meeting, the ANC formally adopted "armed struggle" as one of its principle means for achieving racial equality and democracy in South Africa. The ambiguity of MK's autonomous status was erased as the ANC, under SACP influence, formally committed itself to a military solution. Although strong evidence suggests the ANC arrived at the decision under the undue influence of dual ANC/SACP members, this relationship can also be considered a marriage of convenience that conferred advantages on both parties, however uneven these might be. As Ellis indicates, the ANC's legacy of mass politics provided the SACP with a popular legitimacy it was otherwise unable to attract underground. Furthermore, the ANC—regardless of its earlier reformist ambitions—remained the oldest African political organization and enjoyed an unparalleled familiarity with the intricacies of black political life in South Africa. Likewise, the ANC lacked any experience operating as an illegal organization, thus, greatly benefiting from the expertise of the SACP in such matters. Accepting the armed struggle as the current mode of resistance, the ANC also came to depend on the SACP for its connections to the Soviet Union, a nation that later proved to be its most reliable and generous donor.[22]

Within a few short months, Duma Nokwe, Moses Kotane, and Tambo traveled to various Eastern Bloc nations, assuring socialist countries of the

ANC's newfound commitment to armed struggle and amicable partnership with the SACP.[23] Such arrangements proved timely, when, on July 11, 1963, South African police, acting on a tip from informant and MK commander Bruno Mtolo, raided the Lilliesleif Farm in Rivonia, capturing much of the MK high command (see figure 1).[24] In the chaotic months that followed, further arrests ensued as additional MK cadres cooperated with authorities, while the remainder either went into hiding or exile. This series of arrests forestalled the implementation of Operation Mayibuye—a plan for the mass infiltration of MK cadres trained abroad, which heralded the beginning of guerrilla war aimed at toppling the apartheid state.

Exile

Eloquently captured by Fish Keitseng, an ANC member based in Lobatse, Botswana, the first journeys out of South Africa during this period proved to be both peripatetic and fearful.[25] Keitseng guided dozens of ANC and SACP members on the "Northern Highway," a route passing through Bechuanaland Protectorate to Northern Rhodesia and Southern Rhodesia where contracted flights completed the journey to Dar es Salaam or London.[26] Further complicating this journey, South African police enjoyed a broad network of spies within the Bechuanaland and neighboring territories, often forcing Keitseng to travel on obscure routes and by cover of darkness to evade detection and arrest. Even with all possible precautions, exiles still faced the uncertain prospect of air travel. Pilots occasionally reneged on their contracts by returning their fugitive passengers to South Africa, while problems with payment often delayed contracted flights, and sabotage remained a distinct possibility, as seen in December 1962 when South African agents bombed a plane used to transport exiles.[27]

In these early years, most exiles assembled in Dar es Salaam before embarking on their final destinations. From Dar es Salaam, experienced exiles assumed a variety of posts within the international structures, while less-experienced cadres might be sent to a variety of locations for guerilla training or to complete their formal education.[28] In the early 1960s, ANC guerrillas trained in camps located in Algeria, Morocco, and Egypt, while the SACP handpicked particularly promising candidates for training in the Soviet Union in facilities near Odessa, later sending recruits for specialization in East Germany, Czechoslovakia, and Bulgaria.[29] Prior to the Sino-Soviet split, a small group of cadres led by veteran trade unionist Joe Gqabi prepared in China at a training camp outside Nanking.[30]

Regardless of rank, at this time most ANC and SACP members regarded exile as a temporary condition. Kasrils, himself sent to the Odessa training camp, wrote, "We expected that we would return as a part of a victorious revolutionary army in a couple of years at the most. Not for a moment did we anticipate that we were going into exile for decades."[31] The experience of traveling to the Soviet Union, where would-be "freedom fighters" acquired the esoteric knowledge of warfare from seasoned World War II veterans, all conspired to buffet the hopes of MK guerrillas. This spirit of optimism caused Kasrils to comment, "everyone expected to return home after completing training."[32] Indeed, many guerrillas deliberately left family behind and told them nothing about their secret departure, all because they were confident in forecasts of a temporary exile followed by quick victory.

Although few memoirs and histories provide a picture of life in North African and Chinese camps, several exiles wrote detailed accounts of their experience in the Soviet Union. The accounts of black recruits tend to foreground the racial tolerance of their Soviet hosts.[33] In comparison with many South African whites, the Soviets appeared racially enlightened. Nevertheless, this appearance is belied by other accounts that record some degree of tension.[34] Off base, African cadres and Soviet men occasionally fought over women, while so-called loose forces—drunken ANC cadres engaged in a variety of infractions—sometimes found themselves locked in local jails.[35] On base, cadres drilled in formation, trained in winter conditions, and took courses in heavy artillery, all of which later proved to be unsuitable to the sort of engagements they would later fight in the African bush and South African townships. As indicated earlier, most Soviet instructors were World War II veterans, who based their lessons on the Soviet experience of the Great Patriotic War, which shaped their perceptions of the sort of combat MK recruits might face in South Africa.[36] Although military training adapted over time, the first generation of MK recruits—like their Soviet-aligned Zimbabwean People's Revolutionary Army (ZIPRA) counterparts—returned to Africa to face an unconventional war with a largely conventional orientation.[37]

Securing a stable presence in newly independent African states presented another set of difficulties. By the mid-1960s, the political climate in host states was far from settled and predictable. Within host states, internal factions jockeyed for position amid an uncertain postindependence political environment, leaving ANC leaders with the difficult task of aligning themselves with the most promising contenders, without offending their current hosts. No state better illustrates this sensitive situation better than Tanzania. Under the "African socialist" regime of Julius Nyerere, Dar es Salaam became a mecca for radical politics and exiled liberation movements. The New Africa Hotel served as the watering hole for a veritable who's who of would-be nationalist leaders exiled from remaining colonial states.[38] An alphabet soup of organizations informally crossed paths in this social world, forming loose affiliations with one another and well as with observant foreign sponsors. Out of this ferment emerged a fragile alliance between the Soviet-supported "big five" liberation organizations: Mozambique Liberation Front (FRELIMO), Zimbabwe African People's Union (ZAPU), People's Movement for the Liberation of Angola (MPLA), South West Africa People's Organization (SWAPO), and the ANC. Lesser contenders also moved in and out of this Dar es Salaam, securing funding from often unreliable sources such as the Organization of African Unity (OAU) Liberation Committee and China, all the while capitalizing on the political missteps and internal disputes of their better funded and more visible rivals.[39]

Despite the warm reception offered by Nyerere, Tanzanian officials within the Tanganyika African National Union (TANU) ruling party soon became suspicious of the burgeoning community of liberation movements. In 1964, the government forced all liberation movements to vacate their offices in Dar es Salaam, permitting each group only four representatives in the capital. The ANC relocated its offices to Morogoro, the site of one of four MK guerrilla camps in rural Tanzania. In 1967, Arthur Kambona, a close adviser to President Nyerere and Tanzanian representative to the OAU Liberation Committee, fled the country amid allegations he planned to overthrow the government. As revealed during his trial in absentia two years later, Kambona allegedly propositioned the leaders of several guest armies, including Tambo, then the acting president of the ANC, and Potlako Leballo of the PAC. According to Stephen Ellis, Tambo refused to assist Kambona but neglected to inform Nyerere of the plot. Such revelations soured relations between the ANC and Nyerere, permitting the PAC to manipulate the scandal to their benefit and ultimately leading to the expulsion of MK from Tanzania in late 1969.[40]

Although Zambia was similarly known for capricious internal politics, at the direction of Soviet backers, in 1965 the ANC shifted the bulk of its operations to Lusaka. At the same time, Joe Modise and Matthews began plans for a joint MK-ZIPRA offensive into Rhodesia, where it was hoped that ANC guerrillas might fight their way into South Africa. Although different authors assign differing rationales for this operation, most suggest that at the time, the ANC faced growing dissention from MK guerrillas over the pace and direction of the armed struggle. By this time, many of the earliest trainees had already spent several years in Tanzania and Zambian guerrilla camps, undergoing seemingly endless drills and exercises under an increasingly authoritarian command structure, while the possibility of actual combat seemed ever more remote (see figure 2). In addition to the stalled liberation war, many guerrillas sensed a two-tiered structure emerging between exiles, with military, political, and diplomatic staff living a more comfortable lifestyle, and a Spartan existence endured by the rank and file stationed in the camps. This perception often drifted into charges of corruption levied at select figures within ANC leadership, many of whom stood accused of embezzling funds intended for military purposes.[41]

The Wankie Campaign

In June 1967, with backing from the National Executive Committee, Modise and Matthews began to infiltrate guerrillas across the Zambian-Rhodesia border in preparation for the upcoming offensive. In August, the Luthuli Detachment assembled at two points along the Zambezi River, crossing into Rhodesian territory with the aim of establishing a self-sustained presence in the country that they could later parlay into a corridor to South Africa. Although Ken Flower, then director of the Rhodesian Central Intelligence Office (CIO), recalled that the MK recruits fought surprisingly well, their offensive permitted a much larger Rhodesian force to eventually inflict heavy casualties. Within a few weeks, the Rhodesians, along with an ineffective contingent of South African Police, repelled the joint MK-ZIPRA force back into Zambia, while another group escaped to the southwest into

Botswana. Chris Hani led the contingent in Botswana, and they were all arrested and tried by authorities on weapons charges. Hani and others served two years in prison on these charges.[42]

Morogoro

By all accounts, the Wankie Campaign was a bitter defeat for the ANC, SACP, and their allies, despite its propaganda value to audiences at home and abroad. Guerrillas failed in their objective to establish a transit route through Rhodesia, suggesting to many that the possibility of bringing the battle to South Africa was, at that moment, moribund. Given the circumstances of the defeat—a small force applying classic guerrilla techniques against a significantly larger army followed by the failure to resupply units once "in country"—many speculated that Modise, among others, orchestrated the doomed campaign to rid the ANC of troublesome dissenters. To those holding this view, it was no accident that Hani—among the most vocal critics of the Lusaka leadership—found himself as the head commissar of the unit leading the failed operation. Regardless of the actual inspiration for the Wankie Campaign, its effects on morale within the ANC proved devastating.[43]

Upon his release from prison in 1969, Hani returned to Lusaka and circulated a memorandum in which he lambasted senior leaders for a variety of offenses. Later known as the Hani Memorandum, the document sent shock waves through all quarters of the external mission. Vladimir Shubin, a former Soviet handler for the ANC, suggested that the document laid blame for the failure of the operation on a culture of "careerism" that plagued the exile organization. In essence, Hani's complaint was that the organization grew complacent in exile and that leaders forfeited struggle and sacrifice for a lifestyle of comfort and personal gain. Hani minced few words by calling out specific leaders by name, directly charging veteran ANC lawyer Nokwe with drunkenness, referencing chief representative James Hadebe's expulsion from Tanzania for "counterrevolutionary activities," while sharply criticizing Modise's competency as MK commander. Hani also struck at the growing stratification of the exile structures. He indirectly attacked the privileged sons and daughters of high-ranking leaders who enjoyed scholarships to Western universities and prestigious posts in the diplomatic wing, while highlighting the condition of less-connected, poorer recruits who bore the brunt of the armed struggle in bush camps. Although Hani merely articulated the bitterness felt by many Wankie veterans, some ranking leaders equated his frankness with treason. Indeed, if not for the intervention of Mzwai Piliso, Hani might have faced imprisonment, expulsion, or worse.[44]

Largely in response to the criticisms levied in the Hani Memorandum, in late April 1969, the ANC gathered representatives together in Morogoro for its Third Consultative Conference—the first since its flight into exile. By all accounts, the ANC was in a state of crisis in the late 1960s. The armed struggle ground to a halt in Rhodesia. Erstwhile African hosts proved to be less than reliable when internal and external pressures mounted. Finally, the South African government enjoyed an unparalleled era of peace and prosperity while implementing the basic structures of "high apartheid," accelerating the forced removal of "black spots," installing the first Bantustans, all the while continuing to suppress domestic political dissent. Against the security of its sworn enemy, the exile community found itself largely demoralized by the Wankie Campaign and internally divided along many lines. Although it is tempting to portray these divisions as purely ideological—pitting communists against Africanist factions—this internal dynamic was, in fact, far more complex, encompassing the psychological effects of geography, emergent patterns of patronage, and long-standing personal relationships.[45]

In some respects, the Morogoro Conference marked an important turning point for the ANC. Many commentators often portray these changes made at Morogoro as evidence of the growing influence of the SACP. While the SACP certainly gained leverage within its partner organization at this time, again, the idea that these administrative maneuverings represented clearly define blocs neatly aligned to specific ideological positions obscures more complex motives. Perhaps the most important change made during Morogoro was the inclusion of so-called non-Africans into the External Mission of the ANC. After much debate and consternation, delegates eventually agreed to permit white, Indian, and Coloured membership but added two important limitations: first, non-Africans continued to be barred from the ANC structures within South Africa, and second, non-Africans remained ineligible for membership in the National Executive Committee. Flag Boshielo, a veteran communist, led the case for the inclusion of whites, arguing that at such a critical moment in the struggle, the ANC needed to open its arms to all, while at the same time committing its very organization to principle of nonracialism as outlined in the first clauses of the Freedom Charter. Kotane, also a veteran communist, argued against the inclusion of whites, fearing an influx of whites into leadership positions might further undermine the legitimacy of the organization in the eyes of its predominantly black rank and file. Although a variety of submerged motives accompanied these stated positions, the adoption of limited nonracialism, in effect, opened the door to communists who were previously barred from a variety of decision-making bodies within the ANC.[46]

The decision to include non-Africans had a cascading effect on other decisions made at Morogoro and at corollary meetings held shortly thereafter. Delegates voted in favor of the creation of the Revolutionary Council, a decision that collected previously scattered posts into a single body solely dedicated to the planning and execution of MK operations. The Revolutionary Council, subordinate to the National Executive Committee, fell below the executive level, thus leaving membership open to whites, Indians, and Coloureds—as well as Africans. As a consequence of their specialized training, as well as their connection to Soviet donors, communists of all colors dominated the new policy-making body. As witnessed by the election of non-Africans such as Joe Slovo, Yusef Dadoo, and Reg September, and longstanding "dual members,"—Africans who belonged to both the ANC and SACP—the party achieved an unparalleled level of influence over the Revolutionary Council and, in turn, over the subsequent course of the armed struggle. Exercising this newfound leverage, communists also offered the "Strategy and Tactics" policy document for consideration at Morogoro. Ultimately approved by the Consultative Committee, the Strategy and Tactics document discounted the urban African working class as the most likely source of revolution in South Africa. The authors of the document followed a loose Marxist-Leninist interpretation of the possibility for revolution, while tracing the overthrow of the South African state through the rural locations, strangely bypassing the possibility of revolution in townships. This document further confused the already-muddied theorization that prefaced earlier armed actions, while misaligning future operations from Soviet appraisals of the South African situation.[47]

Malaise

Despite this internal reorganization and external planning, the ANC still lacked the forward bases it needed to stage attacks into South Africa. Making matters worse, immediately following the Morogoro Conference, the Zambian and Tanzanian governments almost simultaneously expelled MK units from their respective territories. Just prior to the Morogoro Conference, Zambia joined other East and Central African states in signing the Lusaka Manifesto, which demanded that liberation organizations desist from the armed struggle in their territories in exchange for a rather hollow recognition of human equality by the remaining colonial powers in southern Africa. Then, in July 1969, Nyerere ordered MK personnel out of the Kongwa camp in southeastern Tanzania, in response to evidence presented at the trial in absentia of Kambona, indicating Tambo knew of the coup attempt but neglected to inform authorities. The expulsion of troops from Kongwa, combined with Zambian reticence about conducting the armed struggle from its soil, eventually forced the ANC to temporarily relocate all MK personnel to Moscow. The uneasy environment in host states also prompted the ANC and SACP to approach even more remote nations such as Sudan in the event of a permanent and total expulsion. Irrespective of the aims expressed at Morogoro, the unpredictable situation in host states compelled the ANC and SACP to devote precious attention to merely remaining on the continent of Africa, rather than fomenting revolution at home.[48]

In the early 1970s, malaise once again descended on the ANC and SACP. At this time, a buffer of unsympathetic states and colonies ringed South Africa, isolating its borders from any sustained incursion by MK guerrillas. Without a reliable path into South Africa, planning for revolution remained an armchair theorizing endeavor. Although the Revolutionary Council endlessly debated the proper technical conditions for fomenting revolution, the failure to establish bases in forward areas, as well as internal structures within South Africa, effectively mooted any prospective conclusion. Nevertheless, the Revolutionary Council made some attempts to remedy this situation, as evidenced in 1971 when Slovo authorized Operation J, a scheme to land guerrillas and weapons on the Transkei coast using a ship moored off the East African coast. However, on the inaugural journey, the engines of the *Aventura* seized off the Tanzanian coast, stalling hopes of any future sea landings. The SACP also attempted to rekindle awareness of the exiled liberation movement within South Africa by staging a number of propaganda spectacles in select cities. Young SACP cadres, such as Jeremy Cronin, Raymond Suttner, and David and Sue Rabkin, planted leaflet bombs outside railway stations and bus terminals, often leaving car radios blasting recorded messages from exile leaders. Spectacular as these operations might have seemed to perpetrators and witnesses alike, they did not attract the kind of popular support the ANC needed to bring the struggle to the home front. Instead, ten years into exile, the core of the ANC-SACP alliance remained a relatively small, increasingly aged group, beleaguered by their precarious foothold in Africa, preoccupied with internecine disputes, and increasingly stratified by the peculiar flows of patronage arriving from international donors.[49]

In April 1974, disaffected army officers overthrew Portuguese prime minister Marcello Caetano. Although the liberation struggle in Angola and Mozambique preceded the coup by nearly ten years, few observers of South Africa predicted the coup or foresaw its impact on the geopolitics of the region. By 1975, both Angola and Mozambique moved toward independence, with the socialist-aligned MPLA and FRELIMO both expected to win preindependence elections. Within South Africa, the decolonization of Portuguese Africa greatly encouraged a new generation of politically minded youths, already articulating their own visions of liberation within the language of the Black Consciousness Movement. The Vorster government, underestimating the strength and commitment of student activists, began to implement language requirements set out in the Bantu Education Act, another in a series of apartheid laws designed to reduce educational opportunities available to blacks, this time by restricting the language of instruction to Afrikaans. A new wave of mass protest swept South Africa, largely independent of the direction of the ANC. In the aftermath of the Soweto shootings, the ANC once again found itself behind the people it purported to lead—struggling to stay ahead of popular calls for political change, all the while maintaining the image of continued relevancy for both domestic and international audiences.[50]

The Post-Soweto Exodus

The massive exodus of South African youths and the collapse of buffer states raised the stakes of the liberation struggle, forcing exiles to capitalize on these changes or be swept aside by other contenders. Over the next several years, the ANC attempted to simultaneously absorb waves of new exiles, building a series of forward bases and safe houses in Angola, Mozambique, Swaziland, and Lesotho, while implanting their model of revolution into the emergent culture of mass protest gripping urban South Africa. Given the complexity of any one of these tasks, taken together these challenges greatly exacerbated preexisting tendencies within the exile community, while introducing a set of previously unknown problems.

Just a few months before the Soweto uprising, under pressure from the SACP, the ANC leadership expelled the "Gang of Eight," a group of veteran ANC members. Several of those expelled claimed ANC membership cards that dated earlier than the Defiance Campaign, while many also enjoyed personal friendships and even familial ties to the old-guard ANC leadership. One member of the Gang of Eight, Makiwane, had been director of international affairs during the crisis years of the late 1950s and early 1960s, a personal friend of Tambo, and cousin to Intelligence Chief Piliso. Although the reasons for their expulsion are complex and vary among different accounts, Tennyson and other dissidents enjoyed high-ranking positions within the ANC prior to the Morogoro Conference but languished thereafter, often assigning blame for their political downfall on the ascendancy of white, Indian, and Coloured communists within the organization. Prior to Morogoro, another of the eight, Themba Mqota, even organized a faction that unsuccessfully challenged the reelection of Tambo to the National Executive Committee. After Morogoro, unbeknown to SACP leaders, Tambo held a secret meeting in the bush with the faction where he offered each patronage positions as advisers to the president. Despite attempts to reconcile with these dissenters, by 1975, the situation came to a head after the eight dissidents used the occasion of a funeral for longtime Africanist Robert Resha to rail against the growing influence of the SACP within the ANC. This provocation proved to be their last, forcing the National Executive Committee to expel the group later that year. As SACP members used their publications to tar the group as "counterrevolutionary" and "reactionary," the Gang of Eight responded in kind, creating a short-lived splinter group known as the *Africanist* National Congress, which issued a number of embarrassing diatribes against the ANC and SACP from its London office.[51]

Like the exodus of old-guard self-proclaimed "Africanists," the influx of the Soweto generation further tested the already-complex relationship between the ANC and SACP. Troubled by divisions within its existing membership, factions within the ANC and SACP competed with one another to imprint their politics on new recruits arriving from South Africa. Many leaders assumed the Soweto generation to be political neophytes devoid of any careful analysis of South African society, politics, and economics and arriving tabula rasa to be molded by various interests. This perception does not meet the reality that incoming recruits arrived with established political sensibilities born from the Black Consciousness Movement. This misperception fostered one of the most significant divides between the older exile leadership and incoming youths. Nevertheless, rival factions perceived recruits in this way and, based on this perception, approached the influx as a means to remake the entire exile community in their respective image.[52]

While the communist-heavy Revolutionary Council controlled the overall planning and strategy of MK, under MK commander Modise, ANC stalwarts retained responsibility for the day-to-day operation of existing guerrilla camps in Zambia and those tentatively reopened in Tanzania. This expansion into Angola, however, provided the party with new means to extend its influence within the ranks of this rapidly expanding army. Political education in the camps was delivered largely by party members who heavily favored a Marxist-Leninist interpretation of the struggle, which shaped the political outlook of thousands of cadres who received training in Angola.

Angola and Armed Propaganda

In May 1977, the Novo Catengue camp opened, followed soon after by the aptly named Funda camp.[53] Among the largest of the Angolan camps, Novo Catengue became known as the University of the South, complete with a heavily Marxist curriculum authored by senior party member Jack Simons. Although any estimates of MK troop strengths or camp output wildly vary, in all likelihood graduates of Novo Catengue numbered in the low thousands, comprising a significant portion of the overall guerrilla army after the late 1970s.[54]

The expansion of training facilities in Angola coincided with a comprehensive strategic review conducted by a senior delegation during a visit to Vietnam in October 1978. General Võ Nguyên Giáp met with the delegation and discussed the prospects for revolution in South Africa. In a meeting that greatly influenced MK strategy and tactics in the next few years, Giáp emphasized the primacy of the political over the military, encapsulated in his concept of armed propaganda, which, in the Vietnamese context, consisted of highly visible military attacks orchestrated primarily for political objectives. Such attacks could result in operational failures when judged in military terms but would, in theory, provide a psychological boost to the masses that might catalyze aboveground political organization. Giáp also stressed the importance of these legal, united front organizations such as school associations and trade unions, which could consistently politicize the masses, augment military activities, and ultimately pave the way for a successful popular revolution. Although Giáp's advice encompassed some strategies long employed by the MK, he provided the delegation with a coherent narrative of how each element worked together to foment revolution, all backed by apparent evidence of their overall success in Vietnam. As Howard Barrell noted in his epic analysis of MK strategy and tactics, the impact of Giáp's guidance resulted in a "Damascene conversion" among delegates. Upon return to Lusaka, delegates penned the Green Book, a document that attempted to combine the political and military struggle, while serving as the theoretical underpinning for the next series of MK campaigns.[55]

Loosely following the principles outlined in the Green Book, MK conducted a series of high-profile attacks within South Africa over the next several years. In January 1980, three MK guerrillas entered the Volkskas Bank in Silverton, taking several hostages before police retook the bank and killed all three as well as one hostage in the melee that ensued. Six months later, MK guerrillas detonated oil tanks at the massive refinery at Sasolburg, creating a spectacular explosion visible for miles around, while destroying precious reserves during an ongoing Arab oil embargo of South Africa. One year later, MK guerrillas launched a rocket attack on the Voortrekkerhoogte military base outside Pretoria. The attack achieved little in military terms but presented the ability of MK to operate within South Africa and to strike at a time and place of its choosing. Finally, on December 20, 1982, just days after the thirty-first anniversary of the inaugural MK operation, guerrillas detonated limpet mines within the Koeburg Nuclear Plant situated outside Cape Town. These attacks occurred in conjunction with coordinated media campaigns announcing a succession of popular slogans best exemplified by named years, with 1979 as the "Year of the Spear," 1980 as the "Year of the

Charter," and 1981 as the "Year of the Youth." The intended combined effect of such efforts was to reintroduce the ANC as a player within the internal political scene and to graft ANC politics over the existing ferment by inserting guerrilla attacks into ongoing mass protest.[56]

INFILTRATION AND MUTINY

South African authorities did not passively await the return of the ANC. Indeed, Pretoria used a variety of means to disrupt and destroy the external mission coordinated by an increasingly powerful shadow state orchestrated by the State Security Council. Among the most successful of these means were infiltrators who entered camps disguised as refugees or were recruited for military training by the ANC itself. According to stories circulated within the ranks, on September 20, 1977, an unidentified saboteur, or group of saboteurs, allegedly poisoned the evening meal in the MK mess. Luckily for the hundreds of cadres poisoned, so these stories went, Cuban personnel dined at another facility and did not rotate kitchen staff, unlike the separate kitchen that was administered by MK administration and fed MK cadres. According to official sources, Cuban doctors quickly identified the toxin and administered an antidote, averting a potential tragedy. Aside from this incident, which remains contested, the work of infiltrators was not limited to poisonings. Some infiltrators achieved leadership positions and applied overly strict punishments and training regimens as a way to foment dissent and disrupt operations. Others deliberately destroyed equipment, wasted ammunition, or committed petty theft in order to seed conflict within the ranks. Still others quietly awaited their return to South Africa, where they might reveal their comrades or flee altogether and later pass valuable information to police and military officials. Not all acts of malingering or disobedience could be linked to such infiltrators; nevertheless, the extensive knowledge of the exile community enjoyed by South African authorities definitely suggests that infiltration was both penetrating and routine. Conversely, MK also knew in advance of several South African Air Force (SAAF) bombing raids and cross-border raids, revealing a common feature of liberation wars in Africa—that ostensible adversaries often possessed an intimate, reciprocal knowledge of each other fostered by the presence of double and even triple agents.[57]

This mutual familiarity does not mean that MK was content with the presence of such spies. In 1979, the National Executive Committee created the core structure of National Intelligence, also known as Nat or Mbokodo. Headed by veteran exile Piliso, Mbokodo became a much feared, ruthless presence in the Angolan camps where accusations of spying and sabotage ran rife.[58] After the assassination of several prominent leaders, followed by the chance discovery of a spy ring in Lusaka, the National Executive Committee afforded Mbokodo an extraordinary degree of autonomy throughout the entire organization and sent promising recruits to East Germany for training in interrogation and intelligence. Mbokodo also assumed control of Pango, Viana, Quibaxe, and Quadro, a set of ANC prison camps in northwestern Angola, constructed in 1977 and 1978 and operated largely in isolation from the rest of MK. Although these "secret" camps housed inmates since their creation, the numbers of prisoners soon multiplied as Mbokodo overextended its authority from suspected spies to disaffected guerrillas. Regardless of the veracity of their crime, those imprisoned in the camps faced poor rations, torture, an excessive work regimen, and, occasionally, arbitrary execution. By the time South Africa began its "destabilization" campaign in the early 1980s, an already-paranoid atmosphere in exile reached hysteric proportions, with few excluded from the terror.[59]

Amid this environment of vituperative accusation and widespread dissent, the MPLA called on MK to help defend Malanje province from a series of attacks by União Nacional para a Independência Total de Angola (UNITA). In August 1983, units commanded by Hani, Lennox Zuma, and Timothy Mokoena began operations against Jonas Savimbi's rebels. At first, MK units fought well, repelling UNITA from their positions in spite of the desertion of several Forças Armadas Populares de Libertação de Angola (FAPLA) units. Bolstered by their initial victories, MK units then crossed the Rio Cuanza into UNITA territory, where they encountered fierce resistance, sustained heavy casualties, and retreated to their bases in the towns of Caculama and Kangandala. In early 1984, the situation deteriorated further, cutting off several units from lines of support, resulting in widespread dissatisfaction. When a National Executive Committee delegation headed by Tambo toured Caculama to quell grievances, an ultimatum arrived from troops at Kangandala demanding an immediate halt to actions in Malanje province and requesting a redeployment against South African troops. The troops threatened a mutiny if Tambo refused to meet their demands. In response, Tambo left for Luanda without addressing the troops at Kangandala or submitting to their requests.[60]

The mutiny that ensued, later known as the Mkatashinga, eventually inspired nearly 90 percent of MK personnel in Angola to take up arms against their superiors.[61] Soldiers left the front in commandeered vehicles, attempted to present their demands to the leadership in Luanda but were intercepted by Mbokodo personnel en route and diverted to the transit camp at Viana, just a few kilometers from the Angolan capital. There, the mutineers sent emissaries to other camps as well as to compounds housing Radio Freedom personnel in Luanda, explaining their demands and encouraging further support. Eventually, Hani visited the camp and suggested that the mutineers elect a committee to negotiate with the leadership. The mutineers selected a "Committee of Ten," who presented a litany of even more drastic demands, including the suspension of Mbokodo, a review of strategic policies, and the election of new leaders. After an attempted invasion of Viana by the Angolan Presidential Guard, Hani returned to address the mutineers, convincing them to disarm without further violence. The Committee of Ten was taken into custody, some imprisoned in Nova Instalação, a notorious Luanda prison, while others were sent to prison camps at Pango and Quibaxe, where, two months later, another mutiny occurred, this time followed by several casualties and seven executions.[62]

Uprisings and Negotiations

Although largely unknown outside the exile community, the entire Mkatashinga episode plunged the ANC, the SACP, and the MK into another period of introspection and reorganization akin to that experienced in the wake of the Wankie Campaign. Unlike the Wankie Campaign, the Mkatashinga was quickly followed by the Vaal Triangle uprising, initiating a period of sustained unrest that rivaled all that preceded it. The impact of the regional insurrection soon spread nationwide, combined with the changes instituted at the Fourth Consultative Conference at Kabwe in early 1985, reoriented the struggle to a decidedly different game, repurposing the armed struggle toward gaining leverage in a negotiated settlement, rather than sparking a popular insurrection through armed propaganda or guerrilla warfare. This shift coincided with a steep increase in the number of MK operations inside South Africa. Despite the increase in operations, the quality of planning, training, and reconnaissance suffered, which, combined with the effects of infiltration and defections, led to extremely high rates of attrition for infiltrated MK cadres. One ANC official estimated that nearly 100 percent of cadres infiltrated from Zimbabwe during this period were either killed or captured within twenty-four hours of their deployment into South Africa, and the structures in Mozambique that serviced the Natal Machinery reported similarly high rates of casualties.[63] This expansion in operations abated by March 1989 when MK began to relocate from Angola to Zambia as a result of the Namibian negotiated settlement and then had its activities severely curtailed in Zambia and moved yet again to camps in Uganda and Tanzania.[64] This move effectively halved the number of operations conducted in 1989 from the previous year's totals. As Thula Simpson notes, despite the precipitous and conspicuous decline in operations, the ANC adeptly managed public perceptions that the armed struggle had resulted in the release of Mandela and other leaders and the unbanning of the ANC in February 1990.[65] This era of dramatic releases and mass rallies were carefully and deliberately festooned with imagery, stagecraft, and performance that emphasized the importance of an armed struggle that was privately acknowledged by ANC leaders as effectively over and were containing an internal revolt when disgruntled MK cadres became aware of their views.

The ANC suspended the armed struggle in August 1990 after it agreed to the terms set out in the Pretoria minute, which guaranteed an end to "political offenses," the release of certain categories of prisoners, and a commitment by the government to lift the state of emergency then in effect in Natal.[66] Although top ANC figures claimed the terms of the suspension were conditional on the behavior of the government, the ANC did not return to armed struggle even after it became the target of government-sponsored violence in subsequent months. A contingent of MK cadres was included in the jointly composed force that safeguarded the elections, but aside from this protective role, MK did not engage in any large-scale military activity during the negotiations or thereafter. MK did not march victorious through the streets of Pretoria, although its image remained politically useful long after it was formally disbanded in a ceremony held in Orlando Stadium on December 16, 1993, thirty-two years to the day after its first operations in 1961.

Notes

1. Mwezi Twala and Ed Benard, *Mbokodo: Inside MK, a Soldier's Story* (Johannesburg: Jonathan Ball, 1994), 150. The network of rumors and gossip that tempered an individual's wider awareness of the war they were a part of was colloquially known in camps as "radio potato."

2. Ben Turok, *Nothing but the Truth: Behind the ANC's Struggle Politics* (Johannesburg: Jonathan Ball, 2003). Ronald Kasrils, *Armed and Dangerous: From Undercover Struggle to Freedom* (Auckland Park, South Africa: Jacana, 2013).

3. Congress of the People, "The Freedom Charter," retrieved June 18, 2016 (http://www.anc.org.za/show.php?id=72).

4. Tom Lodge, *Black Politics in South Africa since 1945* (New York: Longman, 1983), 67–68.

5. Nelson Mandela, *Long Walk to Freedom* (Boston: Little, Brown, 1994), 207–8. Paul Landau. "The ANC, MK and 'The Turn to Violence' 1960–1962," *The South African Historical Journal* 64 (2012): 538–63.

6. A. Lerumo (Michael Harmel), *Fifty Fighting Years: The Communist Party of South Africa* (London: Inkululeko, 1971), 89–92.

7. Lionel Bernstein, *Memory against Forgetting: Memoirs from a Life in South African Politics 1938–1964* (London: Viking, 1999), 138–52. Baruch Hirson, *The Revolutions in My Life* (Johannesburg: University of the Witwatersrand Press, 1995), 274–75.

8. Lodge, *Black Politics in South Africa since 1945*, 201–3. Philip Frankel, *An Ordinary Atrocity: Sharpeville and Its Massacre* (Johannesburg: Jonathan Ball, 2001), 7.

9. Mandela, *Long Walk to Freedom*, 230–40.

10. Ibid. Frankel, *An Ordinary Atrocity*, 60–61.

11. Turok, *Nothing but the Truth*, 99–100. Kasrils, *Armed and Dangerous*, 36–37, 44–48. Mandela, *Long Walk to Freedom*, 270–73.

12. Mandela, *Long Walk to Freedom*, 273.

13. isiXhosa for "Spear of the Nation." Recently, a number of publications refer to Umkhonto we Sizwe by placing "the" before it as in "the Umkhonto we Sizwe." Although I heard a handful of interviewees use this format, no one has offered a clear explanation of the difference between referring to MK as just Umkhonto we Sizwe or "The" Umkhonto we Sizwe. isiXhosa does not have definite article "the."

14. Kasrils, *Armed and Dangerous*, 41–46.

15. Ibid., 47–54. Hirson, *The Revolutions in My Life*, 311.

16. Kasrils, *Armed and Dangerous*, 47.

17. Scott Thomas, *The Diplomacy of Liberation: The Foreign Relations of the African National Congress since 1960* (London: Tauris Academic Studies, 1994), 94.

18. Ibid., 43–49.

19. Mandela, *Long Walk to Freedom*, 287–96.

20. Thomas, *The Diplomacy of Liberation*, 127–48. Stephen Ellis and Tsepo Sechaba, *Comrades against Apartheid: The ANC and the South African Communist Party in Exile* (Bloomington: Indiana University Press, 1992), 53–54.

21. Ellis and Sechaba, *Comrades against Apartheid*, 34–35.
22. Ibid.
23. Thomas, *The Diplomacy of Liberation*, 56.
24. Mandela, *Long Walk to Freedom*, 279–82. Kasrils, *Armed and Dangerous*, 58–66.
25. Fish Keitseng, *Comrade Fish: Memories of a Motswana in the ANC Underground* (Gaborone: Pula, 1999), 61–63, 66, 69, 70–71.
26. Kasrils, *Armed and Dangerous*, 77–80.
27. Ibid., 77.
28. Ibid. Vladimir Shubin, *ANC: A View from Moscow* (Bellville, South Africa: Mayibuye Books, 1999), 62–67.
29. Shubin, *ANC*, 62–83.
30. Ellis and Sechaba, *Comrades against Apartheid*, 58.
31. Kasrils, *Armed and Dangerous*, 74.
32. Ibid., 80.
33. Twala and Benard, *Mbokodo*. Phila Ndlovu, interview with author, June 2004.
34. Kasrils, *Armed and Dangerous*, 84.
35. Ibid., 88, 133. Twala and Benard, *Mbokodo*, 20–24.
36. Kasrils, *Armed and Dangerous*, 89. Ellis and Sechaba, *Comrades against Apartheid*, 48–51.
37. Kasrils, *Armed and Dangerous*, 129–30.
38. Ibid., 78–81.
39. Philip Ata Kgosana, *Lest We Forget* (Johannesburg: Skotaville, 1988), 10.
40. Ellis and Sechaba, *Comrades against Apartheid*, 53–59. Shubin, *ANC*, 67–74, 101–11.
41. Ellis and Sechaba, *Comrades against Apartheid*, 47–68. Shubin, *ANC*, 68–80.
42. Keitseng, *Comrade Fish*, 50, 51. Ken Flower, *Serving Secretly: An Intelligence Officer on Record, 1964 to 1981* (London: John Murray, 1987), 107–9.
43. Flower, *Serving Secretly*, 107–9. Ellis and Sechaba, *Comrades against Apartheid*, 50–51, 53. Lodge, *Black Politics in South Africa since 1945*, 299–300.
44. Shubin, *ANC*, 86–89. Kasrils, *Armed and Dangerous*, 253.
45. Lodge, *Black Politics in South Africa since 1945*, 299–300.
46. Flag Boshielo later disappeared mysteriously while on a mission to South Africa via Namibia. Lodge, *Black Politics in South Africa since 1945*, 300–1. Ellis and Sechaba, *Comrades against Apartheid*, 54–59. Kasrils, *Armed and Dangerous*, 97, 194.
47. Curiously Ellis and Sechaba contend that the Strategy and Tactics document achieved the opposite: a strict Marxist-Leninist approach, focused on the urban African proletariat. This interpretation is not supported by my reading of the Strategy and Tactics document. Ellis and Sechaba, *Comrades against Apartheid*, 59–60. Sol Dubula (Joe Slovo), "Strategy and Tactics," retrieved June 18, 2016, https://www.marxists.org/subject/africa/anc/1969/strategy-tactics.htm.
48. Shubin, *ANC*, 96, 99.

49. Kasrils, *Armed and Dangerous*, 123.

50. Hirson, *The Revolutions in My Life*, 89, 199.

51. Themba Mqota went under the nom de guerre Alfred Kgokong and was the first director of the Department International Publicity. His tenure at the Department of International Publicity is omitted in official ANC histories such as Francis Meli's *South Africa Belongs to Us*. Ellis and Sechaba, *Comrades against Apartheid*, 62–65. Lodge, *Black Politics in South Africa since 1945*, 303. Francis Meli, *South Africa Belongs to Us: A History of the ANC* (Bloomington: Indiana University Press, 1988).

52. Kasrils, *Armed and Dangerous*, 124–29. Marion Sparg et al., *Comrade Jack: The Political Lecture and Diary of Jack Simons, Novo Catengue* (Johannesburg: STE, 2004), 115–212.

53. The word *funda* is isiXhosa for "read" or "learn."

54. Kasrils, *Armed and Dangerous*, 180–81. Sparg et al., *Comrade Jack*, 112. Shubin, *ANC*, 196.

55. Howard Barrell, "Conscripts to Their Age: African National Congress Operational Strategy, 1976–1986" (PhD diss., University of Oxford), 210.

56. Ellis and Sechaba, *Comrades against Apartheid*, 101.

57. Ibid., 116–18. Kasrils, *Armed and Dangerous*, 158–59, 214–43. Jack Simons, *Comrade Jack: The Political Lecture and Diary of Jack Simons, Novo Catengue* (Johannesburg: STE, 2004), 112–14. Twala and Benard, *Mbokodo*, 147–49.

58. *Mbokodo* is isiXhosa for "grinding stone."

59. Ellis and Sechaba, *Comrades against Apartheid*, 118–30. Kasrils, *Armed and Dangerous*, 125–53. Twala and Benard, *Mbokodo*, 78–101.

60. Ellis and Sechaba, *Comrades against Apartheid*, 124–40. Kasrils, *Armed and Dangerous*, 249. Shubin, *ANC*, 260–61.

61. The word *mkatashinga* is Kimbundu for "burden."

62. "Reports of the Commission of Enquiry into Certain Allegations of Cruelty and Human Rights Abuse against ANC Prisoners and Detainees by ANC Members" (Johannesburg, 1993), 106–12. Ellis and Sechaba, *Comrades against Apartheid*. Twala and Benard, *Mbokodo*, 65.

63. Thula Simpson, "Toyi-Toyi-ing to Freedom: The Endgame in the ANC's Armed Struggle, 1989–1990," *Journal of Southern African Studies* 35 (2009): 509.

64. Ibid., 511.

65. Ibid., 512.

66. Ibid., 519–20.

2. "I Am Not Prepared to Answer at This Stage": History, Evidence, and the Mamre Camp, December 26–30, 1962

ON WEDNESDAY, DECEMBER 26, 1962, twenty-seven men traveled by truck to the town of Mamre, about thirty kilometers north of Cape Town. They arrived at a property they thought belonged to an associate but actually belonged to the Lutheran Missionary Society. After unloading a motorcar engine, a chart of the human body, and camping equipment, they set up tents only to be instructed to move to a more concealed location surrounded on three sides by a dense thicket.[1] The purpose of the camp continues to be highly contested, but as camp commandant Denis Goldberg put it in an interview in 1990, "it was hardly a Boy Scouts camp."[2] Both organizers were members of Umkhonto we Sizwe (MK), but others had yet to be oathed.[3] After three days of lectures, exercise, and conversation, the caretaker of the property discovered the camp and called the local supervisor for Coloured Affairs, who then summoned the police from Cape Town. After meeting with Albie Sachs and Denis Goldberg, the police instructed the camp attendees to report to the Calendon Square police station for further questioning. The attendees stayed at the camp overnight, then drove back to the Cape Flats, where they disembarked in formation, marching and singing as they headed home.[4]

This description is an assemblage of uncontested details of what was, or was not, the first guerrilla training camp inside South Africa. Everything else that anyone ever said or wrote about the camp was contested or contradicted, sometimes by the same person. Competing claims over whether this was the first guerrilla training camp operated by MK are less important than understanding how recollections of this camp illuminate a series of broader historiographical questions related to the armed struggle in South

Africa. What we know and cannot know about this camp is determined by the evidentiary paradigms that order knowledge about the past. Descriptions of the Mamre camp surface and submerge in three bodies of evidence: court testimony given during the Rivonia Trial, written reportage in the form of published diaries, and oral testimony of camp attendees.[5] The purpose of this chapter is not to weave together these bodies of oral and written evidence into a convincing and authoritative account of what happened in the camp. Rather, I will consider the way these sources have been invoked in negotiations over the purpose, meaning, and legacy of the camp.

The fundamental question of this chapter is, to what extent can we see through various layers of oral and written evidence? The assumption here, following Luise White's arguments on secrecy, lies, and history, is that "texts, whether written or oral, are not transparent."[6] Anyone reporting on the past is simultaneously engaged in the process of interpretation, and interpretation means the selection and omission of details that trouble a certain narrative account. As White puts it, "these authors, or speakers, mediated the past as much as [historians] will do," and consequently, "we can't see through them to the past."[7] The idea of texts constituting a history composed of layer upon layer of interpretation applies to any number of topics but is a particularly useful way of excavating the historical reckonings of the armed struggle. The Mamre camp is useful not just for its notoriety as a possible point of origin of guerrilla warfare in South Africa, but also because it is called to serve so many rhetorical purposes in these three bodies of evidence. What makes this "secret" camp so interesting is not that it remained unspoken but that so many people could not resist talking about it and talked about it in so many ways. At different times, in different venues, and for different audiences, the Mamre camp stood as a signifier for any number of things: local interpretations of the practice of guerrilla war, a token of resistance in a battle of wills between interrogator and interrogated, a site of production of historical knowledge and meaning. In each of these deployments, the narrative conventions and selective arguments of writers and speakers opened and shuttered windows on the past. Contrary to more positivist assumptions that posit that a clearer picture of the past accrues with time and the accumulation of more evidence, this unruly material demonstrates that the details of the Mamre camp become more incomplete and less self-evident with each successive layer of interpretation.

The chronology of events preceding the Mamre camp cannot be understood without describing how locally specific forms of segregation impacted political developments in Cape Town. For a variety of reasons better described elsewhere, there was no clear correlation of labor and ethnicity in Cape Town.[8] This mixture of a Coloured and African working class did not prevent successive governments from segregating public accommodations or subjecting new arrivals from residential segregation. Later, apartheid brought more strident attempts to divide this mixed working class and reorder it into a hierarchy based on racial classifications. The Group Areas Act 1950 and the designation of the Cape as a Coloured labor preference area hardened the boundaries that circumscribed employment and residence for Africans in the Cape. In an ideal form, the entire African population would be reduced in the Cape, leaving only a pliable, male workforce of migrants living in hostels.

Although the ideal outcomes of these laws did not match the realities of enforcement, the effect of this codification of preexisting forms of segregation had a threefold effect on political developments during the latter half of the 1950s. First, it weakened claims on residency, splitting working-class families and placing entire communities in jeopardy of being endorsed out of the city. Second, these laws attempted to drive a wedge between Coloured and African workers. The twin pressures of residential segregation and the social engineering of labor, following others, radicalized working-class politics in the Western Cape to a degree perhaps unseen in other areas.[9]

This radicalization did not result in a mass following for the Congress Alliance. Rather, as government interventions drove further into the body politic, one could best describe the situation as constituencies in search of a political home in the Cape.[10] And while the Congress Alliance did not automatically benefit from the radicalization wrought from these interventions, it certainly attempted to channel discontent into support for its particular brand of nonracial politics. Attendees at the Mamre camp recalled three organizations—the Modern Youth Society, the Volunteers, and the Nyanga Cultural and Social Organization—as important entry points into Congress Alliance politics. Brief mention of these organizations is warranted not because they were the antecedents of MK or inspiration for the Mamre camp, but they did provide a vocabulary of political expression and a repertoire of tactics that reappeared in a different form and under different circumstances at Mamre.

The first of these organizations was the Modern Youth Society. Established by leftist students at the University of Cape Town in 1952 and faded out sometime after the Treason Trial, this nonracial organization was the off-campus mirror of an exclusively on-campus organization. The society organized social gatherings, night classes for African dockworkers, and served as a forum for debate for all manner of leftist politics. In its manifold tasks, the Modern Youth Society served as an important clearinghouse for disseminating leftist ideas in the form of political education for workers but, more importantly, as a sort of brain trust of up-and-coming thinkers and leaders whose influence extended throughout Cape Town and beyond. At a time when Cape Town became more rigidly segregated, and the Congress Alliance itself was organized along racial lines, the Modern Youth Society opened a nonracial space where members could put their ideals into practice. Most often, this meant social events such as two youth camps held over the Easter holidays but also meant conventional activism such as assisting Herman Andimba Toivo ja Toivo to tape-record and smuggle a statement to the United Nations.[11]

Concurrent with the Modern Youth Society was the Volunteers, a paramilitary formed during the Defiance Campaign.[12] The Volunteers had a nationwide presence with regional chapters in each province. The Volunteers were not a paramilitary in the sense that they were a fighting force or an army in waiting but that they adopted many of the embodied affectations of a uniformed force. Members wore khaki coveralls, armbands, and green berets; marched in lockstep; and performed a variety of ceremonial functions during public events such as funerals. Although some have drawn a straight line between the public symbolism of the Volunteers and the clandestine operations of MK, the former was less an antecedent than the deployment of a repertoire of ideas about militancy. Foremost among these ideas is the notion that military discipline, particularly discipline of the body, is a necessary part of male political practice. In the context of the Defiance Campaign, this practice took the form of nonviolent protest, but by the late 1950s, many of these same ideas were taken up for an entirely different purpose—armed struggle.[13]

The expansion of the African National Congress (ANC) Youth League is another example of the branching out of formations in Cape Town. This expansion occurred during the late 1950s and accelerated in the years prior to the Mamre camp. Sports were the vehicle for recruiting young men and women into the Youth League. Teddington Nqaphayi, a Youth League leader and Mamre camp attendee, recalled that most of the expansion of the ANC Youth League in Cape Town occurred under the auspices of the Nyanga Cultural and Social Organization, which sponsored a rugby club and two soccer clubs, one for young men and another for young women. While playing matches, leaders of the organization introduced discussions of "Congress politics" among members, gradually swelling the ranks of the formal ANC Youth League. By 1962, this chapter had 168 members who then became a recruitment pool for MK and for the Mamre camp. Although the Nyanga Cultural and Social Organization is significant as an entry point to the Mamre camp, it is also part of a wider phenomenon of sports teams overlapping with political organizing in Cape Town and beyond.[14]

The decision to embark on armed struggle is a complicated and contested history better described elsewhere.[15] Most debates over this contentious strategic turn revolve around how different personalities within the leadership viewed armed struggle. Mamre camp attendees identify one particular event—the violent repression of the 1960 stay-away strike—as the catalyst that crystallized popular attitudes toward armed struggle in Cape Town. The violent repression of the strike accelerated ongoing debates about the place of violence in the struggle. The government, nervous about mass protests after Sharpeville, deployed the army and police, sealed off access to Langa and Nyanga, cut off water and food to the townships, and eventually forced people out of their homes and to the workplace at gunpoint. Although the turn to armed struggle was not a fait accompli, as is commonly suggested in official histories, this militarization sent a strong signal to local activists that the era of nonviolent protest had drawn to a close. After the strike, ANC members formed underground cell structures. By 1961, MK had formed a regional command in Cape Town and embarked on a local sabotage campaign, which included fairly unspectacular operations such as cutting electrical and telephone lines and small acts of arson. Men began to leave for military training abroad the following year while the regional command sought to expand the sabotage campaign in hopes that government forces might be stretched enough to permit them to return home to fight. Once driven underground, political organizing took on a darker tone and a more embattled hue. When rendered as such, it became difficult to distinguish between activities. Painting slogans became carefully orchestrated "operations," political education arrived at more aggressive conclusions, and confrontations with the state became more urgent. It is in this context, then, that the Mamre camp represented the militarization of what had been a confrontation between police and protestors, voiced in a vocabulary of politics borrowed from earlier organizations such as the Modern Youth Society, the Volunteers, and the Nyanga Social and Cultural Organization.[16]

In the months after the camp broke up, a few attendees reported to Calendon Square for questioning, others were spirited out of the country, while the remainder faded into obscurity. Denis Goldberg, the camp commandant, went underground in Johannesburg to escape detention under the newly passed General Law Amendment Act of 1963 (aka, the ninety-day detention law), while Looksmart Ngudle, his lieutenant at the camp, remained in Cape Town and died in detention after severe torture.[17]

Command Performances

The high command of MK was arrested at the Liliesleaf Farm on July 11, 1963, and the subsequent trial, known afterward as the Rivonia Trial, began four months later. The state charged that the eight defendants under the Sabotage Act, arguing that they not only orchestrated a campaign of sabotage but that they also embarked on guerrilla war. The Mamre camp directly implicated only Denis Goldberg, but the events there formed a special place in the prosecution's burden of proof because the state claimed it was a guerrilla training camp and thus evidence of a guerrilla war (see figures 3 and 4). To support their claim, the prosecution called two attendees to testify as state witnesses: Cyril Davids and Caswell Nboxele. The defense cross-examined these witnesses but called only Goldberg to testify on his own behalf.[18]

There are a number of reasons not to view this testimony as transparent evidence of the events at Mamre. In reviewing this evidence, I borrow from Michael Johnson's review of the inquiry into the Denmark Vesey conspiracy and from Philippe Riot's analysis of the parricide trial of Pierre Rivière. In the case of Vesey, the honor of the court rested on the discovery of a conspiracy, but confessions made under torture may have produced a more perfect conspiracy than actually existed. Riot describes how both prosecutors and defense attorneys used evidentiary matrices to extract meaning from an ambiguous autobiography penned by the accused. Both Johnson and Riot, who were not simply skeptical about the usefulness of court testimony as evidence for historians, demonstrate how courts hew testimony into coherent narratives of uniform length and consistency. In this regard, they question the way juridical truth arbitrated through layers of exclusion and representation is translated into historical fact years after the trial.[19]

These doubts apply to much of the testimony given during the Rivonia Trial. Percy Yutar, the state prosecutor, argued in his opening address that the Rivonia trialists were engaged in a vast and well-orchestrated conspiracy. By intertwining the tropes of the *swart gevaar* and *rooi gevaar*, Yutar connected internal acts of sabotage to an externally directed guerrilla war, which he claimed would end with the toppling of the government through armed invasion of the Republic.[20] Police and prosecutors knew enough from their informants that MK was not as coordinated as they insisted, but like the Charleston inquisitors who interviewed Vesey's suspected co-conspirators, they had the honor of the court to protect and the heroic myth of the police to uphold. The police did their part to tart up the statements of willing witnesses, and they tortured unwilling detainees into tailor-made confessions.[21] While the prosecution filtered all questioning about the Mamre camp through this matrix, emphasizing aspects that strengthened their claims that this was not just a guerrilla camp but a guerrilla camp tentacled to Moscow. As in the Vesey inquest, the honor of the court was at stake. Producing evidence of a guerrilla camp at Mamre would prevent the high theatrics of the Rivonia Trial from ending in embarrassing denouement of the Treason Trial.

In this respect, the defense strategy bears mention. Two concerns guided the treatment of testimony by the defense. On the one hand, the defense team wanted to avoid death sentences for their clients, and on the other hand, their clients wanted to use the court as a platform for explaining their political program.[22] Further, the defendants refused to give testimony on aspects of their activities that might implicate other comrades. When questioned about their activities, the defendants either refused to answer or shifted the discussion onto political terrain. The matrix born of these concerns crafted an image of principled, disciplined, and sober political activists who had legitimate grievances against an unjust government.

Defense witnesses were hardly silent on the Mamre camp; they claimed it was a camp for "health and spiritual purposes" in line with earlier holiday camps held by the Modern Youth Society. However, there were limits to what they would say about specific activities involving specific individuals, and those limits prevented them from elaborating on certain issues that to some extent hamstrung the defense. These limits also placed the onus of cross-examination on state witnesses.[23]

Johnson's arguments about coerced testimony and imagined conspiracies and Riot's suggestions about interpretive frames of questioning are better suited for retrying the case in the court of historical opinion than for reading oral and written evidence against the grain. The real value of this testimony lies not in what it tells us about guilt or innocence but in what it reveals about local ideas about guerrilla war in the earliest phase of the armed struggle.

However much police coerced certain answers during interrogation, state witnesses often went off-script in court. They forgot or ad-libbed their lines, they talked about things that were irrelevant to the state's case, or they gave deliberately vague answers to very specific questions. What is significant about these unconvincing performances, contra Johnson, was not the ability of the state to coach testimony but the inability of the state to keep its witnesses on message. These improvisations, digressions, and equivocations in testimony not only frustrated the prosecution's line of questioning, but they also produced a text that was, to paraphrase Carlo Ginzburg, both "dialogic and leaky."[24] How could anyone determine whether Mamre was a guerrilla camp if none of the parties involved knew precisely what a guerrilla training camp was? No one speaking—Yutar, Krog, Goldberg, Davids, or Nboxele—had ever been to a guerrilla training camp before, nor did any of them have any formal military training. Neither the prosecution nor the defense called any military experts to offer their opinions. In order for the prosecutors to prove that the Mamre camp was part of an international conspiracy to foment guerrilla war in South Africa, they first had to determine what constituted a guerrilla training camp. This meant entering into a dialogue with witnesses over the meaning of words and "using a shared vocabulary that neither interrogator nor interrogated were entirely comfortable with."[25] The details that leaked out of the margins of this dialogue not only offer telling clues about how camp attendees imagined themselves, but also how the term *guerrilla training camp* was mapped through this shared vocabulary.

The purpose of the camp was an open question, and this indeterminacy gave Davids and Nboxele a space to chart out their interpretation of the events at Mamre. Although Davids and Nboxele claimed this was a guerrilla training camp, they could not remember the organizers explicitly saying as much. At best, Davids claimed that Goldberg explained the curriculum at the outset and said "that it was necessary to know about these things in case of revolution." While Nboxele heard Ngudle say that the purpose was "to help ourselves when we had to fight ... the white people," a Xhosa translation of Goldberg's statement.[26] Joel Joffe, a lawyer for the defense, later noted that it was unlikely that Goldberg and Ngudle were so careless as to explicitly announce that this was guerrilla training camp to a group of strangers and even less likely that they continued to do so throughout the course of their lectures. To make the prosecution's charges stick and to save their own necks, Davids and Nboxele had taken what they knew, what they were given by police, and what organizers inferred and arrange it into a convincing image of a guerrilla training camp. What was rendered in testimony, then, was a composite of bits and pieces of rehearsed lines, remembered observations, and the personal imaginings of what guerrilla war meant for an electrician and a bakery assistant in Cape Town in the early 1960s.

Thinking on their feet, they told a tale of innocent waifs swept up into a lurid conspiracy. Davids and Nboxele portrayed themselves as uninitiated in politics, claimed only casual relations with the organizers, and were shocked to discover that they were not at a holiday camp. To support their narratives, they summoned the following details: attendees were ordered to move the camp to a more concealed location, a mysterious group of whites funded and organized the camp, attendees were placed in a military hierarchy with enforced discipline, guards were placed around the perimeter of the camp, and lectures included not only mundane topics but also selective readings of revolutionary texts.[27]

But these details failed to hold together under cross-examination. Vernon Berrangé, cross-examining for the defense, asked Davids for his definition of the term *guerrilla* to which he replied, "Young soldiers fighting the Govt—the S.A. Gov. with rifles, hand grenades." Neither Davids nor Nboxele mentioned the presence of guns or grenades at the camp nor did police collect any weapons at the camp. Here, Davids offers a definition that fails to fit his narrative and one that, arguably, is off-script from any coached testimony. A particularly revealing exchange between Berrangé and Davids probes the provenance of this term:

> Davids: In September I changed—Lt. Sauerman came to see me. Questioned me again—he asked me purpose G's [Goldberg's] gorillas [sic] were being trained.
> Berrangé: Did he tell [what] you knew?
> Davids: Yes—Oh no it was a slip—it was a slip—the question was not clear. He did not tell me anything else. Exactly the same questions as before—nothing more. He did not suggest that he had evidence which implicated me.
> Berrangé: He did not tell you anything more than before. Never suggested gorillas [sic]?
> Davids: I am telling the truth now.
> Berrangé: What made you change your mind?
> Davids: I felt depressed—had enough of 90 days. Longing to be back at work. I was concerned. I made enquiries from the S/B [Security Branch]—they were alright.[28]

Berrangé wanted to discredit Davids by revealing that the Security Branch coerced him into inserting the term *gorilla* in his narrative. Joffe also portrays Davids testimony as a textbook example of coaching by the police. However, the question of provenance remains open: did the police hand Davids their definition of guerrilla warfare—one that did not fit with the rest of his narrative—or did Davids reverse engineer what he thought the police wanted to hear? Sergeant Card, a detective from Port Elizabeth, gave an apt description of his department's methods: "we just tell him what we know and wait until he confirms it."[29] But Davids himself described the process in the following way: "I had been thinking about it before—I had nothing else to think about."[30] It is just as likely he came up with the definition on his own, cobbling together what he could glean from police questions with his own imaginings of such a war. Distinguishing coaching from imagination might be impossible, but there is enough evidence to suggest that this question be left open to interpretation.

This question demonstrates limitations of court testimony as historical evidence of the Mamre camp and perhaps of most underground activities during the armed struggle. Davids was hardly a willing witness. He maintained that the Mamre camp was for "health and spiritual" purposes for seventy-four days under solitary confinement as authorized by the ninety-day detention law. Davids only changed his statement after a fifth interrogation when police threatened another term of ninety days. On a deeper level, Davids's ambiguous, inconsistent, and partial testimony troubles facile depictions of the state's witnesses as turned comrades. Many defendants felt nothing but bitter betrayal by turned comrades, particularly those who became askaris, those who never appeared in court, and those who invisibly hunted their erstwhile friends.[31] But quite a few acknowledged that everyone has a limited ability to withstand torture, making state witnesses also objects of pity or even sympathy.[32] This indeterminate loyalty meant that state witnesses often played a subtle game. State witnesses could deflect blame for the accused by taking personal responsibility for things that others did, they could sabotage their testimony by riddling it with contradictions, or they could conceal the role of others by telling half-truths and outright lies.

By all indications, Davids did just that by concealing the fact that another attendee, James April, had read the first chapter of *Guerrilla Warfare* by Che Guevara aloud to literate and illiterate attendees. In subsequent interviews April praised Davids for keeping this "smoking gun" out of the hands of the prosecution.[33] The concealment of this recitation also suggests that Davids was far more familiar with at least a textbook knowledge of guerrilla warfare than he was willing to admit in court. Playing dumb allowed him more room to maneuver as he tried to sustain his image as an apolitical innocent against ever more incisive lines of questioning by the prosecution and the defense. But his strategy also included shielding a free comrade from arrest.

Unlike Davids, Nboxele was not detained under the ninety-day detention law. Instead, he was visited three times during the six months after the camp and gave several statements to the police.[34] Although the threat of detention hung over him, his statements and subsequent testimony give a more untutored vision of what he knew about guerrilla warfare, because he was not an instructor like Davids, probably had less to offer to police, and thus would make a less credible witness. This did not make his testimony any more or less true than Davids, but it certainly meant that Nboxele constructed his narrative with different materials and under different conditions. In the end, Nboxele played to the prejudices of the court, giving a more convincing performance as a hapless rube, glossing one term for another, and tripping over his own statements and those of others.

As mentioned above, Nboxele did not use the term *guerrilla warfare* when asked about the stated purpose of the Mamre camp; instead, he answered that they were preparing "to fight the whites." Interestingly, Nboxele traced the origins of "fighting the whites" not to Goldberg or Ngudle but to Davids, who gave a lecture on building field telephones. This admission not only weakened the link between Goldberg and Ngudle and guerrilla war, but it also contradicted Davids's assertion that he played only a casual role at the camp. Nboxele did claim that Goldberg used racial terminology, but it was not to describe the nature of the alleged "guerrilla war" he supposedly encouraged but as a way to explain the political philosophy of the Congress movement. In a particularly telling passage, Nboxele recalled Goldberg's explanation of Congress politics:

Nboxele: [quoting Goldberg] We people of COD [Congress of Democrats] are living in difficulties because we are not wanted by the whites or Xhosas but are on the side of the Xhosas.
Yutar: Did he enlarge on that topic?
Nboxele: He read out of a book by Castro.
Yutar: Did he say in whose favor the COD was?
Nboxele: He said the COD was on the side of the Xhosas. He read out of a book on Castro. I don't know books title. Fidel Castro liberated Cuba.
Yutar: In what way?
Nboxele: Guerrilla war.[35]

The nonracial Congressmen who organized the camp certainly did not envision a guerrilla war as a "war against the whites" but as a war against the racial segregation rent by monopoly capitalism. This passage begs a number of important questions about the discussions that took place at the Mamre camp. Did Nboxele come to the camp with his own ideas about a racial war, collected necessary skills, and then heard what he wanted to hear, or did Goldberg and Ngudle sell him a bill of goods by dumbing down nonracialism to make their politics more accessible to outsiders? Such questions are not simple semantics; they cut to the core of what it meant to negotiate a shared political vocabulary among a racially, linguistically, and culturally diverse body of partisans.

Further complicating matters, Nboxele stated that he had not known the terms *guerrilla* and *guerrilla warfare* prior to hearing them recited during a reading of Xastro's Xuba, the mispronounced title of a pamphlet on the Cuban Revolution.[36] Presumably, the readers explained the term to uninitiated attendees, but Nboxele could provide the court with only the vaguest definition of "guerrilla warfare" as "fighting in the bush." Whether "fighting in the bush" was applicable to the situation in South Africa was an entirely different kettle of fish. Between his examination and cross-examination, Nboxele contradicted himself by paraphrasing Goldberg's interpretation of the text in two ways: first, quoting him as saying it would be difficult to fight a guerrilla war in South Africa, but that if they followed instructions, "they could fight and get through," and, second, while under cross-examination, quoting him as saying that guerrilla warfare "was no good because bush was not dense enough." After this second quote, Nboxele, apparently lost in all his glossing between terms, confessed, "I don't know if he [Goldberg] was training guerrillas. If I was interested to learn more I would have learned a lot more." This confusion extended even to the status of these texts. Nboxele questioned "Xastro's Xuba," and a veiled reference to April's reading of *Guerrilla Warfare* by stating:

> I know only of Fidel Castro's book and another book read by James Apie [April]—don't know if that was a short story or not. I don't know if Castro's book was a short story. It was a description of how he got freedom for his people—I got impression we were being taught g/warfare [guerrilla warfare] from that book. I am not certain.[37]

Goldberg's testimony contains all the usual defenses expected of a man on trial for a capital offense. Most questions did not revolve around Mamre but on his role as a technical officer in MK working in the underground around Johannesburg. But like the witnesses for the prosecution, he could not help but enter into a dialogue with prosecutors about the purpose and meaning of the Mamre camp. His strategy was clear. When unable to shift the discussion toward politics, he placed the Mamre camp in the context of earlier camps and social groups like the Modern Youth Society Easter holiday camps and the Nyanga Social and Cultural Organization gatherings.

He stressed elements of the camp that Davids and Nboxele overlooked; the campers listened to records and sang, there was an area set up for volleyball, and they planned to stage a tableau of African and American history titled, "The Winds of Change." Goldberg admitted that first aid, telephony, and motor mechanics were all part of the curriculum but placed that curriculum not as a preparation for guerrilla war but as a routine part of political education for the now-banned Congress Alliance. If there was a conspiratorial air to the Mamre camp, it was not because they were secretly planning to do illegal things; it was because once-legal things now had to be done in secret.[38]

But all these mundane details did not explain why Goldberg lined the attendees into spans of four, elect sergeants for each span, and then asked attendees to refer to him as comrade commandant. To an educated eye, this resembled the formation of a British army platoon. Accordingly, advocate Krog focused on "comrade" and "commandant" as not only markers of military discipline but also terms linking the Mamre camp to an externally orchestrated guerrilla campaign. Goldberg refused to yield to this interpretation, arguing that these were not military terms at all; "comrade" was a marker of friendship among equals, while "commandant" and "sergeant" were temporary titles meant to maintain a disciplined and orderly environment—not altogether different than Boy Scouts jamboree. In a particularly telling bit of dialogue, Krog tested the rationale for these terms.

> Krog: Mr Goldberg do you know Afrikaans?
> Goldberg: Ek kan Afrikaans praat.
> Krog: Well I think to denote a rank of equals, I think if you had told those people in the Camps they could just call him "Du Pallie" that would...
> Goldberg: Undignified!
> Krog: Oh I see!—undignified. The camp was on a dignified basis too?
> Goldberg: Certainly, we are serious politicians and we are dignified.[39]

When pressed again, Goldberg told Krog that he had been known as Comrade Denis for years and that comrade was the operative term for allies within the Congress Alliance. The defense warned Goldberg against wisecracking in court, but he could not resist this opportunity to exchange blows with Krog, no doubt an Afrikaans speaker. Although this passage demonstrates how Goldberg attempted to picture himself and his comrades as principled political activists, its real significance lies in how it opens an oblique angle into the Mamre camp. Contrary to Goldberg's inference that attendees were seasoned activists, his testimony suggests the opposite. These attendees were green, raw recruits, which made discipline a foremost concern, and that they were unfamiliar with terms of address befitting the political culture of the Congress Alliance.[40]

While "comrade" might have passed as an alien term of affection, "commandant" struck an entirely different chord. It was an incontrovertible sign of martial discipline which lent credence to Davids's and Nboxele's captivity narratives. Here, Goldberg turned Nboxele's cross-examination on its head. When the attendees first arrived at the site, they pitched the tents close to the road. Goldberg ordered them to relocate the entire camp further into the bush, a task they begrudgingly completed. Nboxele referenced this story to show that secrecy was paramount and that Goldberg was an unquestioned leader. Goldberg referred to this testimony to explain away his rank as "commandant" as an ironic moniker closer to taskmaster than quartermaster. Although this was a dodge, the "commandant" story raises a few tantalizing questions. The attendees were willing, but were they committed or even ready? Davids recalled telling Goldberg that he would attend the camp, but only if he could leave early for the Tweede Nuwe Jaar carnival. Likewise, Albie Sachs, another instructor, remembered that attendees had to be prodded awake with sticks during lectures in the hot afternoon sun.[41] If the organizers were prepared to sacrifice their very lives for the cause, were the attendees casual participants more invested in symbolics than substance? Were they more *amavoluntiya* than Che Guevara?

Although Judge Quartus De Wet was convinced of their guilt, Davids, Nboxele, and Goldberg neither confirmed nor disconfirmed that the Mamre camp was a "guerrilla training camp."[42] Their testimony tangled in on itself like a thicket of outright lies, half-truths, fabrications, contradictions, and flights of fancy. These men served several masters: not incriminating themselves, lingering loyalty to comrades, and adopting a certain strategic persona. But beyond mere departures from facile definitions of "the truth," this kind of testimony speaks volumes about the limits of speech among strangers engaged in illegal acts. The organizers of such camps knew the rules of conspiracy, and attendees were warned about agent provocateurs in their midst, who would coax out information from others by making grandly radical statements. And to restate the obvious, they were about to embark on patently illegal acts. If this camp was not a guerrilla training camp, it certainly had all the makings of a sabotage camp and, barring that, a training camp for underground propaganda work. Even in a secret setting and in a cellular organization, organizers were not free to explicitly state the purpose of their actions. Instead, they had to telegraph their intentions through gesture, inference, and oblique reference. The difficulty for historians is this: To what extent were these gestures picked up by attendees? What ideas about conflict did the attendees arrive with? And given the limitations on explicit speech and guided by the rules of conspiracy, what ideas could they return home with? More to the point, what historical arguments can be founded on such shifting sands? This material raises a much more fundamental thesis: was the armed struggle even a stable concept, understood in the same way by all who professed to be partisans? To quote a contemporary of the Mamre attendees, who at the time was a junior member of the Natal regional command, "were we aiming to simply put pressure on the government—to force it to change—or to overthrow it? If so, how? I perceived these questions only dimly at the time."[43]

Jail Diaries; Factography, Reportage, Dramaturgy

Unlike the Treason trialists, the Rivonia trialists were convicted. They escaped the death sentence but spent about three decades serving out life sentences and were released at different times and for different reasons.[44] The theories behind their sentencing are too complex and speculative to address here. More certain is the legacy left by the first wave of prison diaries written in the mid-1960s. From the mid-1960s through the 1970s and into the 1980s, these diaries became important vehicles for explaining the apartheid system and highlighting the abuse of detainees. Some of these texts enjoyed a truly international popularity, unmatched by works written in the same genre in other countries.[45] Much of their popularity lies within not only their explanatory power but also their emotional weight as compelling stories. The purpose of this section is not to question the veracity of these texts as literal truth rendered in narrative form. There are ways of addressing this question, but they are better left to another study. A more appropriate question is how do these authors work within the conventions of the genre while testifying about the recent past? These diaries intervene on the Mamre camp in two ways: first, they blinkered what could and could not be publicly known about this event, and second, the authors' knowledge of the camp served as the pivot of emplotment.

Much of the following analysis is written within and against Peter Steiner's provocative deconstruction of *Notes from the Gallows*, a prison diary written by Julius Fučík, a Czech partisan tortured and executed by the Nazis.[46] Steiner persuasively argues that *Notes from the Gallows*, despite its claim to documentary truth, still falls within generic conventions. Borrowing from Northrop Frye, Steiner posits that Fučík wrote a romantic narrative. He then conducts line item analysis of this prison diary, noting along the way several romantic conventions. These are, in abbreviated form, a concern with a man's vision of his own life as a quest; characters cast as good and evil; a questioning of identity; the bewitching, confusion, or metamorphosis of the hero; and a conclusion where truth, justice, or beauty triumphs over lie, injustice, or ugliness. Steiner introduces two nearly synonymous terms to better explain the way Fučík dabbled in literary tropes. The first is a factography, an embellished text assumed to passively relay a "true story," and the second is reportage, a sort of chronicle of events bearing the stamp of an eye-witness author. Steiner does not reference dramaturgy, but as I will demonstrate, it applies to an unusual prison diary that intersects with the Mamre camp. Although there are faults in Steiner's work, his application of Frye's conventions reveals a lot of rhetorical maneuvers working under the surface of *Notes from the Gallows*.

Three prison diaries address the Mamre camp. In order of completion, they are *The State versus Nelson Mandela* by Joel Joffe, *The Jail Diary of Albie Sachs* by Albie Sachs, and *The Jail Diary of Albie Sachs* by David Edgar. These are very different kinds of works, but all share the romantic characteristics displayed in *Notes from the Gallows*.[47]

Joel Joffe penned *The State versus Nelson Mandela* about his experiences as a defense attorney in the Rivonia Trial. Completed in 1965, Joffe did not publish the manuscript until the late 1980s. In a 2007 edition of *The State versus Nelson Mandela*, Joffe explains his reluctance to publish the book as an act of respect for his clients who remained in prison. Likewise, Joffe did not write *The State versus Nelson Mandela* while in prison nor did he ever serve any sentence. It might be useful to think of *The State versus Nelson Mandela* as a kind of desk novel, written during an authoritarian present but cached away for a more open future. But Joffe has little in common with dissident Soviet writers like Andrei Platonov, Mikhail Bulgakov, and Nadezhda Mandelstam. He was not commenting on the apartheid bureaucracy per se, he did not write an allegory, and his focus was not on a personal tragedy. Further, he was free to leave South Africa, and the authoritarian culture of apartheid and the Soviet bureaucracy were vastly different animals.

The State versus Nelson Mandela may not be a desk novel in the strictest sense of the term but nevertheless exhibits some of the factographic characteristics noted in prison diaries. Joffe wants to recount all of the behind-the-scenes facts of the trial, free from arbitrary rules of evidence, the hostile press, and the rhetorical smoke and mirrors of the prosecution. But his text is more than a mere exposé. Denied a fair trial, Joffe uses his manuscript to retry his case. In the process, he resorts to many of the usual conventions of the romantic narrative, the most significant among these being character development along Manichean lines. Lieutenant Theunis Swanepoel, Yutar, and A. B. Krog appear as morally bankrupt henchmen, while Nelson Mandela, Walter Sisulu, and others, although not entirely saintly, certainly fit the bill as stoic martyrs. Further, Joffe is not boastful about his achievements and does not cast himself as a reluctant hero, but his position as narrator makes him a kind of invisible protagonist locked into a legal quest.

Like Frye's romantic hero and Steiner's reading of Fučík, Joffe fell into a kind of confusion during the trial. Although he was a respected member of the legal fraternity, he was not a "fighting lawyer" like Bram Fischer, Joe Slovo, and Berrangé.[48] As an outsider, he was not privy to many activities, nor was he necessarily an advocate for their brand of politics beyond a lawyerly respect for legal procedure and an intense dislike of apartheid. It is not publicly known how much the accused told him, but prison authorities listened in on consultations between the defense team and their clients, a surveillance that severely limited attorney-client privileges. Further, other MK combatants were reluctant to talk to Joffe, despite the fact that he was an attorney for their comrades. Joffe registered his frustration when interviewing MK members about the prosecution's star witness and turned comrade,

Bruno Mtolo. Joffe writes, "I went off to Pietermaritzburg . . . to find something more about this mysterious character and his testimony [Mtolo]. . . . When I returned from the interview, I knew little more than when I went down."[49] Joffe probably knew more about the Mamre camp than he revealed in court, but there were layers of confidence between counsel and clients. Although it would be a stretch to compare his position to that of Carlo Ginzburg's inquisitor, he certainly negotiated with his clients over the meaning of secret acts. This negotiation was part of an unresolved process of "discovery" that occurred not only between the defense and the prosecution but also between the defense and their clients. This incomplete "discovery," taken together with his clients' desire to put politics at the forefront of their defense, meant that he could put forward only a limited knowledge of the "true" nature of the Mamre camp.

The dramatic flourishes that make *The State versus Nelson Mandela* a compelling read also suggest that Joffe's choice of genre was calculated to generate international appeal. Given this objective, it is important to note that a silent partner wrote alongside Joffe. As Joffe reveals in his introduction, his text was as much a result of his authorship as that of Lionel Bernstein.[50] Bernstein, among other exploits, edited *Fighting Talk*, a broadsheet written by members of the underground Communist Party of South Africa, reconstituted under the name the South African Communist Party. Although Joffe cannot determine which parts of *The State versus Nelson Mandela* belong to whom, it is safe to say Bernstein did not miss this opportunity to broadcast his perspective on the trial. This does not make *The State versus Nelson Mandela* mere agitprop, but the general narrative arc suggests that these authors imagined a particular international audience and tailored facts to fit it. Assuming that the Mamre camp was a guerrilla training camp, would broad-based international solidarity suffer if evidence of armed struggle stood front and center in a sympathetic narrative about the Rivonia Trial?

Unlike Joffe and Bernstein, Albie Sachs placed the Mamre camp at the center of *The Jail Diary of Albie Sachs*, an account of the 130 days he spent in solitary confinement.[51] Although Sachs did not indicate when or where he wrote his text, it was first published in 1966 and reprinted several times thereafter, making it one of the earliest and most widely read anti-apartheid prison diaries. There are any number of reasons for this popularity, not the least of which is Sachs own biography: a young barrister detained under the ninety-day law, his near assassination by apartheid agents, and his work writing the constitution and as a justice on the constitutional court. Biography aside, the real strength of this narrative lies in its ability to report how he evaded his interrogators, particularly when they repeatedly questioned him about the Mamre camp. By all accounts, Sachs played a limited role at the Mamre camp: he attended for one day, gave two lectures on political economy and legal rights, and then left for Cape Town after the police arrived. He did nothing untoward, nor did he remember witnessing anything illegal. But Sachs's refusals and evasions become the device that drives the plot along. His detention was conditional, his freedom depended on answering police questions to the "satisfaction of the attorney general." Like Joffe, Sachs never placed the mantle of heroism on his brow, but his position as narrator assumes that he is, at the very least, a protagonist caught in a just struggle.

The Jail Diary of Albie Sachs is a chronicle of the secret world of police interrogation. Sachs reports on his experiences in two ways: first, he details his observations about police methods, and second, he describes his own responses to these methods. The police know quite a bit about the Mamre camp from other detainees, but they nevertheless pursued Sachs with a dogged intensity. What makes his story interesting is the transformation in his rationale for refusing to answer. Initially, he wants to have his day in court, maintaining that if he answers any questions it will be before a judge after being charged.[52] He later refuses to answer because of fear for his comrades, worrying that any piece of innocent information might be the piece needed to "complete your jigsaw" and make an arrest. But toward the end of his detention, Sachs realizes that he is the only person still held under the 90-Day Act and anyone else implicated in the Mamre camp had either fled or been convicted. At this point, he refuses for refusal's sake alone. Here, the Manichean battle of wills between good and evil takes hold.

The police up the ante, arranging for round-the-clock interrogation teams, in an effort to break him. While not inflicting physical harm in the strictest sense, this form of torture pushes Sachs into a severely suggestible mental state, where he questions not only his identity but also his memory of events.[53] At this point, interrogators leave him alone in a room with a document titled, "Addendum on Mamre Sabotage Camp." After imagining the dossier the police have collected on him, his interrogators entice him to take a look at a chapter and perhaps confuse himself in its details. Sachs writes:

> The months of isolation had tended to wipe my mind clean of past recollection. The constant references by my interrogators to the Sabotage Camp was causing me to wonder whether or not I had knowingly taken part in a sabotage camp.... Reality is something continuous and integrated. If one is abstracted from normal reality one has difficult remembering aspects of the reality of yesterday. Fortunately for me, however, they have not succeeded in substituting their version of reality for my vanishing recollection.[54]

He discovers that a handful of attendees gave information about him, but little of it was accurate enough for a conviction. At this climactic moment, Sachs realizes not only that his mind is sound enough to resist suggestion but that the police already have what they need. They have tortured him for the sake of torture alone.

Sachs never reveals what he did say or did not say after his marathon interrogation. He hints that it might be possible to hand police a few innocuous details but fears even the slightest leak might be exploited for more information. Although we never learn whether Sachs made a statement, he concludes *The Jail Diary of Albie Sachs* after his release. Closing out the romantic narrative, Sachs vows to remain in South Africa until truth triumphs over lies. He waits for the day when he can confront one Detective Rossouw about the physical torture of two acquaintances, a double synecdoche for the entire repressive apparatus of the apartheid state, over the entire body of its victims.

The heroic narrative eclipsed a detailed description of the Mamre camp. Along the way, small details wash up in the monologue, attendees fell asleep during Sachs's lectures, he warned attendees about agent provocateurs, and he remembered some of the curriculum. But Sachs's refrain "I am not prepared to answer at this stage" is as much addressed to his readers as it is to his captors.[55] He is circumspect about revealing the details of the camp to his public, probably because the time was not right. As noted above, Sachs contemplated making a statement, but he worried that even a simple declaration might unleash other secrets, secrets he had not yet divulged to either the police or his readers. The reason for this reticence could be that the mid-1960s was simply not the "stage" for a full reckoning of the Mamre camp. By

1965, Defense and Aid had become International Defense and Aid, the British Anti-Apartheid Movement placed economic sanctions and an academic boycott on the world stage, not to mention the fledgling solidarity campaigns of the ANC in exile. And the need for a compelling account of police interrogation and torture put romantic heroism squarely at the center of his reportage from South Africa. Further, like Joffe and Bernstein, Sachs does not foreground armed struggle, perhaps because his appeal was attended to broaden support among more skeptical readers.

Evidence for this theory appears in the text of *The Jail Diary of Albie Sachs*. Sachs signals his awareness of other prison diaries while contemplating the moral introspection that happens in prison. Specifically, he references Henri Alleg, who wrote an account of his experiences during the Algerian War, as well as Fučík, who needs no further introduction.[56] Sachs is not trying to place his own writing in this canon, although it eventually ended up there anyway. But I would argue that his name dropping suggests that he has been moved by his reading of these "sacred" texts and implicitly expects that others will be moved by his own text. It is clear that Sachs understands the importance of these models, which, to borrow a phrase, are not so much an empire of letters as an internationale of diaries.

In one of the more interesting sections of *Jail Diary*, Sachs imagines his life as a play mise en abyme—a device that allows him to step outside of himself. Picking up on this thread, British playwright David Edgar wrote and staged an eponymous adaptation of *The Jail Diary of Albie Sachs* in 1978. Written after Soweto, Edgar is far less restrained about the place of violence in the anti-apartheid struggle. He knows little more about the Mamre camp, but he presents Sachs as a protagonist who is more certain about the necessity armed struggle. His character suggests as much in a soliloquy;

> It's all too simple, to elevate our lack of courage to a principle, and call that principle non-violence. It's all too easy, build your fear of being hurt and killed into a principle that people should not hurt or kill people who are hurting and are killing them. It's all too, neat, to say that change must be controlled and ordered, that our world here can revolve that far without a revolution, that crops will grow without the plough, that we can have the rain without its thunder, we can seize the sun without the fierceness of its burning.
>
> I'm furious with what my jailors do, but not with what they are.
> I hate the whip but not the men that wield it.[57]

As in the text *Jail Diary*, the plot of this play balances on Sachs's refusal to divulge information about the Mamre camp. His interrogators refer to the "sacred texts" of prison diaries, ask Sachs if he thinks he is the "Freedom Fighter of Algeria" or the "French resistor" under Nazi occupation, and point out that he is not going to the gallows, "just the empty cell, and all those endless days."[58] In a marked departure from Sachs's text, Edgar's character admits to the audience that he will talk but not before undergoing torture, this time at the hands of the infamous Lieutenant Swanepoel. The result is a tape-recorded confession, played for the audience over a darkened stage. Sachs's voice details police methods of torture and makes the singular admission, "The following statement has thus been extracted from me illegally. On the 14th of December 1962 I attended a camp near the village of Mamre. I had been invited to lecture on the history of the white colonization of South Africa."[59]

Dates aside, the subtle changes that separate Sachs's reportage from Edgar's dramaturgy indicate how much had changed between Rivonia and Soweto. Like Sachs, Edgar does not place the details of the Mamre camp on center stage. However, unlike Sachs, he now hints that there was more to the camp than meets the eye. Indeed, Edgar may characterize Sachs in a heroic light, but he also allows him to strike a measured but more aggressive tone on the topic of violence. The late 1970s witnessed the rebirth of armed struggle, after more than ten years of inactivity. Likewise, the Soweto massacre in many ways was a tipping point for international attitudes toward apartheid. In the face of these kinds of shifts, fewer could continue to support the idea that Africans acquiesced to apartheid, more began to see the logic of armed struggle, and a minority began to support it altogether. Acknowledging this new audience, Edgar does not explicitly state that Mamre camp was part of the armed struggle, but he certainly draws the two much closer together.

Edgar's play was first staged in 1979, then adapted for the British Broadcasting Corporation in the early 1980s, and received a special audience in 1989, when it was performed for Albie Sachs as he recuperated after an assassination attempt by apartheid agents. This, then, was the new meaning of Mamre camp for the fiery confrontations of the late 1970s and 1980s. The Mamre camp was still mysterious but not so secret and was certainly linked to armed struggle. Representations of the Mamre camp served as the pivot that leveraged the factography of getting the record straight, to the reportage of getting the message out, to the dramaturgy of getting people in the streets. Throughout these genres and across these decades, the meaning of the Mamre camp hinged on what, when, and how this event entered into public knowledge.

PLASTER BUSTS, THE RULES OF CONSPIRACY, AND THE ACTION HERO

In 2007, James April recalled that when police arrived at the Mamre camp site, they surveyed the scene and told the attendees, "Look, guerrilla warfare can't even work here" (see figure 5).[60] Although this was a remark in passing, it nevertheless explains a lot about how interviewees craft their testimony about the Mamre camp. Beginning in 1985 and continuing to the present day, camp attendees provided their interviewers with a complex set of rationalizations about armed struggle. These rationalizations came at a time when the possibility of a peaceful negotiated settlement eclipsed the armed seizure of power. Memories of what happened at Mamre became intertwined in a contemporary debate over just what went wrong with the armed struggle and how these frustrations folded into an ambiguous postapartheid present. In this respect, camp attendees argued against not only the skepticism of the police who closed Mamre but also with political rivals, factions within their own party, and professional historians. Interviewees share no single rationale; rather, each puts forward their own ideas about why armed struggle was necessary, why it took the form it did, and how the Mamre camp fit into this broader picture. Returning to questions asked of the written record, to what extent does oral testimony allow us to see through these rationalizations into the past?

These interviews not only serve as another body of evidence, but they also test many of the assumptions that underpin the place of oral history in the social history of Africa. Recent scholarship has questioned certain methodological "fetishes" that preoccupy oral historians working in Africa.[61] Foremost among these is the idea that evidence precedes interpretation. Historians have fetishized African voices as representative of collective truth or an individual voice as experiential truth. The problem with these tendencies is that they take what people say at face value. This belief in the literal truth of oral history misses all the interesting ways people interpret the past as they recount it. The Mamre attendees are not only eye witnesses but also incredibly sophisticated interpreters of South African society who provide as much justification as description. In this respect, oral testimony is neither a corrective nor a complement to the written record. Instead, oral testimonies are another layer of sources that are subject to the same rhetorical strategies that guide the written records that lie beneath and between. The extent to which we can see through these rhetorical strategies to the past remains an open question.

Goldberg gave at least three accounts of the Mamre camp: one after his release from prison in 1985, another during negotiations in 1993, and the last with the author in 2008.[62] In his first two interviews, Goldberg responds to skeptics on the left and the right, providing almost sociological justifications for the armed struggle.[63] While Trotskyists critiqued the Congress Alliance for prematurely abandoning the working class for the adventurism of armed struggle, right-wing critics portrayed MK as a fringe group without constituency among the majority of law-abiding Africans. To counter these claims, Goldberg couples a detailed class analysis of the effects of residential segregation with a blow-by-blow chronology of frustrated protests and strikes. Within this context, Mamre became the crest of a growing wave of militarization that swept the Congress Alliance in the early 1960s, which in his view signaled both the theoretical correctness of the turn to violence that he interpreted was a response to irrepressible popular demands for armed struggle.

In his 2008 interview, Goldberg shifted his discussion of Mamre away from sociological justifications of armed struggle and toward the politics of meaning. In the months before this interview, marginalized veterans returned to mainstream politics as partisans in a divisive power struggle within the ANC. These veterans were collectively deployed as the image of the heroic comrade during elections and published a slew of "struggle biographies" that mythologized armed struggle. In this moment, Goldberg used the Mamre camp to complicate the politics of memorialization that lay at the heart of this factionalization of the party. With a light hand, Goldberg works within and against the new heroic narratives of armed struggle. He makes room for the accidental by recalling that the camp was discovered after a comrade visited a local bakery to replace loaves that had moldered in plastic bags. He opens a window onto a moment when camp attendees fashioned their image of an idealized guerrilla from a bricolage of their readings of other armed struggles. Finally, Goldberg questions the appropriateness of expensive monumentalizations in post-apartheid South Africa by citing a poem by Bertolt Brecht. Drawing comparisons between officialdom in post-revolutionary Kazakh Soviet Socialist Republic and post-apartheid South Africa, Goldberg questions the wisdom of buying plaster busts of heroes, instead of bringing dignity and comfort to the lives of ordinary people.[64] His answer is didactic; the Mamre camp should be marked by only a simple plaque.[65]

The tension between these testimonies is an attempt to grapple with what another prominent MK strategist called the "heroic failure" of the armed struggle. Goldberg attempts to soften the historical resonance of both terms. In his earlier testimony, the "failure" of the Mamre camp was due to chance and circumstance and not to the underlying popular legitimacy or the theoretical correctness of the turn to armed struggle. But in later testimony, Goldberg allows the Mamre camp to be a less confident moment than would be allowed in most "struggle biographies." In this respect, he attempts to deflate heroic images of armed struggle summoned in the "usable pasts" during election campaigns. The combined effect is a subtle, yet partisan, rendering of Mamre, one that steers between the dismissiveness of critics and the mythologization by opportunists.

Taking a different tack, in 2007, James April viewed a broad tableau of Cape politics through the lens of the Mamre camp. His testimony is not a stand-in for the "Coloured perspective" but rather, a post mortem of the Mamre camp, rendered in a relational analysis of Congress politics cast against the ethnic and class complexities of the Cape. As he saw it, this political landscape was riddled with secrecy, intrigue, and tangled alliances. The personalities he referenced are not one-dimensional, and relationships are not linear. Rather, bonds of friendship, family, and occupation form the counterintuitive threads that tied together the Unity Movement and Coloured People's Congress, Stalinists and Trotskyists, and activists and police investigators. April presents the Mamre camp as an emblem of this subterranean world, where appearances and affiliations are often not what they seem to be. Without naming names, he comes to the conclusion that the Mamre camp was betrayed by a police spy. Here, the Mamre camp is the final act in a sort of cautionary tale. People had ignored the rules of conspiracy and put personal reputations above operational secrecy. Put more broadly, the Mamre camp is a way of explaining how the Coloured People's Congress fell apart and why the Congress Alliance never assumed hegemony in the Cape.[66]

Christopher Mrabalala's story is an outlier among other attendees but represents a tendency in the narratives of many other kinds of veterans.[67] Mrabalala's not only includes details not mentioned by other attendees, but his description of events also directly contradicts the testimony of others. In both respects, his narrative is interesting not because it is truer than the rest, but because it is a highly imaginative expression of how a forgotten comrade makes sense of the armed struggle in the post-apartheid era. The points of disagreement are worth noting. Mrabalala follows other narratives of the Mamre camp until he comes to the incredible chain of events that followed the arrival of the police. In his version, police surveyed the campsite, then helicopters began to drop scores of police and soldiers, all attendees were ordered to cross a log bridge, at which point he dropped into the water, hid with only his nose above the water, and then returned to the campsite to remove guns. The scene he describes is a massive manhunt conducted by scores of police and soldiers. No other evidence, written or oral, corroborates any of these details, and much disproves it.[68] Most informants suggest that the police left with only Sachs and Goldberg, and no one mentioned guns at the camp, the arrival of helicopters, or the presence of Mrabalala himself.

However tempting it may be to prove this story true or false, determining its literal truth misses ways generic conventions are deployed and the reasons behind these deployments. Suspending claims of historical truth for a moment, the contours of the story strike a familiar chord; the genre is the action movie, and the protagonist is the archetypical action hero. Mrabalala portrays his past self as a skilled practitioner of military arts, a self-sufficient soldier who can evade legions of police and soldiers through a combination of ability and sheer force of will. Most importantly, he uses this archetype to place himself in a historic event.

Why did Mrabalala choose to tell this particular story and pose himself within it in this particular way? Arguably, Mrabalala uses a form of storytelling employed by all veterans. This form is especially common among aggrieved MK veterans who believed they were the sacrificial victims of the negotiated settlement. As MK veterans struggled to insert themselves in an ambiguous post-apartheid world, they adapted material from other conflicts to locate themselves in the armed struggle and explain the significance of the armed struggle in the present dispensation. These heroic episodes form the emotional weight in claims for benefits in this dispensation. The sentiment expressed in these episodes is that the teller is a legitimate, yet unrecognized, soldier who risked his life for the greater good of an indifferent society. Although Mrabalala's version of the Mamre camp is not an exact facsimile of any particular action movie, it certainly resonates with the story of John Rambo, another aggrieved veteran of a forgotten war.[69]

Notes

1. Caswell Nboxele, Rivonia Trial Record, Mayibuye Center Archives. Cyril Davids, Rivonia Trial Record, Mayibuye Center Archives.
2. Denis Goldberg, interview with Howard Barrell, February 7, 1990, Karis Gerhart Collection, Historical Papers Research Archive, Cullen Library, University of the Witwatersrand.
3. Denis Goldberg, interview with author, May 20, 2008.
4. Ibid.
5. High Court of South Africa, Rivonia Trial Record, Mayibuye Centre Archives. Albie Sachs, *The Jail Diary of Albie Sachs* (London: Harvill, 1966). David Edgar, "The Jail Diary of Albie Sachs," *Plays: One* (London: Methuen, 1987). Joel Joffe, *The State versus Nelson Mandela* (Oxford: Oneworld, 2007). James April, interview with author, April 30, 2008. Amy Thornton, interview with author, June 3, 2008. Alfred Willie and Sandile Sejake, interview with author, My 28, 2008. Denis Goldberg, interview with author, May 20, 2008. Denis Goldberg, interview with Howard Barrell, February 7, 1990, Karis Gerhart Collection, Historical Papers Research Archive, Cullen Library, University of the Witwatersrand. Denis Goldberg, interview with John Pampallis, June 13, 1985, Mayibuye Centre Archives. Denis Goldberg, interview with Wolfie Kodesh, August 6, 1993, Mayibuye Centre Archives.
6. Luise White, "'Not Telling': Secrecy, Lies, and History," *History and Theory: Studies in the Philosophy of History* 39 (2001): 11–22.
7. Ibid.
8. Vivian Bickford-Smith, "South African Urban History, Racial Segregation and the Unique Case of Cape Town?" *Journal of Southern African Studies* 21 (1995): 75.
9. Bernard Magubane et al., "The Turn to Armed Struggle," in *The Road to Democracy in South Africa, Vol. 1, (1960–1970)*, ed. Bernard Magubane (Cape Town: Zebra, 2004), 94–102.

10. David Shandler demonstrates the geographic limits of ANC support in the Western Cape. David Shandler, "'Nie Meer in die Nag Nie': Popular Struggles in Worcester 1950–1960" (MA thesis, University of Cape Town, 1985).

11. Denis Goldberg, interview with John Pampallis, June 13, 1985, Mayibuye Centre Archives. Amy Thornton interview with author, June 3, 2008. Peter Mfene (Teddington Nqaphayi), interview with Wolfie Kodesh, February 19, 1992, Mayibuye Centre Archives.

12. The Volunteers are alternately known as *amavoluntiya*.

13. Sandile Sejake and Alfred Willie, interview with author, My 28, 2008. Peter Mfene (Teddington Nqaphayi), interview with Wolfie Kodesh, February 19, 1992, Mayibuye Centre Archives.

14. Peter Mfene (Teddington Nqaphayi), interview with Wolfie Kodesh, February 19, 1992, Mayibuye Centre Archives.

15. Compiling an exhaustive list of publications that address the turn to armed struggle is a near-impossible task. The question of timing and the identity of personalities involved in the debate have preoccupied commentators and participants for decades. The following list comprises the major works that address the subject. Tom Lodge, *Black Politics in South Africa since 1945* (New York: Longman, 1983). Francis Meli, *South Africa Belongs to Us: A History of the ANC* (Bloomington: Indiana University Press, 1988). Howard Barrell, "Conscripts to Their Age: African National Congress Operational Strategy 1976–1986" (PhD diss., University of Oxford, 1993). Lionel Bernstein, *Memory against Forgetting: Memoirs from a Life in South African Politics 1938–1964* (London: Viking, 1999). Stephen Ellis and Tsepo Sechaba, *Comrades against Apartheid: The ANC and the South African Communist Party in Exile* (Bloomington: Indiana University Press, 1992). Baruch Hirson, *The Revolutions in My Life* (Johannesburg: University of the Witwatersrand Press, 1995). Martin Legassick, "Armed Struggle in South Africa: Consequences of a Strategy Debate," *Journal of Contemporary African Studies* 21 (2003): 285–302. Nelson Mandela, *Long Walk to Freedom: The Autobiography of Nelson Mandela* (Boston: Little, Brown, 1994).

16. Denis Goldberg, interview with Wolfie Kodesh, August 6, 1993, Mayibuye Centre Archives. Sandile Sejake and Alfred Willie, interview with author, May 28, 2008.

17. For an extended discussion of the circumstances surrounding Looksmart Ngudle's death, see Joffe, *The State versus Nelson Mandela*, 37–40. See also Beauty Ngudle's testimony before the Truth and Reconciliation Commission. Beauty Ngudle, *Case no. CT/00504*, Truth and Reconciliation Commission.

18. Joffe, *The State versus Nelson Mandela*, 146.

19. Philippe Riot, "The Parallel Lives of Pierre Rivière," in *I Pierre Rivière, Having Slaughtered My Mother, My Sister, My Brother . . . A Case of Parricide in the 19th Century*, ed. Michel Foucault et al. (New Haven, CT: Yale University Press, 1975), 229–50. Michael P. Johnson, "Denmark Vesey and His Co-Conspirators," *William and Mary Quarterly* 58 (2001): 915–76.

20. Police and military officials used the terms *swart gevaar* (black menace) and *rooi gevaar* (red menace) to describe internal and external threats to the apartheid state. The *swart gevaar* referred to the influx of Africans into cities, particularly during the rapid industrialization witnessed in South Africa during World War II. Apartheid planners saw this influx as a mortal danger and responded with a series of residential segregation laws. The *rooi gevaar* referred to internationally sponsored communist subversion. As mass protest in South Africa reached a crescendo in the mid-1950s, police and military officials cast opposition groups as puppets of a conspiracy directed from Moscow.

21. More extreme forms of "coaching" occurred. Vernon Berrangé interviewed Isaac Tlale during an inquest into the death of Looksmart Ngudle. Tlale testified he was electrocuted repeatedly and then presented with a blank piece of paper which he then signed. His "confession" was later typed on this blank page. Joffe, *The State versus Nelson Mandela*, 37–40.

22. See Mac Maharaj's preface to Joffe's *The State versus Nelson Mandela*. Joffe, *The State versus Nelson Mandela*, xix.

23. The Sabotage Act placed additional burden on the defense. Joffe notes that an offense could be legally proven by a single witness. Joffe, *The State versus Nelson Mandela*, 14.

24. Carlo Ginzburg, *Clues, Myths and the Historical Method* (Baltimore: Johns Hopkins University Press, 1989), 156–65. Ginzburg is quoted in Johnson, "Denmark Vesey and His Co-Conspirators."

25. Luise White, *Speaking with Vampires* (Berkeley: University of California Press, 2001), 23–27.

26. Cyril Davids, Rivonia Trial Testimony, Mayibuye Centre Archives. Caswell Nboxele, Rivonia Trial Record, Mayibuye Centre Archives. Joffe, *The State versus Nelson Mandela*, 210.

27. Cyril Davids, Rivonia Trial Testimony, Mayibuye Centre Archives. Caswell Nboxele, Rivonia Trial Record, Mayibuye Centre Archives.

28. Cyril Davids, Rivonia Trial Testimony, Mayibuye Centre Archives.

29. High Court of South Africa, Rivonia Trial Record, Mayibuye Centre Archives. Joffe, *The State versus Nelson Mandela*, 139.

30. Cyril Davids, Rivonia Trial Testimony, Mayibuye Centre Archives.

31. Askari was the term used to describe turned comrades or comrades who willingly assisted police in locating, arresting, or assassinating underground MK operatives. The date when askari became the operative term for these individuals is uncertain.

32. At least one libel case has resulted from questions of the culpability of individuals who testified on behalf of the state or gave statements to the police following torture or prolonged solitary confinement. Bob Hepple successfully sued the publishers of Ben Turok's *Nothing but the Truth*. Please see the note pasted inside the cover of Turok's book held at the Jager African Studies Library at the University of Cape

Town. Ben Turok, *Nothing but the Truth* (Johannesburg: Jonathan Ball, 2003), 118. The court forced Turok to correct the assertion that Hepple had willingly given a statement to the police.

33. James April, interview with author, April 30, 2008.
34. Caswell Nboxele, Rivonia Trial Testimony, Mayibuye Center Archives.
35. Ibid.
36. Denis Goldberg, interview with Howard Barrell, February 7, 1990, Mayibuye Centre Archives. In the Xhosa language, the letter *x* denotes a click. This click is often transliterated into a hard *c* in English phonetics.
37. Caswell Nboxele, Rivonia Trial Testimony, Mayibuye Centre Archives.
38. Denis Goldberg, Rivonia Trial Testimony, Mayibuye Centre Archives.
39. Ibid.
40. Ibid.
41. Sachs quoted in Heidi Holland's "struggle history," *The Struggle: A History of the ANC*. Heidi Holland, *The Struggle: A History of the ANC* (Johannesburg: Ravan Press, 1989), 89.
42. Quartus De Wet, Rivonia Trial Testimony, Mayibuye Center Archives.
43. Ronald Kasrils, *Armed and Dangerous: My Undercover Struggle against Apartheid* (Oxford: Heinemann, 1993), 47–54.
44. The Treason Trial was the first mass political trial of 156 Congress Alliance members begun in 1956 and concluded in 1961. The trial ended in acquittal for all defendants after the state failed to prove that the political activities of the leadership of the Congress Alliance committed treasonous acts.
45. Ruth First, *117 Days* (London: Bloomsbury, 1965). Sachs, *The Jail Diary of Albie Sachs*. Mandela, *Long Walk to Freedom*. Hugh Lewin, *Bandiet* (New York: Random House, 1974).
46. Peter Steiner, "Making a Czech Hero; Julius Fučík through His Writings," *The Carl Beck Papers in Russian and East European Studies* 1501 (2000): 1–61. Julius Fučík, *Notes from the Gallows* (London: New Century, 1948).
47. Joffe, *The State versus Nelson Mandela*. Sachs, *The Jail Diary of Albie Sachs*. Edgar, "The Jail Diary of Albie Sachs."
48. Political activists used the term *fighting lawyer* to describe lawyers who were also members of the Communist Party of South Africa or its underground reincarnation as the South African Communist Party.
49. Joffe, *The State versus Nelson Mandela*, 94.
50. Ibid., x.
51. Sachs, *The Jail Diary of Albie Sachs*. This introduces an interesting topic outside the scope of this book. Given the strictures of prison regulations in South Africa, most jail diaries are accompanied by stories of their writing, usually on scraps of paper smuggled out of prison. The effect of these harrowing stories about writing imbues the resulting text with an air of authenticity. The question that remains is just how much of the "jail diary" was not written in jail but composed from memory after release.

52. Sachs, *The Jail Diary of Albie Sachs*, 38–40.
53. Two psychologists from the University of Cape Town were called by the defense to testify that solitary confinement can cause physical damage to the human brain. Their evidence was ruled inadmissible by the court. Joffe, *The State versus Nelson Mandela*, 194.
54. Sachs, *The Jail Diary of Albie Sachs*, 218.
55. Ibid., 144.
56. Ibid., 90. *Notes from the Gallows* was routinely handed out to new recruits to the South African Communist Party. Sue Rabkin, interview with author, May 12, 2008.
57. Edgar, "The Jail Diary of Albie Sachs," 72.
58. Ibid., 82, 83.
59. Ibid.
60. James April, interview with Nhlanhla Ndebele and Moses Ralinala, in *The Road to Democracy: South Africans Telling Their Stories*, ed. Gregory Houston (Johannesburg: South African Democracy Education Trust, 2008), 47–59.
61. Luise White and Frederick Cooper quoted by Gregg Mann. Gregg Mann, "An Africanist's Apostasy: On Luise White's *Speaking with Vampires*," *International Journal of African Historical Studies* 41 (2008): 117–21.
62. Denis Goldberg, interview with John Pampallis, June 13, 1985, Mayibuye Centre Archives. Denis Goldberg, interview with Howard Barrell, February 7, 1990, Karis Gerhart Collection, Historical Papers Research Archive, Cullen Library, University of the Witwatersrand. Denis Goldberg, interview with author, May 20, 2008.
63. Edward Feit, *Urban Revolt in South Africa, 1960–1964: A Case Study* (Evanston, IL: Northwestern University Press, 1971). Martin Legassick, *Armed Struggle and Democracy: The Case of South Africa* (Uppsala, Sweden: Nordiska Africainstitutet, 2002).
64. Bertolt Brecht, "The Carpet Weavers of Kuyan-Bulak Honour Lenin," in *The Collected Works of Bertolt Brecht* (London: New World Publishers, 1929), 55.
65. Denis Goldberg, interview with author, May 20, 2008.
66. James April, interview with author, April 30, 2008.
67. Magubane et al., "The Turn to Armed Struggle," 101–3.
68. The SADET volume *The Road to Democracy* states that Mrabalala left the country in February 1962, a full ten months before the Mamre camp, yet his "eyewitness" account of the Mamre camp is nevertheless included. Magubane et al., "The Turn to Armed Struggle," 93. Archie Sibeko claims that he never attended the Mamre camp. This claim runs contrary to Mrabalala who claimed to have seen Sibeko there. Archie Sibeko, *Freedom in Our Lifetime* (Durban: University of Natal Press, 1996), 77. The Rivonia Trial Record notes that twenty-right people attended the camp, not thirty-six.
69. *First Blood*, directed by Ted Kotcheff (1982; Santa Monica, CA: Lionsgate, 2004), DVD.

3. The Sight of Battle: Visuality, History, and Representations of the Wankie Campaign, July 31–September 8, 1967

THE OFFICIAL NARRATIVE OF THE Wankie Campaign is a chapter in the South African Democracy Education Trust volume *The Road to Democracy in South Africa*, a compendium bearing an introduction by former president Thabo Mbeki which was sponsored by the South African government, a major cell phone company, and a bank.[1] In this lengthy chapter, Rendani Ralinala, Jabulani Sithole, Gregory Houston, and Bernard Magubane construct a detailed chronological description of the Wankie and Sipolilo Campaigns, organized around topics such as deployment, engagements, casualties, and imprisonment. Their underlying motive in reconstructing an oft-reconstructed set of battles is to open fresh evidentiary ground and determine once and for all who won and who lost these battles. In their view, previous accounts cast these campaigns as failures because their evidence was drawn from contemporary propaganda, political broadsides written by exiled rivals, and pro-Rhodesian war literature. Their hope for a more sympathetic portrayal of the Wankie Campaign rests with the power of oral history. Or as the editors state in the preface, "It is our firm belief that voices and/or experiences of 'ordinary' people, if there is anything of that sort, come much closer to the 'truth' than history books that lack their voices, however skillfully written."[2] Underwriting this argument is the belief that oral testimony holds the promise of a more comprehensive, if not authoritative, version of events—one that will no doubt transparently reveal the fighting abilities of these ANC and ZAPU detachments in a more positive light.

One of the problems with this sort of project is that its unreflective reliance on oral testimony tends to make a cardboard caricature out of combatants. Taking informants at their word leaves us with the images that they themselves construct—that of the forthright soldier who graces the propaganda leaflet, never swaying from his patriotic duty to prosecute this heroic struggle with earnest dedication. Arguably, this is no better than accounts drawn from partisan sources that depict these combatants as amateurs sent on a fool's errand, or accounts that valorize the fighting prowess of the Rhodesian army. I argue that the root of these unproblematic visions of this campaign is an uncritical acceptance of oral and written evidence as historical truth. At no point in these sorts of historical reconstructions do the authors wrestle with the stories told by their sources or place these stories side by side and let them wrestle with one another. In the end, the authors craft sympathetic accounts by simply turning the unsympathetic narrative on its head, invalidating the written sources with oral sources, and reversing the valence of this morality play.

This chapter is a different take on the Wankie Campaign. Rather than restore the image of the combatant through an inversion of one set of sources over another, I will demonstrate how an alternative reading of written and oral sources can take readers behind the representations that loom large over a severely polarized literature.

To get beyond this dilemma, I will present an operational history that foregrounds the experience of soldiers. The purpose of this chapter is to bring visuality into dialogue with experience and show how that experience is then translated in oral testimony and the written record. The battlefield terrain shaped the perspective of soldiers in very specific ways. Reading across the breadth of oral and written sources, one gets the sense that while there is significant overlap between different versions of the campaign, no two accounts entirely agree. These incongruences become all the more apparent when looking closely at eyewitness accounts of individual events.

Visuality also illuminates soldiers' conceptual understanding of war. In an insightful study of World War I soldiers' narratives, Samuel Hynes describes the tension between two concepts, the "war-in-the-head" and the "Battlefield Gothic." Soldiers enter war with a war-in-the-head: an imaginary received from propaganda and from popular culture and past wars.[3] This received image falls away when soldiers finally encounter the gothic strangeness of the battlefield in the present war. During World War I, the imagined landscape of cavalry charges through open fields was shattered by an anti-landscape scarcely recognizable, and scarcely visible, from the trenches. In the case of the Wankie Campaign, combatants could not sustain heroic imaginings received from Sierra Maestras of Cuba and the jungles of Vietnam in an African landscape that screened what could and could not be seen. Their war-in-the-head of idealized guerrilla warfare promised them invisibility through a mastery of the landscape, but the conditions of the bush denied them this possibility.

Evidence of visuality also reveals the imperfections and mistakes that are shaken out of histories concerned with overturning a prevailing narrative. Losing the war-in-the-head is above all else a process of discovery, one of learning how general theories of guerrilla war differed from the practice of combat in a local setting. This discovery did not come easy and was marked with trial, error, and disappointment. Reading evidence against the grain teases out those episodes when combatants got lost, separated, or ambushed or when their pursuers were within earshot and lost the trail. What sympathetic and unsympathetic operational histories have done is confuse the war told in these details for the war-in-the-head reproduced in testimony and record. The result is an all-too-perfect version of history that validates credentials without critically appraising what informants and documents actually say, rather than what they mean to say.

An examination of visuality also contributes to broader critiques of the reliability of experience as a source of historical truth. As Hynes notes, "truth problems" are as much about "infidelities of memory after the event" as they are about the "failures of observation and the confined vision of witnesses." The written and oral record of the Wankie Campaign is replete with conflicting accounts, wavering inconsistencies, and contradictory statements that in many instances have their root in the visual perceptions and misperceptions of informants. Foregrounding these discrepancies not only reveals how the literature on Wankie became so polarized, but also why several accounts taken from one side of the battle could differ so frequently and so widely.[4]

Before delving into the substantive issues of visuality, experience, and the battlefield, I will briefly sketch out the most significant events of the Wankie Campaign.

The reasons behind the timing of the campaign are contested. Those who portray planning as deliberate and careful suggest that the Wankie

Campaign was born out of geographic isolation and solidarity between liberation movements. Beneath these explanations lies a closer reading of conditions within the army. After several years of inactivity, factions developed in the rank and file, arbitrary punishment created simmering resentments against the leadership, all of which led to indiscipline and mutiny. These pressures animate alternative explanations. Were leaders responding to rank-and-file calls to go home? Or was the campaign a convenient way to quiet troublemakers in the camps?

However much contemporary hagiographers reconstruct the Wankie Campaign as a heroic confrontation, it was never originally intended to be an exercise in guerrilla warfare. The strategic goal of this infiltration was first to secretly establish a group in Matabeleland to assist with further infiltrations and second to deliver small groups to four regions in South Africa.[5] The groups bound for South Africa would train recruits inside the country, rebuild the underground structures, and receive guerrillas from outside the country. Both detachments were well armed, and both had instruction to engage the enemy if necessary but were ordered to remain undetected for as long as possible while en route to their final destinations.

The combined ANC-ZAPU force was comprised of two units: the Luthuli detachment, which consisted of around thirty soldiers culled from the Umkhonto we Sizwe, and the Nkomo detachment, which consisted of approximately fifty soldiers culled from ZIPRA. This combined force was to split at two different junctures once inside Rhodesia, the first occurring at the entrance of the Wankie Game Reserve where twenty-three guerrillas would go west through Lupane to an area outside Salisbury where they would base themselves, conduct small operations, and assist future groups in transit. The second group of fifty-seven guerrillas would then head south toward South Africa. Once inside South Africa, this southbound group would further divide into smaller units of four groups each bound for Durban, the Transvaal, the Cape, and the Transkei.[6]

On the night of July 30–31, 1967, both detachments scaled down a deep gorge, then crossed the Zambezi and entered into Rhodesian territory. They fought as a group in three separate engagements. The first engagement occurred on August 13 when the group bound for Matabeleland fought a seven-hour battle with a patrol of Rhodesian African Rifles (RAR) troops and British South Africa Police. The second and third battles occurred on

August 22 and 23 when the South Africa–bound southern group engaged Rhodesian forces. After these much larger battles, this group moved southwest and scattered into much smaller groups while Rhodesian security forces pursued them across the border into Botswana where they were arrested, tried, convicted, and sentenced to prison terms on weapon possession charges.

The Wankie Campaign failed to achieve its objective of establishing a guerrilla presence in Rhodesia that might operate as a conduit for further infiltrations into South Africa. Further, the groups bound for South Africa never arrived at their destinations. Looking at the casualty figures reveals the costs of this failure. Reports of casualties vary widely. ANC lists twenty-five of its members as casualties, various South African government tallies of killed South African guerrillas range from twenty-nine to thirty-five, while other written sources inflate these numbers to as many as forty-seven.[7] Given that the ANC probably gave the most conservative estimate, if thirty-three ANC members were deployed with the original group and twenty-five died, only eight survived. Estimates of Rhodesian casualties vary as well. One Wankie combatant estimated thirty-three deaths, but the Rhodesian roll of honor counts eight, a number that roughly approximates the numbers reported in Rhodesian army situation reports logged during August and September.[8]

Bringing visualization of the battlefield into the picture adds an important layer to interpretations of the Wankie Campaign. In part, it is possible to reconstruct the war-in-the-head that guerrillas carried as they crossed the Zambezi because much of their prior knowledge of the battlefield came from mapping and reconnaissance.

Topographies

Visualization of the battlefield begins with mapping. The ability to imagine terrain, to orient to novel surroundings, and anticipate enemy movements all hinge on a merging of vision with cartography. Despite its importance, the commanders who planned the Wankie Campaign lacked adequate experience in cartography. Ben Turok, an early MK member and an engineer with surveying experience, met with a commander after the campaign and in conversation learned that this senior person lacked any training in mapping and could not even read a compass. When Turok asked how they mapped their way through, the commander responded that "we didn't bother too much about mapping."[9] Turok bracketed this story within complaints about disorganization and his own marginalization from the planning of the armed struggle.

Commanders casually dismissed the importance of mapping because they erroneously believed that others had done adequate advanced reconnaissance of the area. Two accounts present illuminating examples of failures in reconnaissance overlapped with insufficient attention to mapping.

Thula Bopela and Daluxolo Luthuli, both veterans of Wankie, place the responsibility for reconnaissance squarely on the shoulders of Joe Modise, then the highest ranking MK commander. According to their account, Modise allegedly entered Rhodesia with a recce group weeks before the campaign, returning with muddy boots and a report of positive contacts with people in Matabeleland. MK cadres doubted that Modise made contact with people in Rhodesia and named him Nyawo Zinodaka, an ironic moniker undoubtedly made in retrospect, which betrayed not just his faulty intelligence but also his sheepish unwillingness to join cadres in the campaign.[10]

In a self-produced film titled *The Luthuli Detachment*, General Zolile Nqose, a commander in the Wankie Campaign and later a general in the post-apartheid South African National Defense Force (SANDF), omits Modise and instead placed the blame squarely on the shoulders of ZIPRA. Echoing sentiments made by other veterans, Nqose asserts that different duties were assigned to the joint MK-ZIPRA command and that reconnaissance was delegated to ZIPRA. Nqose recalled that when detachments crossed, they found that ZIPRA cadres were not familiar with the area. In frustration, Nqose left with an eight-person team of MK and ZIPRA cadres ahead of the group to survey the territory and recommend a safe route forward. He then sent four back to fetch the main group. These cadres got lost and Nqose went looking for them. When the team returned to the location where the main group had been, they discovered that they had already left.[11]

Taken together, these accounts not only foreshadow the visual handicaps that plagued the entire campaign, but they also illustrate the beginnings of a cleavage between the war-in-the-head that informed expectations prior to crossing the Zambesi and discovery of the Battlefield Gothic that awaited them on the other side. The overlap between these stories suggest how failures in mapping, reconnaissance, and planning resulted in ominous episodes such as Nqose's team getting lost. The inability to visualize terrain caused more significant conceptual problems. This meant that guerrillas entering the field envisioned a campaign with ideas received from other wars, rather than seeing what lay before them. Fresh out of a training camp named Da Nang, when these guerrillas set foot on Rhodesian soil they probably still envisioned a Ho Chi Minh trail unfolding through a savannah populated by willing sympathizers.[12] Without reconnaissance to the contrary, they could not see that conditions on the ground precluded these plans from taking shape.

This is not to say those deployed in Rhodesia were wholly unprepared for the challenges they faced in that country. Graham Morodi stated that the Luthuli detachment spent a year "in the forest" in Zambia prior to deployment.[13] Wolfie Kodesh also asserted that men that trained in the Soviet Union had trained in topography. But Brigadier General Nqaphayi, another veteran, stated that they were issued school maps rather than proper topographical maps, while Morodi noted that both detachments shared one "very old compass."[14] Given that the detachments mostly traveled at night to avoid spotter planes, they were figuratively and literally in the dark much of the time, using stars to navigate their way through the bush. Bopela and Luthuli, two dissident veterans, wrote about this kind of navigation: "we tried to follow the Southern Cross . . . but we were shocked to discover we were right back where we had started . . . navigating by stars obviously wasn't our forte."[15]

The Bush

After splitting up in the Wankie reserve, both groups remained undetected until August 13 when the eastbound group fought a pitched battle with Rhodesian forces. The southbound group, already deep within the Wankie reserve, heard about the battle via Radio South Africa.[16] Over the next three weeks, the southbound group was engaged in a deadly game of cat and mouse through the forests in the Wankie reserve and the dry grasslands on the southwestern border between Rhodesia and Botswana.

There are no narratives of the August 13 battle, but veterans gave several accounts of the two battles fought by the southbound group. In addition to these accounts, Rhodesian security forces filed frequent and detailed situation reports while tracking this group. If these sources are placed within the context of visuality, narratives of heroism and antiheroism give way. This not only opens a window on how landscape influenced perceptions of these events but also reveals a tangled web of evidence that fails to yield to simplistic partisan renderings.

All these sources contain stories about getting lost in the bush. The vegetation was very dense in the Wankie reserve, making it very easy for individuals to become separated from the main group. Where the bush was less dense, it lacked distinguishing features and landmarks that could be used to gauge distance and mark the ground covered. Because most movements were conducted at night, this combination of density and similarity caused a number of individuals to lose the main group. Once separated, they could not call out for fear that the enemy might locate them. By the time of the first sighting of the enemy, the group had already lost two members along the way, while reconnaissance groups sent out to search for them also got lost.[17]

The bush enclosed those within it and limited their field of view, but the lack of any sort canopy left their position exposed from above. After Rhodesians learned of the presence of the southbound group, they sent spotter planes and helicopters to scan the area. To avoid detection, the guerrillas constructed blinds, dug foxholes, and looked for sparse tree cover to avoid detection while they slept during the day. This surveillance became ever more invasive once they traveled beyond the southern perimeter of the Wankie reserve where the bush thinned out, turning to grassland and then brush on the Botswana border. These changes in vegetation are registered by the heightened tension conveyed in several accounts as the group passed from the relative safety of the reserve to the open spaces beyond. As spotter planes patrolled overhead, guerrillas tightened their formations and maintained "a state of combat readiness."[18]

About a week after radio broadcasts indicated their presence, the Rhodesians made their first contact with the southbound group at the southern edge of Wankie reserve. In a desperate bid to find food and water, three men tracked game to a watering hole while the rest hid nearby.[19] Helicopters spotted the men at the dam and radioed their location to Rhodesian ground troops.[20] Five armored personnel carriers passed the group in hiding while on their way to the dam.[21] Shots rang out at the dam, the Rhodesians followed tracks back to the group, yelled for them to surrender, and then fired shots into the bush.[22]

Accounts differ about what happened next. Secondary written accounts suggest that the group patiently waited for the Rhodesians to approach, repelled them in a hail of bullets, and then collected supplies and a field radio they left behind.[23] Oral testimony tells a less dramatic story: the group remained in hiding, waited out the Rhodesians, withdrew to another location, and then returned to the dam at night to look for their two men.[24] The first version is almost certainly a compression of the episode at the dam and the battle that followed the next day. Why this compression appears in certain accounts and not others has more to do with narrative strategy than with the vagaries of memory.

Following game to the dam during the daytime was an act born of desperation. August is the dry season in Matabeleland, a time when seasonal riverbeds ran dry and animals congregated near any available watering holes. Rhodesians interrogated captives from the eastbound group and surmised from those interrogations that the southbound group would be short on food and water.[25] Indeed, this is confirmed in the oral testimony of several veterans, some noting that the group had not eaten for several days while in the reserve, while others suggesting that they survived on leaves and rats.[26] Given all this, the Rhodesians probably concentrated their aerial surveillance on watering holes and waited for the starving band to emerge from the forest.

Contrary to their projected image as self-sufficient fighters, these errors suggest that the detachment found great difficulty living on the land. Planners had not charted the way forward, ZIPRA cadres had not made arrangements in advance with local supporters, and the group did not seem to anticipate the scarcity of water and game in the area. These difficulties resulted in risky decisions such as making premature contact with unknown locals, shooting for the pot, and drawing water from exposed sources.[27]

Not surprisingly, two secondary accounts employ narrative strategies to displace these problems from their accounts. The first account is Michelle Berger's "Chris Hani," based primarily on an article written by Hani in 1986 for an MK journal, but adapted as a biographical school primer.[28] In a literary flourish of derring-do, Berger recounts the encounter at the dam: "Chris's soldiers were eager to open fire, but Chris ordered them not to. 'Our bullets are precious,' he instructed them in urgent but firm whispers. 'Don't shoot until you can see your target clearly. . . .' Chris remained calm until some of the enemy troops stood up trying to spot Chris's unit. His order rang out: 'Fire!' Two of the enemy soldiers were hit." Both soldiers killed were officers, and the remainder of the Rhodesian forces fled in fear. The compression of the dam story into a battle fought the following day turned what was a blunder into a hastily crafted ambush, one that demonstrated the brave assertiveness of the group. The authors of the SADET chapter borrow Berger's heroic tone and even append her version of events with quotes from interviewees, lending an aura of authenticity by invoking the immediacy of oral testimony.[29] The only problem is that Berger and the SADET authors larded their narratives with quotations that are in fact descriptions of a different battle that occurred the following day.

The chronology presented in both the Berger and the SADET volume is at variance with a number of other accounts, particularly those offered by most witnesses. Setting aside questions of factual accuracy for the moment, the real consequence of this distortion is that it makes the first encounter seem too neat. From Hani's article, to Berger's book, to SADET's chapter, the dam encounter is staged as a theatrical confrontation, where the guerrillas used their invisibility to launch a daring attack on an unwitting enemy.

A closer reading of the firsthand account of veterans tells a different and more complicated story. After traveling all night, the southbound group hid themselves and rested during the day. Alfred Willie, Christopher Mampuru, and Ernest Modulo left the group late in the morning, following game to the dam.[30] Their intention was to find water, and they had taken the group's water bottles with them.[31] Away from the dam, Cletus Mzimela awoke a fellow comrade and claimed he saw a radio antenna above the undergrowth. When this comrade disbelieved him, a second radio antenna appeared. Troops came close enough for them to see black berets and rifles while army trucks could be heard in the distance. Mzimela recalled that he somehow fell asleep after the soldiers passed, only to be awoken later by the sound of gunfire at the dam.[32]

Morodi was close enough to see black and white soldiers and five armored personnel carriers pass by his location on their way to the dam. He could hear the commander directing his men to the tracks of the three who went to the dam. When the Rhodesians returned from the dam, they fanned out looking for the others. Morodi claims that he and another comrade were seen by one of these soldiers but that the soldier was too afraid to call to his commander. The Rhodesian commander then directed his men to shoot at the bush in the opposite direction. The group then took this opportunity to withdraw five hundred meters to a wooded area where they dug foxholes and prepared for battle. Morodi claims that reconnaissance helicopters and planes saw them withdraw but could not direct ground forces to their location. The group stayed there the whole day, but the Rhodesians could not find them and kept shooting in the opposite direction. They stayed another day in the same location but secreted away that evening when they heard a big reinforcement arrive.[33]

Although one must read all these accounts with a certain amount of suspended disbelief, they nevertheless illustrate how the landscape screened the visible from the invisible. The Rhodesians were not only within feet of the group, but Morodi also claims one RAR soldier made eye contact with him.[34] Although the line about making eye contact with a reluctant enemy smacks of embellishment, it nevertheless operates as a device in a narrative that demonstrates the restraint and resolve of these men who safely retreated while the Rhodesians flailed about, shooting in the wrong direction. Although Morodi's version runs counter to Berger's more romantic vision of an impromptu ambush and a heroic rout, it still affirms the idea that these men were accomplished guerrilla fighters. Read within the context of mid-twentieth-century writing on guerrilla war, this episode depicts these men as archetypical guerrillas: masters of their environment, deftly moving in and out of view, screening themselves from detection even though they were initially caught off guard by the Rhodesian patrol.[35]

Training and Discipline

The description of withdrawal also lends itself to arguments about the role training played during the campaign. Many commentators attributed the failure of the campaign to inappropriate training.[36] The most common claim was that Soviet trainers instructed their African trainees in mobile warfare. This form of warfare was largely derived from the experience of Soviet partisans during World War II and was thus inferred to be ill suited for the realities of an asymmetrical bush war. Morodi foregrounds his detailed account of the withdrawal to counter these claims.

As noted in Rhodesian writings, the numerically superior guerrilla group could have mounted a successful attack on the eighteen Rhodesian soldiers but instead chose to withdraw.[37] On the surface, this seems like a panicked response, and it very well could have been. But Morodi narrates this withdrawal by appealing to their reading of the landscape. The group had been caught resting in a thicket surrounded by tall grass. As the Rhodesians searched around, the group remained still until spotter planes and helicopters appeared overhead. Morodi suggests that the decision to retreat underneath a tall stand of trees was a conscious effort to seek adequate cover from the aerial surveillance. But because the forest floor was more open than the nearby bush, the men quickly dug foxholes to literally and figuratively embed themselves in the terrain. In this reconstruction of events, the men resisted their gut instinct to fire back and instead calmly applied their knowledge of tactics, which in practice are demonstrated to be appropriate to the situation at hand.[38]

The first full battle did not occur until August 22, two whole days after this first encounter. Aside from the superimposition of this battle over the engagement at the dam, accounts of this battle also carry contradictions in testimony born of visuality and the landscape.

Most accounts agree that after two nights, the group left the dam and headed south to the Tjolotjo Tribal Trust Land. There they found a sparse grove of bushes, dug foxholes, and set up a perimeter of guard posts. But the details of the contact are a major point of disagreement. Some said that one guard spotted the Rhodesians through binoculars, then surprised the Rhodesians with a burst of fire; another account argued that the Rhodesians took them by surprise because one guard group did not camouflage themselves properly; still another asserted that the Rhodesians heard guards bickering and surprised the group.[39] All accounts admitted that the group suffered about four casualties in the opening volley of shots. The length of the battle differs, but by the end, the southbound group killed two Rhodesian officers, Lieutenant Nick Smith, and Warrant Officer Timitiya. Guerrilla accounts mentioned killing fifteen other RAR troops, all of them black noncommissioned soldiers, although official histories of the RAR make no mention of these deaths.[40] After the death of Smith and Timitiya, the fifty or so RAR soldiers fled, leaving behind food, uniforms, radios, topographical maps, the bodies of Timitiya and Smith, and Timitiya's gold watch.[41]

The reasons why different accounts diverge at the point of contact again relates to many of the rhetorical strategies employed in narrations of the dam encounter. As in that incident, disagreement in sources signals the displacement of events that do not fit certain kinds of narratives, while other events are expanded over these incongruent details. Many of these histories are sourced from eyewitness accounts that cannot seem to agree on even basic details such as who saw who first. But who saw who first is not just about gaining the initiative in battle; it also relates the importance of training versus discipline in the field. In many ways, how people chose to depict training over discipline and vice versa shape their ostensibly factual accounts of "what actually happened" and with it all of the judgments about the fitness of the guerrilla detachments.

Sympathetic accounts such as Chris Hani's written and oral testimony, the SADET book, and Berger's derivative account all suggest in varying degrees that the guerrillas saw the Rhodesians first and launched a preemptive attack.[42] As in the withdrawal at the dam, they took the necessary preparations by setting up an all-round defense with sentry posts around the group.[43] The SADET account describes how one sentry, Peter Mhlongo, spied the Rhodesians as they advanced on their tracks, giving enough forewarning for Hani to call out orders to the rest of the group. At this point, the SADET authors depart into an almost novelistic description of Hani giving orders—he called on his men to remain hidden and in silence until the Rhodesians advanced within a hundred meters. According to this set of accounts, the men followed these orders, waited, then returned fire, instantly killing the radio operator and driving back the rest of the Rhodesians.[44]

Alternative accounts hinge on the indiscipline of sentries. When the guerrillas set up camp after their night march, they positioned the group destined for the Northern Transvaal at one sentry post. In Zolile Nqose's film, *The Luthuli Detachment*, Alfred Willie describes how this group wore black jackets and placed those said jackets overhead in the branches of a bush, presumably to shield themselves from the sun while they rested. Willie recalled that these men were warned about placing the jackets in full view but that they refused to take them down. The jackets made their position clearly visible, both exposing themselves and the entire group.[45] By implication, when the Rhodesians passed through the area, they caught the group by surprise, launched an attack on this sentry post, and killed Barry Masipa, Robert Baloyi, and Charles Sishuba, while mortally wounding Sparks Moloi and Peter Mhlongo. In one swift attack, the Rhodesians eliminated most, if not all, of the Transvaal unit. These five men were the only guerrilla casualties incurred during the ensuing battle.

Bopela and Luthuli elaborate on this account but put a greater emphasis on indiscipline. Writing partially as dissidents and partially as loyal opponents, Bopela and Luthuli allow for more critical events than the final edit of *The Luthuli Detachment* and certainly Hani, Berger, and the SADET authors. These authors mince no words: "the first action we became involved in was the result of the indiscipline of a particular group."[46] Undisclosed grievances caused the Transvaal-bound men to threaten to shoot their commander, which is inferred from other accounts to be Julius Maliba (aka Manchecker), a storied veteran of many subsequent MK campaigns. Sishuba took over the group when Maliba fled, but "feeling flushed with their victory over their commander, the group became absolutely uncontrollable."[47] Diverging from either account, Bopela and Luthuli suggest that the Rhodesians did not see this group but heard them arguing loudly. Again, this breach of discipline came with consequences, as the Rhodesians fired first at their position and lobbed grenades into their blind.

It is quite possible that all three versions of this event happened. Mhlongo could have spotted the Rhodesians, not had time to warn the rest, while the jackets and the loud argument attracted additional attention. Most of the southbound group probably heard shots after the initial contact. An official history of the RAR suggests that Rhodesians were tracking the group when they were fired on, suggesting a properly staged ambush laid by the guerrillas. The contact diagram included in this history shows that most guerrillas outside the sentry post could not see the Rhodesians approach.[48] Most guerrillas were positioned some distance away, and dense brush obstructed their line of sight. Because dead men tell no tales, we cannot be sure what Baloyi, Sishuba, and Matsipa did or did not see when the Rhodesians approached. What is left is an imperfect field of evidence based on the limited experience of witnesses and post mortem reconstructions of the battlefield conducted by either side after the rout. Few, if any, viewed the battlefield in its entirety, rendering most accounts partial, myopic, and conflicted.

Genealogies of "Struggle History"

There is another way to read these sources besides from battlefield topography, vegetation, training, and discipline. The heroic counternarrative of Hani's oral testimony, the SADET chapter, and Berger's book all descend from the same source, "The Wankie Campaign," a 1986 article written by Hani for *Dawn*, the official journal of MK.[49] Although these sources vary somewhat in consistency, chronology, and detail, they all share the same fundamental sentiment. Hani expresses this best in the original article: "We had undergone training in the Soviet Union . . . and had looked forward to this historical engagement. . . . For a trained soldier it is always important to participate in battle because that is where you prove the merits of your training and at the same time there is nothing so scintillating and stimulating to a soldier as to test his whole reactions in actual battle, your responses when you are under fire. I think every soldier looks forward to this and we were no exception."[50] As in the dam engagement, this narrative is designed to emphasize the tactical prowess of the guerrillas. This is not only a matter of record but also a didactic history directed at a frustrated readership in MK training camps in the 1980s. But Hani's article lived a second life as the source for subsequent official anthologies and school textbooks—casting this sanitized version of the Wankie Campaign over a much wider public audience.

General Zolile Nqose's film *The Luthuli Detachment* bears a resemblance to the lineage of representations described above, but this similarity is limited to sentiment rather than content. *The Luthuli Detachment* is a nostalgia film.[51] Nqose conducted interviews with veterans, most of whom were commanders or commissars. He then edited segments of these interviews into a montage that traces the entire narrative arc of the detachment: from camp life, to training, to deployment, and to battle. But unlike Hani's article, which is narrated by one voice, the narration of this film is split between several veterans' testimony with segues provided by Nqose. This creates a tension between Nqose, who wants to anthologize the veterans as heroes, and the veterans themselves, who are in turn both critical and sanguine about their experiences. Although Nqose tries to portray the detachment in the most positive light, his film cannot contain all of the alternative explanations of events offered by his interviewees. When read against other sources,

Alfred Willie's comments about the Rhodesians spotting the black jackets take on a different significance. Nqose shoehorns his story into the frame of tragic sacrifice for a noble cause, but if it is placed within the dissident frame, it hints at tensions submerged beneath the surface of more heroic accounts.

Bopela and Luthuli expand on these tensions in their book, *Umkhonto we Sizwe: Fighting for a Divided People*, a collaborative effort that promises readers "to tell it the way it was and not as we wish it had happened, or as somebody else might prefer us to tell it."[52] Part autobiography and part exposé, the resulting narrative draws much of its rhetorical power from its authorship: Bopela and Luthuli are dissident rank-and-file members of MK. This authority does not make their narrative any more or less true than any other, but it does present an explanation of events that is wholly absent from the Hani lineage and almost displaced from Nqose's film. Bopela and Luthuli draw a straight line between the authoritarian culture of the training camps and indiscipline in the field. Simply put, the Rhodesians spotted the group because commanders could not control those under their command.

The Chinese Kamikaze

The second battle occurred the following day, on August 23. After they routed the Rhodesians on August 22, the group left that night; they opted not to stay in a nearby forest and instead set up camp in a patch of bush surrounded by open fields. Accounts differ on why they stopped in this location; some say that carrying a wounded guerrilla slowed their progress, while others suggest that the location was less conspicuous than a nearby forest.[53] In either case, their location was fortuitous because the Rhodesians launched airstrikes on the forest at 4:00 p.m. and 6:00 p.m. In between airstrikes, two platoons of RAR troops set up camp next to the guerrillas in the same bush. Their intention was to conduct mopping-up operations on any survivors of the airstrikes. John Dube, the commander of the southbound group, dressed in a captured RAR uniform walked into the army camp, and either spoke with some of the troops in Sindebele, fired on these men, and walked away without shooting, or was chased out with the Rhodesians in pursuit.[54] The guerrillas quickly assembled an advance team to attack the Rhodesians. Once again, they routed the Rhodesians, killed two officers, captured an assortment of supplies, and withdrew.

Like the two previous engagements, this battle occurred in very dense bush with limited visibility at close range; but in this case, fighting continued into twilight. This limited visibility and the abruptness of the attack not only left a bit of sway in eyewitness accounts, but it also produced one of the more imaginative situation reports of the entire Wankie Campaign. A report filed by RAR officers the day after the battle relayed an unconfirmed report that a Chinese commander led the guerrilla detachment. The next day, this commander multiplied into two Chinese or Malay men and one Chinese woman were leading the guerrillas. A subsequent report repeated the same claim, only this time adding that "drug use [was] not discounted."[55]

Needless to say, there were no Chinese guerrillas leading the group. Nevertheless, Rhodesian and South African security forces remained preoccupied with the story long after it was presumed to be false. Captured guerrillas recalled being questioned about it during interrogations, and newspaper accounts sensationalized the confiscation of Chinese-made weapons. This fascination with Chinese intervention in southern Africa is seen elsewhere and draws from a Cold War imaginary of communist subversion. Ideas about the hidden hand of international communism lent itself to overestimations of guerrillas' fighting abilities. However, the real value of this story lies not only in what it reveals about the anxieties of security forces, but also in a broader sense how bush warfare lent itself to the generation of legends.

The last battle was marked by two cases of mistaken identity. As noted earlier, Dube had discovered the Rhodesian encampment by walking into it while in an RAR officer's uniform. But Dube was not the only guerrilla in a captured uniform. James April, one of two Coloured guerrillas in the detachment, also wore an RAR uniform. As the advance team prepared to attack the encampment, April leaped ahead and charged enemy positions at point-blank range. In most accounts, his gun jammed and was then pinned down under heavy fire when the rest of the team rescued him. Patrick Matanjana suggested April's light complexion and officer's uniform and hat confused the enemy long enough for him to penetrate deep into their positions.[56] Bopela presented a slightly different version, suggesting that April acted rashly and wore a white headband that caused him to be mistaken for a Chinese kamikaze.[57]

The idea that battle produces all sorts of figments of imagination is not a new concept in histories of conflict. What people think they see and hear often gets inscribed as fact, especially when these stories are accompanied with the kind of truth that can only come from eyewitness accounts. But what is noteworthy about the Chinese kamikaze legend was that it was so easily debunked, but it nevertheless fed into exaggerated estimates of guerrilla strengths. Ron Reid-Daly, leader of the Selous Scouts, hints at this in his appraisal of Operation Nickel, the name given to the counterinsurgency operation that combated the guerrillas. Reid-Daly attributes unusually high RAR casualties to the fear and inexperience of African troops. These figures led commanders to the conclusion that "the terrorists were credited with a military skill and aggressiveness that they did not actually possess." Reid-Daly suggests that this overestimation led RAR commanders to misapply tactics learned during the Malaya emergency.[58]

Bopela hints at how this process of turning fiction into fact emerged from his interrogation by Rhodesian police. A homicide detective named Stanley Peters asked Bopela about Dube entering the camp in RAR uniform and the presence of Chinese soldiers in the group. Bopela and his comrades knew that Dube blundered his way into the camp and that April broke discipline by going it alone. However, he surmised from questioning that the Rhodesians thought these actions were deliberate and a demonstration of determination and bravery. Bopela played along, suggesting that Dube had been trained "to occasionally do such things to put the fear of God into our enemies." He also let the Chinese kamikaze story stand, content in the knowledge that April's "totally irresponsible" behavior "had actually caused panic in the enemy ranks."[59]

Even after the Chinese portion of the story had been discounted, the wild-eyed kamikaze legend lived on. April recounted that South African security police confronted him with a version of the story after he was arrested while doing underground work in South Africa in 1971. During his interrogation, the police confronted April with a detailed description of his exploits in battle and charged that he had boasted to his comrades about killing a number of Rhodesians. April denied ever making such claims and argued that he acted in self-defense during the attack. April traced the provenance of this story to Zolile Nqose, who escaped from prison in Botswana, was captured in South Africa, and returned to exile under suspicious circumstances. Once in custody, April deduced he was the source for the South African version of the kamikaze attack—the implication being that the South African security police knew details about the attack that could only be known by eyewitnesses such as Nqose.[60]

These details of the Wankie Campaign proved significant during the trial because physical evidence alone was not enough to convict April of plotting to overthrow the government. However, the addition of April's activities in Rhodesia might result in a conviction under the Terrorism Act of 1967. Prosecutors relied heavily on the testimony of Leonard Nkosi, a Wankie Campaign veteran turned askari. Nkosi testified that April had fired on the Rhodesians and single-handedly killed several. However, under cross-examination, he admitted that he could not see April but made the dubious claim that he heard a distinctive burst of fire from his pistol and submachine gun. In his final judgment, Judge J. Kennedy could not determine what Nkosi did or did not see during the battle but was convinced that April was part of premeditated conspiracy to overthrow the governments of Rhodesia and South Africa. Nkosi's version of the kamikaze story did not entirely convince Judge Kennedy, but it did play an important part in casting April in the image of an idealized "communist terrorist."[61]

From an evidentiary perspective, the kamikaze demonstrates how conflicting eyewitness accounts from a chaotic battlefield can reverberate through interrogation, court testimony, and rumor until they ring forth as accepted fact in the historical record. The abruptness and ferocity of the attack, combined with the dense thicket and waning daylight, made it difficult for the Rhodesians to see or to be sure of what was seen. This is a moment of rupture between the Battlefield Gothic of warfare in the bush and the war-in-the-head that the Rhodesians carried over from Malaya and elsewhere. Out of this breach grew fantastical stories of guerrilla detachments led by Chinese soldiers who drove their men with an almost suicidal fervor. The retrospective process interrogation might have shed some more implausible aspects of these battlefield accounts, but captives were more than willing to allow interrogators to continue to believe their own fantasies about guerrilla strengths. These fantasies were then reinscribed in court cases where prosecutors hoped to win convictions by constructing the bogeyman of the menacing "communist terrorist."

Jailhouse Forensics

The southbound group did not fight any other significant battles after August 23. They meandered around Tjolotjo, eventually heading southwest for the border with Botswana.[62] All accounts depict a bleak scene: Rhodesians began to napalm the grassland and mopane trees to increase visibility and to flush out guerrillas, RAR units advanced to border towns to intercept anyone crossing over, aerial surveillance was stepped up, and the group was perilously low on water.[63] Making matters worse, the landscape became more open and arid the closer they moved toward Botswana.

This change in the landscape required a change in tactics. The guerrillas moved strictly at night and became more dependent on local villages for food and information. James April provided a vivid description on how different ways of seeing mitigated the risk of these nighttime visits: "We saw these little fires and we thought it could be the enemy camping out there, because we just saw these little fires. You see nothing else. You don't see any hut, nothing! I thought, my word, I'm not used to rural areas like this! I'm from an urban area. But these guys know what is what, Chris [Hani] and them because they grew up in rural areas and they could see there is a hut next to that little fire there."[64]

The theme that connects various descriptions of the final days of the campaign is that of being lost in a harsh and undifferentiated wilderness. A few days after the battle, a number of men fell behind, and the group split into two groups: seven sent to look for food and water, while the remainder waited in a dry donga for their return. According to April and Morodi, the group sent out tried to mark their path by breaking twigs and counting stones. But when they became lost, they fired shots in the air to communicate with the others only to receive no response.[65]

The confusion caused by the landscape had a serious effect on morale. After separating from the main group, the party of seven also separated. April remembered that three men—Hani, Dube, and another ZIPRA cadre—left to locate a nearby village and find food. When these men failed to return, the remaining four began to argue over whether to leave.[66] According to Berger, Hani's departure left the four men distraught over the absence of their noble leader. Berger quotes an unnamed man implausibly lamenting the loss: "How will we be able to carry on if anything happens to Chris? He is always willing to help us with our problems. I often ask him for advice, and he gives it to me. Where could we find another commissar like him?"[67] James April casts the departure in a less cloying way. According to him, when Hani and the others left, those who remained behind immediately suspected that they were "gone for good." April chastened the others for doubting Hani, but eventually, they gave up hope and moved on. Other accounts indicate that Hani and his men were spotted by a plane and decided that a rendezvous with the others would put both groups at risk.[68]

Various accounts ascribe different intentions to their escape into Botswana. Hani and others suggested that the foray into Botswana was a strategic withdrawal; after replenishing supplies and ammunition, the men would return to Rhodesia to finish the fight.[69] Mzimela maintained that the group did not know where they were going and stumbled into Botswana by accident.[70] But Morodi and Duka claimed that the men had no choice but to enter Rhodesia after Rhodesian troops entered nearby villages looking for the guerrillas.[71] Whatever their intentions were, no veteran described this scattering as breaking rank, although many mentioned that they were eventually arrested as individuals. Most made it to Botswana where they were reunited in prison. Those unfortunate enough to remain in Rhodesia were killed in pursuit, transferred to South Africa, or imprisoned in Rhodesian prisons. Those in Botswana received two- to four-year sentences, while others sent to prison in Rhodesia remained there until independence in 1980, and the few transferred to South Africa served fifteen- to twenty-year sentences on Robben Island.

Upon their return from prison in Botswana, a group of Wankie veterans levied several severe accusations against the leadership in Tanzania. One version of these complaints came in the form of the Hani Memorandum, most commonly attributed to Chris Hani but was said to be collectively authored by a faction of Wankie veterans from the Cape.[72] The group named certain leaders and decried their lack of seriousness about the armed struggle. After this, they were threatened with court martial but were instead expelled from the organization. Interpretations of the memorandum ranged from mild critiques of planning, to calling into question the character of certain leaders, to dark allusions to suicide missions and the purging of dissidents.[73] The authors of the memorandum only returned to the organization after the Morogoro Conference, when many of their criticisms were addressed in a full strategic review of the armed struggle.

Veterans did not limit their recriminations about the failed campaign to critiques of the leadership. The process of reconstructing exactly what went wrong with the campaign began in prison as soon as it ended and, in some respects, continues to this day. Some believed that spies in Zambia had given the Rhodesians prior notice before their crossing. Bopela and Luthuli follow this line, suggesting that the Rhodesians were tipped off and began tracking the group as soon as they crossed the Zambezi.[74] They narrate their account by foreshadowing their inevitable defeat, the detachment was the victim of an elaborate hammer-and-anvil operation orchestrated by the Rhodesians who placed one RAR unit in pursuit while another waited ahead. Advance notice meant that the Rhodesians could plot their movements and had a general sense where the group was and was going without actually seeing them. But a variety of sources, ranging from RAR official histories, to Reid-Daly's analysis of the campaign, to situation reports, all contradict Bopela and Luthuli.[75] These sources indicate that the Rhodesians did not know about the guerrilla presence until August 10, suggesting that they were as surprised by the discovery as the guerrillas were at being discovered. This plot device works well in a dissident account preoccupied with conspiracy but probably lends the Rhodesian forces a devious omniscience they certainly did not possess.

Other explanations of the undoing of the campaign look inward. The case of Peter Tladi (aka Lawrence Phokanoka) presents an illuminating example of how eyewitness accounts fueled accusation and insinuation long after the conclusion of the campaign. Tladi, known by the traveling name Black Mambazo, lost his AK-47 on the trail about nine days into the campaign, was sent back to find it, became lost, and a search party sent out failed to locate him.[76] Tladi wandered for a few days before being arrested on August 14 by a railway security inspector at a siding. Eventually, the Rhodesians turned Tladi over to South Africa, where he was subsequently tried in the Pietermaritzburg terrorism trial and served a long sentence on Robben Island.

At some point after his capture, rumors began to circulate that Tladi had a hand in revealing the detachment. Graham Morodi gives only a hint of the rumor in an interview; after his capture, Tladi was seen in a Rhodesian helicopter pointing out the crossing point on the Zambezi.[77] Presumably, the Rhodesians went to the crossing point and then tracked the spoor that eventually led them to the guerrillas. It is not at all clear who started the rumor about Tladi, but it certainly circulated among the men in prison in Botswana and perhaps traveled with them when they began to be released in late 1969. Once out in the exile community, these rumors traveled widely and became a part of the unofficial reckoning of the campaign.

When Morodi was released from prison in 1971, he returned to Zambia where Oliver Tambo debriefed him. Tambo specifically asked Morodi about the cloud of suspicion around Tladi. Morodi dismissed the rumors by relating what Nqose had told him—the same Nqose noted before who escaped to South Africa, was held for three months, and was then repatriated to Botswana with secret instructions to lure the guerrillas back home. Nqose exposed the plot to his cellmates, gave them detailed information about the capabilities of the security police, and staunchly defended Tladi against these rumors. Morodi recalled that these strength of Nqose's stories persuaded Tambo to change his mind about Tladi. It is unclear whether Tambo's endorsement fully restored Tladi's reputation, but he later returned to exile, contributed to official debates on the armed struggle, and received honors and a post in provincial government after the transition.[78]

Was Tladi flying around in a helicopter directing Rhodesian security forces? Rhodesian situation reports indicate that a captured guerrilla was taken to Victoria Falls and identified a crossing point. Given that Tladi was the first guerrilla captured, it would make sense that those in prison suspected his complicity. But beyond this assumption and given the benefit of hindsight, there is no evidence to suggest that this captured guerrilla was Tladi or that the location of the crossing doomed the campaign. The flight to Victoria Falls occurred long after the Rhodesians first detected the infiltration. Official RAR histories date the initial detection to August 10, when a game warden reported the chance discovery of a suspicious set of footprints that led to the eastbound group.[79]

Given this, it is unlikely that anyone actually saw Tladi in a helicopter. However, the transformation of an alleged sighting into a rumor about betrayal is part of a larger construction of the meaning of defeat. No one ever personally claimed to see Tladi in the helicopter, and yet the rumors about him carried the weight of an eyewitness account. What may seem peculiar to an outsider—an eyewitness account without a witness—is a generic form of explanation that shapes much of the testimony of former guerrillas, particularly those who spent time in prison. Jailhouse narratives that debate the complicity of comrades are a genre of storytelling too vast and complicated to fully address here. However, I suggest that these sorts of stories condense experiences of the Battlefield Gothic in the bush. Contrary to prescriptive accounts of other guerrilla wars, these detachments experienced a different kind of war, one that had local specificities.[80]

NOTES

1. Many thanks to Sharon Hutchinson for the inspiration for this title. Rendani Ralinala et al., "The Wankie and Sipolilo Campaigns," in *The Road to Democracy in South Africa: Volume 1 (1960–1970)*, ed. Bernard Magubane (Cape Town: Zebra Press 2004), 479–541.

2. "Preface," in *The Road to Democracy in South Africa: Volume 1 (1960–1970)*, ed. Bernard Magubane (Cape Town: Zebra Press, 2004), xix.

3. Samuel Hynes, *The Soldiers' Tale: Bearing Witness to Modern War* (New York: A. Lane, 1997).

4. Ibid.

5. Ralinala et al., "The Wankie and Sipolilo Campaigns," 497.

6. Ibid., 494.

7. "*List of ANC Members Who Died in Exile*," accessed June 19, 2016 (http://www.anc.org.za/show.php?id=100). Ralinala et al., "The Wankie and Sipolilo Campaigns," 511–12.

8. Justice "Gizenga" Mpanza, interviewed by Jabulani Sithole and Bernard Magubane, in *The Road to Democracy: South Africans Telling Their Stories: Volume I (1950–1970)*, ed. Gregory Houston (Edenvale: Mutloatse Arts Heritage Trust, 2008), 337–49.

9. Ben Turok, interview with Wolfie Kodesh, March 8, 1993, Mayibuye Centre Archives.

10. *Nyawo Zinodaka* translates to "Dirty Boots." Thula Bophela and Daluxolo Luthuli, *Umkhonto we Sizwe: Fighting for a Divided People* (Alberton: Galago, 2005), 55.

11. Zolile Nqose, *The Luthuli Detachment* (2007; Johannesburg: Qoma Film Productions), DVD.

12. James April, interview with author, April 30, 2008.

13. Graham Morodi, interview with Wolfie Kodesh, March 23, 1993, Mayibuye Centre Archives.

14. Ibid. Peter Mfene (Teddington Nqapayi), interview with Wolfie Kodesh, February 19, 1992, Mayibuye Centre Archives. Nqose, *The Luthuli Detachment*.

15. Bophela and Luthuli, *Umkhonto we Sizwe*, 77.

16. Cletus Mzimela, interview with Jabulani Sithole, 2001, South African Democratic Education Trust.

17. Patrick Matanjana, interview with author, November 25, 2007. Lawrence Phokanoka (Peter Tladi), interviewed by Siphamandla Zondi, in *The Road to Democracy: South Africans Telling Their Stories: Volume I (1950–1970)*, ed. Gregory Houston (Edenvale: Mutloatse Arts Heritage Trust, 2008), 409–23.

18. Cletus Mzimela, interview with Jabulani Sithole, 2001, South African Democratic Education Trust. Morodi, interview with Kodesh, March 23, 1993, Mayibuye Centre Archives.

19. Alfred Willie provided these details when interviewed by Zolile Nqose. Nqose, *The Luthuli Detachment*.

20. Matanjana, interview with author, November 25, 2007.

21. Morodi, interview with Kodesh, March 23, 1993, Mayibuye Centre Archives.

22. The Matanjana interview held at the Mayibuye Center Archives indicates that the men sent to the dam had all of their water bottles, which were then taken after the two were shot by the Rhodesians. The interviewee conducting the interview is not identified. Patrick Matanjana, interviewer not indicated, date not indicated, Mayibuye Centre Archives.

23. Ralinala et al., "The Wankie and Sipolilo Campaigns," 504. Chris Hani, "The Wankie Campaign," *Dawn* 10 (1986): 4–6.

24. Morodi, interview with Kodesh, March 23, 1993, Mayibuye Centre Archives.

25. Alexandre Binda, *Masodja: The History of the Rhodesian African Rifles and Its Forerunner the Rhodesian Native Regiment* (Johannesburg: 30 Degrees South Publishers, 2007), 214–24.

26. Morodi, interview with Kodesh, March 23, 1993, Mayibuye Centre Archives.

27. Bophela and Luthuli, *Umkhonto we Sizwe*, 59–82.

28. Michelle Berger, "Chris Hani," in *They Fought for Freedom*, ed. John Pampallis (Cape Town: Maskew Miller Longman, 1994), 19–24.

29. Ralinala et al., "The Wankie and Sipolilo Campaigns," 489. Hani, "The Wankie Campaign," 4–6.

30. Sandile Sejake, "Inside the Wankie Campaign: ANC-ZAPU Armed Actions in Rhodesia during 1967–68," accessed June 19, 2016 (http://panafricannews.blogspot.com/2007/11/inside-wankie-campaign-anc-zapu-armed.html).

31. Matanjana, interviewer not indicated, date not indicated, Mayibuye Centre Archives.

32. Ralinala et al., "The Wankie and Sipolilo Campaigns," 504.

33. Morodi, interview with Kodesh, March 23, 1993, Mayibuye Centre Archives.

34. Ibid.

35. Robert Taber, *The War of the Flea* (New York: L. Stuart, 1965). Ernesto Guevara, *Guerrilla Warfare* (Lincoln: University of Nebraska Press, 1985). Alberto Bayo, *Ciento Cincuenta Preguntas a un Guerrillero* (Havana: International Publishers, 1961).

36. Stephen Ellis and Tsepo Sechaba, *Comrades against Apartheid: The ANC and the South African Communist Party in Exile* (Bloomington: Indiana University Press, 1992), 46–47.

37. Binda, *Masodja*, 214–24.

38. Morodi, interview with Kodesh, March 23, 1993, Mayibuye Centre Archives.

39. Ralinala et al., "The Wankie and Sipolilo Campaigns," 505. Nqose, *The Luthuli Detachment*. Bophela and Luthuli, *Umkhonto we Sizwe*, 68.

40. Binda, *Masodja*, 214–24.
41. Bophela and Luthuli, *Umkhonto we Sizwe*, 70–71.
42. Ralinala et al., "The Wankie and Sipolilo Campaigns." Berger, "Chris Hani," 19–24. Hani, "The Wankie Campaign," 4–6. Chris Hani, interview with Wolfie Kodesh, date not indicated, Mayibuye Centre Archives.
43. Maps included in Rhodesian contact reports confirm this. Binda, *Masodja*, 214–24.
44. Ralinala et al., "The Wankie and Sipolilo Campaigns," 505–7. Binda, *Masodja*, 214–24.
45. Nqose, *The Luthuli Detachment*.
46. Bophela and Luthuli, *Umkhonto we Sizwe*, 68.
47. Ibid.
48. Binda, *Masodja*, 214–24.
49. Ralinala et al., "The Wankie and Sipolilo Campaigns." Berger, "Chris Hani," 19–24. Hani, "The Wankie Campaign," 4–6. Hani, interview with Kodesh, date unknown, Mayibuye Centre Archives.
50. Hani, "The Wankie Campaign," 4–6.
51. Nqose, *The Luthuli Detachment*.
52. Bophela and Luthuli, *Umkhonto we Sizwe*, 13.
53. Norman Duka, *From Shantytown to Forest* (Vancouver, BC: LSM Press, 1974). Bophela and Luthuli, *Umkhonto we Sizwe*, 71. Hani, interview with Kodesh, date unknown, Mayibuye Centre Archives. Morodi, interview with Kodesh, March 23, 1993, Mayibuye Centre Archives.
54. Binda, *Masodja*, 214–24. Ron Reid-Daly, "War in Rhodesia: Cross-Border Operations," in *Challenge: Southern Africa within the African Revolutionary Context*, ed. Al Venter (Johannesburg: Ashanti, 1989). Duka, *From Shantytown to Forest*. Morodi, interview with Kodesh, March 23, 1993, Mayibuye Centre Archives. Bophela and Luthuli, *Umkhonto we Sizwe*, 71.
55. This quote was taken from a selection of RAR sitreps submitted between August 1967 and October 1967. Many thanks to Nicky Van Driel for access to her personal collection of these documents.
56. Matanjana, interviewer not indicated, date not indicated, Mayibuye Centre Archives.
57. James April is referenced by his nom de guerre, George Driver. Bophela and Luthuli, *Umkhonto we Sizwe*, 73–76.
58. Reid-Daly, "War in Rhodesia."
59. Bophela and Luthuli, *Umkhonto we Sizwe*, 73–76.
60. April, interview with author, April 30, 2008.
61. Leonard Nkosi, *State vs. James April*, Pietermaritzburg: High Court of South Africa, 1971.
62. Duka, *From Shantytown to Forest*.
63. RAR sitreps written between August 1967 and October 1967 record these activities. Duka, *From Shantytown to Forest*.

64. April, interview with author, April 30, 2008.

65. Ibid. Morodi, interview with Kodesh, March 23, 1993, Mayibuye Centre Archives.

66. April, interview with author, April 30, 2008.

67. Berger, "Chris Hani," 22.

68. Ralinala et al., "The Wankie and Sipolilo Campaigns," 509.

69. Hani, interview with Kodesh, date unknown, Mayibuye Centre Archives. Duka, *From Shantytown to Forest*, 90.

70. Ralinala et al., "The Wankie and Sipolilo Campaigns," 508.

71. Morodi, interview with Kodesh, March 23, 1993, Mayibuye Centre Archives.

72. Hugh Macmillan, "The Hani Memorandum: Introduced and Annotated," *Transformation: Critical Perspectives on Southern Africa* 69 (2009): 106–29.

73. Tom Lodge, *Black Politics in South Africa since 1948* (New York: Longman, 1983). Ellis and Sechaba, *Comrades against Apartheid*.

74. Bophela and Luthuli, *Umkhonto we Sizwe*, 77–79.

75. Rhodesian African Rifles, "Situation Reports: Operation Nickel, August 1967 to October 1967," Nicky Van Driel Collection. Reid-Daly, "War in Rhodesia." Binda, *Masodja*, 214–24.

76. Morodi, interview with Kodesh, March 23, 1993, Mayibuye Centre Archives. Ralinala et al., "The Wankie and Sipolilo Campaigns," 533.

77. Morodi, interview with Kodesh, March 23, 1993, Mayibuye Centre Archives.

78. Ibid.

79. Binda, *Masodja*, 214–24.

80. Taber, *The War of the Flea*. Guevara, *Guerrilla Warfare*. Bayo, *Ciento Cincuenta Preguntas a un Guerrillero*.

4. Losing the Plot: Mystery, Narrativity, and Investigation in Novo Catengue, May 1977–March 1979

THIS CHAPTER IS BOTH THE story of how one training camp was bombed flat and an explanation of how investigations of infiltration flattened the history of it.[1] The training camp in question is Novo Catengue, a railway depot turned army barracks that operated from May 1977 to March 1979 in southern Angola. This particular camp is significant because it was a threshold: an entire generation of cadres marched through its parade ground into the ranks of MK. Known collectively as the Soweto generation, thousands of young people left South Africa after the student uprisings in June 1976 and formed the first new detachments since the mid-1960s. Their entrance breathed new life into the stalled armed struggle, revived the international relevance of the exiled leadership, and held the promise of forming a youthful constituency within South Africa. However, the camp also suffered an alleged poisoning and was closed after an aerial bombardment by the SAAF. Despite the ignominious end of this camp, the story of the alleged poisoning and bombing are the most common ways of narrating this episode. Novo Catengue was both an instructive lesson on the dangers of infiltration, a justification for the necessity of investigation, and the perseverance of a just cause. In the end, the camp succeeded in turning students into soldiers, completing a transformation that marked the beginning of an upward swing in violence throughout the 1980s and early 1990s.

This narrative is born from investigative reports written after the closure of the camp. A long line of internal documents place the alleged poisoning and the aerial bombardment at the beginning of a decades-long chronology of infiltration. These authors interpreted the causes and effects of subsequent infiltrations differently, but all assumed that an unknown number of agents organized these first attacks and then passed through this camp into the army. Accordingly, the incidents at Novo Catengue were the first in a cascade of occurrences identified as either suspicious or malicious. In 1981, security officials uncovered a spy ring. In 1984, they suppressed a mutiny of suspect origin. In the late 1980s, high casualty rates among infiltrated cadres warranted investigations of infiltration in underground structures. At each of these junctures, the security department reexamined earlier events and saw patterns of infiltration that linked the destruction of equipment, to theft of supplies, to training accidents, to mysterious disappearances, to indiscipline and insubordination, to orchestrated mutinies and unsolved murders. At these three points, the commissariat, security officials, and commissions of inquiry called on witnesses to detail circumstances of certain events and speculate on their causes. Investigators then gathered this new evidence, referenced it against what they knew or thought they knew about Novo Catengue, and wrote texts that connected past events and personalities together into conspiracies of varying size and configuration. Ultimately, their reports became a genre of writing, a form of storytelling where all events had causality, and the meanings of events like the alleged poisoning and aerial bombardment could only be interpreted through the frame of investigations of infiltration. I argue that over time, the narrativity of report writing fixed the meanings assigned to Novo Catengue. Narrativity structured this evidence in a particular way, making it difficult for historians to separate the social world of Novo Catengue from the rhetorical duty this camp was called to serve in investigative reports and histories written from these reports.

The historiographical effects of this narrativity can be summarized in the following way. As each layer of writing and testimony accrued, it became more and more difficult to discern the relations that governed accusations in the camp apart from the kinds of relations that governed other times and places. With each passing retelling, the story of Novo Catengue became less an episode with its own history and own political valence and more a way of explaining subsequent infiltrations by organizing a series of texts and testimonies into a coherent pattern within an accusation intended to convince readers. A backward glance across these references reveals the complexity and intertextuality of these texts: submissions to the Truth and Reconciliation Commission (TRC) reference reports into a mysterious death in 1989, which reference security reports presented at a party congress in 1985, which reference interrogations conducted in 1981, which reference a code of conduct drafted in 1980 in response to the alleged poisoning and bombing that occurred in Novo Catengue in 1977. The combined effect of this intertextuality constitutes a circular and self-referential discourse, one that grows more confident and presumptuous with each layer of writing. In present literature, infiltration is a foregone conclusion, and there is little ambiguity about causality. A symptom of this problem is that now one cannot speak about Novo Catengue other than first prefacing it as the entry point for agents who were responsible for the alleged poisoning and bombing there and were later responsible for subsequent intrigues, murders, and mutinies in other places and at other times.

But the evidentiary effects of narration are more an opportunity than a problem. Novo Catengue offers a pathway into understanding how narration structures histories of the liberation struggle and the armed struggle within it. All of the evidence that references Novo Catengue—whether interrogation reports, conference proceedings, counterintelligence training manuals, security bulletins, oral testimony, TRC perpetrator hearings, and published memoirs—contextualize this event within their potted histories of the armed struggle. These potted histories pose a protagonist, the morally righteous liberation struggle, against an antagonist, the morally bankrupt apartheid regime. Infiltration becomes one of the main themes that distinguishes the characteristics of both protagonist and antagonist. Unpublished reports written in the late 1970s and 1980s set this narrative scheme, and truth commission submission given in the 1990s reproduce it by drawing on these earlier documents.[2] Over time, neither body of evidence could narrate the entire span of the armed struggle without reference to infiltration, and the events at Novo Catengue became the first and most significant in a long line of crimes. In other words, if infiltration was the theme that united the last few chapters of the armed struggle, then Novo Catengue was the most convenient example for what lay ahead.

In reading through all these layers of writing, I return to the following questions: To what extent can we now separate the social world of the post-Soweto exodus from the rhetorical uses this camp performed in narratives about infiltration? Further, is it possible to rescue the specificity and contingency of this moment from later accusations of infiltration? The assumption underlying these questions is that the more people wrote about Novo Catengue, the less their readers seemed to know about accusations in the camp. How and why this came to be is a matter that cuts to the core of the historiographical certainties that govern histories of the armed struggle and the entire liberation struggle. To introduce a problematic borrowed from an intrigue in another liberation struggle, "how do we write the history of the guerrilla apart from the history of the guerrilla war?"[3]

What method might rescue the contingency of Novo Catengue from the way people write about accusation? Fortunately, two separate genealogies of texts describe the events at Novo Catengue. Aside from investigative reports, Jack Simons recorded his perceptions of this camp in two diaries.[4] Simons was a party stalwart and academic who taught at the camp during two separate stays: the first in late 1977 through early 1978 and the second in late 1978 through early 1979. During both stays, Simons trained instructors in political education using a syllabus composed of materialist history, the philosophy of Marxism-Leninism, and a review of ANC politics. Given his position as teacher of teachers, his diaries are a very intimate chronicle of everyday life in the camp, the relationship between the camp administration and Cuban instructors, and the theoretical debates that occurred during classes. Simons also gave very frank appraisals of significant events. These events included the passing-out ceremonies for both detachments; serious incidents of malingering, indiscipline, and insubordination; and, of course, the alleged poisoning, known in later camp lore as Black September. Simons records only secondhand reports of the bombing in his second diary because he was evacuated from the camp a week before the event. Simons's diaries and syllabi began as unpublished documents but were edited over two decades and finally published as an annotated volume in 2001.[5]

Reading Investigative Reports

What is the most useful way to read investigative reports turned memoirs? Given that so many of these reports were preoccupied with making accusations, the ethnographic literature on witchcraft accusation is a useful place to start. The study of witchcraft beliefs and witchcraft accusations in Africa began with E. E. Evans Pritchard.[6] Pritchard used local terms to describe witchcraft accusations but ultimately wanted these beliefs to seem rational to his audience. To do this, he argued that Africans accept the empirical causes of events, even while they use witchcraft belief to explain why misfortune happens to one person and not another. Monica Wilson continued Pritchard's rationalization, quoting her informant's apt logic: "I know that typhus is caused by lice, but what I want to know is who sent the lice?"[7] This sort of logic is all too easily shoehorned into accusation of infiltration in the camps: "I know that the bad roads cause car accidents, but why has this particular comrade wrecked so many times, and who sent him to cause so many problems?" But Pritchard, Wilson, and others do not go beyond who gets accused and why. Rationalizing belief does not begin to explain how written accusations constitute "the infiltrator" or how the narration of infiltration fixes the meaning of Novo Catengue.

The limitation of early ethnographies of witchcraft is that they neglect to explain why accusations occur when they do. Mary Douglas makes this same point in a review essay.[8] Above all else, she urges anthropologists of witchcraft to think more like historians and place witchcraft in time. Nodding to the early work of Max Marwick and Clyde Mitchell, Douglas argues that witchcraft accusation was less of a way of preserving the old order from change and more a line of attack when relationships are ambiguous. Her point is that anthropologists need to examine the symbolics of these definitions without returning to the homeostatic thesis. In times of flux, witchcraft affirms certain social definitions, while simultaneously amounting "to a denial of common bonds and responsibility." Treating the witch as a symbol demonstrates how it shapes social definitions during moments of rupture. Symbols arrange boundaries, marking individuals as within or without a community, and this delineates how insiders can cause harm in a way outsiders cannot. The import of this kind of ethnography is clear: investigative reports written after the discovery of spy rings or the suppression of mutinies develop symbolic "infiltrators" to affirm social definitions.

John and Jean Comaroff also place witchcraft in time but see symbolics as less revealing than ritual.[9] In their view, ritual is "a powerful tool for making sense of the world, and expressing the meaning of novel conditions after dramatic historical changes."[10] Moving from semiotics into linguistics, the Comaroffs suggest that one needs to read ritual for all of the poetic tropes, juxtaposition, and redundancy that are "deployed to work their magic."[11] This approach has many implications for accusations of infiltration. Because investigative reports come out of inquiries and tribunals, what, then, are these bodies but another form of ritual, both rituals of discovery and rituals of accusation? How, then, might we read their written product, the genre of report writing?

As useful as ethnography may be for understanding the logic, symbolism, and encoded meanings, all these theories are derived from participant observation rather than written texts. This ethnographic literature tends to deal with accusations made in the present, in person, and as they happen, rather than the arrangement of a number of incidents into a convincing accusation, perhaps written years after the events in question. Clearly, there is a temporal dimension to written texts, especially those that justify their explanations, by placing events in historical narratives. How do you detect the generic rules that quietly pattern this writing over time? What are the shared tropes used to connect multiple persons to multiple crimes?

Literary criticism of the detective novel may further these questions. It is tempting to call investigative reports one long detective novel, one written by several authors over several decades. But investigators did not adapt the detective novel to write their reports, even though Nelson Mandela, as commander of MK, was once dubbed the Black Pimpernel, and ANC used the term *red herring* in its submissions to the TRC.[12] I am not making the argument that investigative reports are direct descendants of detective novels, nor am I making a claim that investigative reports are entirely fictive. Instead, I am suggesting that literary criticism may offer strategies of reading both of these similar but unrelated genres. Both attempt to convince audiences of the validity of their conclusions by closing off alternative possibilities. The strategies of reading provided by literary criticism can reveal the historiographical aftereffects of this kind of closed text.

Investigative reports mirror features found in two eras of crime fiction: the golden age of the nineteenth-century detective novel and the hard-boiled postwar detective novel.[13] Both forms of detective novels interpret evidence of the past, attempt to debunk falsehoods, develop detailed arguments, and offer convincing conclusions. This last point is the most significant: these genres are about formulating accusations that stick, and each form arrives at these conclusions in different ways. In golden age detective novels, the crime is committed in a hermetically sealed environment, the officially sanctioned detectives advance incorrect theories, at which point the amateur detective intervenes, discounts red herrings, turns clues into fact, and explains the commission of the crime by establishing motive, means, and opportunity. Most importantly, he or she sets wrong right by correctly identifying the perpetrator. Moral boundaries are never in question; the detective is unimpeachable, the victim innocent, and the perpetrator incorrigibly evil. The hard-boiled detective novel employs many of the same conventions but troubles these clear moral lines. These novels are set in cynical urban landscapes where the moral boundaries that separate detective from criminal are constantly in question. Detectives and criminals inhabit the same seedy space and often trade favors for information quid pro quo. In addition to these trade-offs, hard-boiled detectives employ the "police procedural," an "excessively detailed official methodology" derived from modern science. Like the golden age detective, the hard-boiled detective delivers a similar sense of closure but with a different combination of evidence: ill-gotten tips and scientific facts. Also, breaking with earlier forms, moral ambiguities remain.

Investigative reports exhibit elements of both periods. Above all else, investigators and infiltrators inhabit a world ordered on strict moral lines. As guardian of the liberation movement, the security department writes itself as unimpeachable and presents its authority to accuse as morally justified. But following hard-boiled detective novels, they establish the authority of their accusations by foregrounding their own police procedural, a combination of almost infallible Eastern Bloc interrogation techniques, biography writing, and careful recruitment procedures. This structure runs through the entire body of investigative reports and is only somewhat disrupted by victim testimony during the TRC, which inferred that the police procedural, which may or may not have included methods of torture, itself interrupted moral lines.

Peter Hühn sees the detective novel as the authoring and deciphering of "plots" in both a literary sense and in a criminal sense.[14] In this formula, detective novels are two stories in one: first, it is the story of the investigation, and second, it is the unveiling of a crime—a hidden story "authored" in the past by the criminal. This crime is a destabilizing event that upsets all of the "systems of norms and rules" regulating life in the community. When monopolizing the authority to accuse, only the detective can reveal the hidden text and thus restore order to the community. His or her discovery and reading of the first story—the hidden text of the crime—"reintegrates this aberrant event" and thus "reaffirms the validity of the system of norms."

For Hühn, detective novels, with their stories about discovering stories, constitutes a hermeneutic circle. The crime is an uninterpretable sign that calls into question the validity of the established order. As a consequence, everyday events "are made strange" and lose the "usual automatically ascribed meanings and signify something else." The task of the detective, then, is to break through the preconceived notions that hampered official investigations and then illuminate the clues hidden in the ordinary. Having gathered enough clues, the detective then sets about sorting through different possible interpretations, reduces polyvalence to one meaning, and reveals the great singular truth that closes the circle. "The fundamental premise of the classical formula," Hühn writes, "is that there ultimately exists one true meaning." The closure of the hermeneutic circle is at the heart of how Novo Catengue gets flattened in investigative reports.

The Police Procedural

There are few uncontested details about Black September and the aerial bombardment at Novo Catengue. The total number of cadres sickened during the Black September incident shifts from report to report, as does the number and type of planes flown over the camp during the bombing two years later. A survey of sources that reference Black September shows that few accounts match, despite some parallel details that span different accounts.[15] In the early evening on September 29, 1977, a few hundred cadres fell ill with severe intestinal cramps and diarrhea. Some say the entire camp was affected while others suggest that only a majority of cadres fell ill. Many mention the heroism of female cadres who assisted the sick, inferring that they were unaffected. Whatever their numbers, the sickness was so severe that many were incapacitated. After some time, Cuban doctors arrived, determined the cause of the illness to be poisoning, and administered antidotes. Most accounts credit the survival of the camp to the quick actions of the Cuban doctors. Investigations at Novo Catengue revealed the poison to be administered in food, and the immediate consequence was ending the rotation of kitchen duty, which limited access to food to a handful of trusted cadres.

The bombing occurred on March 14, 1979. Most accounts note that the movement had advance warning of an impending attack but offer different explanations of how they knew. All accounts note that in the weeks preceding the bombing, all cadres evacuated the camp early in the morning and disrupted their routines to avoid being in a predictable location at a predictable time. The bombing came at the precise time that the camp would be at assembly in the parade grounds. Authors include these details to infer that the SAAF had good information about routines and that this information could only come from an infiltrator in the camp. Most accounts suggest that three people were killed, two ANC cadres and one Cuban.[16] Accounts differ on the response of anti-aircraft batteries. Some say that one Canberra was hit and credit MK cadres who fired their guns. Others make no mention of the crash at all. All note that the immediate consequence of the bombing was the closure of the camp.

The first report written in response to these events was a code of conduct drafted in late 1977 and revised at least through 1980.[17] Andrew Masondo authored these drafts while he was the national commissar and thus head of the commissariat at Novo Catengue. By virtue of his position, Masondo had an intimate knowledge of both Black September and the aerial bombardment and morale in general in the camp. He testified before a closed hearing of the TRC that he wrote the code of conduct in response to the attacks.[18] Early drafts of the code are presently unavailable, but several sets of written comments on the 1980 version survive.[19] It is possible to infer a number of omissions, substitutions, and additions in the first drafts of these comments are placed against the final version of the code adopted at the Kabwe Conference in 1985. Above all else, these documents are early attempts to define crimes against the movement, establish the justifications for investigation, and formulate the procedures of tribunals. Likewise, these comments are a reflection of official thinking on Black September and the aerial bombardment. In this sense, these writings are the first attempt to uncover the "hidden text" of the infiltration at Novo Catengue. Following Hühn's diagram of the detective novel, they also represent the failure of official investigators to solve the crime and mark a moment just prior to the intervention of the detective.

Comments on the draft suggest an as-yet-undeveloped police procedural and very broad definitions of what constituted a "grave crime against the movement." The comments on the draft record a heated debate over the necessity of definitions, the legitimacy of tribunals in sovereign states, and the severity of the penalties. Albie Sachs wrote the most critical comments.[20] Sachs, a distinguished lawyer and longtime human rights activist, wrote that he had "fundamental reservations" about the document. He saw it as too severe, too premature, and perhaps disrespectful of the jurisdiction of criminal courts in host nations. Sachs was against the formation of tribunals and instead suggested that most infractions could be solved with political reeducation or simple expulsion. In his view, most crimes within the movement were too petty to warrant formal tribunals, while serious crimes had to be handled by courts in host countries. He does make exception for clear threats to security in combat situations. Borrowing from the Mozambique Liberation Front's (FRELIMO's) experience of guerrilla warfare, "assassins" and "traitors" may be executed by the military but only in liberated zones and not in host states. But above all else, he demanded a clear statement against the use of torture and reserved capital punishment for the extraordinary circumstances of combat or an imminent threat to the leadership. Sachs is unambiguous; the draft overreaches its authority, fails to justify the necessity of its severity, and collapses minor infractions into grave crimes against the struggle. His statements are a telling index of grave crimes in the movement at that particular time. In his mind, judicial procedure should be geared toward politically rehabilitating errant comrades, and aside from a few individual infiltrators, there was no evidence of fifth column in the ranks. The language of an "enemy in our midst" is entirely absent from this document.

Comments written by the political department—the parent body of the commissariat—show the official mind of investigators. These comments clearly depict a group of novices struggling to define a grave crime and, instead, broadening the definition to include pretty much any act deemed suspicious, granting them the power to detain people at will. The political department stated in unambiguous terms: the time has come to "once and for all punish those who have chosen to stand as barricades against the freedoms of our people. It comes at a time when a precise line has been drawn between ourselves and the enemy by the people themselves, without any clouds."[21] Unlike Sachs, the political department accepts the draft but tips the balance of power on the tribunal: it should include at least one security official and one commissar. Because these two officials would be the primary investigators of the crime, prosecutors would also serve as judges.

As these comments demonstrate, after the closure of Novo Catengue, official investigators had few methods in their police procedural and no clear idea whom they were looking for. As Sachs suggests, the broad definitions of grave crimes allowed tribunals to assign severe punishments for trivial offenses. The power grab encoded in broad criminal definitions resonates with infiltration in ZANU, where security departments needed to monopolize the authority to levy accusations lest accusations get out of control and damage morale in combat zones.[22] But contrary to monopolizing the authority, this heavy-handedness and dull definition indicates that investigators had a real inability to separate suspects from innocents and thus needed sweeping powers and severe penalties to control a situation they did not entirely understand. At the time, the formal investigative department was under reorganization, and Masondo, a former mathematics instructor turned national commissar, had to set the parameters of investigation as the default investigator.[23] Simply put, a trained body of investigators had not yet assumed authority for all investigations, and in the gap, the commissariat, a guardian of political lines, stepped in to install iron discipline by criminalizing minor infractions as grave crimes.

Illuminating the Everyday

This situation changed in a matter of months. The discovery of a spy ring in late 1981 signaled both the arrival of "the detective" in the form of the Department of National Security (NAT) and the first sign of extensive infiltration.[24] The spy ring is significant for four reasons. First, it caused widespread paranoia among the leadership. The size and extent of the network indicated a coordinated and successful conspiracy, one linked to the events at Novo Catengue and was thus capable of inflicting many more casualties. This also was the first indication that South African intelligence services had a coordinated and long-term plan to infiltrate the military and political leadership. Second, this investigation provided security with an opportunity to deploy their newly trained staff, as well as test and develop the police procedural given to them during specialization in the Soviet Union and the German Democratic Republic.[25] Success during a time of paranoia lent security more authority to detain, question, and punish suspects. In theory, their official role was only investigation, but in practice, they could interrogate and punish almost anyone.[26] Third, the spy ring sketched out a profile of suspect groups. The accused came from the best and brightest of the Soweto generation, all had passed through Novo Catengue, and were quickly promoted into leadership positions. Two had even had positions within security itself. Fourth and perhaps more importantly, this investigation linked events at Novo Catengue to ongoing infiltrations and began to weave a narrative of infiltration into summaries of the armed struggle. What we can see here are the first furtive attempts by "the detective" to see the "strange in the familiar" and illuminate a set of clues that might explain Novo Catengue.

This atmosphere of suspicion coincided with growing resentment in the camps. By 1982, deployment to South Africa slowed to a trickle, and many Soweto-generation recruits grew restless after training for five years in the camps. Suspicion and indiscipline rose in tandem and reached a crescendo in the Mkatashinga mutiny in late 1983 and early 1984, where cadres in several camps rebelled, executed a few camp leaders, were suppressed by loyalists and Angolan forces, and several faced summary executions.[27] Internal documents show a struggle over how to interpret the meaning of this event. An independent inquiry known as the Stuart Commission found legitimate grievances, abuses by security officials, and slight evidence of infiltration.[28] Writing against this report, security officials defended their performance over the past few years and maintained that the mutiny was not the result of growing resentment over the poor conditions and a repressive atmosphere in the camps but of a large, well-orchestrated, and patient conspiracy. To prove their accusation, they gave the first instance of a narrative of infiltration and its effects on the armed struggle.

The most significant investigative report written during this period was *Some Aspects of Counter-Guerrilla Tactics Based on Our Experience* authored two months after the Stuart Commission Report and four months after the mutiny.[29] This document shows a far more confident investigation than the 1981 Code of Conduct. Investigators portray themselves as capable of reading the clues in the everyday and thereby able to begin to decipher the hidden text of the crime. They narrow down potential suspects through a typology of profiles, an assessment of motives, and a clearer definition of different crimes. This is a document that begins to close the noose around those responsible for the events at Novo Catengue. Black September is referenced as a specific crime, while an entire category of crimes specific to the camps derives from analysis of the aerial bombardment.

How did they see the clues in the everyday? Investigators claimed they had the ability to read the true identity of infiltrators in the ordinary details of their biographies. Using a typology of profiles to interrogate and screen new recruits, investigators discerned two types of agents: the short-termers, who gather information or commit assassinations in a matter of months, and long-termers or "sleepers," who sought leadership positions and slowly orchestrated their crimes over a number of years. The typology explains their motives by virtue of their class positions; short-termers are most likely to be lumpens or criminals swayed by quick money or early release, whereas sleepers tend to be desperate workers or frustrated petit bourgeois intellectuals with ambitions for prestige or lucrative police salaries.[30] Investigators also knew that infiltrators would attempt to hide their true identities using legends but remained confident that their typology could detect the generic characteristics of these false stories, as well as in the discrepancies between written biographies and personal details revealed in casual conversation.[31] The most successful legends used by sleepers were the persona of students or former Black Consciousness Movement (BCM) activists. Because most of the Soweto generation was composed of these two kinds of recruits and these recruits predominated at Novo Catengue, investigators clearly attributed the poisoning and aerial bombardment to enemies within.

Investigators also presented a more sophisticated view of "the crime." After the spy ring and the mutiny, in the official mind, infiltration became part of a grand strategy of subversion. The enemy would continue to attempt massacres like those averted at Novo Catengue, but the ultimate objective of infiltration was undermining the leadership and demoralizing the rank and file. Beneath explicit crimes like poisoning and bombings lay a subtext of more subtle implicit offenses, ones that were previously invisible to investigators. Spreading a rumor, crashing a car, stealing supplies, or complaining about shortages were acts of demoralization and could now get you labeled as an infiltrator.[32] Where there was smoke, there was fire, so in many ways, a high frequency of seemingly mundane problems could indicate the presence of short-termers and sleepers acting in tandem. Based on the past experience of the spy ring and mutiny, investigators believed they now had the power to connect seemingly unrelated occurrences, and predict big attacks from a number of petty but demoralizing offenses. In this new awareness, a broken movie projector was no longer just a broken movie projector; it was a harbinger of mortal danger.

Some Aspects of Counter-Guerrilla Warfare from Our Experience clarified the relationship between the spy ring and the mutiny and, in this sense, rewrote a new interpretation of Novo Catengue in these terms.[33] Investigators did not reveal the names of those responsible for the poisoning and the bombing, but they clearly placed these events within this elaborate schematic of infiltration. In a list of "missions performed by enemy agents in the ANC," Black September is the only event mentioned by name, while the precision of the aerial bombardment is clearly the result of inside information passed along by an infiltrator. Simply put, these were the biggest near massacres ever perpetrated by the regime. But as yet, they are unable or unwilling to name the criminals responsible for both crimes. Part of this inability may be a function of this kind of report. It is more a training manual than a formal indictment. But another part of it may be lingering doubts about their powers of identification. They mention that sleepers have infiltrated security itself and are accusing innocents of being infiltrators. These red herrings no doubt preoccupied investigators, and short-termers gummed up their screening. This document is less a lifting of the veil and more a finalization of their claim on the authority to accuse. Challenged by an independent commission that criticized its methods, investigators demonstrated their capability by using their police procedural to align numerous clues into a convincing, linear but as-yet-inconclusive narrative.

In May 1985, delegates from all ANC structures met in Kabwe, Zambia, for the first national conference held in exile.[34] With recent crises on their minds, delegates debated past mistakes and suggested future reforms, all under the watchful eye of members of security.[35] First and foremost was a review of the Code of Conduct, which was abrogated during the mutiny.[36] The most significant changes between the 1981 draft and the 1985 draft are the detailed criteria for the use of "intensive interrogation methods," an ambiguous prohibition on torture, and a sharper delineation on the composition and function of tribunals.[37]

Like *Some Aspects of Counter-Guerrilla Warfare from Our Experience*, security responded with a document that uses narration to assert both the effectiveness of its methods and its moral righteousness. *The Report on Security and Intelligence* recapitulates the typology of criminal profiles, but for the first time, this document builds a chronology.[38] It first cites Black September and the aerial bombardment as evidence of the mortal threat posed by infiltrators. The authors then turn to a detailed narration of the investigation of the spy ring, suggesting that it was part of a two-pronged method to elect sleepers in the executive leadership by provoking a crisis, in this case a mutiny. This narrative includes a character sketch of an as-yet-unnamed infiltrator.

Above all else, this document uses a narrative of infiltration to deny the existence of legitimate grievances against its authority. The authors introduce Novo Catengue as evidence of the mortal threat posed by infiltration and signaled the presence of sleeper agents. Because the mutiny was the result of a long-term strategy of infiltration, the ruthless suppression of mutineers was entirely justified, and any attempt to curtail security or elect a new leadership would further the aims of the infiltrators. Although security officials acknowledged that innocents were harmed in the course of both investigations, these abuses were isolated incidents, and calling attention merely sowed division and again furthered the aims of the infiltrators. Despite these lapses, the authors write "that the task of the movement and the leadership" "is to defend the security department . . . and increase its numbers and improve its training."[39] In the span of two reports, the noose tightens. The investigators have the means and the motive; all that remains is identity.

The Red Herring?

Commission of Inquiry into the Death of Thami Zulu is an example of how a complex biography tested the limits of the typology of profiles.[40] The subject of the inquiry, Thami Zulu, was among the best and the brightest of the Soweto generation, who quickly rose through the ranks at Novo Catengue, commanded a successor camp, was then deployed to the forward areas, and sent cadres and arms into Natal. But from the early 1980s onward, the underground structure he commanded suffered an inordinate number of casualties.[41] Investigators tolerated these anomalies until 1988 when nine cadres died in a single ambush. Security took Zulu into custody, held him for fourteen months, and released him. Days after his release he died under mysterious circumstances and was ominously denied an official funeral. A month later, amid rumors, speculation, and a growing rift between the military and security, the executive leadership called an independent inquiry into his death.

There are two levels to the report. First is the investigation into the cause of death. Zulu tested positive for HIV, left custody in an emaciated state, and his autopsy revealed both tubercular spots on his lungs and lethal levels of a commercial pesticide in his blood. After a long review of the sequence of diagnoses, witness testimony on his conditions and treatment during custody, and a reconstruction of his movements after release, the commission of inquiry kept to the middle ground. It decided that AIDS wasted his body, tuberculosis put him in a critical condition, and diazinon was inferred to have dealt the final blow. The inquiry discounted rumors that Zulu was tortured or starved by security.

The second level of the report is a debate over evidence that Zulu had committed "grave crimes against the struggle" and was thus a sleeper. This designation would illuminate clues in his biography, perhaps indicating his involvement in the poisoning and aerial bombardment at Novo Catengue, where he served as platoon commander. This independent commission was in some sense a referendum on the effectiveness of investigative techniques. Security demonstrated the ability to critically appraise evidence and discount a red herring. Security needed only the thinnest evidence of a "grave crime" to bring Zulu before a tribunal and therefore did not need a smoking gun. But despite this low burden of proof, security released Zulu without charge. The commission even related how security systematically picked apart the confession of a police agent who fingered Zulu as a spy. The conclusion of the report states that these were "skilled interrogators who prepared carefully, basing themselves on logic, probabilities and attention to detail."

In terms of narrativity, this evaluation of a suspect demonstrates the rejection ambiguity found in the falling action of detective novels. Although commissioners left enough sway on either side to suggest that Zulu was or was not a spy, its line of questioning is still locked into an either-or formula. On the one hand, the type of poison used indicated a method of assassination commonly used by South African agents, suggesting he was in the employ of the enemy and silenced to prevent a deathbed confession. On the other hand, a skillful investigation found no evidence linking him to a "grave crime." The report holds out the possibility that evidence may turn up in the future, but for now, Zulu remains not innocent but suspect. The presumption in all of this is that conclusive evidence will eventually determine his guilt or innocence in terms of one crime, but in terms of Novo Catengue, he is not our man. In this sense, this is the penultimate chapter in the long novel of infiltration, where the identification of the true criminal is premature but both possible and immanent. The only persons indicted in this report are the membership at large, who cast Zulu out of their community using the unofficial category of a "not cleared."

Above all else, the *Commission of Inquiry into the Death of Thami Zulu* demonstrates power of security to exclude a range of possibilities, possibilities that suggest a more complex set of relations. As Luise White noted, poisoning is a crime of intimacy. This is particularly true with diazinon, a poison most likely administered via alcoholic beverages. If Zulu accepted a drink, it was from a known acquaintance. Was this acquaintance another agent, a jealous rival, a righteous avenger, or a regretful friend tasked with a necessary duty? Or, transcending the logic of the investigative report, could the perpetrator have encompassed all four of these personas? Histories of other exiled liberation movements agree with oral histories of this movement: old comrades might have suspected friends were agents but tolerated them for personal reasons or because they posed no real threat.[42] Accusations and assassinations only ignited when history intervened, shifting the power relations that lay hidden beneath the face of party unity. The last months of 1989 are easily characterized as such a historical moment, although morally inscribed investigative reports could not sustain such complexities and still tell the story they do.

Spots of Blood

The ANC's *Statement to the Truth and Reconciliation Commission* is the final chapter in the investigation into the events at Novo Catengue.[43] This document is actually two separate submissions: *The First Submission* was delivered in August 1996, and after further questioning by the TRC, *The Second Submission* was delivered in May 1997. These two submissions are the final expression of the narrative of infiltration at Novo Catengue, nested within the overarching story of the armed struggle and, within that, the entire liberation struggle. *The First Submission* provides a long, elaborate defense against allegations of human rights abuses, presented before a commission purposed with finding a singular truth about such abuses. To contextualize abuses committed by the ANC, the author gives a grand narrative of human rights abuses committed against the black majority, tracing a historical arc that begins with the moment of colonization and extends into the present. The ANC, as legitimate modern representative of the black majority, is the latest victim in this chronology of violence. The author presents the armed struggle as a justified response to the violence inflicted by the regime. Above all else, the ANC prosecuted the armed struggle with restraint, it remained committed to the avoidance of civilian casualties, and in this regard, it stood above both the regime and less disciplined anticolonial movements. The ANC never endorsed the torture of infiltrators or enemy captives as a matter of policy, and when abuses occurred, they were the result of "bad apples" or incidents when a "ticking time bomb" threatened innocent lives.

Novo Catengue is the lynchpin that binds these historical frames of reference with these moral justifications. As narrated by *The First Submission*, the armed struggle entered its most dangerous phase after 1976, when thousands of recruits brought an unknown number of infiltrators into the ranks. These infiltrators laid low until they orchestrated Black September and passed on information that aided the aerial bombardment. These events were the opening volleys of Total Strategy, a master plan created by South African securocrats who coordinated domestic counterinsurgency, regional destabilization, and infiltration of the anti-apartheid movement. Black September and the aerial bombardment are key because they not only demonstrated the presence of infiltration but also showed its lethality and, thus, justify the extraordinary excesses committed to prevent further attacks. *The First Submission* names seven individuals as responsible for both attacks at Novo Catengue. They include a camp commissar, a camp commander, a physical trainer, a member of security, a politics instructor, and an agent who fled to South Africa to become the first askari. The Novo Catengue case broke after the discovery of the spy ring in 1981. Thami Zulu is mentioned in another section of *The Second Submission* and, while never fully exonerated of his own crime, is not implicated in the Novo Catengue case and appears here as a red herring.

But both *The First Submission* and *The Second Submission* leave one question open: how did investigators know what they knew? The narrative given in *The First Submission* falters a bit in *The Second Submission*, which was a response to a more aggressive line of questioning by the TRC. In response to questions on the "excesses against cadres and captured agents," the author backs up his contextualization by summoning details contained in the Shishita Report, the official report of the spy ring investigation.[44] This unreleased internal report reconstructs the extent and activities of the spy ring presumably on evidence obtained through interrogations of the accused. *The Second Submission* extracts details about one cadre in particular, Kenneth Mahamba. Mahamba was a graduate of Novo Catengue and, at the time of his arrest, was camp commander at another camp. Once in custody, Mahamba allegedly confessed to recruitment by the police, that he received special training at a military base prior to deployment, and, along with other accomplices, poisoned Novo Catengue and passed information that assisted the aerial bombardment. According to *The Second Submission*, a tribunal convicted Mahamba, and he was executed along with several coconspirators.

Contrary to the intent of the author, TRC questioning forced a mention of the Shishita Report, which then opened a further line of questioning into the methods used to extract confessions, the reliability of information contained in such confessions, and the moral lines established by *The First Submission*. *The Second Submission* was supposed to supply additional details to support several assertions that abuses were isolated and never part of official policy. The author mentions the Shishita Report as a way of demonstrating an effective investigation into a very real conspiracy. Mahamba was meant to serve as an example of the observation of codes of conduct amid extraordinary danger. But the mention of his name inadvertently connected *The Second Submission* to victim testimony provided by one of his cellmates, who reveal an alternative account of his death. This alternative account opened a breach between the kind of stories told in *The First Submission* and *The Second Submission*. A former detainee testified to the TRC that he had seen Mahamba in a detention facility just prior to his death. In his account, Mahamba was so disfigured by beatings that he was recognizable by his voice alone. Mahamba's last words to this detainee reportedly were "tell them anything they want to hear."[45] Instead of a fair trial in front of an impartial tribunal, this detainee maintained that security tortured Mahamba to death. As *The Second Submission* itself admits, abuses could occur when "a known infiltrator . . . refused to divulge information despite being confronted with prima facie evidence." *The Second Submission* gave no indication what prima facie evidence Mahamba saw or did not see and neglected to discuss the meaning of "intensive methods of interrogation" allowed for in the Code of Conduct adopted at Kabwe in 1985.

Reading *The Second Submission* against testimony given in victim hearings introduces an alternative interpretation that threatens to upset the entire system of order restored by all these layers of investigative reports. Did the force used during interrogation lead to a cascade of false confessions? If so, what, if anything, do we really know about Novo Catengue? Because all but one of the named coconspirators were also "executed by a tribunal," the TRC had little hope of further corroborating these claims through addition witness testimony. And while the ANC provided the Shishita Report to the TRC, it cited concerns about the confidentiality of witnesses and argued that it not be released to the public. Aside from testimony from the detainee and Mahamba's own brother, the "author as detective" had eliminated all other possible explanations by eliminating almost all who could offer such explanations.[46] The implicit sentiments of *The First Submission* and *The Second Submission* borrow from a clichéd phrase often used in crime fiction: "That's our story and we're sticking to it."

As noted by other commentators on the TRC, the breach between *The First Submission* and *The Second Submission* troubled the categories of victim and perpetrator. The blurred categories of victim and perpetrator parallel the moral coordinates inscribed between detective and criminal in the two types of detective novels. In *The First Submission*, the grand historical narrative of colonial violence, and Novo Catengue placed within it, depicts a world of clear moral lines, with the ANC firmly positioned on the high ground. The disbelief of the TRC, as revealed in its continued question, in many ways begs a rewrite of this story. And the author largely does that in *The Second Submission*, even though they maintain that "this is a supplement to, and not a substitution for, [*The First Submission*]." But the blood spots that drip from the mention of Mahamba and the Shishita Report both suggest that *The First Submission* suppressed a much darker, much more ambiguous world inhabited by infiltrators levying false accusation as investigators and investigators making infiltrators out of innocents. When read alone, *The First Submission* does restore the "system of order," but *The Second Submission*, with its link to victim hearings, leaves the hermeneutic circle wide open. Taking this beyond Hühn, *The First Submission* and *The Second Submission* constitute a palimpsest: as hidden clues are aligned into the explanation of one crime, they are arranged in such a way as to conceal another. The end of one investigation leaves the blood spots that begin another.

Are these concealments deliberate or a product of the mediation of texts through a narrator? As Hühn noted, classic detective novels are often narrated by an uninformed acquaintance of the detective. The uninformed acquaintance tries to decipher the incomprehensible investigation of the detective, while the detective tries to decipher the hidden text authored by the criminal. The archetype of the uninformed acquaintance is Sir Arthur Conan Doyle's Dr. Watson, who, despite being a close associate of Sherlock Holmes, is utterly reliant on the detective's informed explanation of his investigation and the crime itself. By all indications, the "Dr. Watson" who narrated *The First Submission* and *The Second Submission* is Thabo Mbeki, who at the time of the TRC was deputy president of the republic. It comes as little surprise, then, that the heir apparent of a party of state might be complicit in the deliberate concealment of crimes committed in the investigation of another crime. But at same time, Mbeki was a prisoner of the same frames of reference reinforced again and again in this genealogy of investigative reports. He had never visited Novo Catengue, he was not a member of security, and he was only privy to the details of investigations as a member of the executive committee and the politburo of the South African Communist Party (SACP). It is even possible to say that Mbeki is not the narrator at all, given that *The Second Submission* is a response to questioning from another imperfectly informed acquaintance, the TRC. The result is a text that is mediated four times over, first by the criminal, second by investigators, third by Mbeki, and fourth by the TRC. In this way, Mbeki's reading of previous texts, just like the TRC's reading of his text, is as mediated as our own, and their interpretations, just like ours, are subject to the meanings already inscribed within this genre.

Comrade Jack

In some regards, the Simons diaries, like the testimony of the detainee, offer a way to step outside this dilemma.[47] Jack Simons's diaries not only serves as a counterpoint to the interpretations of the alleged poisoning and aerial bombardment but also goes beyond these narrow concerns to capture something of the complex set of relations and negotiations that governed Novo Catengue. Reading the diaries against investigative reports is not another attempt to lift the veil and rewrite the last chapter of this detective novel. Neither Simons nor I play the role of Dr. Watson in the sense that either of us pose the second genealogy as the "real solution" to the mysteries that preoccupy the first genealogy. To start with, the Simons diaries are hardly conclusive. These texts leave more questions than they answer but pose the kind of questions left out of investigative reports. Further, I do not assume that the authors of diaries passively and impartially record all the details that they witness. Diaries are as mediated as other texts, they contain omissions and displacements, and they are limited by the perceptions of the author. However, diaries are subject to certain documentary conventions.[48] They are detailed chronicles limited by what can be known in the present. In this sense, the author of a diary surrenders a certain amount of authority over the narrative arc of his or her text, allowing for a number of loose ends often closed in investigative reports.

Above all else, the Simons diaries capture the moment after Soweto. Likewise, understanding this moment is the key to understanding Black September and the aerial bombardment. Scholars often pose Soweto as *the* event of the 1970s but assign it different meanings. For Baruch Hirson, a Trotskyist academic and longtime activist, Soweto demonstrated the poverty of Black Consciousness as an ideology.[49] The student revolt was spontaneous violence uniformed by Marxist theory. Gail Gerhart took the opposite view, arguing that Black Consciousness had sophisticated vision for post-apartheid future, one that had currency among an influential black elite.[50] The significance in terms of the Simons diary is clear: this debate among scholars paralleled arguments going on in political education classes at Novo Catengue. Political education was meant to be the finishing school anticipated by Hirson, albeit rendered in the SACP's interpretation of Marxist theory and praxis. The degree to which students accepted the premise that Black Consciousness was incomplete without Marxist-Leninist theories of revolution determined the tenor of relations between students and the camp administration.

But ideology captures only a narrow spectrum of relations recorded in the Simons diaries. Jonathan Hyslop provides a wider picture of the resources of revolt during school riots.[51] Hyslop argues that specific acts of student protest must be interpreted in Freudian terms. Power relations within the school setting do not permit overt forms of protest and stifle honest expressions of root grievances. The result is a condensation of meanings around symbolic acts of disobedience. What connects student protests across time and space are repertoires of resistance. Although Hyslop uses the concept of repertoire to draw a conceptual circle around mission school riots in the 1940s and student protests in 1976, another circle certainly encompasses Soweto and the camps. The grievances that animated either setting had nothing in common. However, in order to understand the meanings condensed in acts of disobedience, one must look to the repertoire that students carried into the camps. While Afrikaans might have been a convenient rallying point for a set of other grievances that had little to do with the language of instruction, in the camps ideological dissidence might have been signifier for a set of tensions that could not be openly expressed in an environment of ratcheting military discipline born from suspicions of infiltration.[52]

As noted previously, Simons wrote two diaries, one from his stay from August 1977 to February 1978, and another from December 1978 to March 1979. The picture captured in the first diary is of an army in flux. Around five hundred recruits arrived in mid-1977: some from a previous camp in Benguela, some freshly recruited from South Africa, and others finding their own way into the exile and the ANC. Simons is disappointed to learn that the ranks of this new revolutionary army are not working class; rather, they are largely students and the lumpen proletariat. This presents two problems. First, students were intellectuals who could challenge the authority of Marxist-Leninist theory. Second, many lumpens were undereducated criminals fleeing prosecution, rather than committed and capable revolutionaries. While reliable students could be placed in an endless revolving door of instruction at the party school or military training in the Soviet Union or elsewhere in the Eastern Bloc, irredeemable criminals and dissidents could neither be expelled nor sent abroad. The result was a residual population that grew increasingly restive with each passing day.

Theoretical and strategic concerns narrowed this bottleneck. After the early 1960s, exiles lacked an internal mass constituency within South Africa. Although a few Robben Islanders left prison in the early 1970s, they hardly comprised a viable underground that could receive trained cadres.[53]

So military strategists struck a middle path; they formed an elite "special operations" unit that orchestrated spectacular attacks aimed at reigniting popular support, while internal political structures mobilized support among the working class. This twin strategy saw mass deployment as a distant possibility. In the meantime, only a very small number of cadres would leave the camps.

Later in the diary, Simons notes the disorganization that plagued the early camps. Military leaders created Novo Catengue as a successor to the Benguela camp, which was an unmitigated disaster plagued by flies, insufficient supplies, and at least one suicide. Simons also notes that Novo Catengue almost "collapsed" during the first few weeks of operation and was only saved by the intervention of Cuban administrators. This chronic disorganization points to three related problems. First, the ANC military staff, never known for their organizational efficiency, exhibited insecurity about their ability to restart a stalled armed struggle. Second, this defensiveness plagued fraternal relations between the Cuban reservists who took over the camp administration. The Cubans questioned the decision to favor political mobilization over immediate armed struggle, while the ANC staff felt that their military expertise was not recognized. Third, this souring of relations led to a struggle over authority that affected the coherence and quality of the training program. Should trainees be trained into focoist guerrilla bands, or should they become political educators who might induce class consciousness among the workers? These inconsistencies certainly did not escape the attention of the rank and file, many of whom had arrived with belief that they would simply "pick up a gun and go home."[54]

The administration could not openly acknowledge shortcomings in demographics, strategy, and organization. Instead, it introduced a vocabulary of infiltration to paper over the difficult questions. The Simons diary clearly records this semantic shift after Black September. His account of the investigation into Black September showed how this language fused dissidence with subversion and subversion with infiltration. At the same time, accusations gain real teeth.

Simons's eyewitness account of this "alleged poisoning" profoundly disrupts the version found in investigative reports. To put it bluntly, Simons remained unconvinced that this was a poisoning and was also skeptical about the presence of infiltrators. He strongly believed that this was a generic case of food poisoning and cites several pieces of evidence to support his claim. As noted earlier in the diary, camp sanitation was not a priority. Toilets were blocked, there were no pit latrines, and excreta was "all around"; food remains were dumped near the kitchen; flies abounded in the eating hall; and unboiled stream water was used for drinking and washing. Further, the camp had no designated health inspector. This was all contrasted with the Cuban section, which had a separate kitchen, boiled water, and different supplies of food.

Simons's description of symptoms and treatment also troubles the accepted version of events. Andrew Masondo testified to the TRC that the poison used was thallium, a highly toxic element readily absorbed after ingestion.[55] But contrary to several investigative reports, Simons recorded that a fifth of the camp did not fall ill. This included Simons himself, who as a vegetarian had a special diet. The Cubans also did not suffer from any symptoms. Presuming the poison was placed in food, why did some, but not all, suffer symptoms. Further, not everyone who exhibited symptoms suffered the same degree of illness. Some ended up in triage, while less severe cases awaited later treatment. Perhaps the most curious discrepancy between the Simons diary and accepted accounts regards treatment. Instead of immediately administering antidote by injection, Cuban doctors waited four days to administer five injections to everyone in the camp. If the poison was as lethal as accepted accounts claim, why did the Cubans wait so long? Further, why would everyone receive the "antidote" regardless of whether they were sickened or not? And why did Cubans administer five injections simultaneously, when the treatment for thallium poisoning, Prussian blue, is administered orally within six hours of ingestion and followed up by two weeks of daily dosages? Finally, Simons did not record the hair loss or neurological problems that are the lingering effects of thallium poisoning.

There are certainly enough contrary details to question the accepted version of Black September, but the real significance of the event lies in the investigation that followed. Simons thought investigators had jumped to conclusions and refused to entertain the possibility that the mass illness had "nonhuman agency." Simons wrote that the investigation was a "witch-hunt," and much to his chagrin, his room was searched, once in his presence, another time when he was not. When Simons went on his daily walk the following afternoon, an armed guard of Cuban soldiers picked him up and returned him to the camp. In this atmosphere, no one was above suspicion, so-called dissidents and stalwarts alike.

The question remained: was the recoding of indiscipline into subversion a way of disciplining an unruly population, was it a way for rival administrations to monopolize authority, was it a simple matter of security, or a combination of all three possibilities? Simons, never one to shy away from constructive criticism of the movement, duly noted all of these problems as he recorded incidents of indiscipline in his diaries. As the "dean" of all political education instructors, he constantly received reports about class discussions that served as a barometer of discontent among the rank and file. Over time, a few instructors singled out a core of students whom they labeled as "dissidents." Tellingly, the strongest accusations came from Thami Zulu, then a platoon commander and close confidant of Simons.

Simons's reaction to these accusations is revealing. Throughout the rest of this diary, he never fully accepted the language of subversion; he placed the word *dissident* in quotation marks throughout his text. When Zulu singled out one student in particular, Absalom Mampe, as the ringleader of the dissidents, Simons took the time to hold a discussion class with them. Mampe, a graduate of Turfloop, asked the most incisive questions about lectures and expressed a genuine interest in this critical dialogue with Marxist theory. Contrary to reports received from his instructors, Simons did not find "dissidents" committed to an oppositional political line, nor was this a group of subversives bent on making trouble. Instead, he found the best and brightest of the camp. Why were they labeled as "dissidents"? The administration could not publicly admit its impossible situation. Even though they had capable, willing cadres, demographic, strategic, and organizational problems prevented their rapid deployment. Also, with nowhere to go, these capable cadres would compete with instructors for positions out of the camp. When these cadres realized their predicament, they would start to ask difficult questions about the progress of the armed struggle and challenge the authority of instructors. Simons records this with each passing act of defiance, ending with their total refusal to attend class, march, or sing. This last episode was deemed insubordination, and the fourteen were then packed off in the middle of the night to another camp.

The second diary suggests the success of this vocabulary of infiltration. As Len Smith noted, discipline is often negotiated by officers and enlisted men in the field.⁵⁶ Looking at Novo Catengue through this lens, the introduction of this vocabulary shifted the balance of power in debates over the meaning of discipline during a time of growing frustration. By the second trip, roughly August 1978 to March 1979, many of the "dissidents" had transferred to other camps, while Novo Catengue received elite cadres who finished their first round of specialization in Moscow.⁵⁷ Simply put, this was a much different camp than before: all cadres had taken the MK oath which bound them to the military code of conduct, and security officials warned the camp on the danger of saboteurs and agent provocateurs in their midst. The language of infiltration was so firmly entrenched that Simons noted that he joked about it in his diary: he called lost mail and power outages acts of sabotage.

Unfortunately, Simons did not witness either the aerial bombing or the investigation that followed. He was evacuated in early March 1979 and only learned details of the attack from secondhand reports. Investigative reports that reference this attack hinge on two points: first, that intelligence had advance warning of the aerial bombardment and thus were able to prevent mass casualties, and second, that an informant had passed along the routine and layout of the camp. The first point is supported by the diary, although later accounts differ on how the administration knew what they knew about the impending attack; Simons notes that they were hiding in railway culverts several weeks before the actual bombardment. On the second point, Simons is silent but comments on a draft version of his published diary note one salient fact overlooked in all investigative reports: the camp was a former railway barracks adjacent to the highly trafficked Benguela Railroad, the only railway that connected the Zambian Copperbelt to the Atlantic coast. This student noted that cadres used to break the monotony of camp life by "peeping and waving" at people on trains passing by. He regretted this after the bombing because "we made it easier for whoever was reconnoitering."⁵⁸ Access to the camp was not a problem, and as later writings on Angola attest, Angolans could tell South Africans were foreigners, often dubbing them *kaas-kop* after their telltale shorn scalps.⁵⁹ These details alone certainly complicate the notion that information about the whereabouts, layout, and routine of the camp could come from only an infiltrator.

The differences between the Simons diaries and the investigative reports are more than discrepancies between versions of the same narrative; they are texts of an entirely different order. The genre of investigative reports, with all its similarity to detective novels, not only does not entertain the possibility of nonhuman agency, but also its most basic premise totally precludes it. Likewise, investigative reports also have to uphold the moral lines of armed struggle and really cannot accommodate the unacknowledged problems that plagued not only Novo Catengue but successor camps as well. But the gap between the two best shows the superimposition of a vocabulary of infiltration over what was a much more complicated set of relations and contingent events. Max Gluckman commented on this very issue in a set of lectures on witchcraft.[60] Turning Pritchard on his head, Gluckman does not seek to find comparable rationalities inscribed in different local logics; he wants to show how both African and Western systems of belief irrationally impose their rationality on situations without causality. Gluckman writes that both systems of belief "cannot accept that social disturbances are an inevitable fact of life" and instead "ascribe quarrels in society to the vicious characters of certain categories of belief." Gluckman does not deny the fact that people never "intrigue and damage" but all too often witch hunts persecute category of persons for "ills that are due to physical causes or the working of society itself."[61] Taking the example of dockworkers, Gluckman suggests that union leaders were all too quick to blame disputes on agitators rather than the "occasional social breakdown." Rather than accept this, people take the easy route and "blame failures on red-tape civil servants, inefficient executives, counter-revolutionaries, saboteurs, and the like."[62] Whatever the circumstances surrounding the alleged poisoning and the aerial bombardment, these events subsume an entire set of complex relations and unacknowledged problems into discrete narratives of infiltration.

The publication history of the Simons diaries demonstrates the final act of leverage, forcing the two genealogies together. Almost immediately after the destruction of Novo Catengue, the SACP asked Simons to edit his lecture notes into a textbook for the newly built Solomon Mahlangu Freedom College. This project stalled until 1984 when the politburo tasked Marion Sparg with assisting the editing this textbook into a primer for the underground.[63] In 1986, Sparg was captured on a mission and the manuscript languished until the early 1990s until project again got off the ground, this time under a new editor who collected oral histories with former instructors and students at Novo Catengue. This version also added selections from Simons's second diary and posed the book now as a textbook, a history of Novo Catengue, and a testament to a trusted stalwart. Once again, Simons dropped the project, citing sensitivities over the integration of his former students in the new South African National Defense Force (SANDF), but these former students later endorsed the publication of what had become both a tribute to their former teacher and their own liberation credentials. Completion of this tribute became ever more pressing after Simons's death in 1995. In the late 1990s, three party members collected more oral histories, finalized the draft, and posthumously published the edited volume under the title *Comrade Jack: The Political Lectures and Diary of Jack Simons, Novo Catengue*.[64]

The long and convoluted publication history of *Comrade Jack* is significant because it details the process of turning a chronicle of an unruly camp into a set piece of struggle history. The function of the text is both memorial and didactic: it celebrates the accomplishments of a great struggle hero, while preserving his teachings for future generations. In this, diary excerpts appear as documentary truth; they are evidence of the success of his program, as well as the dangers posed by the aerial bombardment. In this sense, *Comrade Jack* is another in a long line of other celebratory volumes and fits within the overall narrative arc that guided the ANC submission to the TRC. Although these are vastly different texts, the editors preface *Comrade Jack* with certain familiar heroic themes and moral coordinates. Given this compatibility, it comes as little surprise, then, that the book bears two forewords, one by Oliver Tambo, the deceased president of the ANC in exile, and Kgalema Motlanthe, then secretary general of the ANC and later interim president of South Africa. This is, then, a text doubly stamped with official authorization.

The question for the editors must have been how do you maintain the status of this text as struggle history while preserving its authority as documentary truth? First and foremost, the excerpts included consist of most of the second diary. The only sections excised are notes from an executive meeting that detailed squabbles between the SACP and the ANC and the political and military wings of the exile apparatus. This exclusion certainly tidies up the narrative but could reasonably fall under edits done for the sake of brevity.

The heavy hand of officialdom falls most conspicuously on a more significant omission. Although editors acknowledge that Simons kept two diaries, they also claim that they found only the second diary and entirely exclude the first diary from their final draft. Unlike the second diary, the first diary gave a detailed picture of the dilemmas faced by the administration and their imposition of the language of infiltration over legitimate grievances. The exclusion of the first diary also excludes alternate interpretations of the alleged poisoning, records the removal of "dissidents," not to mention salacious details such as an attempted rape committed by the Cubans and a subsequent retaliation by the rank and file.

The status of the first diary at the time of publication is unclear. It is possible that they had the first diary and deliberately omitted it, they were genuinely unable to locate it, or that Simons withheld the diary. Whatever the case may be, the absence of this text severely limits public knowledge of Novo Catengue and preserves the integrity of official explanations of Black September and the aerial bombardment. In effect, this volume is an example of one genealogy grafted onto another. Because readers can access only the second diary, which shows a more placid camp, they lose the complexity of the first diary, for the "useful history" of the investigative report. The meaning of Novo Catengue remains undisturbed: it was a promising camp ruined by the two most lethal atrocities that ever happened. Further, the lesson to be taken from this story is that the means of investigation, even when practiced in excess, were both necessary and good because they clearly saved innocent lives. In this, Comrade Jack and *The First Submission* and *The Second Submission* share a common trait. As private texts move closer to publication, they are shorn of all the thorny details that might trouble the overarching narrative of the liberation struggle and the armed struggle within it. This clipping of genealogies is but one example of the policing of public knowledge of this history.

Notes

1. This title is borrowed from Mwezi Twala's dissident autobiography. Twala spent significant time in the camps in Angola as a cadre. Along with other cadres, he cleared land and built The Plot, a base that supplied the MK troops that put down the 1984 mutiny of MK cadres. "Losing the Plot" is a serviceable metaphor for the suppression of memory of this mutiny, as well as the culture of accusation and suspicion born from misreadings of the causes of the alleged poisoning at Novo Catengue five years earlier.

Mwezi Twala and Ed Benard, *Mbokodo: Inside MK: A Soldier's Story* (Johannesburg: Jonathan Ball, 1994), 56, 64.

2. "Statement to the Truth and Reconciliation Commission, August 1996," accessed June 20, 2016, (http://www.anc.org.za/show.php?id=2639). Hereafter referred to as *The First Submission*. "Questions from the TRC to ANC in Response to the ANC First Submission to the TRC, November 1996," accessed June 20, 2016 (http://www.anc.org.za/show.php?id=2644). "Further Submissions and Responses by the ANC to Questions Raised by the Commission for Truth and Reconciliation, 12 May 1997," accessed June 20, 2016 (http://www.anc.org.za/show.php?id=2645). Hereafter referred to as *The Second Submission*. Author(s) not indicated, "Minutes of the First Session of the Dar es Salaam Zonal C. C. Conference Held at the Zone II Cultural Club on Wednesday 17th April 1985 at 10:25 AM," Karis Gerhart Collection, Historical Papers Research Archive, Cullen Library, University of the Witwatersrand. Author(s) not indicated, "Report on Security and Intelligence, 1985," ANC Collection, Mayibuye Centre Archives. Author(s) not indicated, "Political and Ideological Work in the Region, 1985," ANC Collection, Mayibuye Centre Archives. Author(s) not indicated, "Commission Five—Theoretical Paper on the Armed Struggle = 1959/84," ANC Collection, Mayibuye Centre Archives. Author(s) not indicated, "The Role and Place of the Youth in Society, the Struggle, and in the ANC, 1985," ANC Collection, Mayibuye Centre Archives. "NEC Working Committee Minutes, 22/08/79–21/11/80," Karis Gerhart Collection, Historical Papers Research Archive, Cullen Library, University of the Witwatersrand. Author(s) not indicated, "Some Aspects of Enemy Counter Guerrilla Tactics Compiled from Our Own Experience, May 1984," Karis Gerhart Collection, Historical Papers Research Archive, Cullen Library, University of the Witwatersrand. Commission of Inquiry (chair James Stuart [Hermanus Loots]), "Report: Commission of Inquiry into Recent Developments in the People's Republic of Angola 3/14/1984," Karis Gerhart Collection, Historical Papers Research Archive, Cullen Library, University of the Witwatersrand. Hereafter referred to as the Stuart Commission Report. Author(s) not indicated, "Guidelines on Underground Construction, 1988," Karis Gerhart Collection, Historical Papers Research Archive, Cullen Library, University of the Witwatersrand. Author(s) not indicated, "Extracts from the Confessions of an Enemy Agent Ralph Mgcina Alias Fear Who Died of Natural Causes Recently, 8/3/1988," Karis Gerhart Collection, Historical Papers Research Archive, Cullen Library, University of the Witwatersrand. NAT, "A Report on Some Aspects of NAT Work, 20/2/88," ANC Collection, Mayibuye Centre Archives. Jack Simons, "Jack Simons to Ray Simons, correspondence, 5/3/1978," Jack and Ray Simons Collection, Manuscripts and Archives, University of Cape Town. Jack Simons, "Jack Simons to Ray Simons, correspondence, 30/9/77," Jack and Ray Simons Collection, Manuscripts and Archives, University of Cape Town.

3. Luise White, *The Assassination of Herbert Chitepo: Texts and Politics in Zimbabwe* (Bloomington: Indiana University Press, 2003), 1–15.

4. Jack Simons, "Novo Catengue Diaries, I and II," Ray and Jack Simons Collection (BC1801), Manuscripts and Archives, University of Cape Town.

5. Marion Sparg et al., *Comrade Jack: The Political Lectures and Diary of Jack Simons, Novo Catengue*, (Johannesburg: STE Publishers, 2004).

6. E. E. Pritchard, *Witchcraft, Oracles and Magic among the Azande* (Oxford: Clarendon, 1937).

7. Max Gluckman, *Custom and Conflict in Africa* (Oxford: Blackwell, 1956).

8. Mary Douglas, *Witchcraft Confessions and Accusations*, (London: Tavistock, 1970), xxv–xxvi.

9. Jean Comaroff and John Comaroff, *Modernity and Its Malcontents: Ritual and Power in Postcolonial Africa* (Chicago: University of Chicago Press, 1993), 15.

10. Ibid.

11. Ibid.

12. The security services allegedly first dubbed Mandela the Black Pimpernel, but this term was quickly popularized in domestic and international media. "South Africa: The Black Pimpernel," *Time*, August 17, 1962. ANC, *First Submission*.

13. "Detective Fiction," in *Oxford Dictionary of Literary Terms*, ed. C. Baldick (Oxford: Oxford University Press, 2007), 332–37.

14. Peter Hühn, "The Detective as Reader: Narrativity and Reading Concepts in Detective Fiction," *Modern Fiction Studies* 33 (1987): 451–66.

15. Eleanor Morse, *White Dog Fell from the Sky* (London: Penguin, 2013). James Ngculu, *The Honour to Serve: Recollections of an Umkhonto Soldier* (Cape Town: David Philip, 2009), 61–62. Wonga Welile Bottoman, *The Making of an MK Cadre* (Pretoria: LiNc Publishers, 2010). Stephen Ellis, *External Mission: The ANC in Exile, 1960–1990* (Oxford: Oxford University Press, 2013). Stephen Ellis and Tsepo Sechaba, *Comrades against Apartheid: The ANC and the South African Communist Party in Exile* (Bloomington: Indiana University Press, 1992). Hugh Macmillan, *The Lusaka Years: The ANC in Exile in Zambia, 1963 to 1994* (Johannesburg: Jacana, 2013). Sifiso Mxolisi Ndlovu, "The ANC's Diplomacy and International Relations," in *The Road to Democracy in South Africa: Volume 2, 1970–1980*, ed. Bernard Magubane (Pretoria: University of South Africa Press, 2006), 658–60. Ndlovu incorrectly suggests that the Pango camp was renamed "Novo Katengue, the University of Umkhonto we Sizwe." Novo Catengue was a separate camp located about thirty kilometers inland from Lobito and predated Pango, which was located northeast of Luanda. Novo Catengue was colloquially referred to as the "University of the South" by camp staff and cadres, but no interviews or published accounts suggest that it was called the "University of Umkhonto we Sizwe." Jacob Dlamini, *Askari: A Story of Collaboration and Betrayal in the Anti-Apartheid Struggle* (Auckland Park: Jacana, 2014), 155–56. Janet Cherry, *Umkhonto we Sizwe* (Auckland Park: Jacana, 2011), 69. Cherry indicates that the poisoning occurred in 1978. Almost all sources date it to September 1977.

16. Ronald Kasrils, *Armed and Dangerous: My Undercover Struggle against Apartheid* (Oxford: Heinemann, 1993), 176. Sipho Binda, interview with Wolfie Kodesh, March 24, 1993, Mayibuye Centre Archives.

17. "Masondo, 12 October 2001," accessed June 21, 2016 (https://cryptome.org/za-masondo.txt).

18. Ibid.

19. Department of Legal and Constitutional Affairs, "Departmental Report for the NEC, 25 Sep 1986," Karis Gerhart Collection (microfilm), Center for Research Libraries. Nelson Miya (Department of Legal and Constitutional Affairs), "The ANC Code of Conduct, 28 Jan 1988," Karis Gerhart Collection, Historical Papers Research Archive, Cullen Library University of the Witwatersrand. Albie Sachs, "Civil and Criminal Code of the People of South Africa, 1980-10-29," Karis Gerhart Collection, Historical Papers Research Archive, Cullen Library University of the Witwatersrand. "Documents and Draft Documents Relating to the ANC Disciplinary Code," Karis Gerhart Collection (microfilm), Center for Research Libraries.

20. Albie Sachs, "Civil and Criminal Code of the People of South Africa, 1980-10-29."

21. ANC Political Department, "Politics Department on Civil and Criminal Code of the People of South Africa, 1980-11-12," Karis Gerhart Collection, Historical Papers Research Archive, Cullen Library University of the Witwatersrand.

22. White, *The Assassination of Herbert Chitepo*.

23. Andrew Masondo, interview with Hilda Bernstein, date not indicated, Mayibuye Centre Archives.

24. Macmillan, *The Lusaka Years*, 144, 164. Macmillan makes the point that until the discovery of the spy network in 1981, the security department, known colloquially as NAT, was a relatively small and "amateurish" outfit, but its enlarged authority and power is reflected in reports filed about the mutinies in MK camps in 1984.

25. Peter Motaung and Katleho Moloi, interviewed by Hilda Bernstein, no date indicated, Mayibuye Centre Archives. This interview provides a detailed account of intelligence training in the German Democratic Republic, as well as its application in exile structures, particularly focusing on biography writing as a screening method.

26. Ellis and Sechaba, *Comrades against Apartheid*. Tom Lodge, *Black Politics in South Africa since 1945* (New York: Longman, 1983). Paul Trewhela, "Inside Quatro: End of an Era," accessed June 21, 2016 (https://www.marxists.org/history/etol/revhist/supplem/hirson/quadro.html). Paul Trewhela, *Inside Quatro: Uncovering the Exile History of the ANC and SWAPO* (Auckland Park: Jacana, 2009). Thula Bopela and Daluxolo Luthuli, *Umkhonto we Sizwe: Fighting for a Divided People* (Alberton: Galago, 2005), 173–77. Mark Gevisser, *Thabo Mbeki: A Dream Deferred* (Johannesburg: Jonathan Ball, 2007), 392–93. Gail Gerhart and Clive Glaser, *From Protest to Challenge: Challenge and Victory, 1980–1990, Vol. 6* (Bloomington: Indiana University Press, 2010), 133–34.

27. Bottoman, *The Making of an MK Cadre*, 139–54. Stanley Manong, *If We Must Die: An Autobiography of a Former Commander of uMkhonto we Sizwe* (Pretoria: Nkululeko,

2015), 204–14. Twala and Benard, *Mbokodo*, 49–66. Ngculu, *The Honour to Serve*, 155–75. Janet Smith and Beauregard Tromp, *Hani: A Life Too Short* (Johannesburg: Jonathan Ball, 2009), 173–88. Ellis and Sechaba, *Comrades against Apartheid*, 189–96.

28. African National Congress, "Stuart Commission Report."

29. Author(s) not indicated, "Some Aspects of Enemy Counter-Guerrilla Tactics Compiled from Our Own Experience, May 1984."

30. ANC, *First Submission*. Author(s) not indicated, "Some Aspects of Enemy Counter-Guerrilla Tactics Compiled from Our Own Experience, May 1984." The direct parallels between the typologies of infiltration deployed in accounts of this period in both documents are striking despite the fact that they were written ten years apart.

31. Peter Motaung and Katleho Moloi, interviewed by Hilda Bernstein, no date indicated, Mayibuye Centre Archives.

32. "Masondo, 12 October 2001," accessed June 21, 2016 (https://cryptome.org/za-masondo.txt). Mthembu, Mtunzi Gabriel, "10 October 2001," accessed June 21, 2016 (https://cryptome.org/za-mthembu.txt).

33. Author(s) not indicated, "Some Aspects of Enemy Counter-Guerrilla Tactics Compiled from Our Own Experience, May 1984."

34. For a balanced appraisal of the Kabwe Conference in terms of shifts in strategy and tactics in the armed struggle, see Padraig O'Malley's *Shades of Difference*. Padraig O'Malley, *Shades of Difference: Mac Maharaj and the Struggle for South Africa* (New York: Penguin, 2007), 133–38.

35. Gerhart and Glaser, *From Protest to Challenge*, 137. Mkatashingo, "The ANC Conference: From Kabwe to Johannesburg," *Searchlight South Africa* 6 (1991): 91–94. Twala and Benard, *Mbokodo*, 104.

36. This is weakly inferred in the Stuart Commission Report.

37. National Executive Committee and Politico-Military Committee, "NEC and PMC Documents, Document B1(b)—Codes of Conduct, 1985," Mayibuye Centre Archives. Senior Organ, T/Q Area, "Rules of Security, Defence and Code of Conduct, March 1981," Karis Gerhart Collection, Historical Papers Research Archive, Cullen Library, University of the Witwatersrand.

38. Author not indicated, "Report on Security and Intelligence (1985)," Mayibuye Centre Archives.

39. Ibid.

40. Commission of Inquiry, "Report of a Commission of Inquiry Set Up in November 1989 by the National Working Committee of the National Executive Committee of the African National Congress to Investigate the Circumstances Leading to the Death of Mzwakhe Ngwenya (Also Known as Thami Zulu or TZ)," Special Collections Library, University of Cape Town. Hereafter abbreviated as "Commission of Inquiry into the Death of Thami Zulu."

41. No author indicated, "Report on the Activities of the Natal Machinery during the Period 1983–1988 When It Was under the Command of Muzi Ngwenya Alias Thami Zulu." Provided to author by Stephen Ellis.

42. Luise White, "Poisoned Food, Poisoned Uniforms, and Anthrax: Or, How Guerrillas Die in War," *Osiris* 19 (2004): 224. White, *The Assassination of Herbert Chitepos*.

43. ANC, *First Submission*. Truth and Reconciliation Commission, "Questions from the TRC to ANC in Response to the ANC First Submission to the TRC, November 1996." ANC, *Second Submission*.

44. No author indicated, "Report on the Subversive Activities of Police Agents in Our Movement, 1-7-81." Provided to author by Stephen Ellis. Hereafter referred to as the Shishita Report.

45. Gordon Moshoeu, TRC Testimony, CT02913/OUT.

46. Joseph Seremane, interview with author, November 13, 2007. Seremane gave similar testimony to the Truth and Reconciliation Commission. "Joseph Seremane, 22-7-1997," accessed June 21, 2016 (http://www.justice.gov.za/trc/special%5Cprison/seremane.htm).

47. Sparg et al., *Comrade Jack*. Simons, "Novo Catengue Diaries, I and II."

48. Philippe Lejune, *On Diary* (Manoa: University of Hawaii Press, 2009).

49. Baruch Hirson, *Year of Fire, Year of Ash: The Soweto Revolt, Roots of a Revolution?* (London: Zed, 1979).

50. Gail Gerhart, *Black Consciousness: Evolution of an Ideology* (Berkeley: University of California Press, 1978). Leslie Hadfield describes the partial implementation of Black Consciousness's ideology in community projects. Leslie Hadfield, *Liberation and Development: Black Consciousness Community Programs in South Africa* (East Lansing: Michigan State University Press, 2016). See also Dan Magaziner's work on theology and Black Consciousness. Dan Magaziner, *The Law and the Prophets: Black Consciousness in South Africa, 1968–1977* (Athens: Ohio University Press, 2010).

51. Jonathan Hyslop, "Food Authority and Politics: Student Riots in South African Schools 1945–1976," in *Regions and Repertoires: Topics in South Africa Politics and Culture*, ed. Stephen Clingman (Johannesburg: Ravan, 1991), 84–116.

52. Ibid.

53. Bernard Magubane and Gregory Houston persuasively argue that internal activists in the early 1970s did carry out the task of recruiting students for training abroad. However, networks remained unable to *receive* significant numbers of cadres that expected to return to South Africa a short time after their training. Gregory Houston and Bernard Magubane, "The ANC Political Underground in the 1970s," in *The Road to Democracy in South Africa: Volume 2, 1970–1980*, ed. Bernard Magubane (Pretoria: University of South Africa Press, 2006), 371–72. Mac Maharaj points to the uneven quality of military recruits sent out of the country by these networks after the Soweto uprising and stated that there "was no political underground" in the late 1970s. O'Malley, *Shades of Difference*, 218–19.

54. Sipho Binda, interview with Wolfie Kodesh, March 24, 1993, Mayibuye Centre Archives.

55. "Masondo, 12 October 2001," accessed June 21, 2016 (https://cryptome.org/za-masondo.txt). Compare the symptoms described by Simons and others with a

diagnosed case of thallium poisoning. "Joyce Mthimkhulu, 26-06-1996," accessed June 22, 2016 (http://www.justice.gov.za/trc/hrvtrans%5Chrvpe2/mtimkhul.htm).

56. Leonard Smith, *Between Mutiny and Disobedience: The Case of the French Fifth Infantry Division during World War I* (Princeton, NJ: Princeton University Press, 1994), 21–22.

57. The fates of these dissidents remain a point of disagreement in autobiographies and reports. Twala and Benard, *Mbokodo*, 38. Douglas Commission, "The Report of the Douglas Commission," 60. Ngculu, *The Honour to Serve*, 85–87. Trewhela, *Inside Quatro*, 158–65. Six of the fourteen gave depositions in 1993, discounting allegations that they had been mistreated during their detention at the Quibaxe camp in Angola. Ben Lekalake, Duncan Khehla Dlamini, Percy Mokonopi, Victor Ngwenya, Alec Chief Tshabala, and Mandla Daka in affidavits taken in February 1993, provided to author by Stephen Ellis.

58. Marion Sparg et al., *The Angolan Diaries of Jack Simons*, Karis Gerhart Collection, Historical Papers Research Archive, Cullen Library, University of the Witwatersrand. This is an unpublished manuscript of the much modified version that was published in 2004. The final draft of the manuscript was published in 2004 as *Comrade Jack*. Sparg et al., *Comrade Jack*. Reggie Mpongo's statement about waving at trains passing by the camp appears in both versions.

59. *Kaas-kop* is Afrikaans for "cheese head," meaning the smooth texture of the shorn scalp. Hein Grosskopf, *Artistic Graves* (Johannesburg: Ravan, 1993).

60. Gluckman, *Custom and Conflict in Africa*, 90–109. Pritchard, *Witchcraft, Oracles and Magic among the Azande*.

61. Gluckman, *Custom and Conflict in Africa*, 106.

62. Ibid.

63. Sparg et al., *Comrade Jack*, v–x.

64. Sparg et al., *The Angolan Diaries of Jack Simons*.

Fig. 1. Aerial photo Liliesleaf Farm, Rivonia, the headquarters of the MK High Command. Photo credit: Liliesleaf Archive.

Fig. 2. MK Cadres drilling in formation in the late 1960s. Photo Credit: UWC-Robben Island Museum Mayibuye Archives.

Fig. 3. Denis Goldberg in disguise. Photos taken after his arrest at Liliesleaf Farm, 1963. Photo Credit: Liliesleaf Archive.

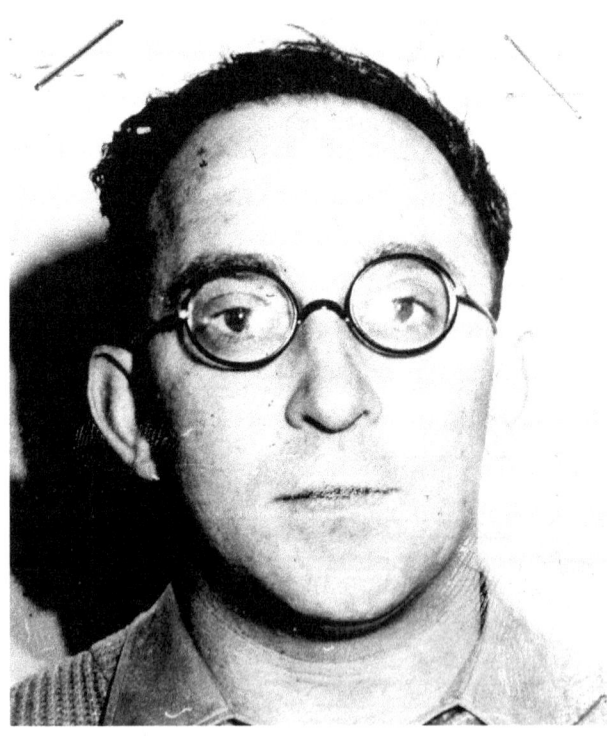

Fig. 4. Denis Goldberg out of disguise. Photos taken after his arrest at Liliesleaf Farm, 1963. Photo Credit: Liliesleaf Archive.

Fig. 5. The location of the Mamre camp on Louw's Kloof Farm, Mamre. Confirmation of location provided by Denis Goldberg and John Maree, son of the late David Pick, another camp attendee. Photo credit: © 2016 Digital Globe © 2016 Google © 2016 AfriGIS (Pty) Ltd.

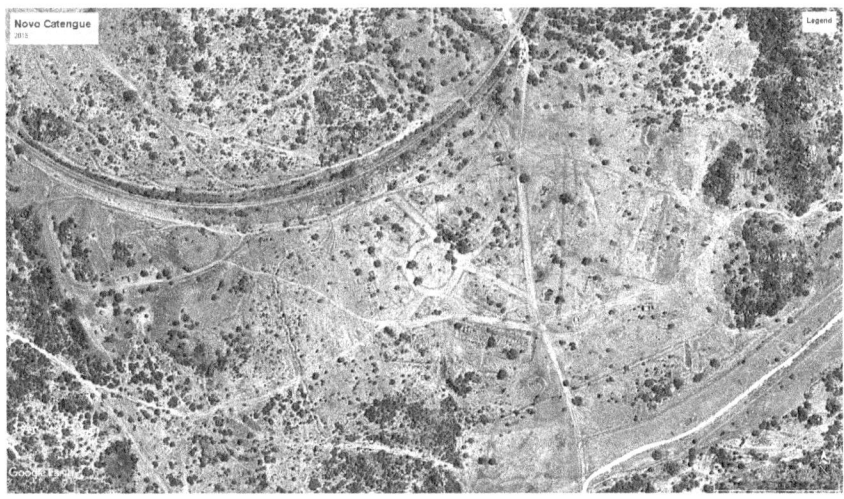

Fig. 6. Satellite photo of location of Novo Catengue camp in 2016. The Benguela Railway is shown passing within full view of the camp. Location confirmed by Warrant-Officer Peet Coetzee, photo interpreter for SAAF bombing raid that destroyed Novo Catengue camp. © 2016 Digital Globe, © 2016 Google.

Fig. 7. A sample page of a propaganda booklet titled, "The Story of Simon and Jane," conceived in the form of a comic book and distributed in South Africa by London recruits in the early 1970s. Source: Carter Karis Gerhart Collection. Historical Papers Research Archive, Cullen Library University of Witwatersrand.

Fig. 8. The Isivivane at sunset, overlooking the Unisa campus. Photo credit: author.

Fig. 9. Gallery of Leaders, photographed 2015. Banners of leaders pictured from left to right; Helen Joseph, Lilian Ngoyi, Robert Sobukwe, Steve Biko. Photo credit: author.

Fig. 10. Paleontological fossils presented without identification in the gallery titled, "Ancestors." Photo credit: author.

Fig. 11. The aftermath of an SADF raid on three ANC residences in Matola, Mozambique (January 29–30, 1981). Photo credit: UWC-Robben Island Museum Mayibuye Archives.

Fig. 12. The body of Sgt. Robert Hutchinson, member of the SADF 6 Reconnaissance Regiment, killed in the Matola raid. The circumstances of Hutchinson's death remain unclear, but eyewitness accounts and some press reports suggest he was killed by MK cadres resident in these houses. This image and the one preceding suggest a sort of combat that was atypical to the rest of the armed struggle. They nonetheless were widely circulated by the ANC and FRELIMO after the raid. Photo credit: UWC-Robben Island Museum Mayibuye Archives.

5. Everyday Life during Wartime: Experience, Modes of Writing, and the Underground in Cape Town during the Long Decade of the 1980s

GILLES PERRAULT'S *THE RED ORCHESTRA* opens with a fictional account of the search for a secret radio transmitter in Norway operated by the Rote Kapelle, the German name for an extensive network of communist spies that "performed" throughout Nazi-occupied Europe during the first years of World War II.[1] As Perrault narrates his highly imaginative account of the episode, he sketches the character of the Wehrmacht radio operator searching the ether, describes his consternation over a storm brewing over the gray Baltic, notes the migration of gulls overhead, and ends with the resignation of a man aware of, but ultimately frustrated by, the invisibility of his foes. Perrault spends the next few paragraphs telling his audience how he made the entire passage up, albeit anchoring his fictional flourishes with the known facts of the Norwegian transmitter and those hunting for it. He then lays out before his readers the thin, lifeless litany of uncontested details about Nazi radio monitoring and the operation of this particular "soloist" in the orchestra performing for an audience in Moscow. These details, while truthful, clearly lack the novelistic beauty of the preceding more literary account, which is drenched with experience, psychology, and drama. The juxtaposition of both modes of writing is stark, polemic, and deliberate.

The Red Orchestra is relevant here because it was a book that was read in the African National Congress (ANC) underground in Cape Town in the 1980s. But more importantly, it is a book that speaks to broader historiographical problems with the writing and revision of the historiography on "resistances" everywhere, the entire anti-apartheid struggle in South Africa, and the ANC underground within it. Perrault's point in contrasting these of modes of writing history is twofold. His account not only makes claims to historical truth and peels away epistemological curtains with "thick descriptions" of interviews and interviewees, but he also entreats his readers to allow him to tell a compelling, yet novelized, story—a narrative arc that he imaginatively sketched at the end of his litany of bare facts: "these quiet beginnings heralded a campaign which was to become a nightmare to . . . the heads of Germany's two secret services, and which eventually prompted Adolf Hitler to declare, on May 17th, 1942, 'The Bolsheviks are our superiors in only one field—espionage.'"[2]

With his conclusion in his preamble, Perrault infers that writing in an imaginative mode, rather than in a strictly factual mode, will give his readers access to authentic historical experiences of an underground that was almost invisible to its adversaries and became somewhat more opaque in subsequent postwar historiography on resistances in Europe. The poetic way he constructs his narrative of the interview process and the narratives contained in oral testimonies end up as a celebration of the secret work of a spy network that he infers was either maligned, marginalized, or wholly unrecognized after the war. With poetic license in hand, he transformed the ambiguous legacy of the fallen leader of a broken spy ring into a heroic narrative of defiance and skill and thus saves the memory of the Rote Kapelle from being plowed under in a highly contentious historiography on "resistances" or a singular notion of "The Resistance" in Europe. Simply put, the very publication of *The Red Orchestra* is one grand historiographical rescue attempt, albeit one that rescues its subjects not from physical danger but from obscurity itself. Perrault's broader purpose is not only in lionizing this conductor and his players but also in breaking them into the pantheon of European resistance fighters by using a key fashioned with particular modes of writing.

The Red Orchestra presents too many theoretical issues on the historiography of other resistances to unpack in a single chapter. In terms of the history of the underground in South Africa in the 1980s, Perrault's method of framing his work on the Rote Kapelle provides historians with a useful way to think about the ongoing conceptual crisis in this literature.[3] *The Red Orchestra* is instructive not only because historical writing on resistance to Nazi occupation in Europe captured the imaginations of many anti-apartheid activists in Cape Town, but also because this particular book occupied a central part of the syllabus of at least one underground unit operating in that city in the 1980s. *The Red Orchestra* outlines the central problem of writing about the 1980s, the entire history of resistance in South Africa, and the place of the armed struggle within this narrative.[4] That problem is that few have found a way to get past explaining the history of the ANC underground without making claims about the end of apartheid and, in turn, avoid conflating the history of the underground with the history of the struggle. The vast body of claims and counterclaims made in this ever-expanding literature are all part of one elaborate exercise in valorizing experience. However, few explanations of the "end of apartheid" have taken the underground in the 1980s on its own terms. In this regard, *The Red Orchestra* is instructive because it points to an unresolved dilemma in resistance historiography: how is the turn to experience justified in particular modes of writing?[5]

This chapter is a review of the literature on the underground in the 1980s and a microhistory of distinct groups of combatants working in Cape Town at three specific historical junctures. This localized history complicates prior generalizations about organizational politics and political orientation and troubles any notions of a singular experience of the underground. An examination of these experiences divorced from claims-making about particular modes of writing and the post-apartheid positioning that these claims entail tells a much more intimate story. In this review of my material, I answer two sets of questions. First, how do we write a history of experience that doesn't confuse the orchestra for the players? In other words, how do we write a history of experience that does not foreground organization over experience? And what can an alternative history of experience thus conceived tell us about the intellectual worlds evident in the everyday lives of the "invisible" underground units in Cape Town?

Perrault's book is merely one useful example of a dilemma that crosses disciplines, geographies, and theoretical concerns. The vast literature on this dilemma circles around a series of important questions about the status of oral testimony and written evidence—in this case, testimony and evidence drawn from the underground in the Western Cape in the 1980s. Are the established modes of writing—namely, social histories, nationalist "struggle histories," and apartheid apologias—the best way to arrange the rich hues of experience captured in the oral archive? Can you reach a definitive answer about the relationship of the underground and the armed struggle to the struggle with such an incomplete written record? Does all evidence need to be framed within an interpretative narrative invested in claims of causality in the "end of apartheid" and thus the legitimacy of the post-apartheid state? Conversely, is it enough to let the evidence speak for itself, or is it better to allow competing claims about particular modes of writing, resistance, and armed struggle made by veterans and scholars wrestle with one another? Perrault took the literary route to bind heroic narratives of experience to explanations of particular modes of writing. Should historians of South Africa adopt a similar mode of writing for the material on the underground in Cape Town in the 1980s?

Because locality and time are critically important in understanding experience, this chapter is bounded geographically and chronologically. Following Vivian Bickford-Smith's injunction to appreciate all the regionally contingent ways segregation manifested itself, I argue, following many others, that the only way to make sense of "the struggle" is to look at it one region at a time, because the dismantling of localized forms of segregation was equally replete with local specificities of resistance.[6] Like previous chapters, I draw from Cape Town and the Western Cape and, when necessary, from other cities and regions. I made contact with members of four or possibly five cells that operated in the ANC underground in the Western Cape during the 1970s and 1980s. A majority of these interviewees were formally inducted into MK, and a majority of these interviewees operated in Cape Town.[7] What follows is a meditation on modes of writing based on oral and written evidence taken from these underground structures during the second phase of the armed struggle, roughly from 1976 to 1993.

As noted in chapter 1 and elaborated at great length by Bickford-Smith, the historical specificities and state social engineering of the Western Cape distorted more typical social and demographic processes witnessed in other urban areas in South Africa during the period of "informal" segregation and apartheid. Economically, socially, and politically, the Cape was and still is unique within South Africa, although not so on the rest of the continent.[8] As oral and written evidence will show, the material on the underground in Cape Town is alternately unique, familiar, and general. Sometimes, it is all of these things at once.

Accordingly, I present experiences that may or may not align with the experience of the underground in other regions. The idea that one experience drawn from one locality at one moment trumps another from a different person, place, and time is patently absurd, but many nationalist "struggle historians" and a few social historians often make these sorts of claims. In any case, I make no claim to "representativity," whatever that might mean in the context of oral testimony and written documents drawn from a network of groups in one locality at several different moments.

The conclusion I posit is that particular modes of writing—namely, social histories, "struggle histories," and apartheid apologias—are all locked in the parlor game of a particular kind of truth-telling, and representations of experience are the cards played in these sorts of contests. This trivialization of complex oral and written evidence hinders the future development of historiography on the 1980s in South Africa.

Arguably, most social histories of the struggle build on Marxian social histories written in the 1970s. The pioneering work of Marxian social historians took experience seriously, but their conceptual basis was based on claims-making about abstract social processes, and their analytical eye was always fixed on the macrohistorical level. Such claims based on experience bore much fruit over the next few decades but not without critique.[9] The most incisive critique came in a 1993 review article by Frederick Cooper.[10] Cooper's point is that resistance—narrowly conceived as indirect and direct rejection of the power of mine bosses, farmers, factory owners, and ship captains—tends to flatten experience into one-dimensional confrontations and neatly tucks away loose ends, missed opportunities, and alternative options. Perhaps most damningly, this mode of writing misses all of the other ways people conceived of their worlds, aside from their subtle and not-so-subtle protests against wretched socioeconomic conditions.

My purpose is not to link experience of the underground to grand historical narratives about social change in South Africa, nor is it to prop up the sagging legitimacy of the post-apartheid state. Also, I will certainly not write an apologia for apartheid. To be sure, I locate my subjects within the broader social and racial milieu of Cape Town and the Western Cape, and I do not deny the existence of vicious forms of racial and class oppression. But unlike other studies, I take experience as a way of illuminating several individuals' understandings and thoughts about the conflict they were in. So this chapter is not referring either to the lower-case r or upper-case R forms of Marxian concepts of resistance referred to in Cooper's critique. This chapter is not an elaboration or rejection of the important work of Marxian scholars concerned with mines, farms, factories, and ships.

So my quarry is different from that of 1970s-era social history and its 1980s-era descendants. My use of the term *resistance* refers to what was known in European languages as "The Resistance," and later glossed in South Africa, as the combination of its overt and covert forms, or "the underground" and "the aboveground." "The Resistance" in Europe is also a term in dire need of retooling and specificity but generally glosses as formal structures and organizations that played an active role in strategizing, theorizing, frustrating, or confronting an illegitimate regime or foreign occupation. In my mind, the historiography on "The Resistance" in Europe, rather than the Marxian literature on practices of "resistance" by the working class, provides the most fruitful points of comparison for understanding "everyday life" during wartime.[11] As noted above, South Africans read about mid-twentieth-century Europe, fantasized about the possibilities of "The Resistance" to their own struggles, and to some degree refashioned themselves after these partisans and patriots. This history of experience is more about breaking the social and political mise-en-scène through secrecy and illegality than it is about the practice of secretly breaking tools.

A definition of periodization and terminology precedes any discussion of the complex historiography on the underground in the 1980s. In temporal terms, the 1980s should be thought of as a long decade whose time line begins somewhere in the restive early to mid-1970s and perhaps bled into the violent early years of the 1990s. This not-so-unique periodization is already tacitly accepted in much of literature, although scholars argue over precise years for very interesting reasons. The underground resistance and counterinsurgency/repression comprises the activities of all disparate parties involved in the strategization, planning, and command and control of political violence perpetrated with the declared intent of bringing about the end of apartheid or the defense of the existing social order, however these ends were disparately conceived and disingenuously effected. In terms of the armed struggle, this could be formal exile armies infiltrating cadres into underground cells, less formal groups formed sui generis within the country, or so-called spontaneous violence often provoked during public demonstrations, forced removals, or retaliations against collaborators or insurgents both real and imagined.

The underground is a more nebulous term. At its most basic level, it is the subterranean architecture of formal hierarchies, informal networks, and personal relationships that underlies more obvious forms of oppositional protest. The dichotomies most often used to delineate this nebulous term are the following: the underground versus the aboveground, the armed versus the unarmed, the military versus the political, the vanguard versus the masses, legal versus illegal, the visible versus the invisible, the known versus the unknown, and the overt versus the covert.[12] In various ways, others have commented on how all of these dichotomies break down under the weight of this complex oral and written evidence. Parts of this rubric holds up better than others, but a good definition of what is and what is not the underground and how the underground relates to the broad field of struggle historiography awaits more careful theorization of this evidence.

For the intents and purposes here, I simply apply the label *underground* to whatever my interviewees say is underground and pay close attention to formal affiliations, initiations, oathing, and practices. This passive definition runs certain risks about establishing facts, but it was very difficult for an interviewer to determine the precise affiliation of many interviewees.[13] Likewise, the level of secrecy afforded to documents and the patterns of their circulation at the date of "publication" is only a rough indicator of whether a certain document came from the underground. These operative terms guide my review of the historiography on the "experience" of underground, particular modes of writing in the historiography of Cape Town in the 1980s, which review precedes my own reading of localized oral and written evidence both new and old.

Experience and Modes of Writing

The best place to address issues of experience and the underground is a review of dissertations submitted in the last decade. These past ten years have been boom years for scholarship on the underground, and judging by the titles and content of these specific dissertations, there is a pressing need to move beyond the political and social histories that predominated in the 1990s.[14] The three dissertations under review here are Rachidi Molapo's "Aspects of the South African Youth Experiences in Exile, 1960–1994," Raymond Suttner's "Rendering Visible: The Organizational Experience of the ANC-Led Alliance until 1976," and Lynda von den Steinen's "Experiencing the Armed Struggle: The Soweto Generation and After." Molapo, Suttner, and von den Steinen examine different subjects—youths in exile, the underground, and Umkhonto we Sizwe (MK) and the African People's Liberation Army (APLA) in toto—but all of these subjects find some degree of overlap in the underground.[15]

These three recent dissertations on the armed struggle collectively argue that there is an "organizational experience" that can be explained through careful synthesis of primarily oral evidence. Although their rationales for moving into the experiential realm vary slightly, all three note the paucity of the written record and argue for an acceptable evidentiary bias toward oral sources, which they then claim are the locus of authentic and verifiable "experience." All three share a positivist orientation toward oral history—namely, that with time and openness, previously silent struggle veterans may open up, allowing for a "now it can be told" oral record. Further, they suggest that by corroborating "scarce" written record with authenticated oral testimonies and unauthenticated oral testimonies with authenticated oral histories, the opening and growth of archival collections in recent years will yield a revised, full, and accurate picture of the recent past.

These evidentiary claims are born of dissatisfaction with the top-down organizational histories that preceded this scholarship. Much of their dissatisfaction stems from the two most significant organizational histories on these topics: *The UDF* by Jeremy Seekings and "Conscripts to Their Age" by Howard Barrell. Both of these pioneering organizational histories of the United Democratic Front (UDF) and MK, while scrupulously factual, exhaustively researched, and absolutely seminal, lack the human dimension promised in histories "told from below." So the turn to "experience" in all these dissertations is justified in the same vein as E. P. Thompson's oft-quoted call to rescue the "poor stockinger" and the "obsolete hand-loom weaver... from the enormous condescension of posterity."[16] The only difference between these historiographical rescue attempts and Thompson's work on the early working class in Britain is that histories of exiles, the underground, and the armed struggle are linked to a vast claims-making complex enmeshed in contemporary post-apartheid state legitimacy. In many ways, rescuing the ordinary youth, operative, or cadre from the "condescension of posterity" is simultaneously about breaking them into the pantheon of more elite struggle heroes—a pantheon conceived, built, and beholden to the post-apartheid state. This "temple to the heroes of the struggle" occupies the center of the claims-making complex that maintains the legitimacy of the post-apartheid state. The degree to which each of these scholars meets this problem head-on, acknowledge his or her role within or without this claims-making complex, and problematize experience and its relationship to particular modes of writing largely determines the success of his or her research agenda.[17]

In this regard, the conspicuous deployment of the term *experience* is telling. Each of these recent dissertations uses the term *experience* in their titles. But what precisely does *experience* actually mean? Molapo does not directly define the term. The closest he comes in the introduction is the "lives and situations of South African exiles."[18] Perhaps this is a history of experience based on biography? If so, where is the requisite problematizing of struggle biography addressed by Suttner, von den Steinen, and others?[19] Suttner avoids the evidentiary pitfalls of struggle biographies altogether but also neglects to define his usage of *experience* in any explicit way. Instead, he adds a modifier to the term, calling his work a history of the "organizational experience" of the underground, in which the "organization" looms large over three fields that he argues comprises experience: gender relations, romantic love, and the sacrifice of the personal for the political. Von den Steinen follows a similar schema in her review of the armed struggle but changes the organizational locus of her study from the underground to liberation armies, particularly the MK and APLA. All three studies justify their turn to experiential history as more a neglected addendum to the grand narrative of the struggle and less as a conceptual corrective to a struggle literature gone awry. Von den Steinen explains that the recent turn to experience, however ill-defined, is nonetheless justified because "ordinary soldiers deserve their place in history as well."[20]

The inclusion of the ordinary soldier is necessary, good, and overdue, but none of these scholars question just what sort of history they might be placing their ordinary soldiers into. Even though these authors might be loath to admit this, they are writing struggle histories masquerading as social histories. And struggle history, with its subsets of exile, popular protest, organized protest, underground protest, and the armed struggle in toto, suffers from a severe case of whiggishness. Coined in *The Whig Interpretation of History* in 1931, Herbert Butterfield used the term *whiggishness* to describe the historiography on the Whig Party in Great Britain.[21] The term has since taken on a life of its own, so it is important to briefly return to the definition that Butterfield laid out in 1931. Butterfield made three claims, first that nineteenth-century Whig historians failed to appreciate the "unlikenesses between the past and present," likewise failed to place "individuals and parties in their proper context" and were thus "prone to base the story upon a single person or party, rather than explore the complexities of the entire historical process."[22] Two consequences flow from these problems: the complexity of the historical process is flattened into a morality play between "heroes" and "villains," and there is a "persistent confusion of the outcomes of actions for the intentions of the actors."[23] A history preoccupied with personality, progress, and particular modes of writing could not admit the full complexity of the "historical process."[24] Butterfield claimed that the way out of this dilemma was a return to rigorous "methodological particularity" that would end the "abridgement" of history and arrive at the proper contextualization of the past.

Butterfield rightfully critiqued overdetermined historical narratives, but the solution he offered had its own problems. As Sewel notes, Butterfield merely replaced the idolatry of progress with the idolatry of process. E. H. Carr noted similar problems, suggesting that Butterfield's renewed call for empiricism came dangerously close to Ranke's theoretically agnostic call to describe the past "wie es eigentlich gewesen ist."[25] Although experience was clearly not on Butterfield's agenda, others later suggested that an experiential dimension could occupy the vacuum left by the demolition of whiggish history. Experience can satisfy the call to particularism and a rigorous reading of sources that particularism entails. But what can experience deliver that whiggish history cannot? Further, how can experience rescue exiled youths, the underground, and the comrade from the condescension of posterity without adding them to the "pantheon of struggle heroes"?

As witnessed in previous chapters, I follow the definitions of experience deployed in microhistory. Carlo Ginzburg's *The Cheese and the Worms* is instructive in this regard.[26] Ginzburg's trouble with social history is not in its ability to locate individuals within a class-based schema or to give voice to ordinary people or the idea of class conflict itself. What he seems to be doing with experience is problematizing the social historian's obsession with particular modes of writing. This is hardly a retreat into an apolitical netherworld of anecdotes and obscurantism. Rather, he is making a very political claim that the intellectual lives of individuals matter, that they can be recovered through a dialogue with evidence, and that social historians, and in this case struggle historians, have been derelict in their duty to bring these experiences to the surface of their grand theories of social change.

In *The Cheese and the Worms*, Ginzburg challenges social historians to see the broader implications of the peculiar weltanschauung of one sixteenth-century miller as a lens into the largely invisible dynamics of popular culture. In this way, Menocchio's peculiarity, and unique, uncorroborated, and perhaps "unrepresentative" testimony, opens a window into the intellectual lives of peasants, a world overlooked by others devoted to constructing a quantifiable, verifiable, and generalized body of evidence. On an evidentiary plane, Ginzburg restores some balance between the validity of oral and written evidence. Most of his evidence is oral testimony given by Menocchio, albeit compelled by church authorities during heresy trial. But Ginzburg is primarily concerned with Menocchio's reading and interpretation of texts. His subtle treatment of the interplay between Menocchio's readings of texts, explanations of the historical status of the texts he read, and the intellectual improvisations Menocchio derived from these interpretations deeply upset the underlying political and scholarly agenda of social history as practiced in the mid-1970s. Experience, then, is not only the lived conditions of forgotten people but also how they interpreted these conditions as mediated through their engagement with a world of ideas. In this regard, Ginzburg argues that social historians, even those who use experience to explain lived conditions, have missed the forest for the trees.

With this definition of experience in mind, I have three counterclaims to make in regard to recent scholarship on experience, whiggish struggle histories, and social history. First, in much of this literature, there are implicit demotions of the written word vis-à-vis the spoken word and explicit complaints about the paucity of documents. Neither of these contentions is true. The written record of the struggle, while fragmentary, policed, and encoded, is not any more or any less incomplete than the oral record. Nor are these documents as scarce as many assume. The problem is not in the quantity or quality of written evidence vis-à-vis oral testimony but in the conceptual tools brought to bear on both bodies. Second, Molapo, Suttner, and von den Steinen lay out three rather contentious claims: first, reading oral testimony in isolation from this written evidence; second, assuming that oral testimony presents a more accurate and authentic of rank-and-file experience; and third, the possibility of validating and corroborating "representative" testimonies from "unrepresentative" testimonies all miss the important historiographical points made by Ginzburg. Oral testimony is not the sole font of truth, and neither is the written record. Even when read in conversation with each other, the written and the oral do not comprise two halves that fit together to constitute a truthful whole, social, political, or otherwise. Understanding the gaps between the oral and written record addresses many of the problems Perrault noted in the Rote Kappelle, Ginzburg confirmed in Menocchio, and what I will attempt to prove in my reading of evidence of the underground in Cape Town during the long decade of the 1980s.

The Forensic Archive: Dimensions of Resistance and Repression in Cape Town

Following all this, I argue that historiographical claims and counterclaims made in the published literature on organizational and political history and unpublished dissertations on experience lack a sustained engagement with the words and evidence of one localized set of combatants. In other words, the reliance on an ill-defined experience and the assignment of particular modes of writing that this reliance entails are too mired in contemporary politics of representation and the politics of post-transition careerism to take seriously the written and spoken words of combatants themselves. This problem became most apparent after my interviews with individuals who participated in underground structures in Cape Town. When held against the explanations offered by commentators over the last three decades, these testimonies reveal entire worlds of experience rendered in readings, improvisations, and performances of texts. All these facets of experience are captured in oral testimony and many of the original texts read at the time survived the "secret" war waged in South Africa. In a case of the snake swallowing its evidentiary tail, the reading of texts and the improvisations and performances derived from their interpretations are further debated and critiqued in oral testimony. This folding and refolding of comments and dialogue and reading and writing is utterly missing from social history that is concerned with locating the bedrock of social truth in experience, in the statist cottage industry of struggle histories, and plausibly deniable apartheid apologias.

Madeleine Fullard's "The State and Political Struggle in Cape Town" is a useful starting point for reconsidering concepts of everyday life and experience in the underground in Cape Town.[27] Fullard's study is not a struggle history or a social history, and it certainly is not an apologia for apartheid. Instead, her work is part of a separate genealogy of fact-finding and truth-telling that began with the Truth and Reconciliation Commission (TRC) and continues into the present day. Her reconstruction of the political landscape of Cape Town in the 1980s is a means of accounting for deaths caused by resistance and repression. Although she meticulously names individual casualties, testimony is not in the foreground of her analysis. Consequently, her concern is less with excavating hidden social truths through explanations of lived experience rendered in oral testimony and more with measuring the dimensions, quantity, and quality of state and anti-state violence practiced in one specific locality. Freed from the sort of claims-making implicit in the genealogies of social history, struggle history, and apartheid apologias, this work does two things that other modes of writing do not. First, it conceptualizes different political constituencies without making claims to their legitimacy or illegitimacy. Second, it deploys a very different chronology to explain the violence practiced by these political constituencies. What emerges is a broad tableau of violence in Cape Town in the 1980s, an engaged but dispassionate consideration of its consequences, and, as I argue, a useful frame for reevaluating the concept of everyday life in the underground.

Fullard begins her narrative with a detailed reconstruction of the state security apparatus that operated through the 1980s, follows that with a description of the three "sites of resistance," and then draws conclusions based on her analysis of the deaths caused by repression and resistance. Although she draws heavily from testimony presented during various commissions and public inquiries, her primary concern is with tallying the numbers of deaths and assigning specific deaths to different categories of political violence. In this regard, her inquiry into the "forensic archive" provides a useful backdrop for evaluating the perceptions of repression and resistance in the underground.

Fullard places a detailed description of the evolution of state security ahead of her narrative on resistance politics. She recapitulates evidence collected during the Harms Commission and the TRC but focuses on the deployment of these structures and strategies in Cape Town.[28] Understanding the deployment of the security state at the local level is critical, not only because it predated transformations in resistance groups but also because it shaped the operational space inhabited by resistance groups. In addition, the specificities of state counterinsurgency strategies created gaps between general Soviet doctrines on how to conduct underground work. Underground cadres saw these gaps and attempted to inform their practice with readings of Soviet texts on underground work. If the Soviet texts failed to satisfy their needs, they turned to a bricolage of other texts. When Soviet doctrine and alternative texts failed to fit the situation they saw on the ground, state counterinsurgency strategies formed much of the context of underground improvisations.

The apartheid state shifted its approach to public order and public relations after failing to anticipate the scope and intensity of violence witnessed during the Soweto uprising. Almost immediately, military and intelligence officials began to characterize domestic unrest as a manifestation of "total onslaught," a vast conspiracy orchestrated by communist-backed exiles, whose ultimate objective was the armed overthrow of the state after a popular insurrection.[29] The state crafted "total strategy" in response: a two-pronged plan that eliminated the threat posed by exiles by destabilizing hostile neighboring states, while undermining mass protest and armed activity within South Africa through targeted violence and the cultivation of a moderate black constituency. Total strategy borrowed heavily from classic counterinsurgency doctrines deployed in conflicts in Malaya, Vietnam, Rhodesia, and Namibia. Foremost among these adapted theories was John McCuen's concept of "winning hearts and minds," known also by the acronym WHAM.[30] The central tenet of WHAM is that insurgencies cannot be defeated by conventional warfare alone but must consist of a coordinated program composed of 80 percent welfare and 20 percent warfare. Translated into the South African situation, welfare was adapted to court "moderate" middle-class black Africans, Coloureds, and Indians through an array of political reforms, legal concessions, and economic incentives. According to McCuen, the "silent majority" of a populace could be swayed by limiting popular grievances, providing a viable alternative to the revolutionary project, and delegitimizing insurgent propaganda. Examples of this strategy included the expansion of local government in the townships in 1982, the tricameral elections held in 1984, and the razing and rebuilding of Crossroads in 1986/87. While never truly successful, the government did not entirely give up on this prong of total strategy and consistently introduced a range of largely unconvincing welfare efforts throughout the entire decade.

Learning the lessons of the Soweto debacle, the warfare component of total strategy was designed to avoid public displays of violence committed by recognizable state agents. Above all else, counterinsurgency warfare should be inconspicuous, discriminate, and plausibly deniable. By 1979, security forces executed dozens of operations through a nationwide hierarchy of joint commands that coordinated the police, the military, intelligence services, black proxies, and white auxiliaries. This highly integrated structure was collectively known as the National Security Management System (NSMS).[31] By the mid-1980s, the NSMS had become a shadow state led by securocrats who commanded vast budgets and seemed to supersede civilian rule. As in welfare efforts, intentions did not match outcomes, and an ostensibly silent war often devolved into very public displays of low-intensity conflict. In spite of these lapses, the government's repression of the 1984/85 unrest, while bloody and mostly visible, saw far fewer deaths than the repression that followed the Soweto uprising.[32]

Having sketched the development and implementation of state repression, Fullard then turns to resistance to state authority. Addressing a question asked by so many others but as-yet unsatisfactorily answered, Fullard attempts to map a decade when resistance came from many quarters and use this topography to explain the consequences of each form of protest. To make sense of this complex terrain, she divides the broad and varied forms of resistance into three categories or "sites of struggle." The first category, popular protest, was comprised of a sort of ad hoc, spontaneous, and largely unorganized contestations of state power. This form of protest could be passive evasions of pass laws or more violent forms of confrontations such as attacking agents of the state with homemade weapons. The second category, organized protest, was composed of the "campaigns and protests organized by activists and supporters of the liberation movements through their organized formations such as the UDF and its affiliates."[33] This form of protest included strikes, boycotts, and demonstrations and shared the common characteristic of public displays of mass strength. The third category, underground protest, includes the armed formations of exiled liberation movements. This form of protest is by definition planned in secret and included "attacks on property and persons" involving the use of "formal weaponry such as firearms and explosives."[34] Underground protest was generally geared toward "armed propaganda," highly visible spectacles of violence that demonstrated the destructive capacity of underground units.[35] However, underground protest also had more prosaic functions such as political education and quiet operations such as the assassination of traitors, rivals, and uniformed and ununiformed agents of the state.[36] She argues against seeing these sites of resistance in isolation from one another but rather considers these sites to be guideposts for her chronology of protest, which is the centerpiece of her study.

Fullard then presents an overlapping chronology of confrontations between the repressive apparatus of the state and these three sites of struggle. She implicitly and explicitly identifies three periods of resistance. The first period, roughly from 1976 to 1983, saw the repression of student organizations after Soweto, the beginning of a new phase of armed propaganda and the return of student activism during the school boycotts of 1980. The launch of the UDF in August 1983 opened the second period of confrontation, which saw the return of mass protest, a resurgence in the trade union movement, and the real possibility of a national insurrection. The pinnacle of organized protest was the successful boycott of the tricameral elections held in August 1984. This early success signaled the arrival of a year-old organization capable of coordinating mass protest throughout South Africa, and low-voter turnout was an indication of the alignment of popular protest with the UDF.[37] The third phase began with the eruption of nationwide unrest that followed Vaal Triangle uprising in 1984/85 and the consequent declaration of a state of emergency in 1985, which was extended to Cape Town in 1986. This period saw popular protest at full boil, marked a steep escalation in violence in all forms, and ended with the hobbling of the armed struggle and the disruption of the UDF. The most emblematic manifestation of this phase of struggle in Cape Town was the clearing of Crossroads squatter camp in May 1986. The events at Crossroads were a convergence of popular protests against forced removal, overlapping with street warfare between comrades, vigilantes, civilians, and the state. The final stage saw a lull in organized protest and popular protest during the state of emergency but a steep increase in the frequency of armed actions.[38] Organized protest and popular protest were severely interrupted by mass arrests and detentions. At the same time, separate lines of top-secret commands within state security—namely, the Civil Cooperation Bureau and Vlakplaas—assassinated popular UDF leaders and known or suspected underground cadres.[39] Although the underground conducted more armed operations during this time, Fullard notes that these operations were increasingly small in scale, and infiltrated comrades faced almost suicidal survival rates. Her study concludes with the final wave of mass protest leading up to and following the release of most political prisoners in 1989.

Unlike many other struggle histories that conflate the entire landscape of resistance with a unitary liberation movement or apartheid apologias that exaggerate the mortal threat posed by total onslaught, Fullard's chronology accepts the existence of moments of overlap between these sites of struggle but rejects the idea that "resistance" equaled "a Resistance," while simultaneously delving deeply into the cynical complicities of state security strategies. Her grasp of the entire landscape of violence in the 1980s is breathtaking. Fullard paints a picture of a widely fragmented topography of resistance and, to a lesser degree, the scatterbrained implementation of repression in the townships. As Fullard considers evidence of competition and conflict between different sites of struggle and contradictions and failures within total strategy, she distinguishes between intentions of historical actors and the outcomes of their actions.

This distinction is made all the more obvious in her provocative review of quantitative and empirical evidence of deaths in Cape Town in the post-1985 period. After 1985, when violence was at its worst, most civilian deaths were caused by other civilians. Perhaps more provocatively, she found that the underground killed more civilians than state agents, and contrary to more maudlin and elitist struggle histories, the rank and file suffered the highest likelihood of torture and death. The numbers of deaths, the causes of deaths, and the relationship between deaths and repression and resistance cut through the heart of oral narratives that portray strategy and practice as identical, describe the practice of political violence as purposeful and coherent, and foreground the experiences of political elites above a nameless and instrumentalized "crowd."

Case in point is how the forensic archive maps the complex topographies of political affiliation. Fullard's most important insight is her novel conceptualization of categories of affiliation. In this scheme, she preserves of the category of the "civilian," and applies this category in her review of forensic evidence. Glossed elsewhere as "the crowd," "the masses," or "the silent majority," the rhetorical uses and abuses of these terms dull the conceptual edge of much of the literature on the 1980s. At the time, all sides claimed to represent the will of the people, and unwatchful commentators, more often than not, have tended to reiterate these claims in their writing. Cutting against this tendency, Fullard introduces her provocative finding: the fact that civilian groups caused the majority of deaths after 1985, which contravenes the widely held assumption that most deaths occurred during clashes between the state and resistance groups.

This finding inspires Fullard's thoughtful delineation of the term *civilian*. She, following Barrell and Seekings, points to the tenuous connections between exiles and their underground structures, the UDF and its affiliates, and to a lesser extent the state and its proxies and vigilante groups. Between and beyond these tenuous connections, she points to what I would call a "franchising of political representation," where many groups affected a militaristic presence; mouthed what they knew of Congress politics, cultural tradition, or the anticommunist rhetoric of the state; and embellished themselves in flags, uniforms, and other accoutrements. The lack of command and control between exiles, the underground, and their constituents on the one hand and the state and their allied civilian groups on the other hand meant that at the street level, there was a fair share of what Lenin called rustic craftsmanship. This descriptive term captures all of the organization, activity, and theorizing that goes on in the name of a particular party but is the result of isolation, decentralization, or outright autonomy of branch structures and hangers-on.[40] In Cape Town, one could extend this definition beyond branch structures of either resistance groups or state proxies and include all those claiming membership, those too junior to become members, and those advertising affiliation or effecting verisimilitude. This was the case particularly in areas where state authority receded, but the UDF and underground leadership did not or could not assume authority. The purpose of this chapter is to explore how this lack of command and control extended within more formalized underground structures and the effect that stretched lines of communications had on the everyday experience of underground work.

Military and Combat Work

Turning to the underground itself, the topography of resistance and repression in Cape Town left a tight space for the deployment of classic theories of underground work. Despite the iconic images of white troops barreling through the townships in armored vehicles, Fullard correctly points out that black vigilantes, deputized militias, and third force agents composed the cutting edge of government forces during the 1980s. The dimensions of the government's repressive capacity in Cape Town also should give pause to triumphal struggle historians who emphasize an omniscient and mobile underground presence. Fullard notes that in Cape Town alone, some eight thousand African men were deputized to be kitkonstabels—a militia of sorts that literally translates into "instant police"—and the witdoeke—a conservative vigilante group that was primarily Xhosa in ethnicity—showed up in the thousands during the political cleansing of Crossroads squatter camp in June 1986.[41] Add to this the ability of the state to recruit agents within the ranks of the mass movement through detention. Max Ozinsky, an underground operative active in Cape Town in the mid- to late 1980s, estimated that nationwide, tens of thousands of individuals were detained during the state of emergency first declared in October 1985.[42] He then hypothesized that if only one out of a hundred detainees turned, the state returned hundreds of agents into the ranks of organized protest groups. Although Fullard revised Ozinsky's estimate downward in Cape Town, Herman Stadler maintained that nationwide the state recruited secret agents with great ease. If this former head of intelligence for the Special Branch is to be believed, the 1 percent hypothesized by Ozinsky is a very conservative estimate of actual rates of recruitment.[43] Thus the underground found itself facing a severe numerical disadvantage, a terrain littered with violent and secretive elements shielded and abetted by a powerful if not always effective state, and dependent on alliances with a heavily penetrated mass movement.

How did underground cadres make sense of their predicament? What were their expectations of revolution within the claustrophobic space between repression and resistance? How did the limits imposed by repression and resistance affect their perceptions of the situation in Cape Town and influence their practices and improvisations there?

The urtext of underground work is a useful place to begin this conversation. The official primer of the underground in the 1980s was a Soviet doctrine known as Military and Combat Work (MCW).[44] Although MCW is hardly the Rosetta stone of archival sources on the underground, it is difficult to make sense of subsequent discussions of everyday life without some understanding of the myriad meanings associated with this text. The problem with interpreting the meanings of MCW is that it is a notoriously tricky text to pin down. It is difficult to identify the precise moment when MCW became the operative doctrine for fomenting revolution. Cadres trained in the 1960s do not mention it by name, rank-and-file cadres in the 1970s and 1980s seemed to have limited exposure to it, and many homegrown units given quick crash courses had only fleeting glimpses of these theories. Judging by my own reading of oral testimony and Vladimir Shubin's recollection of training programs, MCW occupied a central place in advanced training courses in the Soviet Union and Angola from the mid-1970s onward.[45] Accordingly, references to MCW appear most frequently in interviews with elite units drawn from the first generation of post-Soweto cadres who trained in Angola and the Soviet Union. Thereafter, leading internal structures and exiled theorists debated this text heavily and recapitulated their debates in contemporary interviews. In a sense, these debates never really ended but were resurrected in retrospective explanations of the failures of the armed struggle. More often than not, "literary critiques" of this text form the basis of post-transition political maneuverings and character assassinations in oral testimonies.

The status of this text among others is even less clear. Underground cadres read widely about revolution. And while MCW was the primer of most extended training programs abroad, it is difficult to determine whether the significance assigned to it in the post-transition period matches the significance it held in the underground at the time. Did trainees consider it bone-dry, doctrinaire, and ill-suited to the specificity of the South African situation, did it measure up in the minds of trainees to other texts in their own personal "syllabi," or was it a powerful and illuminating blueprint faithfully mapping the path to liberation?

The oral archive offers some clues to perceptions of MCW. Cadres, particularly the angry young students who went into exile for military training after Soweto, speak about MCW in tones of awe, almost as if it were

Promethean fire. The hottest students describe the reception of MCW as almost an anointment into revolutionary personhood.[46] The standard narrative here was that where once they were naïve firebrands who went into exile to pick up guns, they now picked up MCW and underwent a Damascene conversion into disciplined revolutionary personhood. Further, MCW bore the imprimatur of Soviet experts who counseled above all else caution, deliberation, and preparation in the planning of revolution. Although these trainees had a variety of political affiliations, most respected the Soviet Union as a liberating force or at least a stalwart ally of the liberation movement. After receiving this text from on high, these students-turned-cadres had the utmost confidence in the text as a workable plan that warranted iron discipline and operational restraint in the practice of political violence. In many ways, their adherence to the text justified their acceptance of the more depersonalizing aspects of everyday life in the underground.

Others, such as Sue Rabkin—an underground cadre in Cape Town in the 1970s and strategist in exile working in Maputo in the 1980s—suggested that MCW lost importance after cadres were deployed into the underground.[47] Faced with the realities on the ground, Rabkin noted that while her group diligently followed the "rules of secrecy," they were an onerous burden that actually limited what they could accomplish. Although improvisation was marked as a sign of indiscipline, she noted that "we were more successful when we ignored the textbook."[48] Although Rabkin maintains the effectiveness of her severely proscribed underground propaganda unit, she also reveled in the innovations she employed and speculated that they could have accomplished much more had they been freer to improvise more.

Aside from oblique mentions and incomplete descriptions in interviews, my only access to MCW in document form is a forty-page photocopy of a manual found in the Liberation Archive at Fort Hare.[49] This manual bears no date but most likely dates to the mid- to late 1980s and describes elaborate sets of tasks necessary to prepare an underground capable of becoming a vanguard during a revolutionary moment. MCW was primarily urban in focus and advised careful, deliberate, and incremental conscientization of the masses by underground units situated in the community. These units were to be organized into distinct political and military wings, and while their primary responsibility was conscientization, military units were later expected to embark on armed propaganda as a component of conscientization, all with the ultimate goal of drawing the people into a people's war or general insurrection. Concurrent with conscientization, MCW dictated that the task of the underground also included infiltration and conversion of state structures of repression—namely, the army and police. MCW, as understood by Soviet theorists, never presumed to induce a revolutionary moment but held out the promise that a properly constructed political and military underground could seize initiative when the balance of forces tipped away from state hegemony and toward dual power. Only after a long period of underground work and the contingent arrival of a revolutionary moment could the underground become a vanguard and clear a path to state power, either through people's war or by general insurrection.[50]

This document is highly unusual in that most trainees emphasized that no written or photographic materials left training facilities. One could safely assume that the documents used for training in Angola stayed in the hands of trainers and returned with the Soviet officers contracted by the ANC. If copies circulated in underground units within South Africa, they would have been jealously guarded, given that the content of MCW would be quite the trophy to any curious state agent. The fact that this document was not widely circulated has two important implications for understanding theoretical debates in underground cells.

First, once infiltrated, underground cadres recalled the lessons of MCW from memory. Like formulas for invisible ink, schematics of explosives, and methods of cryptography, the theoretical interpretations of MCW were only as good as the recollections of the interpreter. This left a wide field for debate and opportunities for improvisation through misremembered lessons or deliberate inventions. The written version of MCW demonstrates a drift between how interviewees described MCW from long-term memory and put its lessons into practice and how the doctrine was described in its original written form. The most interesting discrepancy between oral interviews and written text is the emphasis interviewees placed on the tactical details of underground work, such as dead letter drops, arranging secret meetings, signaling, losing tails, and other forms of spy craft. My text is almost entirely composed of the strategy of subversion and mobilization and contains virtually no content of these sorts of clandestine techniques. Whether the emphasis on spy craft above conscientization and infiltration was an inadvertent conflation, a profound omission of the theoretical context of clandestine techniques, or a deliberate reprioritizing of tactics over strategy is unclear but hotly debated in written evidence and oral testimony.[51]

Second, knowledge of MCW was a source of power for infiltrated cadres inserted into existing underground structures.[52] Underground structures recruited entirely within South Africa may or may not have had extensive exposure to MCW. Conversely, cadres deployed from the elite Angolan camps or elite cadres trained abroad had or at least assumed a stance of authority on all matters pertaining to "proper" underground work. This does not mean that their authority went unchallenged by experienced, "home-schooled" cadres, but it certainly set the stage for power struggles based on knowledge of authorized texts. Pulling rank by "knowing what works" is a common theme in oral testimony. Knowing what works is largely a debate between memory of texts on the one hand and experience, practice, and improvisation on the other hand.

How did MCW frame debates within underground cells? Above all else, this text is a profoundly historicist understanding of revolution-as-process. Although one can never pinpoint the date of a revolutionary moment, the underlying theoretical assumption of MCW is that one can reasonably read social and economic conditions, anticipate the coming of a revolutionary moment, and exploit popular grievances and weaknesses in the state to hasten its arrival. MCW conferred a confidence in social and economic interpretation in a properly initiated reader, one that added to the presumed authority of Marxist theory in toto and thus gave a profoundly historicist flavor to the memories of many of trained cadres.[53] Time and time again in oral testimony, former underground cadres who can admit the ignominious denouement of the armed struggle still largely presume that the underground failed to seize state power because of one or another misapplication of strategies or tactics.[54] Further, their adherence to historicist reading of the armed struggle excludes a wide range of other reasons and rationales. In terms of MCW, most debates circle around whether enough attention had been paid to political mobilization vis-à-vis military operations. On one side of this debate stands Ozinsky who felt that not enough attention was paid to infiltrating the repressive apparatus of the apartheid state and that the "military work" side of MCW was often misinterpreted to mean merely building the underground and not compromising, converting, or subverting soldiers, police, and intelligence agents.[55] On the other side of this debate stands

Mac Maharaj, who spent most of the 1980s leading the reconstruction of the underground and cited the preoccupation with "military work," however defined, as a drain on, what he argued, was the more important work of political conscientization within a committed popular constituency.[56] What is most interesting about this debate is not why these arguments conflict or finding a way to reconcile them but rather the common premises that they are built on. Both Ozinsky, Maharaj, and others assume that there is a right and a wrong way to build the underground and conduct the revolution, and their explanations of the 1980s both presume that along the way, someone, somewhere read something wrong and did something wrong.

The historical theories that animate MCW are based on historiographical manipulations perpetrated in official Soviet narratives on the Russian Revolution and partisan warfare in Eastern Europe during World War II.[57] The manipulations are particularly glaring in state histories of these revolutions and in a separate genealogy of Soviet writings on Cuba.[58] Above all else, these manipulations place the agency of the party over the contingency of events. In the mildest form, the status of MCW as the blueprint of an effective underground reserves all authority on revolutionary strategy and tactics for the CPSU and the CPSU alone.[59] This authority presumes that there is a right way and a wrong way to plan for revolution, and the Soviet model—while subject to the odd authorized revision here and there—was the most tried and tested because it "worked" in Russia in 1917 and again in Eastern Europe in the 1940s.

In its most extreme form, the official thinking behind these manipulations and the misreadings cadres derived from them can best be described in an example of a common misreading of Marxist historicism. In the minds of the more incautious historicists, "men make their own history." These same historicists often forget that man does not "make it out of conditions chosen by himself."[60] So with some sort of version of this selective quotation in mind, many exiled strategists conceded that while the underground led popular protests from behind and was out of joint with organized protest, they still vigorously maintain that the underground was not entirely subject to contingent forces beyond their control or anticipation.

Their assertions fail to hold up to voluminous oral and written evidence. In the case of large uprisings such as the Soweto or the Vaal Triangle uprisings, exiles did not predict, control, or entirely understand situations unfolding within South Africa.⁶¹ Recently released Robben Islanders might have seen more but remained focused on workers and peasants and maintained only casual contacts with mainstream student groups. In short, both exiles and released Robben Islanders probably knew something was happening but did not know what it was. And, as I will later argue, in subsequent years, the underground seemed unaware of these tectonic social shifts or at least unable to exploit their effects.⁶² In short, historicism set the stage for the marked gaps that opened up between the theory and practice of underground work, creating a space for imagining new ways of performing the revolution most exiles and underground cadres believed was on the horizon.⁶³ Further, the degree to which interviewees still accept the historicist view greatly colors their oral testimony and the interpretive styles deployed therein.

The Danie Theron Combat School: Basic Tactics of the ANC offers a number of practical counterpoints to historicist narratives of the 1980s.⁶⁴ The Danie Theron Combat School, established in 1967, operated as the proving grounds for an entire generation of SANDF counterinsurgency specialists. My version of the training manual dates to July 1985, which provides a window in the official mind of SANDF trainers at the cusp of the state of emergency that followed the Vaal Triangle uprising as well as a catalog of strategic thought about the last ten years of the armed struggle. In short, this document provides an excellent segue for discussing the vignettes of everyday life in the underground that follow.

How does one characterize the status of this text vis-à-vis my version of MCW manual? *Basic Tactics* can be best described as an imperfect mirror of MCW. Whether it was drawn from a captured version of the formal MCW manual, or it was intuited from observed practice and operation experience, it is a snapshot of what SANDF knew, the activities and tactics they anticipated, and perhaps an explanation of necessity of improvisation in Cape Town. In short, it is an index of what was known and anticipated about the underground. The predictive power of anticipation speaks volumes about the depressing rates of survival for underground units.⁶⁵ It also throws into high relief the successes of those units that evaded detection and capture for a long time. In this regard, the Basil February MK Squad is noteworthy because it lasted for two years, perhaps longer than any other publicly known infiltrated unit in South Africa during the 1980s.⁶⁶

Basic Tactics is organized into four sections: basic background on ANC strategy, the recruitment and deviation of aspirant terrorists, training programs, propaganda, the operation of MK, ANC rural operations, summary of strong and weak points, and a conclusion. Each section contains bulleted lists of the primary strategies and tactic employed by the underground to undermine the state and bring about a people's war. *Basic Tactics* provides two important points for evaluating readings of MCW in the underground. First is the hierarchy of threats. The state recognized the threat posed by popular protest, organized protest, and underground protest but did not treat all three equally. The ranked threats in *Basic Tactics* suggests that popular protests—the running street battles and ad hoc confrontations in the townships—was the most easily managed threat. Organized protest had a greater potential to disrupt the established order than popular protest, but tellingly, the author(s) of *Basic Tactics* singled out efforts directed at whites as the most threatening. This priority is repeated again in discussions of underground protest. Clearly the state saw the splitting of its white constituency and the subversion of the security apparatus inherent in this cleavage as the most pressing threat to the state. This meant that the state placed "military work"—the infiltration, subversion, and neutralization of the police, army, and intelligence services—above "combat work," which was defined by the Soviets as the implementation of an underground capable of leading a people's war but misread by many in the underground as actual combat or a theatrical obsession with secret work. The order of importance of these lists is telling, particularly in the sections on recruitment and subversion. The state was most concerned with anticonscription campaigns among whites and propaganda that convinced whites of the impossibility of the maintenance of the status quo. Beneath these primary concerns were students not defined by race. *Basic Tactics* sees popular disturbances as one way that the underground dislodges students from campus politics and funnels them into military training. This text seems least concerned with the running battles in the townships, which lies contrary to received image of the conflict in the 1980s. In addition, the discussion of tactics of the military side of the underground gives the impression that security forces could and did anticipate infiltration and operations. The author(s) of *Basic Tactics* both knew that the underground deployed cadres from their home areas and thus could be easily identified, located, and captured and that homegrown units that received blitz training conducted poor-quality operations, on occasion blowing themselves up in the process. Simply put, the state's reading of MCW, either in actual text or observed practice saw military work rather than combat work as the potential existential threat to state security. The degree to which underground units had the same readings and applied them in practice determined the degree to which they were perceived as an actual existential threat.

Interestingly, both MCW and *Basic Tactics* deploy the same mode of writing. Both texts project a tone that imbues the reader with a sense that they now have the interpretive power to read the landscape of resistance in South Africa in the 1980s. For the reasons noted above, both doctrines fail to anticipate the profoundly uncanny, contingent, and imaginative lived experiences of underground cadres and their adversaries. Following the arguments explained above, struggle histories and social histories written from these proscriptive documents can assume a convergence between intentions and outcomes. Instead of positioning these documents as blueprints, the unwary struggle historian or social historian might substitute them for the lived experience of the underground and those searching for it. Returning to Perrault and Ginzburg, these are the litany of factual details that cause the unwary to miss the forest for the trees.

The Habituated Eye

The composition of my vignettes follows a metaphor I developed in conversation with Shirley Gunn.[67] Gunn's biography and record of underground activity is far too complicated to exhaustively describe here.[68] Suffice to say, she was an elite cadre who received advanced combat training in Angola and training in secret work at a facility in Cuba. She excelled at marksmanship in Angola and reveled in her mastery of underground work. About midway through my fieldwork, Gunn granted me three wide-ranging interviews that covered any number of topics.

One of the most interesting aspects of these interviews was her description of the clandestine photography techniques she learned in Cuba as part of a training program in secret work. The Cubans taught Gunn how to photograph strategic installations and potential targets by displacing the secret subject of her composition. This meant taking a picture of someone or something conspicuous and unimportant in the foreground while capturing the actual subject far off in the distance or in a corner of the frame. The purpose of this technique was to create plausible deniability should police confiscate the film as evidence. A picture with a waving, smiling figure in the foreground could be interpreted as innocent, despite the fact that an army barracks, power transformer, or government building lies off in the distance.

This form of clandestine photography manipulates routinizing effects of a common compositional convention to conceal the true meaning of their photographs. In particular, clandestine photography manipulates the Pythagorean theorem, which is an almost ubiquitous compositional convention in Western pictorial art. Compositions that follow this theorem focus the action of the eye in certain predictable zones—namely, at the four intersections formed by dividing the frame into fourths and thirds.[69] This theorem is so commonly used in pictorial art that the eye of the viewer is, in a very strong sense, habituated to a certain predictable arrangement of visual elements. This habituation causes the viewer to anticipate that important visual elements will appear in these four intersections and that other visual elements lying beyond and between these zones can be disregarded. Photographers, clandestine or otherwise, are aware of the habituating effects of this theorem on the eye and that viewers cannot "see" without these conventions.[70] Thus, the photographer is able to exploit this phenomenon to great effect when concealing, distorting, or demoting composed meanings or narratives.[71]

Gunn reminisced that she practiced this technique in Cuba by photographing ordinary Cubans going about their day. She described this work as a sort of social documentary rendered in the style of secret work.[72] Cuban regulations prevented cadres from keeping any written or photographic materials after their departure. After a pause, she expressed regret that she did not have these photographs today and longed to continue this sort of social documentary via candid camera. My eye was somewhere between habituated and unhabituated when I met Gunn.

This technique informs my reading of the oral testimony of former underground cadres. I argue that the habituated eye is a good metaphor for describing the compositional strategies deployed by interviewees. Like the clandestine photographer, interviewees encode meaning by displacing certain elements of their oral "compositions." For example, in several instances provided here, my interviewees mentioned important aspects of everyday life in passing. When pressed on these points, they downplayed the importance of these experiences and then returned my attention to a narrative of their more illustrious activities. This demotion of experience over grand narrative may be a deliberate concealment, either because such details conflict with intended narrative or because social tensions among cadres prevent them from addressing certain topics, or interviewees themselves cannot "see the forest for the trees." Learning to "see" around these strategies and unhabituate the reader's eye is more about selectively recentering demoted experiences than transparently reproducing foregrounded historiographical "rescue attempts."

Much of the evidence of experience presented in the vignettes foregrounded a historicist narrative over aspects of everyday life, as defined by Ginzburg. For example, when Cecyl Esau mentioned *The Red Orchestra* and John Le Carré novels, he did so only in the context of a more conventional syllabus he drew up as the political commissar of his unit.[73] *The Red Orchestra* and Le Carré's writings only assumed importance after they were cut off from exile structures in Botswana and denied access to more "textbook" materials on underground work. But his mention of these fictional and nonfictional texts unlocked the meaning of many of his subsequent stories, which foregrounded rich images of "tradecraft" relayed with an obvious sense of pride. Esau also casually flagged two genealogies of fiction and nonfiction that turned up in other oral testimonies and decrypted intelligence reports presented in court.[74] Only a few interviewees saw any value in recounting the routine, the seemingly mundane, or the burdensome aspects of everyday life. For these interviewees, the stuff of history came from a recitation of events. They positioned the litany of facts ahead of a history of imagination, improvisation, and performance. The mode of writing employed below attempts to allow the reader to see foregrounded and displaced evidence at the same time. One way of doing this is to constantly switch between habituated and unhabituated ways of seeing.

Not all foregrounding and displacement is the result of deliberate manipulations. As Judith Van Allen pointed out to me, the enclosed vision of a tightly organized cellular underground is not unlike the limited horizon that plagued guerrillas fighting in the bush in the Wankie Reserve.[75] As former cadres stress again and again, their vision of their world was hemmed in by a need-to-know existence or was occluded by the walls of secrecy erected between cells. After 1980, the underground in Cape Town began to be organized into cells of three or four individuals, and only one of these three could access the cell above. These horizontal and vertical limits are evident in oral testimony—the memory of many underground cadres was segmented by the formal structure of a cellular underground. In other words, many did not know what was going on in the next cell over or if the next cell over even existed.[76]

This circumscribed vision has a number of important implications when assessing oral evidence of everyday life in Cape Town. First, no individual testimony can be considered as representative—the evidentiary shibboleth that validates much social history and underwrites struggle history. Second, because no individual testimony can be characterized as representative, the purpose of this chapter is not to place these vignettes together to form some cumulative truth. Third, the subject position of the author, and by extension the reader, permits them a wider field of vision than most interviewees. Fourth, the limits imposed by vision and the limits imposed on memory are not an obstacle to be overcome; it is evidence in and of itself. An important part of evaluating oral evidence experience is recognizing an interviewee's awareness of its limits. What this means, by extension, is that oral testimony of this kind is by nature unique and anecdotal. From this, one could make a reasonable claim that the quest for representivity is at best misleading and at worst Quixotic. A more fruitful exploration of experience must begin and end with an appreciation of difference, rather than a plowing under of the anecdotal and unique. Accordingly, I chose to flag the limits of vision of my interviewees in each vignette and avoid generalized comparisons.

Finally, I use written evidence to curate these oral testimonies. They include oral interviews conducted by myself, oral interviews conducted by others, novels, published memoirs, operational histories, affidavits, confessions and court testimony, TRC testimony, and documents such as an MCW manual and encoded field notes captured in a raid and later decoded by police cryptographers. Each kind of written evidence can flag instances of displacement that are deliberately and inadvertently reproduced in these vignettes.

Three Vignettes

In order to place these vignettes into some sort of structure and chronology, I provide the following narrative summaries of relevant facts.[77] As evident in chapter 1, underground activity in Cape Town dated to the very first months of the armed struggle in 1961. However, much of this underground activity either disappeared or lay dormant after the Rivonia Trial in 1964. Although this periodization is contested by recent scholarship, most earlier works locate the second phase of the underground to 1976.[78]

Born in England, Sue Rabkin came from an active trade unionist background and met and fell in love with David Rabkin in London. After being recruited by "Frank" sometime in 1969 or 1970, they joined the SACP and underwent explosives training at a rural cottage in the Cotswolds and secret work in flats around London. They married shortly before departing by ship for Cape Town in late 1970.[79] Following this, they were deployed to Cape Town. In an episode that foreshadowed the world of disguises they would come to inhabit, they were met by David's cousin, who, according to Sue, was going through a "transvestite phase and was dressed in full regalia."[80] They stayed in Clifton with David's wealthy aunt, presumably in a grannie flat or spare apartment. Following this, they had a child together, operated a secret print shop at their residence, and built and planted bucket bombs around Cape Town for the next four and a half years (see figure 7). They were joined by Jeremy Cronin after he returned to South Africa from the Sorbonne in the early 1970s. All three remained active and undetected until July 1976, when the police arrested Sue, David, and eventually Jeremy. Sue gave birth to her second child in detention but was spared a significant prison sentence and left South Africa for work in the exile structures. David and Jeremy were convicted and sentenced to seven years in prison. Following their release, David trained in Angola and elsewhere, and Jeremy remained in South Africa working with the UDF and ANC underground. Sue later played an integral role in the underground structures in Mozambique that serviced KwaZulu and Natal from the early 1980s onward.[81]

The second cluster of underground cadres grew up in the winelands and the Boland but particularly in townships in and around Worcester. Cecyl Esau was part of this group, which included several individuals who fled for exile and trained in Angola and several individuals who remained in South Africa and formed underground units.[82] Esau remained in South Africa, attended the University of the Western Cape, and participated in student politics there. As conditions turned more violent in Cape Town in the first few years of the 1980s, Esau noted a distinct personal drift toward the armed struggle, while maintaining his status as a student activist. At some point, Esau joined others and formed an underground unit, presumably part of MK. Eventually, Esau ended up in a cell commanded by Lizo Ngqungwana, which was organized in an unusual manner.[83] These cadres were part of an Area Politico-Military Committee (APC), which was an integrated, nonparallel structure that folded military and political wings into one structure. At some point in 1985, the police discovered the unit and successfully arrested, tried, and convicted Esau and his comrades. Esau spent the next few years on Robben Island. The dates of his political and military activity extend roughly from the mid-1970s until his capture in 1985.

My best evidence comes from interviews with former members of the Basil February MK Squad. The Basil February MK Squad assumed authority for underground operations in the Western Cape after the collapse of Ngqungwana's unit in 1985. Although personnel rotated in and out of the unit, it was composed of three integrated branches: the leadership was composed of highly trained exiles successfully reinserted into South Africa, the propaganda unit consisted of activists-cum-cadres recruited at the University of Cape Town (UCT), and the military wing included cadres from the Cape Flats, primarily Crossroads but also other locations as well. The two subjects of the vignette below, Chris Giffard and Max Ozinsky, were recruited as student activists at UCT, began with propaganda work, and eventually took separate paths into intelligence work and military work, respectively.[84] In terms of the vignette below, this integrated structure meant that cadres shared a number of responsibilities and could comment on both political and military matters.[85] All three branches of this unit conducted a significant number of operations.[86] Finally, significant evidence suggests that this unit, unlike others before it, had extensive connections to organized protest groups within and without the UDF. This evidence does not suggest that the unit was the puppet master of organized protest groups, but intelligence was collected on and shared with a wide array of aboveground formations. Finally, as noted above, this group has the distinction of being one of the longest surviving publicly known underground units. In the late 1980s, the estimated time of survival for infiltrated cadres ran around four to six months.[87] In contrast, the Basil February MK Squad operated for more than two years. A complex tangle of reasons explains the longevity this group, but many of these reasons can be inferred from the vignettes below.

Their trial was the last terrorism trial of the 1980s and ended with the state dropping its case against the accused.[88]

Legendary Performances

In a series of extended interviews over the past three decades, Sue Rabkin provided the most significant description of the underground in the 1970s and 1980s, as told by both an underground cadre and exiled strategist.[89] Consequently, her testimony casts a long shadow over the oral record as presently composed. Noting this significance is important for two reasons. First, she has such an extensive archive of stories and chronological accounts that it is impossible to arrive at a representative summary of her testimony. What follows is a selection of stories from one interview she gave me in May 2008 and a second interview with Wolfie Kodesh, a party stalwart who conducted a series of interviews in 1993.[90] Second, Rabkin served on both sides of the border, first as a cadre and then as a strategist. Likewise, it is sometimes difficult to disaggregate observations drawn from one locale or in one capacity and projected over another. This does not mean this testimony is disorganized; it is simply important to note that her experiences as an underground cadre in Cape Town in the early 1970s are often indexed against her experiences as an exiled strategist in Maputo during the 1980s. This reflexive quality infuses her testimony with a simultaneity: she is interpreting as she is telling and telling as she is interpreting.

The material presented here is limited to her experiences in Cape Town in the early 1970s. Rabkin provided a loose chronology, but the real richness of her testimony lies in the stories she tells. She described this period as the "Dark Ages." Her group was isolated, beholden to the Revolutionary Council in London, and under constant threat of arrest. Jeremy Cronin, a cadre who later joined the unit, implicitly contrasted the underground of the 1970s with the underground of the 1980s.[91] Underground cadres in the 1980s could rely on a fairly extensive network of politically engaged sympathizers who assisted with safe houses, medical treatment, and temporarily caching propaganda and ordinance. For instance, in the mid-1980s, Cronin, then on the run, was able to visit his wife and newborn son after visiting hours because the hospital was staffed by sympathetic doctors and nurses. Cronin also gave the sense of mobility and awareness that contrasted with the immobility and the limited field of view that plagued units in the 1970s.

The sense one gets from Rabkin's testimony is that networks of politically engaged sympathizers, if they existed, were out of reach of this unit, which was under strict orders to avoid any contact that might reveal their political leanings. This was the era before popular and organized protest, when underground work was a lonely, isolating affair that bonded units together in constant theoretical discussions and the intimacies of everyday life.

Their assigned duties were severely curtailed by a number of factors. This was a propaganda unit, directed to reproduce and distribute material authored by the leadership in London. Rabkin noted two frustrations with this top-down arrangement. First, the unit could not produce materials in reaction to events on the ground; it had to wait for material authored by the Revolutionary Council. Because these were loyal, committed party members, on the whole they obeyed these directives, often allowing opportunities for agitation to pass by because of delays in communication with London. This led to periods of "enforced boredom," a phrase I use to describe not inactivity born of laziness but inactivity born of being disciplined but disconnected from distant party leaders. This time was not idle but spent endlessly theorizing revolutionary politics, while enduring a constant fear of arrest. Eventually, the unit grew impatient with these delays and began to write and distribute their own material. When the unit finally struck out on their own, they published *Umsebenzi*—a double-sided sheet that paired an analysis of news on the front page with lessons on secret work on the back page. Tellingly, their lessons on secret work did not come from their formal training in London but rather was drawn from their experiences on the ground in Cape Town. To quote Sue Rabkin, "You learned on the job." Accordingly, when they offered "job training" to others, they did not tear a page from the textbook; they borrowed a page from their notebooks. In turn, their improvisations became an authentic underground document for their readers and lent an aura of authority to secret work derived from improvisation.

But who was reading what they produced? The Rabkins had smuggled an address list of trade unionists, church members, and stalwarts presumably compiled in the years before exile. Sue noted that the unit mailed their cyclostyled pamphlets in the mail, but they had no way of knowing whether anyone actually received them. She speculated that the post office could have easily intercepted the material and burned it. Because they were forbidden contact with any political groups, they literally received no feedback. Therefore, the unit inhabited an insular space, broken only by intermittent contact with the Revolutionary Council in London, and infrequently reproducing material for an unknown number of readers. These limitations meant that everyday life in this unit became primarily the maintenance of appearances through the performance of legends.

Sue provided a cavalcade of rich stories about these performances. The Rabkins lived with David's aunt in a flat beneath her house in Clifton. Their day-to-day task was to maintain the appearance of a young, fashionable, and worldly couple.[92] This meant quietly acquiescing to the willful ignorance that permeated the polite, refined circles they traveled in. Sue was acutely aware of the ever-present oppressive effects of apartheid and, as a committed communist, felt a duty to confront those who turned a blind eye to the situation. However, maintaining her legend meant the outward acceptance of the status quo, even while and inward self-hatred boiled into rage. This directive not to break character took an enormous psychological toll. Every off-color remark, every casual instance of racism, every contentious political point had to be left alone by committed communists maintaining the pretense that they were apolitical, if little bohemian, sophisticates. As Sue noted, "Eventually you learn to dislike yourself, although it might be for a higher cause." At the beginning of her four years, Sue hated guns; by the end of her four years, she wanted to pick up every gun she saw.[93]

In a sense, one can read Sue's stories about legends and disguises as evidence of sublimation. While never "fun" in any sense, her stories do convey at least a satisfaction in her powers of deception, as well as a sense of accomplishment in her specialty in the unit—secret work. This satisfaction was born out of the somewhat unsatisfying work of being the local print shop for a distant Revolutionary Council. Case in point was her story about purchasing a birthday gift for David's uncle Vic. Uncle Vic was the arts editor for *Die Burger*, a man who saw himself as part of the artistic intelligentsia of white society in Cape Town. Accordingly, he saw David and Sue as social assets, as recent arrivals bringing to parochial Cape Town some of the cosmopolitan culture of London. The Rabkins were aware of the uncle's perceptions and needed to live up to the expectations of others by offering a stylish gift befitting their status. This posed a dilemma for underground cadres living on operational funds. Sue stated that they agonized for weeks over the gift.

Eventually, they settled on a little pot of caviar and went to the food section of Stutterfords. Confronted with dozens of different kinds of caviar, Sue turned to David.

> I said to David... "the whole point is we've got to get him the best. You know what the best caviar is; I haven't got a clue." So David stood there, really he was very resourceful, David. And he said to me completely straight-faced, "I think it is beluga." So I said, "How do you know? You've never even had it." And he said, "James Bond eats beluga caviar, and I think Ian Fleming always did his homework."[94]

Sue then stated that they gave Vic the caviar wrapped in gold paper and that he and his guests were duly impressed.[95]

Sue recounted another story that illustrated the subtlety of disguises and their reception by different audiences. Typing two thousand names and addresses was an onerous, time-consuming task that increased the chances of exposure during their brief windows of production.[96] To increase their productivity, Sue located the supplier of an addressograph, which used specially treated plates to mechanically address printed material. With an addressograph, the unit could crank out an edition in a shorter window of time, which was a key improvement because neighbors had to be away from the adjacent apartments in order to operate the cyclostyle machines. But the gains in efficiency had to be weighed against the risks associated with picking up the addressograph and etching plates from the supplier. Such material was closely monitored by security police, and this sort of point of contact could become a breakthrough as investigators honed in on the unit.

Sue disguised herself in a motley mix of accessories and affectations. Calling herself Tina Davis, Sue affected a French accent, took off her wedding ring, and wore a doek and heavy makeup. She avoided buying a wig for fear that the police would take notice of the purchase. Her goal was to look "as nondescript as possible." The crux of the story is contained in two epilogues. First, when Sue was arrested, she was introduced to the whole of the security police as Tina Davis. She later learned that the police had been looking for her alias for two years. For someone who assumed responsibility for secret work within the unit, this successful deception was an enormous source of pride. Second, the Coloured stock clerk who had helped her load the plates at the supplier presumably had the best chance of identifying the defendant as Tina Davis. When he took the stand at her trial, he stated that he could not positively identify Tina Davis as Sue Rabkin. On the stand, this man, as Rabkin quoted him in a Coloured accent, squinted his eyes and stated, "'Maaaybe she is . . . and maaaybe she isn't. . . .'"[97] This dent in the state's case against the accused came not in her ability to fool the stock clerk—he was the audience of a disguise, not a legend—but in her mastery of secret work that allowed for the visual ambiguity that could later be exploited by reluctant state witnesses.

After her description of her arrest, time in jail, and trial, Sue then attempted to sum up the accomplishments of the unit. She called on two stories to summarize their activities. Because the unit was never assured that their printed material reached its intended readership, the true measure of their success was the length of their survival. Survival depended on their mastery of secret work, rendered in performances before an audience of rarified acquaintances and close family. The fulfilled expectations of this audience came in a story that overlapped fashion, disbelief, and legends. Sue prefaced her story by stating that black nail polish was in vogue among "trendy" Capetonians in the mid-1970s. After her capture, one of Sue's acquaintances confided in her father-in-law, "I simply don't believe Sue is a communist. I mean, she wears black nail polish!"[98] To which her father-in-law allegedly retorted, "I find Sue's politics more acceptable than the way she dresses."[99]

Later on, she told a story about footwear. Prior to their first rendezvous with Jeremy Cronin, Sue sent recognition signals to London written in secret ink. Sue told the revolutionary that she would be wearing red satin espadrilles as her signal for the meeting. "Apparently, Dr. Dadoo said to Frank, 'Who is this? What are red satin espadrilles?'" Dadoo, then a ranking member of the Revolutionary Council, had to turn to Frank's wife, Eleanor, who informed him that red satin espadrilles were the "latest style of fashionable shoe."[100] Dadoo's lack of knowledge about current fashion was less about the stodgy unhipness of an older generation of party leaders and more about how far Sue Rabkin had drifted away from standard tradecraft and into her own refashionings of secret work.

With these stories in mind, I asked Sue what sort of fantasies she harbored about underground work. Her answer took these stories in a different direction. Her fantasies did not include playful reminiscences of posing as a socialite; instead, she recalled that her time in Cape Town was "absolutely the worst four years of [her] life."[101] She harbored fantasies about the ANC underground itself, which she initially believed was "an organization which was populated by strong, clear, principled, brave warriors." When the unit repeatedly failed to receive copy from the Revolutionary Council in London, the veil dropped on the transparent, well-functioning machinery they thought they had joined. More skeptical than the others, Sue pressed the matter with Frank on a visit home. She asked Frank about the apparent lack of activity inside the country, aside from their propaganda unit. At the same time, she suggested that if this was the case that the unit be allowed to produce more. Frank gave her a dressing down and said, "Why do you think you are the only unit?" Humiliated by this exchange, Sue returned to Cape Town and said to David and Jeremy, "You know, I'm never doing that again, because he made me feel like such an ass that I'd even asked such a question. That I'd doubted the movement. We are obviously part of a huge network." Six months after Sue was arrested and released, she returned to London and learned that "[they] were indeed the only unit."[102]

Tinker, Tailor, Soldier, Cadre

On a hot, dry afternoon spent in the shade of a community gymnasium, Captain Mahlale, a longtime activist and later underground cadre, described how elements from popular and organized groups were formed into underground protest cells in the early 1980s.[103] The arc of his narrative traced shifts in organization, training, and recruitment during the reconstruction of the underground in Cape Town. Mahlale saw two important shifts in the years after the Soweto uprising but before the Vaal Triangle uprising. First was the creation of a skeletal underground organized in a classic cellular structure. From the early 1980s onward, underground cadres would be placed into groups of no more than five people, with only one cadre in contact with the next cell above or below. This renewal of underground protest groups was born from both inserted exiles and the remains of organized protest groups—primarily student organizations—that were banned or decapitated by the repression after 1976. In this schematic, the division between aboveground and underground organizations should be maintained. The schematic could be interpreted as an application of the M-Plan followed a generic blueprint for a cellular organization that was widely followed in a number of conflicts.[104]

The second shift was in recruitment. Once formed, this nucleus of underground cadres provided political education to a new generation of radicalized youths. These classes allowed cadres to gauge the aptitude and commitment of potential recruits, select and vet potential recruits, and funnel them off to cells. This transmission belt ended in formal oathing and training in combat tactics and the rules of secrecy. Mahlale then gave a long description of the common procedure for arrest and interrogation.[105] If captured, a cadre was bound to uphold one rule: say nothing for twenty-four hours. Holding out allowed others in his cell to note his absence and then go into hiding or leave the country. Mahlale had confidence in these and other rules. If properly applied, the overall integrity of all cells could be maintained after a single arrest. Disregard for the rules and sloppy behavior could lead to multiple arrests that could bring down the entire structure. The most serious threat to the new cellular structure came from informants and agents. He provided a long litany of textbook processes for vetting recruits. In many ways, his account is the bare litany of details that Perrault counterposed against his more literary account.

The procedures described by Mahlale, while instructive and chronological, do not match other testimonies in form, content, or richness of detail. Case in point is testimony provided by Cecyl Esau, which serves as a colorful and instructive counterpoint to more idealized versions.[106] Esau gave me a nearly complete life history that traced his involvement first in student politics, then in UDF structures, and finally, his descent into an underground cell of MK. This chronology is traced above, but across this arc, Esau foregrounds practices of recruitment and training in secret work.

Following his student activism on the UWC campus, his work as a rural recruiter for the UDF, Esau and his associates began to question the utility of nonviolent aboveground organizing. When I asked if this turn to armed struggle generated any debate within his group, Esau abruptly answered no. His answer was a familiar refrain among students-turned-activists-turned-cadres—that "they couldn't continue to go on mobilizing and organizing in the same way." Around the time of the campaign against the tricameral election, this group began to seek out individuals in the know about possible MK contacts. Much of the rest of his testimony dealt with learning about attempting what I would call "the approach" and later how to handle those who tried the approach on his fully formed underground unit.

Marking a departure from Mahlale's account, Esau noted that this group was not actively recruited but rather sought out someone whom they thought had a connection to MK.[107] In order to receive formal training, oath allegiance to a chain of command, and thus become a "real" underground unit, they needed to link up with someone on the inside. They knew that such individuals traveled in their circles, and as the list narrowed, Esau identified the most likely candidate. The way Esau later described the approach—the narrative conventions he deployed, the images he selected, the aura of suspense he conveyed—are at least as important as the mechanical details. Esau had met a man in Victor Verster Prison while briefly imprisoned in 1976. He later served with him on the Student Representative Council at UWC in 1977, and in 1979, this man held a discussion group with several of the members of Esau's future unit. This was a man who was both known and unknown, inconspicuously stood on the periphery of wider networks of student activists and was continually present at the formation of important activist groups. When Esau finally made the approach, he met the man at night and told him of his intentions of forming a unit. The man laughed and then told him, "Let's go for a walk."[108]

Like many testimonies from underground cadres, Esau is not primarily concerned with building a chronology of events. His narrative does dovetail with Mahlale's description of shifts in organization, training, and recruitment on one vital point. In the first years of the 1980s, the exile structures servicing underground units took several casualties after the SADF launched a series of cross-border raids into Lesotho, Botswana, and Mozambique. With several linkages severed and the possibility of mass infiltration in question, internal reconstruction of the underground took a different tack. Instead of recruiting untrained cadres, sending them into exile for formal training, and then returning them wholly formed units, the task was now to insert just a handful of individual cadres from exile who would then conduct the entire training program inside the country. Barring this, recruits could be sent into a neighboring country for crash courses in MCW, here interpreted as handguns, explosives, and the basics of secret work.

As the political commissar of the new unit, Esau was charged with collecting literature for political education and training. For a time, the unit had a connection to the exile structures servicing the Cape from Botswana, but a series of quick arrests and the departure of key individuals severed the link. Prior to this, Esau assembled training materials from whatever could be smuggled into the country, which was then mixed into a bricolage of other sources: the odd copy of *Umsebenzi* or *African Communist*, journalism on contemporary struggles elsewhere, and memoirs and fiction. Esau listened to the January 8 addresses by Oliver Tambo on Radio Freedom, but reception of exile broadcasts in Cape Town was intermittent at best.[109] After the quick departure of key members around Christmas 1984, the severing of the "interlibrary loan" with official exile structures in Botswana, and the infrequency of contact with cadres coming into the country, Esau had to look elsewhere for reading material.

In response, Esau assembled a reading list of fiction and nonfiction to complete his syllabus in secret work. In particular, Esau remembered reading *The Red Orchestra* and the spy novels of John Le Carré to round out his knowledge of secret work. *The Red Orchestra* provided invaluable lessons in how to structure an underground group, while Le Carré, himself once a spy, gave the group a rich repertoire of examples of tradecraft that could easily be translated into the Marxist-Leninist vocabulary of secret work. In an example of centering versus displacement in oral testimony, Esau vigorously maintained that they read these works strictly for content, but one could not help but notice the seepage of stylistics in the examples provided above and below. The worlds created by Le Carré and lived in by Leopold Trepper were places where the worth of an agent or cadre was based on the integrity of their tradecraft or secret work. Agents and cadres properly initiated into this culture of secrecy and precision talked about the quality of one another's work, sometimes to the exclusion of much else. Esau clearly articulated how secret work fit within the overall chain of cause and effect that he believed would collapse the regime. But in a condition where fiction was read as fact and factual accounts were embroidered with fiction, one could easily see how the importance of secret work metastasized within the imaginations of those in the underground.[110]

This was most apparent when Esau's unit, not yet active, began to receive the approach by interested parties. With a wry sense of pride, Esau discussed an approach made at a youth camp he attended at a university in Lenasia in February 1984. Because infiltration is the most pressing threat to an underground unit, such encounters were delicate affairs, full of observation, tacit knowledge, and gesture. At some point, a young man approached Esau and indicated that he wanted to be in the organization. As Esau pointed out, the nuance of his phrasing allowed the approach to continue. Esau recalled, "He said, 'I didn't say you, but that you would know people who know.'" Esau instantly recognized that the man was offering him a safe way to express interest but remain indirect enough to give both men the option to walk away. As Esau read the situation, this was an initial indication that the man was sophisticated enough to handle this kind of work. After the encounter, another member of the unit investigated this man. They asked him to do political discussions and then waited for him to come back. Eventually, they instructed the man to go to a meeting where he would finally meet his MK contact. When the man walked into the meeting, he was flabbergasted to see only Esau sitting there. The man had pictured the MK contact being a taller man without a limp, and there was Esau laughing at the man's surprised look.[111]

Following a successful approach, newly recruited cadres were then asked to conduct a series of low-level operations that served as a sort of practicum in secret work. Core members of the unit were already in the clear by virtue of the fact that they all had known each other for a long time. However, new recruits had to cut their teeth doing propaganda work such as cutting stencils and spray painting slogans around town. These sorts of tasks could gauge the commitment and abilities of new recruits in two ways. First, it tested their ability to select targets and plan and execute a successful operation. In terms of the practical mechanics of transporting material, orchestrating the action, and making a safe getaway, propaganda work differs only in degree from armed actions such as setting a limpet mine. Second, this sort of propaganda work forced the recruit to assume a significant risk for the cause. This is not altogether different than the gerontocracy of "The Circus" in Le Carré, where junior agents did menial clerical duties such as receiving coded calls over dedicated lines and perhaps graduated to the "lamplighters" who arranged safe houses for debriefings, all with the intention of becoming ringmaster. Within underground units, there was a clear division of labor among seasoned veterans and green recruits that mirrored "The Circus."[112] In many ways, this testing the mettle not only served the practical purpose of conscientizing the masses but also reinforced the line between the trained and untrained within the unit. A straight line cannot be drawn between Le Carré's fiction and this sort of proving, but the way Esau positions this story within his narrative—immediately after his discussion of his new syllabus—suggests that while content certainly informed their practice, the stylistics also fed their imagination of the possibilities offered by secret work.

Leaflet Men, Ordinance Men, and "Hitting Back"[113]

About five months into my fieldwork, I made contact with several former members of the Basil February MK Squad as well as one person who recruited several members into the unit. This group is unique in two respects: first, they were one of the longest surviving active underground units; second, they were last in a series of major units uncovered, arrested, and tried in Cape Town in the late 1980s.

My interviewees left a good deal of the events of their experiences and their conflicted subsequent interpretations of these events in the margins of their composed testimonies. What they did provide, and provided in great detail, was the outlines of the practice of underground work, on both the political and military sides of their unusually structured unit. The Basil February MK Squad was unique in that it was an APC, which integrated both military and political branches into a single cellular structure. This is significant because interviewees had a much broader view of a wider range of activities than cadres in other units divided by distinct parallel lines of military and political structures. Accordingly, they were uniquely qualified to comment on the practice of underground work. This sort of testimony is invaluable for breathing life into the thin litany of factual details and chronologies provided in court records. Prosecutions establish the facts of a crime and build a case for conviction; however, an extended dialogue on practice, free from the adversarial constraints of the courtroom and legal rules of evidence, provides a fuller picture of what the underground meant to those who worked within it.

This dialogue on the practice of underground work also captures a very important moment in the history of the underground in Cape Town in the 1980s. As noted above, after 1985 the total number of armed operations within South Africa increased dramatically.[114] This quantitative increase coincided with a qualitative decline. Not only were the armed actions after 1985 smaller in scale and more modest in aims, but the selection of targets also suggested a lack of theoretical clarity. As the struggle lurched toward the negotiating table and away from the seizure of power, what was the purpose of the underground?[115] Several former cadres characterized certain armed operations as retributive—born of anger over cross-border raids and assassinations, rather than some clearly articulated strategic objective.[116] These former cadres often referred to this retributive cycle as "hitting back." Did cadres within the Basil February MK Squad see their practice of underground work as synonymous with hitting back? If so, how did they rationalize this with the sort of proscribed and historicist readings of revolution contained in MCW?

Alan Feldman offers one way of framing this complex field of evidence in his brilliant ethnography of violence during The Troubles in Belfast.[117] Feldman delineates different ethics of violence according to two local categories placed in historical succession: the hardman—old-style toughs beholden to a code of honor bound with ideas of fairness and proper conduct—and the gunman—no-holds-barred killers whose political objectives override socially accepted expectations of decorum and restraint. Among the many distinctions listed by Feldman, one of the most important is his concept of technoethical opposition, which he defines as "the distinction between violence as a performative component of an individual agent and violence as a mechanized component of the gun, in which the human bodies at both ends of the instrument fulfill purely transitive functions."[118] Here, Feldman uses a technoethical opposition to draw out a rubric that distinguishes the individualized violence practiced by hardmen against the autonomous, collective violence practiced by the gunmen of the paramilitaries.

One cannot apply the same rubric to underground units in South Africa, not only because of the localized specificities of its historical succession of formations of violence, but also the specific instruments used by the Basil February MK Squad can reconstruct the technoethical oppositions in their conception of various forms of underground work. The Basil February MK Squad used four basic functions: to print and distribute propaganda leaflets; to transport, stockpile, and distribute firearms, ammunition, and explosives; to conduct armed operation against a variety of targets; and to funnel intelligence about the political situation in the Western Cape to exile structures. The materiality of these four functions focused on three classes of instruments. The first were mechanisms for disseminating propaganda. The most spectacular mechanism was the bucket bomb, a container filled with leaflets and fitted with an explosive charge that when detonated, dispersed its contents into the air. More commonly, leaflets were simply delivered in bulk to organized protest groups who passed well-worn copies hand to hand. The second was ordinance, which comprised the materiel smuggled into the country from exile. This included firearms such as AK-47s and Makarov pistols, ammunition, or limpet mines and grenades. Evidence presented in court showed that cadres in the Basil February MK Squad stockpiled these weapons in secret caches, trained others in their use, and used them in bombings and assassination attempts. The third class is different methods of secret writing, which included invisible inks, photographic equipment used to produce microfilm, and throwaway codes. Court records featured hundreds of pages of decoded notes on intelligence collected on the organized protest groups, observations of police activities, and evaluations of individual underground cadres, all encoded onto strips of microfilm that could be hidden behind postage stamps on posted letters. Arguably, the materiality of these instruments, adapting Feldman's terminology, the "leaflet man," the "ordinance man," or the "microfilm man," is one way of decoding evidence of everyday life captured in testimony on the practice of underground work.[119]

Chris Giffard and Max Ozinsky provided the most significant evidence of these practices. Giffard recruited Ozinsky into the Yengeni-Schreiner unit in 1986. They had met each other while students at UCT and served in a variety of student activist groups on campus. Their first assignment was to produce printed propaganda leaflets for dissemination on the UCT campus and deliver them to organized protest groups elsewhere in Cape Town. After completing this work, they were eventually given additional responsibilities. Both cadres made runs to neighboring states to deliver reports, collect cadres from exile, and transport ordinance. In addition, both received crash courses in firearms and basic MCW.[120] However, Giffard later collected intelligence on different academic units on campus, as well as learned techniques of secret communication that included the microfilm technique described above. Ozinsky moved on to the planning and execution of armed actions and provided a detailed description of an aborted attempt to place a limpet mine at a military hospital in Wynberg in July 1987. Although their narratives on practice are topical rather than chronological, their testimony details their transition from leaflet men into a microfilm man and an ordinance man, respectively. But because both men were part of a unit that integrated political and military structures and received all-round training, they commented on a wide range of practices beyond their ultimate areas of expertise.

What is most interesting about Giffard and Ozinsky's testimony is that by the mid-1980s the leaflet man did not use bucket bombs. The Rabkin unit used bucket bombs with varying degrees of success, but this heavily circumscribed group had no other method of distribution. They were ordered to steer clear of all organized protest groups and were never given instructions to conduct armed activities. These limitations made the bucket bomb not only a practical instrument for distribution but also a spectacle that both announced their presence and sublimated their desire for more aggressive forms of practice. Sue Rabkin noted that her unit could not remember the precise formula for the explosive charges used in bucket bombs, leading to at least one situation where the charged destroyed the leaflets it was intended to disperse. In her view, the destruction of the leaflets was regrettable, but the explosion itself served the purpose of the operation. The means of delivery became an end in itself. A group beholden to party discipline and circumscribed by a hostile environment could take pride in an operation that may not have delivered its payload but at least announced their presence and did so in a way that hinted at their capacity to do more.

What is interesting is that the leaflet men of the Basil February MK Squad did not mention bucket bombs. The absence of bucket bombs is all the more significant given that the state seized a detailed manual on bucket bombs after their arrest. This absence speaks to shifting definitions of underground work in the changed operational environment of the 1980s. Unlike Sue Rabkin, by the 1980s underground had a wide-ranging aboveground distribution network they could rely on. They did not need to cast leaflets to the four winds; well-placed individuals within organized protest groups handed their materials to readers. Further, the Basil February MK Squad, active as it was in armed actions as well as propaganda work, did not need to sublimate its desire to hit back. After all, who needs a bucket bomb when you have limpet mines.

In an article presented as evidence during trial, and perhaps seized as evidence from a residence, Alexander Sibeko wrote in a theoretical treatise on the value of propaganda work: "a well-worn leaflet passes from hand to hand and forms an invisible link between those who read it; an invisible link capable of being concretised into a material force under a given set of circumstances.¹²¹ This is what we mean by the 'qualitative' value of an item of propaganda, be it a leaflet, wall slogan, radio broadcast or clandestine journal." Writing in 1977, Sibeko noted a shift that Giffard confirmed in his testimony on the mid-1980s. The materiality of the leaflet took on a greater importance given the emergence of an aboveground organized protest movement. The leaflet was the primary means that the underground vanguard gave guidance to organized protest groups. To reinforce his point, Sibeko then quotes the author of another *Sechaba* article: "in a situation reminiscent of the terror conditions of Nazi occupied Europe, a single leaflet or slogan daubed on a wall brings hope and inspiration to the oppressed and breathes defiance of the tyrant."¹²²

So the technoethical opposition of the leaflet men shifted with the renewal of armed struggle after 1976, the expansion of organized protest in the early 1980s, and the explosion of popular protest after 1984/85. Someone like Giffard, who disliked guns but saw their necessity for the struggle at large, could print and deliver leaflets while others dealt with planning and executing armed operations. This did not mean Giffard lacked commitment and shirked risk; many leaflet men before him spent years in prison and even died under torture. But after the mid-1980s, there was technoethical opposition between what he did and what other cadres did, even in a unit where political and military activities were integrated.

The experience of ordinance men also demonstrates a shift in technoethical opposition in the mid-1980s. Ozinsky noted that overstretched lines of communication with the exile leadership forced units to do their own targeting and planning. His testimony about one particular aborted operation reveals a wealth of details about the consequences of this break in the chain of command. In July 1987, Ozinsky was instructed to scout out targets at a military base in Wynberg. He reconnoitered three targets within the base: a hospital, the officers' residence, and the barracks. When he returned with this information, his commander instructed him to place limpet mines in the hospital. Ozinsky stated that he could not do it. Ozinsky did not say he would not do it, which would have been grounds for insubordination, but that there was a boundary that prevented him from targeting a hospital. Although security around the base tightened, and thus prevented Ozinsky from completing this operation, he did indicate that in the interim, his target had changed; he intended to place a limpet mine in the stairwell of the officers' residence rather than the hospital. The subtext of his response to a direct order suggests that local commanders and cadres did not always share the same definition of a legitimate target. Further, this seems to coincide with Len Smith's finding that discipline is not something that is assumed but is negotiated in the field.[123]

Moreover, preserving the long-standing ethic of preventing civilian casualties in a time when definitions of legitimate targets expanded and contracted meant some consideration for the technical characteristics of the preferred instrument of the ordinance man—the limpet mine. Limpet mines can be detonated any number of ways, but most operations used timers for detonation. This not only allowed for the placement of the mine well in advance of the explosion, but it also meant that the ordinance man could not anticipate who would or would not be near the mine when it exploded. If the limpet mine was placed in a certain kind of facility, cadres could set the timer to detonate when few would be around—for example, between trains on a train platform or after hours at a courthouse. A review of the list of charges for the Basil February MK Squad reveals that several limpet mines were set but not all of them detonated.[124] Were the timers so imprecise that one could not synchronize separate explosions? If so, were they so imprecise that they allowed enough time for a bomb squad to safely detonate the unexploded mines? Was this a deliberate way to demonstrate the lethal capacity of the unit while limiting the potential for civilian casualties? Were cadres responsible for making these decisions, or were these questions answered by the very materiality of the instrument? Such questions intervene directly with Feldman's assertion that "violence as a mechanized component of the gun."[125] Following this, were the human bodies at both ends of the limpet mine fulfilling purely transitive functions? Such questions of materiality and culpability have also been explored by Sharon Hutchinson among the Nuer, who considered the materiality of weapons in their designation of different categories of death and their concomitant rituals of atonement.[126]

Ozinsky's operation was part of a series of bombings that occurred in late July 1987. The Basil February MK Squad claimed responsibility for the attacks in a letter mailed to several newspapers. The justification for the attacks given in the letter offers a local definition of hitting back derived from the situation in Cape Town during the late 1980s. Taking the name of Basil February, a son of Cape Town and mgwenya killed in Rhodesia during the Wankie Campaign, the authors amplified the stated rationale for the bombings—namely, that "we are paying our last respects to and honoring our late Commander and leader Comrade Cassius Make, Ashley Kriel and all other heroes and martyrs of the struggle."[127] The bombings in late July were not tit-for-tat attacks. These operations did not include eye-for-an-eye assassinations of prominent state agents. However, the wording of the letter suggests that these operations had a retributive function beyond a clear articulation of MCW. The targets suggest a drift away from the stated goal of attacking recognizable agents of the state. In addition to a police station, other targets included gas stations and auto repair shops, certainly not part of the repressive apparatus of the state or even an economic target when placed against the grand blow dealt at the Sasolburg oil storage facility in 1980. Giffard subtly registered his own unease with the wisdom of hitting targets such as gas stations, while Ozinsky himself criticized this drift in a broader critique of strategy and tactics given earlier in his testimony. In Ozinsky's view, the problem of the underground during the 1980s, and perhaps the reason why the armed struggle was ultimately unsuccessful, stemmed from a profound misreading of MCW. He lamented that there was too much emphasis on armed actions for the sake of hitting back and not enough emphasis on infiltrating, subverting, and converting the repressive apparatus of the state. Military work—the penetration of the army, police, and intelligence services—was more often than not defined solely as secret work and armed actions. Regardless of its historicist foundations, MCW was an authoritative blueprint for the erosion of state power through simultaneous organization and infiltration, which had little room for hitting back. As Bill Anderson noted, the uneven exposure to the actual text left middle cadres recruited in the late 1970s with the best definition derived from their memory of advanced training courses in the Soviet Union, rank and file had another version of the definition intuited from what they heard from middle cadres, while older leaders, whose training predated MCW, knew little or nothing of the actual doctrine.[128] All of these competing definitions were several times removed from readings of the actual text. Anderson noted that while notes were smuggled out of Soviet training facilities, these were disseminated as really bad photocopies and were partial and also sometimes derived from memory. The process of assembling these notes into a cobbled-together MCW manual did not begin until late 1988.

How was hitting back expressed in verbatim testimony? Ozinsky gave the most cutting description of the sentiments and equivalencies behind hitting back:

> Ozinsky: In a war situation, we saw ourselves as soldiers. You know, they would kill any MK cadre anywhere. . . . The anger would build up . . . you know? Those were our comrades. We must do something to show that we are surviving. Because there was quite a lot of MK activity in Cape Town. So you known, you would have to one, resist that. But you also have to show the people that even though they have arrested twelve MK people that MK is still here. Within a few days there must be a retaliation, there must be a response. . . .
>
> Davis: I remember seeing in a book of struggle art a graffito, "You ANC Nothing Yet." Do you remember that?
>
> Ozinsky: [laughter] Look, I must tell you if MK hit the Boers anywhere in the country anywhere, anywhere, we used to literally cheer those things. We used to be very happy. Whatever the consequences were. You know? I remember . . . I must tell you I was never one who was strongly opposed to necklaces and those kinds of things; to me, war is war. And the masses must . . . this is . . . [in] people's war the masses must be involved in war. You couldn't tell people that it's OK to shoot someone but not burn them to death. What's the difference? In my mind . . . I'm not saying you must. . . . You must hit the right targets; there is no doubt about it. You cannot just hit indiscriminately. You know if someone is a police informer or police himself or black soldiers. To me, they are soldiers . . . it doesn't matter . . . how you hit them doesn't worry me. As long as you . . . I was very . . . I felt very strongly at the time. . . . We were signatories to the Geneva Convention and trying to avoid civilian casualties, and all those things, there is no doubt about that. But to me, there's no difference between shooting someone and burning them. . . . To me, it doesn't make a difference.[129]

Here, Ozinsky is drawing the technoethical opposition between the leaflet men and ordinance men within an organized underground unit and the gunmen and necklace men who appeared in aboveground popular protests. There are two maneuvers at work here. Ozinsky is drawing underground and popular protest together within the broad semantic field of hitting back. Both "we," meaning those who were formal members of the ANC underground, and "people," meaning those popular protesters aligned with but not formal members of the ANC underground, were all prosecuting the same war. But there is a profound technoethical difference between a soldier in an underground unit and the someone who is a soldier in the army of the crowd. In this formulation, the materiality of instrument, a gun or a petrol-filled tire, matters less because the crowd can positively identify state agents. There is an intimate immediacy to shooting someone or burning someone alive. The presumption Ozinsky holds about the gunman and the necklace man is that because they can see their targets and maybe even know them, they can positively identify them. Thus, the materiality of their instruments means something different and their bodies are less transitory. This immediacy and intimacy is not part of the experience of planting a limpet mine, where the ordinance man can target only general populations by location, rather than identifying an individual state agent by sight. Further, an ordinance man, unlike a gunman or a necklace man, does not watch his target die. The technoethical distinctions between this class of instruments—guns and petrol-filled tires—is markedly different than the technoethical concerns governing the class that includes ordinance like limpet mines.

As Ozinsky concluded, the drift from clear expressions of authorized doctrines of military and combat work became part of the justification for Operation Vula. The overstretched lines of communication between internal underground units and exiled lines of command led to the rustic craftsmanship that distracted from the real work of undermining the repressive apparatus of the state. These distractions signaled a need for the insertion of exiled leaders who claimed ultimate authority for knowing what works.[130] After his departure into exile, Ozinsky was intimately involved in the planning and execution of this operation. Operation Vula was organized into several different regional commands, covering all provinces in the republic. Although Ozinsky was deployed to the Cape, Mac Maharaj noted that planners decided to include the fledgling structure in that region. As Maharaj noted in a recent (auto)biography, Cape Town "was not far enough along" to be included in Operation Vula.

Conclusion

Returning to Perrault's stark juxtaposition of different modes of writing, the written record on Max Ozinsky poses a number of provocative questions. Aside from the extensive interviews referenced above, Ozinsky appears in only two written sources. The first is the arraignment of the Basil February MK Squad delivered in the high court in Cape Town on March 20, 1988. Because Ozinsky evaded arrest, he was not formally charged, but as this arraignment shows, he was known by name and deed. The second source is *Operation Vula*, a memoir by Connie Braam, a Dutch anti-apartheid activist.[131] What follows is a summary of the bare litany of facts taken from the arraignment and a paraphrased summary of a more literate description. The arraignment mentions Ozinsky in two charges:

> During August/September 1987 on the instruction of accused number one [Tony Yengeni] accused two [Jenny Schreiner] and Max Ozinsky traveled to Botswana to assist Mzwandile Vena ... to enter the Republic unlawfully and to transport him to the Western Cape.
>
> During the period 1986 to 1987 accused nine [Chris Giffard] received a number of draft copies of leaflets containing ANC propaganda from accused two [Jenny Schreiner].... Some of these leaflets were distributed on the campus of the University of Cape Town by accused nine [Chris Giffard] and Max Ozinsky.[132]

Ozinsky, like the operators of the Norwegian transmitter, was known but invisible to those hunting for him. He was also part of an "orchestra," and like the Rote Kapelle, this performance was eventually interrupted. Beyond this, there is little evidence of experience captured in court records.

Operation Vula, provides the more literary account, one that is steeped in psychological observation, convincing performance of legends, and celebrations of improvised disguises. Braam is uniquely poised to write this account: not only was she an ANC-aligned anti-apartheid activist, but also prior to this memoir, she authored several works of historical fiction and had extensive ties to theater people, many of whom were recruited for Operation Vula. Likewise, *Operation Vula* is a memoir of her activities as the go-between between Dutch makeup artists and costumiers as much as it is a record of the activities of the cadres themselves. Her group provided the disguises upon which underground legends were built.[133]

Braam describes "Christopher" as "tall and slender with a pale face and a deer's sad eyes" who nevertheless had "something strong and steadfast concealed by the frail exterior." In a long passage, "Christopher" reveals the painful truth about his past to Braam: he lost a relationship to his rigorous devotion to the struggle, a loss that Braam represents as a noble, if psychologically costly, sacrifice. In choosing to frame this sacrifice in this way, Braam taps into a trope of the self-sacrificing cadre that is deeply rooted in genealogies of fictional and nonfictional writings on other struggles, particularly narratives of World War II partisans like Perrault's *The Red Orchestra*.[134]

Here is a place to pause and reconsider Raymond Suttner's concept of "rendering visible." Suttner's study of organizational experience seeks to render visible those aspects of underground life that were overlooked in earlier organizational histories—namely, gender relations, romantic love, and the sacrifice of the personal for the political. Elaborating on Suttner's arguments and pairing them the metaphors of testimony as composition, what is not rendered visible between the factual litany on Ozinsky and the literary account of "Christopher"? What is displaced into the margins? What is placed in plain sight of the habituated eye?

I could provide a line item comparison of these texts with my interview with Ozinsky. However, all these points of interest center on one tendency in Braam's mode of writing. Her struggle history, written as it is in the experiential dimension, composes instances of everyday life within a heroic narrative of good and evil.[135] Operation Vula, maligned in the media as a last-ditch communist plot to seize state power and an operation kept secret from even the highest echelons of the leadership, is clearly an episode due for a historiographical rescue attempt. But is this mode of writing the best vehicle for rescuing these cadres from the "condescension of posterity." Is it not mired in the condescension of eliding complexities evident in testimony the cadres themselves? Her characterization of "Christopher" poses him as the sacrificial victim of a morally pure struggle. Does this characterization displace Ozinsky's evidence of technoethical oppositions implicit in hitting back? Does the gap between "Christopher" and Ozinsky constitute an example of the instability of the subject? Is this instability a problem to be solved or an evidentiary effect worthy of further consideration?

Moving inquiry closer to the mechanics of writing struggle history, Braam's text exhibits a common characteristic of this mode of writing.

Rather than limiting her memoir to a first-person narration, Braam tells her story in a series of dialogue between herself and cadres and among cadres themselves. Where do these snippets of dialogue come from? Her memory? Unreferenced diaries? Out of thin air? What does this novelistic style mean in terms of the status of the text as historical evidence? Can one quote dialogue rendered as evidence? Operation Vula is laced with the "now it can be told" quality of many other struggle histories. Who is doing the telling here, and what are they saying and not saying about the underground?

Whenever people sit down to write a history of the underground and whatever mode of writing they deploy, one must ask how they locate themselves in contemporary debates about the meaning and legacy of the struggle. In my estimation, there are three general positions: the true believers who are the high priests of historicism handed down from on high by Soviet ideologues, the skeptics who took stock of 1989 and saw the underground with a greater level of complexity, and the realists who are the post-apartheid elites who bemusedly recall their misspent youth as heady Marxists. For the true believers, MCW still stands as an operable plan for revolution; for the skeptics, ends of social progress did not justify the means of armed struggle; and for the realists, the past is another country. Testimony from each kind of informant shows evidence of displacement. This chapter hopefully begins the task of retelling the history of everyday life in the underground by curating what a prominent exile derided as "funny stories."[136]

I began my research into the underground with what might seem to some to be a flippant question: do underground cadres ever resurface? One wife of a former cadre told me about how her husband still writes down phone numbers with a deliberately altered digit—a digit he remembers to correct when dialing. Much of my evidence shows that those who performed legends in the underground can sometimes restage them aboveground. In rarer instances, they became prisoners of their legends, either typecast in the role by their adherence to historicist narratives or unable to imagine themselves playing any other role. Connie Braam noted this trap in her account of Dutch perceptions of the underground during World War II, writing, "it was only when they had grown old, and I had grown older too, that I understood that escape and hiding go together with survival and the fear of death, and that it can be easier to go underground than to go back out into the open."[137]

Notes

1. Gilles Perrault, *The Red Orchestra* (New York: Simon & Schuster, 1969), 9–11.
2. Ibid.
3. Philip Bonner, "Fragmentation and Cohesion in the ANC: The First 70 Years," in *One Hundred Years of the ANC: Debating Liberation Histories Today*, ed. Arianna Lissoni et al. (Johannesburg: University of the Witwatersrand Press, 2012), 7. Jon Soske et al., "One Hundred Years of the ANC: Debating Struggle History after Apartheid," in *One Hundred Years of the ANC: Debating Liberation Histories Today*, ed. Arianna Lissoni et al. (Johannesburg: University of the Witwatersrand Press, 2012), 29–53. Raymond Suttner, *The ANC Underground in South Africa, 1950–1976* (Boulder, CO: First Forum Press, 2009), 5. Hilary Sapire and Chris Saunders, "Liberation Struggles in Southern Africa in Context," in *Southern African Liberation Struggles*, ed. Hilary Sapire and Chris Saunders (Cape Town: University of Cape Town Press, 2013), 1–31.
4. Wilmot G. James et al., *The Angry Divide: Social and Economic History of the Western Cape* (Cape Town: David Philip, 1989), 180–92. Cecyl Esau, interview with author, November 14, 2007. James Ngculu, *The Honour to Serve: Recollections of an Umkhonto Soldier* (Cape Town: David Philip, 2009).
5. Belinda Bozzoli, "Experience, History and Culture," in *Town and Countryside in the Transvaal: Capitalist Penetration and Popular Response*, ed. Belinda Bozzoli (Johannesburg: Ravan, 1983), 1–47. Joan Scott, "Evidence of Experience," *Critical Inquiry* 17 (1994): 773–97.
6. Vivian Bickford-Smith, *Ethnic Pride and Racial Prejudice in Victorian Cape Town: Group Identity and Social Practice, 1875–1902* (New York: Cambridge University Press, 1995). This approach has been intuitively taken by veterans themselves in self-published commemorative works and semiofficial publications. Archie Sibeko, *Archie Sibeko's Roll of Honour: Western Cape ANC Comrades* (Bellville: University of the Western Cape, 2006). Oscar Mabuyane, ed., *Umbutho Wesizwe: The African National Congress of the Eastern Cape* (London: Harry's Printers, 2012).
7. Sue Rabkin, interview with author, May 12, 2008. Gertrude Fester, interview with author, January 29, 2008. Brett Myrdal, interview with author, July 2, 2008. Max Ozinsky, interview with author, January 24, 2008. Captain Mahlale, interview with author, January 25, 2008. Jeremy Cronin, interview with author, June 2, 2008. Shirley Gunn, interview with author, January 18, 2008. Cecyl Esau, interview with author, November 14, 2007. Chris Giffard, interview with author, January 30, 2008. Chris Giffard, interview with author, June 14, 2016. Malixoli Hadi, interview with author, January 12, 2008. Kennedy Rampeng, interview with author, December 15, 2007.
8. One could make a reasonable argument that most port cities in Africa, particularly port cities on the Atlantic, shared some basic similarities in economic, social, and political trajectories. In terms of the liberation movements in southern Africa, the obvious case of Luanda comes to mind.

9. Martin Legassick and Gary Minkley, "Recent Trends in the Production of South African History," *Alternation* 5 (1998): 98–129. Leslie Witz and Carolyn Hamilton, "Reaping the Whirlwind: *The Readers Digest Illustrated History of South Africa* and Changing Popular Perceptions of History," *South African Historical Journal* 24 (1991): 185–202. Isabel Hofmeyr, "'Wailing for Purity' Oral Studies in Southern African Studies," *African Studies* 54 (1995): 16–31. Belinda Bozzoli and Peter Delius, "Radical History and South African History," in *History from South Africa: Alternative Visions and Practices*, ed. Joshua Brown (Philadelphia: Temple University Press, 1991): 4–25. Peter Delius, "Thompson's Child or a Relative from the Colonies: A Footnote from a Foot Soldier in South Africa's History Wars, 1970–1990," unpublished conference paper, *History after E. P. Thompson*, November 16, 2015.

10. Frederick Cooper, "Conflict and Connection: Rethinking Colonial African History," *The American Historical Review* 99 (1994): 1516–45.

11. James Wilkinson, *The Intellectual Resistance in Europe* (Cambridge, MA: Harvard University Press, 1981). Allesandro Portelli, *The Order Has Been Carried Out: History, Memory and Meaning of a Nazi Massacre in Rome* (New York: Palgrave Macmillan, 2003). The history of Italian anti-Fascist resistance is but one example of the complexities within this literature. Charles Delzell, "The Italian Anti-Fascist Resistance in Retrospect: Three Decades of Historiography," *The Journal of Modern History* 47 (1975): 66–96.

12. The term most often used by my interviewees to distinguish between armed and unarmed comrades, particularly my interviewees operating in the aboveground structures of the UDF, was "carrying the gun." If one was known as "carrying the gun," it marked you as a literal combatant and, in most instances, a fully oathed and trained member of MK. In practice there was a good degree of operational overlap between the two, as UDF aboveground activists were sometimes asked to house cadres and weapons in their homes or were wittingly or unwittingly transporting weapons across borders and through the country. Still, these individuals are today, as yesterday, very vigilant about claiming the status inferred by the phrase "carrying the gun." My interviewees expressed their self-identifications with dead seriousness, an indicator of the rigidly segmented power of claims-making in remembrances of the armed struggle the post-apartheid present. For example, countless interviewees began their interview by carefully pointing out that they were or were not formally in MK. Claiming historical membership meant the power to activate certain claims in the present, as well as conveying a set of assumptions about the limits of their perspective on the past.

13. This has a lot to do with post-apartheid monumentalization, the monument-industrial complex, and lingering fears of prosecution for human rights violations. None of the interviewees here had these reservations.

14. Howard Barrell's dissertation "Conscripts to Their Age" deals primarily with organizational history of the exile apparatus and the military leadership of MK. Howard Barrell, "Conscripts to Their Age: African National Congress Operational Strategy, 1976–1986" (PhD diss., Oxford University, 1993). Likewise, Jeremy Seekings's *The*

UDF is also an organizational history, albeit of the primarily aboveground formations of the UDF. Jeremy Seekings, *The UDF: A History of the United Democratic Front in South Africa, 1983–1991* (Athens: Ohio University Press, 2000). Madeleine Fullard's thesis, while not an organizational history, is keyed into the organizational dynamics of violence in Cape Town but does so not through experience but through a categorization of types of violence and an exhaustive quantitative survey of statistics on deaths and injuries. Madeleine Fullard, "The State and Political Struggle: Strategies of Repression and Resistance in the Greater Cape Town Area from 1985 to 1989" (MA thesis, University of the Western Cape, 2000).

15. Rachidi Molapo, "Aspects of the South African Youth Experiences in Exile, 1960–1994" (PhD diss., University of the Western Cape, 2005). Lynda von den Steinen, "Experiencing the Armed Struggle: The Soweto Generation and After" (PhD diss., University of Cape Town, 2007). Raymond Suttner, "The Underground Organizational Experience of the ANC-Led Alliance until 1976" (PhD diss., University of the Witwatersrand, 2007). Suttner's dissertation formed the basis of his published monograph. Suttner, *The ANC Underground in South Africa*.

16. E. P. Thompson, *The Making of the English Working Class* (New York: Vintage, 1963), 11.

17. Von den Steinen and Suttner are more explicit about the consequences of this rescue attempt and installation within the pantheon.

18. Molapo's book is about exiles, but insofar as these exiles comprised the underground within South Africa, many of his arguments overlap into the "organizational experience" of the underground as well. Molapo, "Aspects of the South African Youth Experiences in Exile, 1960–1994," 1.

19. Bill Nasson, "The Was, the Is and the What-Might-Have-Been: Political Leadership in Post-Apartheid South Africa," *Journal of African History* 49 (2008): 467–74.

20. Von den Steinen, "Experiencing the Armed Struggle."

21. Herbert Butterfield, *The Whig Interpretation of History* (London: G. Bell, 1931).

22. Ibid., 56. Kenneth Sewell, *Herbert Butterfield and the Interpretation of History* (New York: Palgrave Macmillan, 2005), 32.

23. Sewell, *Herbert Butterfield and the Interpretation of History*, 33.

24. Sewell credits Butterfield with clearing the way for a new historiographical and methodological agenda but finds fault with his replacement of progress with providence and particular modes of writing with process.

25. Translated into English as "how it actually was." E. H. Carr, *What Is History?* (New York: Vintage, 1961), 43.

26. Carlo Ginzburg, *The Cheese and the Worms: The Cosmos of the 16th Century Miller* (Baltimore: Johns Hopkins University Press, 1980).

27. Fullard, "The State and Political Struggle."

28. "Harms Commission of Inquiry Evidence," accessed June 22, 2016 (http://www.historicalpapers.wits.ac.za/?inventory/U/collections&c=AK2300/R/). Independent Board, *Who Lied?: Discussion of the Findings of the Harms Commission of Inquiry Prepared*

by the Independent Board (South Africa: Independent Board of Inquiry into Informal Repression, 1991). "The TRC Report," accessed June 22, 2016 (http://www.justice.gov.za/trc/report/).

29. Gail Gerhart and Clive Glaser, *From Protest to Challenge: Challenge and Victory, 1980–1990, Volume 6* (Bloomington: Indiana University Press, 2010), 31–37. Willie Esterhuyse, *Endgame: Secret Talks and the End of Apartheid* (Cape Town: Tafelberg, 2012), 54.

30. John McCuen, *The Art of Counter-Revolutionary War: The Strategy of Counter-Insurgency* (Harrisburg, PA: Stackpole Books, 1966).

31. "SADF Involvement in the Internal Security Situation in the Republic of South Africa," accessed June 22, 2016 (http://www.justice.gov.za/trc/hrvtrans/submit/sadf.htm). F. W. De Klerk, "Submission to the Truth and the Reconciliation Commission by Mr. FW De Klerk, Leader of the National Party," accessed June 22, 2016 (http://www.justice.gov.za/trc/hrvtrans/submit/np_truth.htm). One illuminating example of the functioning of the NSMS is depicted in Shirley Gunn's account of the Trojan horse massacre. Shirley Gunn, *If Trees Could Speak: The Trojan Horse Story* (Cape Town: Human Rights Media Centre, 2007).

32. Fullard, "The State and Political Struggle."

33. Ibid., 22.

34. Ibid.

35. The epiphenomenality of "armed propaganda" is often explained by former underground cadres as a way of conscientizing and mobilizing the masses. Whether armed propaganda actually accomplished this goal, or remained "a thing that went bump in the night" is a question of continual debate.

36. An oft-rumored but thinly substantiated claim is that one other secret component of underground protest was what I would term "creative fund-raising." Several authors make the claim that high-ranking exiles ran stolen car rackets, smuggled diamonds, and were the premier traffickers of Mandrax in Lusaka. These activities, while anecdotal at this point, appear on the margins of testimony and in a few scant notes in the archive. Ellis and Sechaba note the stolen car rackets, and I heard as much from cadres in the Cape Flats. A perhaps apocryphal story that circulates in Pan-Africanist Congress circles recounts drug smuggling in the context of sourcing local arms. Former African People's Liberation Army cadres recall arriving at a dead drop where they expected to find arms deposited by their exile structures. When they dug up the container supposedly containing the weapons, they instead found bags of Mandrax and a note telling them to sell the drugs and buy arms on the black market within South Africa.

37. This was most evident in Cape Town, particularly among Coloured voters. However, these voter turnout statistics are far from transparent. Was this stay-away part of the heritage of the NEUM's advocacy of noncollaboration, cascading popular enthusiasm for the UDF that was launched at an electrifying assembly in Mitchell's

Plain the year before, or the simple disinterest of an unconvinced body of voters? See Neville Alexander's piece for more on the complexities of noncollaboration in the Cape Province. Neville Alexander, "Non-Collaboration in the Western Cape," in *The Angry Divide: Social and Economic History of the Western Cape*, Wilmot G. James et al. (Cape Town: David Philip, 1989), 180–92. Tom Lodge, "Rebellion: The Turning of the Tide," in *All, Here, and Now: Black Politics in South Africa in the 1980s*, ed. Tom Lodge et al. (New York: Ford Foundation, 1991), 58–64. Seekings, *The UDF*, 91–119.

38. The contradiction between the uptick in operations and downfall of the armed struggle can be explained as a function of diminishing returns. While sheer numbers of attacks ramped up, epic and significant blows like the rocket attack on the Sasolburg oil storage complex in 1980, the detonation of limpet mines in the Koeberg Nuclear Plant in 1982 became few and far between after 1985, while the small-scale operations that typified this period demonstrated a lack of purpose, confusion about targeting, and the splintering of decision making within the exile apparatus. Thula Simpson, "Toyi-Toyi-ing to Freedom: The Endgame in the ANC's Armed Struggle, 1989–1990," *Journal of Southern African Studies* 35 (2009): 507–21.

39. Jacob Dlamini, *Askari: A Story of Collaboration and Betrayal in the Anti-Apartheid Struggle* (Auckland Park: Jacana, 2014).

40. Vladimir Lenin, *What Is to Be Done* (New York: International Publishers, 1902).

41. Cornelius Odendal, Testimony to the Truth and Reconciliation Commission. Catholic Institute for International Relations, *Now Everyone Is Afraid: The Changing Face of Policing in South Africa* (London: Catholic Institute for International Relations, 1988), 20–30.

42. Max Ozinsky, interview with author, January 24, 2008.

43. Herman Stadler, interview with Howard Barrell, date not indicated, Karis Gerhart Collection, Historical Papers Research Archive, Cullen Library, University of the Witwatersrand.

44. Author not indicated, *Military and Combat Work*, ANC Archives, University of Fort Hare.

45. Vladimir Shubin, *The ANC: A View from Moscow* (Bellville: Mayibuye Books, 1999), 311, 329, 345, 350, 381.

46. Raymond Suttner, "Culture(s) of the African National Congress of South Africa: Imprint of Exile Experiences," *Journal of Contemporary African Studies* 21 (2003), 305.

47. Sue Rabkin, interview with author, My 12, 2008. Sue Rabkin, interview with Howard Barrell, November 26, 1990, Karis Gerhart Collection, Historical Papers Research Archive, Cullen Library, University of the Witwatersrand.

48. Sue Rabkin, interview with author, May 12, 2008. Sue Rabkin, interview with Howard Barrell, July 7, 1989, Karis Gerhart Collection, Historical Papers Research Archive, Cullen Library, University of the Witwatersrand. Sue Rabkin interview with Howard Barrell, November 26, 1990, Karis Gerhart Collection, Historical Papers

Research Archive, Cullen Library, University of the Witwatersrand. Sue Rabkin, interview with Howard Barrell, November 27, 1990, Karis Gerhart Collection, Historical Papers Research Archive, Cullen Library, University of the Witwatersrand.

49. Author not indicated, "Military and Combat Work," ANC Archives, University of Fort Hare.

50. But even while elite armed combatants received training in MCW, older focoist strategies held sway among a significant portion of theorists and formed the strategic theory that underwrote a number of campaigns throughout the 1980s. Solly Shoke, interview with Wolfie Kodesh, July 4, 1993, Mayibuye Centre Archives. No author indicated, "Planning for People's War Discussion Document, November 1983," Karis Gerhart Collection, Historical Papers Research Archive, Cullen Library, University of the Witwatersrand. Martin Legassick suggests that the impression that "people's war" replaced focoist concepts is false. He suggests that in practice, the two concepts were indistinguishable and that focoist "detonator theories" informed much of the strategic thinking of the military leadership in the 1980s. Operations that could only be described as focoist persisted, the last significant operation being the failed Ingwavuma operation in late 1987. Martin Legassick, "Armed Struggle in South Africa: Consequences of a Strategy Debate," *Journal of Contemporary African Studies* 21 (2003): 191. Author(s) not indicated, "Typed Version of a Diary Recovered at Ingwavuma on December 14, 1984," Karis Gerhart Collection, Historical Papers Research Archive, Cullen Library, University of the Witwatersrand. Concurrent with this was internal reconstruction and development, a parallel program of underground building and political conscientization that in theory harmonized with armed propaganda but in practice suffered from parallelism, infighting, and disjointedness. Barrell, "Conscripts to Their Age."

51. Cecyl Esau, interview with author, November 14, 2007. Mac Maharaj, interview with Howard Barrell, November 30, 1990, Karis Gerhart Collection, Historical Papers Research Archive, Cullen Library, University of the Witwatersrand. Sue Rabkin, interview with Wolfie Kodesh, March 24, 1993, Mayibuye Centre Archives. Sue Rabkin, interview with author, May 12, 2008. Author(s) not indicated, "Repot [sic] of Commission on Military Training Improvement of Skills and Deployment," date not indicated, Mayibuye Centre Archives. Commission 3, "General Report of the ANC Vanguard Role since 1959," Mayibuye Centre Archives. Bill Anderson, interview with Howard Barrell, April 8, 1991, Historical Papers Research Archive, Cullen Library, University of the Witwatersrand. Max Ozinsky, interview with author, January 24, 2008. Chris Giffard, interview with author, January 30, 2008. Meshack Mochele, interview with Wolfie Kodesh, December 15, 1992, Mayibuye Centre Archives. Ngculu, *The Honour to Serve*.

52. Cecyl Esau, interview with author, November 14, 2007. Sue Rabkin, interview with author, May 12, 2008. Shirley Gunn, interview with author, December 19, 2007.

53. Spencer Hodgson, son of the legendary Jack Hodgson, a founding member of MK and longtime SACP member, remembered seeing banners in Angola proclaiming

in Portuguese that "Marxism-Leninism Will Win Because It Is True." This anecdote preceded a critical, but measured, appraisal of the mentalité of the movement in the 1970s and 1980s. His comment was delivered in a distinctly ironic tone. Spencer Hodgson, interview with author, December 13, 2007. Historicism is also present in debates within the military leadership about the composition of the MCW manual used in training. Mac Maharaj, interview with Howard Barrell, November 30, 1990, Historical Papers Research Archive, Cullen Library, University of the Witwatersrand.

54. This attitude resounds in Howard Barrell's many conversations with Mac Maharaj who believed too much emphasis was placed on military operations. Mac Maharaj, interview with Howard Barrell, November 30, 1990, Karis Gerhart Collection, Historical Papers Research Archive, Cullen Library, University of the Witwatersrand. Mac Maharaj, interview with Howard Barrell, November 20, 1990, Karis Gerhart Collection, Historical Papers Research Archive, Cullen Library, University of the Witwatersrand. Wolfie Kodesh also framed his interviews with struggle veterans as a kind of post mortem of a revolution, although Kodesh himself often defended the compromises made by the leadership during the transition. This is most apparent in his interview with Meshack Mochele. Meshack Mochele, interview with Wolfie Kodesh, December 15, 1992, Mayibuye Centre Archives.

55. Max Ozinsky, interview with author, January 24, 2008.

56. Maharaj suggests that in practical terms "military work" meant acts of violence, known in many testimonies as "hitting back," which he interprets as largely epiphenomenal to developments happening in other quarters of the anti-apartheid struggle. In his view, an orthodox interpretation of military work would be the infiltration of security structures, not direct military operations, at least at an initial stage. "Military work" and "combat work" meant so many different things to so many people that it is difficult to determine precisely what interviewees meant when they referenced either term in interviews. Clues provided in examples of actual operation usually suffice as a marker of one definition over another. This problem of conceptual clarity was not overlooked by underground cadres, who saw the theoretical confusion writ large in the gap between their commands and their operations in the field. Padraig O'Malley, *Shades of Difference: Mac Maharaj and the Struggle for South Africa* (Viking: New York, 2007). See also Howard Barrell's interview with Bill Anderson. Bill Anderson, interview with Howard Barrell, April 8, 1991, Historical Papers Research Archive, Cullen Library, University of the Witwatersrand.

57. Sheila Fitzpatrick, *The Russian Revolution* (New York: Oxford University Press, 1994), 166, 176.

58. An idea that, at least in the 1960s, conflicted wildly with the narratives offered by Castro's "struggle heroes." See Che Guevara's articulation of third world revolutions in *The African Dream*. Cold War alliances aside, Guevara's ideas draw from his representations of the Cuban Revolution would be considered "revisionist" in terms of official Soviet interpretations of the lessons of the Russian Revolution and the

communist partisan warfare in World War II. Ernesto Guevara, *The African Dream: The Diaries of the Revolutionary War in Cuba* (London: Harvill, 2000). Piero Gleijeses, *Conflicting Missions: Havana, Washington and Africa* (Chapel Hill: University of North Carolina Press, 2002), 373–78. Arne Odd Westad, *The Global Cold War* (Cambridge, UK: Cambridge University Press, 2007), 175–80.

59. See literatures on conflict between communist states claiming global revolutionary expertise. The debates grow heated as anticolonial struggles increased in frequency in the 1960s and 1970s. See Westad, *The Global Cold War*. Mac Maharaj claimed that Soviet instructors were not pleased with some of the deviations they saw in a version of MCW penned by military leaders in MK. Mac Maharaj, interview with Howard Barrell, November 20, 1990, Karis Gerhart Collection, Historical Papers Research Archive, Cullen Library, University of the Witwatersrand.

60. Karl Marx, *18th Brumaire of Louis Napoleon* (New York: International Publishers, 1852), 9.

61. Jack Simons, "Novo Catengue Diaries, I and II," Ray and Jack Simons Collection (BC1801), Manuscripts and Archives, University of Cape Town. O'Malley, *Shades of Difference*, 189. Linda Schuster, *A Burning Hunger: One Family's Struggle against Apartheid* (Athens: Ohio University Press, 2004), 97. Mark Gevisser, *Thabo Mbeki: A Dream Deferred* (Johannesburg: Jonathan Ball, 2007), 320. Tom Lodge, "Resistance and Reform, 1973–1994," in *The Cambridge History of South Africa, Volume 2, 1885–1994*, ed. Robert Ross et al. (Cambridge, UK: Cambridge University Press, 2012), 427–29. Hugh Macmillan argues that the ANC was better aware of the situation prior to the uprising than has been previously assumed but strictly maintains that it did not foment the uprising itself. Hugh Macmillan, *The Lusaka Years: The ANC in Exile in Zambia, 1963–1994* (Auckland Park: Jacana, 2013), 112. For an interview that runs wildly against most evidence, see Jacob Zuma, interview with Howard Barrell, August 18, 2008, Karis Gerhart Collection, Historical Papers Research Archive, Cullen Library, University of the Witwatersrand.

62. Even wholly internal organizations such as the UDF led popular protests from behind after the Vaal Triangle uprising. Seekings, *The UDF*, 147.

63. To elaborate on this point, underground cadres active in the 1980s repeat the idea again and again that revolution is not contingent and layered with causes but is a recipe that if properly applied will yield a certain correct result. These two interviews are representative of these attitudes in both the leadership and in the middle ranks. Ronnie Kasrils, interview with Howard Barrell, October 28, 1990, Karis Gerhart Collection, Historical Papers Research Archive, Cullen Library, University of the Witwatersrand. Meshack Mochele, interview with Wolfie Kodesh, December 15, 1992, Mayibuye Centre Archives. Although many exiles and underground cadres are loath to admit this, many "successful" revolutions were as much about being in the right place at the right time as they are about having the tightest organization among other political contenders. Barrell's dissertation, *Conscripts to Their Age*, is a more

sophisticated take on this notion, persuasively suggesting that "the ANC succeeded in spite of itself." Barrell, "Conscripts to Their Age." Howard Barrell, interview with author, November 1, 2007.

64. Author(s) unknown, *Danie Theron Combat School: Basic Tactics of the ANC*, Andrew Masondo Library, South African National Museum of Military History. Hereafter referred to as *Basic Tactics*.

65. Author(s) not indicated, "Report on the Activities of the Natal Machinery during the Period 1983–1988 When It Was under the Command of Muzi Ngwenya Alias Thami Zulu." Provided to author by Stephen Ellis. Bongani Jonas, interview with author, July 12, 2006. Politico-Military Committee, "PMC Organizational Report," Karis Gerhart Collection (microfilm), Center for Research Libraries. Sue Rabkin, interview with Howard Barrell, July 7, 1989, Karis Gerhart Collection, Historical Papers Research Archive, Cullen Library, University of the Witwatersrand. Garth Strachan, interview with Howard Barrell, December 28, 1990, Karis Gerhart Collection, Historical Papers Research Archive, Cullen Library, University of the Witwatersrand.

66. Chris Giffard. "Statement," *State vs. Yengeni and 13 Others*. Supreme Court of South Africa, Cape of Good Hope Provincial Division.

67. Shirley Gunn, interview with author, January 18, 2008. Shirley Gunn, interview with author, December 19, 2007. Shirley Gunn, interview with author, November 20, 2007. Errol Morris describes many of the conceptual issues related to framing and staging photographs and the production of meaning in history. Errol Morris, *Believing Is Seeing: Observations on the Mysteries of Photography* (New York: Penguin, 2011).

68. "Shirley Gunn, Human Rights Violation Hearing Testimony, 7-August-1996," accessed June 23, 2016 (http://www.justice.gov.za/trc/hrvtrans%5Chelder/ct00792.htm). Johan van der Merwe, "Recall of Gen Johan Velde van der Merwe, July 20, 1998," accessed June 23, 2016 (http://www.justice.gov.za/trc/amntrans%5C1998/98072031_pre_cosatu7.htm).

69. Stephen Edwards, *Photography: A Very Short Introduction* (New York: Oxford University Press, 2006), 40–76.

70. John Berger, *Ways of Seeing* (New York: Penguin, 1990).

71. Conversely unhabituated viewers who are not routinized with these conventions do not automatically fix their eyes on the usual intersections and, in certain instances, can see displaced subject encoded in the composition. Shirley Gunn, interview with author, January 18, 2008. Shirley Gunn, interview with author, December 19, 2007. Shirley Gunn, interview with author, November 20, 2007. Christopher Chabris and Daniel Simons, *The Invisible Gorilla: How Our Intuitions Deceive Us* (New York: Harmony, 2007).

72. This social documentary through candid camera is reminiscent of Ruttman's *Berlin: Symphony of a Great City*. *Berlin: Symphony of a Great City*, directed by Walter Ruttman (USA: Fox Film Corporation), DVD.

73. Cecyl Esau, interview with author, November 14, 2007.

74. Ozinsky mentions Le Carré and snippets of microfilmed intelligence reports in Yengeni Trial documents make mention of *The Red Orchestra*. Max Ozinsky, interview with author, January 24, 2008. "Evidence," *State vs. Yengeni and 13 Others*, Supreme Court of South Africa, Cape of Good Hope Provincial Division.

75. Judith Van Allen, conversation with author, April 11, 2010.

76. Which is not to say that underground cadres did not hear rumors or that rumors were not valid sources of knowledge about the activities of other cells.

77. I foreground these particular groups above others for their explanatory power and conceptual richness. At another level, I selected individuals from these groups primarily because I was most confident in my evidence on these individuals. This should not be taken as an implicit hierarchy of the importance of one or another group over others not mentioned here.

78. The exile structure responsible for rebuilding the underground after 1976 was known as Internal Reconstruction and Development. The fact that this name uses the term *reconstruction* seems to imply that this was a new underground rather than the activation of a long dormant but otherwise intact underground.

79. Sue expressed concern about perceptions of marriage in her interview. This concern stems less from her love for David and perhaps more from her desire to be taken seriously as an independent entity within the often chauvinistic culture of the underground. See Pregs Govender for more on chauvinism in the Natal underground. Pregs Govender, *Love and Courage: A Story of Insubordination* (Johannesburg: Jacana, 2007). Raymond Suttner has written at length about gender politics within the movement at large and the underground in particular. Suttner, *The ANC Underground in South Africa*.

80. Sue Rabkin, interview with Wolfie Kodesh, March 24, 1993, Mayibuye Centre Archives.

81. After the 1984 Nkomati Accord between South Africa and Mozambique expelled the majority of known underground MK in Mozambique, the ANC was allowed to keep a skeleton crew of five or six representatives in Maputo. Sue Rabkin was one of those people.

82. Cecyl Esau, interview with author, November 14, 2007. Jama Matakata, *Hills of Hope* (Pietermaritzburg: Nutrend, 2004). Subsequent interviews with others from the Worcester area in other units added context to the background of Esau's unit. Ish Moss, interview with author, September 25, 2007. Kennedy Rampeng, interview with author, December 29, 2007.

83. For more on Ngqungwana's contribution to the underground structures in Cape Town, see his trial record. *State vs. Lizo Bright Ngqungwana and 14 Others*, Supreme Court of South Africa, Cape of Good Hope Provincial Division. See also the unpublished biographical files of the Karis Gerhart collection. "Ngqungwana, Lizo Bright," Karis Gerhart Biographical Files.

84. Chris Giffard, interview with author, January 30, 2008. Max Ozinsky, interview with author, January 24, 2008. Gertrude Fester, interview with author, January 29, 2008. Bongani Jonas, interview with author, July 12, 2006.

85. This was largely a consequence of the merging of political and military structures after the Kabwe Conference in 1985. Despite the shared space, there remained firewalls within units between political and military functions. Chris Giffard, interview with author, June 14, 2016.

86. The unit successfully placed a bomb outside of the magistrate's court in Athlone on June 12, 1987, a gas station on July 19, 1987, detonated a bomb outside an apartment building housing primarily South African Air Force officers, located on Tennant Street in the central business district on July 20, 1987, and bombed a women's restroom in Jan Smuts Airport on July 21, 1987. The propaganda unit printed large amounts of leaflets and pamphlets for several years. These materials were distributed by the propaganda unit themselves but were more widely circulated by cadres on the Cape Flats who distributed them to their end readership. On occasion, the propaganda unit assisted with the transport of weapons and personnel to and from Botswana, Cape Town, and other regional locales.

87. Sue Rabkin, interview with Howard Barrell July 7, 1989, Mayibuye Centre Archives.

88. My interviewees suggested that the state did not so much drop the case out of a lack of evidence but that it lost the "trial within a trial" concerning coerced confessions. Chris Giffard, interview with author, June 14, 2016.

89. In the parlance of the underground, a legend is the combined false biography, physical disguise, and performed persona of an underground cadre. The word has a specificity in the context of secret work that terms like *incognito, alias,* and *secret identity* fail to capture.

90. Sue Rabkin, interview with Wolfie Kodesh, March 24, 1993, Mayibuye Centre Archives. Sue Rabkin, interview with author, May 12, 2008. Additional interviews conducted by Howard Barrell focus on her years working in Maputo. Sue Rabkin, interview with Howard Barrell, July 7, 1989, Karis Gerhart Collection, Historical Papers Research Archive, Cullen Library, University of the Witwatersrand. Sue Rabkin, interview with Howard Barrell, November 26, 1990, Karis Gerhart Collection, Historical Papers Research Archive, Cullen Library, University of the Witwatersrand. Sue Rabkin, interview with Howard Barrell, November 27, 1990, Karis Gerhart Collection, Historical Papers Research Archive, Cullen Library, University of the Witwatersrand.

91. Jeremy Cronin, interview with author, June 2, 2008.

92. Sue Rabkin, interview with author, May 12, 2008.

93. Ibid.

94. Sue Rabkin, interview with Wolfie Kodesh, March 24, 1993, Mayibuye Centre Archives.

95. Rabkin followed this story up with another anecdote about maintaining the impression that they were moneyed sophisticates. Periodically, she would remove "operational funds" from a separate account, flash the wad of bills in front of her family and acquaintances, and then return the money to the same account. In actuality, the Rabkins lived on a shoestring budget. All operational funds went to the purchase of equipment and material for reproducing propaganda. Sue Rabkin, interview with author, May 12, 2008.

96. Sue Rabkin, interview with author, May 12, 2008.

97. Sue Rabkin, interview with Wolfie Kodesh, March 24, 1993. Sue Rabkin, interview with author, May 12, 2008.

98. For more on fashion and the culture of the South African Communist Party, see Gillian Slovo, *Every Secret Thing*. Gillian Slovo, *Every Secret Thing* (New York: Brown, Little, 1997).

99. Sue Rabkin interview with Wolfie Kodesh, March 24, 1993, Mayibuye Centre Archives. Sue Rabkin, interview with author, May 12, 2008.

100. Sue Rabkin interview with Wolfie Kodesh, March 24, 1993.

101. Sue Rabkin, interview with author, May 12, 2008.

102. Sue Rabkin, interview with Wolfie Kodesh, March 24, 1993.

103. Captain Mahlale, interview with author, January 25, 2008.

104. Raymond Suttner and others have made claims about the survival of a functional if dormant underground within South Africa in the lean years following the arrest of the MK high command in 1963. Many of these claims hinge on an analysis of the cellular structure prescribed by the M-Plan. Raymond Suttner, *ANC Underground in South Africa*, 18–59. Bernard Magubane et al., "The Turn to Armed Struggle," in *The Road to Democracy in South Africa, Volume 1 (1960–1970)*, ed. Bernard Magubane (Cape Town: Zebra Press, 2004), 112–17.

105. Captain Mahlale, interview with author, January 25, 2008

106. Cecyl Esau, interview with author, November 14, 2007.

107. This sort of bottom-up approach carried enormous risks, particularly later in the decade when counterinsurgency units posed as MK recruiters. *The Gugulethu Seven*, directed by Lindy Wilson (2007: Wilson Films), VHS. In other parts of the country, agents posing as trainers took would-be recruits to remote areas and had them "practice" with tampered grenades. "Joseph Titus Mazibuko, Human Rights Violation Hearing Testimony, February 4, 1997," accessed June 23, 2016 (http://www.justice.gov.za/trc/hrvtrans%5Cduduza/mazibuko.htm).

108. Cecyl Esau, interview with author, November 14, 2007.

109. Ineke Van Kessel, conversation with author, 2007.

110. Cecyl Esau, interview with author, November 14, 2007.

111. Ibid.

112. "The Circus" is the nickname for Le Carré's fictionalized British intelligence service, based on his experience working for MI6. John Le Carré, *Tinker, Tailor, Soldier, Spy* (New York: Penguin, 2011).

113. The use of the term *men* is used to maintain the analogy with, and valence of, Alan Feldman's term for the "hard men" in the Irish Republican Army. In this context, I use *men* in a gender-neutral sense, given that the Basil February MK Squad was co-led by Jenny Schreiner, four out of the thirteen trialists were women, and women performed as "ordinance men" and "leaflet men" alongside their male comrades.

114. Figures for acts of terrorism abound but are not comprehensive for the entire decade of the 1980s. Pieces of these statistics appear in "Terrorisme in die RSA" a table presented as evidence during the Yengeni trial, also in Tom Lodge's compilation of statistics from the early 1980s, and can be sourced from printouts of police statistics held in the Carter Karis collection at the University of the Witwatersrand. "Terrorisme in die RSA," *State vs. Yengeni and 13 Others*, Supreme Court of South Africa, Cape of Good Hope Provincial Division. Tom Lodge, "Rebellion: Turning of the Tide," in *All, Here, and Now: Black Politics in South Africa in the 1980s*, ed. Bill Nasson and Dan O'Meara (New York: Ford Foundation, 1991), 178. Gregory Houston, "The ANC's Armed Struggle in South Africa," in *The Road to Democracy in South Africa, Volume 4 (1980–1990)*, edited by Gregory Houston (Pretoria: University of South Africa Press, 2010), 1142–68. Houston suggests that the ANC's own accounting of MK actions is inaccurate and primarily drawn from press accounts rather than military documents. "Further Submissions and Responses by the ANC to Questions Raised by the Commission for Truth and Reconciliation, 12 May 1997," accessed June 24, 2016 (http://www.anc.org.za/show.php?id=2645).

115. Although several groups representing business interests and the government made overtures to the ANC in exile beginning in the mid-1980s, the degree to which these overtures were known and discussed in the ranks of MK is an open question. Certainly, those closely following events on the ground had a sense that commitment to the armed struggle was in question. One document of this situation came from a report of a vitriolic meeting held in Zambia in 1989, where the author of the report, Ronnie Kasrils, noted that cadres expressed severe anger that they had not been consulted during negotiations and that deployments were few and far between. The report also reveals that cadres had already been disarmed and were complaining about their lack of security in the townships around Lusaka. Gail Gerhart, conversation with author. Ronnie Kasrils, "Report from Women's Day Meeting at Kaunda Square, August 9, 1989," Historical Papers Research Archive, Cullen Library, University of the Witwatersrand.

116. Captain Mahlale, interview with author, January 25, 2008. "Hitting back" is a constant theme in critiques of the militarism inherent in the way that military structures implemented armed struggle. The most vocal critic of this militarist tendency and the negative impact hitting back had on long-term political mobilization is Mac Maharaj. A range of interviews done by Howard Barrell address the dynamics of retributive violence versus political mobilization. Mac Maharaj, interview with Howard Barrell, November 30, 1990, Karis Gerhart Collection, Historical Papers Research Archive, Cullen Library, University of the Witwatersrand. Mac Maharaj,

interview with Howard Barrell, November 20, 1990, Karis Gerhart Collection, Historical Papers Research Archive, Cullen Library, University of the Witwatersrand. Mac Maharaj, interview with Howard Barrell, February 3, 1991, Karis Gerhart Collection, Historical Papers Research Archive, Cullen Library, University of the Witwatersrand. Mac Maharaj, interview with Howard Barrell, November 19, 1990, Karis Gerhart Collection, Historical Papers Research Archive, Cullen Library, University of the Witwatersrand.

117. Alan Feldman, *Formations of Violence: The Narrative of the Body and Political Terror in Northern Ireland* (Chicago: University of Chicago Press, 1991).

118. Ibid., 52.

119. Interviewees did not use these terms to describe themselves or their work. The operative terms they would use would be political cadres involved in propaganda work and military cadres involved in military work. I adapt Feldman's terminology not to elide their specific terminology, but because it is a useful shorthand that allows me to talk about the theoretical implications of technoethical oppositions that interviewees tacitly understood but did not explicitly express.

120. Ozinsky later attended an advanced course in intelligence in Moscow after he fled for exile when his unit collapsed in 1987. This course no doubt prepared him for his involvement in Operation Vula. Max Ozinsky, interview with author, January 24, 2008.

121. Alexander Sibeko is the nom de plume of Ronnie Kasrils. Alexander Sibeko, "The Underground Voice," *The African Communist* 68 (1977): 48–58.

122. Jethro Ngani, "Voice of Freedom," *Sechaba* 10 (1976): 38–49.

123. Which is not to say discipline in an underground unit should be seen as identical to the French army during World War I. Leonard Smith, *Between Mutiny and Disobedience: The Case of the French Fifth Infantry Division during World War I* (Princeton, NJ: Princeton University Press, 1994). In a command structure that emphasized loyalty to party line as well as discipline, it effected its control through secrecy as much as martial authority. While underground commanders and cadres did not always agree about practice of violence, individual cadres who took a position at variance with the party line were not always as successful as Ozinsky. Anne Mager elaborated on this concept by describing "cooking" or "cooking a line." Cooking a line is a sort of secret collaboration among several individuals interested in ensuring that one member accepts a particular line. It is about working a person over in successive way. Suffice to say, it is not a humane practice by a legitimate authority but a way of enforcing discipline and stamping out free thought. Rank-and-file cadres might have negotiated discipline but were bargaining from a weak position in a decidedly rigged exchange. Anne Kelk Mager, conversation with author, 2008.

124. "List of Charges against Yengeni et al.," *State vs. Yengeni and 13 Others*, Supreme Court of South Africa, Cape of Good Hope Provincial Division.

125. Feldman, *Formations of Violence*, 54.

126. Sharon Hutchinson, *Nuer Dilemmas: Coping with Money, War and the State* (Berkeley: University of California Press, 1996), 103–57.

127. Basil February MK Squad, "Letter to Reporter, 23 July 1987," *State vs. Yengeni and 13 Others*, Supreme Court of South Africa, Cape of Good Hope Provincial Division.

128. Bill Anderson, interview with Howard Barrell, April 8, 1991, Historical Papers Research Archive, Cullen Library, University of the Witwatersrand.

129. Max Ozinsky, interview with author, January 24, 2008.

130. This operation was kept secret not only from the enemy but also from the entire chain of command in exile. Connie Braam, *Operation Vula* (Bellevue: Jacana, 2004), 25. Stephen Ellis, *External Mission: The ANC in Exile, 1960–1990* (Oxford: Oxford University Press, 2013), 233–35. O'Malley, *Shades of Difference*, 239, 259. State agents had so heavily penetrated exile structures that many began to suspect that the high casualty rates were not only due to the efficiency of the state but also due to cadres within the movement betraying a number of operations. Garth Strachan, interview with Howard Barrell, December 28, 1990, Karis Gerhart Collection, Historical Papers Research Archive, Cullen Library, University of the Witwatersrand.

131. Braam, *Operation Vula*.

132. "List of Charges against Yengeni et al.," *State vs. Yengeni and 13 Others*, Supreme Court of South Africa, Cape of Good Hope Provincial Division.

133. Curiously, Ozinsky's face, both incognito and otherwise, graces the cover of *Operation Vula*. However, Braam then conceals his identity with the pseudonym "Christopher." Most peculiarly, Braam finally reveals his identity in the dramatis personae on the last page of her book. Braam, *Operation Vula*, 269.

134. *Operation Vula* bears more than a passing resemblance to books such as *The Red Orchestra*; Braam equated the underground in South Africa with Dutch experiences of Nazi occupation during World War II. In a telling passage, she recalled how her father had hidden from the Nazis in a pit dug out under the floor. Seeking out others for her tasks, she wrote, "I had underestimated the fact that many of my generation, born as I had been under the shadow of war, were quite familiar with ideas like resistance and hiding.' Braam, *Operation Vula*, 29. The degree to which Dutch anti-apartheid activists superimposed these experiences over their understanding of the struggle in South Africa is evident in other material. See material in the Karel Roskam Collection on Anti-Apartheids Beweging Nederland (AABN) support for Radio Freedom. Karel Roskam Collection, Mayibuye Centre Archives.

135. Case in point is her description of "Christopher's" disguises. Braam describes at great length the transformations she affects on "Christopher." She develops three personas for him: a brutishly masculine "Rhodie," a self-centered yuppie, and a Coloured man. Although she spends the least time on the Coloured man, she revels in her construction of the "Rhodie" and the yuppie. Her description of the "Rhodie" persona gives some clues to the moral calculus implicit in her mode of writing: "a Rhodie, one of those whites still reminiscing sentimentally about old Rhodesia. Rough and racist,

and with a completely unfounded conviction of his own superiority which by comparison made all Africans seem the epitome of culture and refinement." To effect this transformation, Braam had "Christopher" watch "*Rambo* One and Two, *First Blood*" to "assimilate the essentials of macho-aggressive behavior." This is an odd choice of films for developing an authentic persona but one that draws a wide circle around who is who in the Manichean constructions of struggle history. Braam, *Operation Vula*, 167, 169–70.

136. I inferred that this informant used "funny" in the sense of the uncanny or peculiar.

137. Braam, *Operation Vula*, 29.

Conclusion: Making the Struggle Concrete; Nationalist Historiography at Freedom Park

THIS BOOK USED EPISODES TO reflect on the ways in which struggle history lays claim over the entire liberation struggle, flattens the armed struggle, and hitches it to a contemporary political project. Looking at the armed struggle through episodes rather than constructing grand narratives with neat beginnings, middles, and ends is one way to reveal the historiographical problems that result when this past is bundled into a nationalist discourse. I have presented alternative ways to understand both these episodes and liberation struggle at large by retracing evidence used before, foregrounding overlooked evidence, and bringing both new and old evidence into view in alternate ways. This concluding chapter begins by stepping outside of the episodic mode to examine how struggle history is made concrete in contemporary memorialization in South Africa. Close readings of the conceptualization of post-apartheid monuments and memorials are useful because they throw issues raised in previous chapters into high relief. Above all else, monuments and memorials are about permanence and memory. Monuments and memorials are attempts to literally and figuratively set narratives about the past in stone. But the inherent instability of the history of the armed struggle and its susceptibility to contestation means its inclusion in monuments threatens to subvert this intended permanence. These problems are most obvious at Freedom Park, the most significant memorial constructed in the post-apartheid era.

Although Freedom Park was originally intended to be a single memorial to victims of human rights violations, it became, as promotions now proclaim, an all-encompassing "one-stop heritage precinct."[1] In its present iteration, Freedom Park eclipses the TRC with a grand epic of national liberation whose chronology extends not just into the recent past but into geologic time itself, locating the founding moment of the South African nation to the emergence of single-celled life fossilized in the Barberton rocks. Centuries of struggles for freedom issue forth from this moment of origin. These struggles for freedom include freedom from natural forces, freedom of consciousness, freedom through technology, freedom from fear of death, among others.[2] Freedom Park presents the liberation struggle as the last and most important struggle. Needless to say, including a largely unsuccessful armed struggle into a "one-stop heritage site" as the capstone of freedom struggles plotted on a geologic time scale proved difficult for planners.

Successful wars of national liberation are part and parcel of what makes nationalist monuments successful both in terms of their emotive impact and in their ability to disseminate a convincing historical narrative that establishes legitimacy of a liberation movement turned ruling party. This is as true in southern Africa as it is elsewhere.[3] However, if the ANC—ever anxious about its credentials as "Africa's slowest liberation movement"—was to take its place among other liberation movements turned ruling parties, how would its showcase monument address its armed struggle, which was anything but linear? How can the history of an army that spent most of its existence in exile be represented as solely part of a national liberation? According to ANC statistics, approximately the same number of combat and noncombat deaths occurred in Angola and South Africa.[4] Do those deaths in Angola count as casualties of a war of national liberation, or at least martyrs for the cause, in the same way as deaths that occurred within South Africa? If so, should the names of those casualties be inscribed in some way? And which national liberation struggle gets to claim them as its own—Angola or South Africa? Is the material and psychological suffering of those who were never deployed and languished in camps a sacrifice to national liberation? If so, what sort of museum exhibit does that story make? Could the history of a war that was fought in secret, on countless different terrains, and executed in any number of different modes of combat be characterized as a single conflict with an overarching character and experience? Could the unresolved complexities of events in this war be retold without resorting to the useful narratives constructed at the time under the guise of armed propaganda? And could the multiple ways the events were remembered and the unresolved meanings of events survive their subordination to the useful histories necessary to construct a convincing nationalist monument? Finally, is it possible to claim the armed struggle as a war of national liberation if it resulted in a negotiated settlement and not a military victory?

Despite its overtly African architectural vocabulary and nods toward the uniqueness of South Africa's post-TRC reconciliation, Freedom Park is a rather generic nationalist monument.[5] The national epic told in its exhibits, memorials, and galleries recounts a familiar litany of nationalist tropes: the projection of the nation into a distant and foggy mythic past, the creation of a pantheon of nationalist heroes to be emulated and the excoriation of enemies of the nation to be reviled, and the sacralization of the nation through quasi-religious ritual. Although Freedom Park is the first major memorial site built in twenty-first-century South Africa, in form and function it follows the modular nationalist model applied throughout the world but here articulated in a self-consciously African architectural vernacular. Following the standard ideological program, Freedom Park extends the temporal boundaries of the nation, in this case by linking the post-apartheid era to the precolonial period and beyond through an essentialized reading of a transhistorical African culture. From there, Freedom Park purports to restore the South African nation to its original state of being by resurrecting precolonial African authenticity from the degradations inflicted by colonialism and apartheid—a ritual of purification and salvation that is a quintessential function of generic nationalist ideologies adapted from the Americas and Europe.

The technologies of memorialization deployed at Freedom Park are similarly borrowed from nationalists elsewhere. These include the inscription of the names of the fallen or celebrated on a cenotaph or wall, an eternal flame set within a reflection pool that memorializes fallen unknown or unnamed heroes, a pantheon that defines heroes of the nation, and a museum of national history rendered in natural history, which plots the development of the nation from the emergence of life itself to the end of the liberation struggle and through the present and beyond.[6] The result is a memorial that retells the history of liberation after liberation as an unapologetic celebration of Africanness—broadly defined in the negative as that which is not non-African. But this celebratory history uses ideas about memorialization and technologies of memorialization that are anything but autochthonous to South Africa. The result is not just a pervasive irony that becomes acutely apparent in memorials and exhibits that reference the armed struggle but a "forced fit" between these ideas and technologies and the archive of the armed struggle.

The conundrum that faced Freedom Park's planners was how to maintain the continuity of this grand epic of national liberation when the liberation war in question did not end in total military victory but a negotiated settlement? The answer provided at Freedom Park is to redefine the armed struggle as a largely symbolic war, whose greatest achievements could only be measured in cultural, not military, terms and only celebrated rather than interrogated. Peculiar transformations of this history follow. At Freedom Park, MK training camps become incubators of cultural expression rather than contested sites of memory and flashpoints of rank-and-file frustrations that later become lodestones of controversy in the post-apartheid era. Armed operations conducted by MK are deemed successful if they energized mass protests in the townships and gave added symbolic weight to the singing of freedom songs and dancing the toyi-toyi, rather than having achieved some appreciable military objective.[7] Finally, the genealogy of the armed struggle is curiously denuded of the adventitious roots that connect it to the underground Communist Party, leaving only a taproot that extends to an overtly African ANC. These reconfigurations of history are a subtle decentering of the long-standing stated objective of the armed struggle: the seizure of state power, which is sublimated into a vaguer set of goals; stiffening the resolve of mass protestors; forcing the hand of the government to negotiate; providing justification for international solidarity; and perhaps most importantly for the purposes at hand, producing great material for songs and dances.

All along the way, the domestication of the history of the armed struggle is reinforced by an unassailable affirmation of African culture, where critique and contestation of this history are muted or neutralized altogether as un-African or colonialist.[8] This remapping is attempted through the exclusion of troublesome narratives, avoidance of specificity and context, and the flattening of the history of a war that progressed in fits and starts and ended without closure. The armed struggle and cultural nationalism are thus imbricated in both a figurative and literal sense. If the tiles that inscribe the names of the fallen on the Wall of Names are removed, rearranged, added to, or subtracted from, then the central memorial loses its structural and conceptual integrity. Remove, rearrange, add, or subtract the narratives that comprise the linear history of the liberation struggle set within the museum as a national epic of cultural restoration and Freedom Park, then it loses its spatial and temporal coherence.

The other side of the equation is that the imported technologies of memorialization—the Wall of Names, the museum of national/natural history, the eternal flame, the reflection pool—are ill suited to adequately capture the complexities of this particular war. Further, the forced fitting of those ill-suited technologies does violence to the complexities of the archive left by that war. The armed struggle was fought across a subcontinent engulfed in separate but interrelated conflicts and was fought by individuals under two and sometimes three assumed names, who collectively comprised an army that was riven with factions and run through with informants and spies. This army engaged in not one mode of combat but several that included a few conventional engagements, many more street battles and gunfights with police, and still more bombings and acts of sabotage calculated less for their military advantages and more as spectacles for public consumption or personal revenge. The archive of this war is further complicated by the secrecy of their opponent, the apartheid state, which generally preferred to fight MK out of public view through its shadow state of security apparatuses. This secrecy left a body of evidence that is far more incomplete, contradictory, and partisan than the conventional wars fought by national armies commanded by states against states, which were more sufficiently memorialized through lists of names organized by more discrete categories of warfare and casualties. In spite of this complexity, in all my research into the conceptualization of Freedom Park, I have yet to come across evidence that anyone questioned the suitability of technologies of memorialization like cenotaphs and eternal flames for a conflict where unstable identities were the norm and the existence of a complete roster of soldiers remains an open question. Rather than letting the archive be the driving force behind conceptualization, the planners of Freedom Park let the cart lead the horse and sought to force this archive into imported memorial conventions. A closer look at the final products of this forced fitting reveals as much about the nature of the conflict itself and the archive it bore as it does about the limits of imported memorial technologies in South Africa.

Read against the episodes described in previous chapters, the history told at Freedom Park appears as a palimpsest, where traces of other stories are still legible beneath the engraving and re-engraving of officially approved African culture and the domestication of the armed struggle. What follows is a close reading of three most important features at Freedom Park: the Isivivane, an outdoor ritual performance space; the Wall of Names, a space for listing the names of the dead to be remembered, the heroes to be celebrated, and everyone else in between; and the //hapo, a museum that explains the anti-apartheid struggle as part of a national liberation struggle that spanned 3.6 billion years. Each of these elements represents attempts to fill all spaces within the history of the liberation struggle with a useful history of uniform consistency and structural integrity. But the rough and uneven contours of the armed struggle left pockets and gaps. These spaces contain the lives and experiences of individual cadres and episodes that refuse linear interpretation and incorporation into useful histories. The faults created by these spaces can be used as points of leverage for prying apart the layers of maneuver and manipulation present in a struggle history laid on thick. This chapter combines a reading of theoretical literature on public heritage and more recent work on the construction and conceptualization of Freedom Park, although my primary source material comes from field notes and photographs taken during two visits to Freedom Park—the first in 2008, when the site was still under construction, to my last in 2015, when most features were complete.[9]

The Sikhumbuto: What's in a Name?

I first visited Freedom Park in March 2008.[10] It is difficult to date the official opening of Freedom Park because the government held several opening ceremonies as individual features were completed over the past fifteen years.[11] At this point and for a long period before and after, the park remained in a liminal state between under construction and open to the public. Initially, gate guards were reluctant to permit me to enter and pointed to ongoing construction and made reference to safety regulations. However, I knew from conversations with other researchers and veterans that many members of the public had already toured the site and that several thousand names had already been added to the Wall of Names, which forms the exterior of the Sikhumbuto, a composite structure that houses a sanctuary and the Gallery of Leaders and is adjacent to a reflection pool featuring an eternal flame, all of which appeared to be complete when I was finally granted permission to enter the park.

I conducted a second visit in May 2015, some two years after the last official opening ceremony, of which there were several.[12] At this point, entry was a simple transaction: purchase a ticket and wait for the golf cart driven by a tour guide that would take me up the koppie. Structures that had not yet been built in 2008 were now open. Foremost among these was the national/natural history museum named the //hapo. A majority of exhibits within the //hapo were populated with artifacts and narrative panels containing thousands of words of text, and video monitors replayed loops of talking head interviews with experts and struggle veterans. At the same time, several hundred artifacts were on display without dates or identification. The Wall of Names appeared to have more tiles with names added, and new organization schemes seemed to be applied to name tiles both new and old. But without access to a database of names, it was nearly impossible to identify new names from old or even calculate how many of the tens of thousands blank tiles on the wall had been engraved with names between visits.

Comparisons between visits yielded a number of important insights. Foremost among them, the sense that the park seemed to be in a state of perpetual becoming. The modularity of buildings and features and the sheer acreage of the site offer planners limitless opportunities for adding features as needs change, although the original cluster of structures is undoubtedly permanent.[13] The core functions of Freedom Park—as a place of historical explanation, a site of remembrance for heroes and victims, and a ritual space for healing and closure—are today more or less fixed in concrete and only movable with the greatest amount of effort and intervention. But as my tour guide on the 2015 visit reminded my group, the remaining empty land on the koppie will allow for more dramatic additions should the present narrative need correction in the future. On this note, he indicated that future plans included another multistory conference center that would feature a larger-than-life statue of Nelson Mandela.[14]

The Wall of Names is the name given to the southern and eastern exterior of the Sikhumbuto, the core cluster of buildings that comprise the main memorial components of Freedom Park. The Wall is 697 meters long and clad with approximately 140,000 tiles, each of which have room for one name and, less frequently, a date of death. Although the criteria for inclusion on the wall are more complicated than they first appear, tour guides and promotional materials suggest that this tiled wall is reserved for the names of those who either died or participated in the liberation struggle. It seems as though names can be added only posthumously, although an individual need not have died during the liberation struggle itself, given that many individuals recently added presumably died of natural causes after the transition. The flexibility of these criteria suggests that this is not only a memorial to fallen martyrs but also a monument containing the names of heroes to be celebrated.

The intended emotional effect of the Wall of Names is reflected in the linear flow of visitors from preceding features. Prior to arriving at the Wall of Names, visitors are presented with the Eternal Flame.[15] What does one borrowed memorial design mean in this context? It represents a catch-all that burns for "heroes and heroines who we will never know."[16] Thus it heralds the problematic way lists of names are deployed on the wall and points to one of the fundamental problems of memorializing the armed struggle and the liberation struggle at large through naming.

The Wall of Names represents a desire for comprehensive memorialization through the inscription of lists of names. Toward this end, Freedom Park employs a research department that verifies names on an ongoing basis. However, the desire for comprehensive verification and memorialization is belied by the fact that many of the histories it references do not easily yield neat and complete lists of names. Foremost among these difficult histories is the armed struggle. The armed struggle was conducted by individuals who were known by their given name by some, by their MK name by others, and a third or fourth name when deployed in the underground.[17] The attachment of multiple names to single individuals is complicated by the compartmentalization of secret knowledge and the fact that the liberation movement was comprised of multiple organizations that were waging an aboveground and underground struggle, in many instances from far afield and under circumstances that did not allow for the record keeping commonly associated with statutory armies. The Eternal Flame burns not only for those "we will never know" but also for those we know by any number of names and those who are lost within the instability inherent in producing lists of names in an army such as MK.

These hints of problems multiply when visitors approach the Wall of Names. Implicit in the very idea of a Wall of Names is having a list of names for the nation to memorialize. However, the Wall of Names contains lists from not just the liberation struggle but seven other earlier conflicts dating back to precolonial conflicts in time immemorial. The sourcing of names from precolonial wars to the present means relying on very different sorts of archives.[18] Setting aside precolonial oral tradition, the colonial archive did not capture precolonial peoples and colonial subjects as individuals in the same way that twentieth-century archives did for the colonized, and the archive left by anti-apartheid groups is not the most reliable or consistent record for sourcing names. The three conflicts with the most comprehensive, accurate, and logically coherent lists of names are from the Anglo-Boer War, World War I, and World War II—conventional wars fought by modern states against modern states. The pairing of conventional conflicts with unnamed precolonial conflicts alongside social and economic institutions such as slavery topped off by the liberation struggle creates a set of jarring juxtapositions that diminishes the seamlessness of the time line that planners of the wall intended to create and the sense of comprehensiveness they desired to project.

These juxtapositions are clear examples of the sedimentation of purposes that is writ large over all of Freedom Park. The TRC report clearly specified that victims of human rights violations should be the focus of a memorial, and that report is the germ of what became the Freedom Park project.[19] However, the commissioners did not provide much guidance in the way of design or conceptualization, aside from a brief discussion of existing models elsewhere.[20] The "Conceptual Framework" document was the first attempt made by the Department of Arts and Culture to define who would and who would not be included in the proposed monument.[21] Here, "victims of conflict" rather than "victims of human rights violations" are the primary subject of Freedom Park.[22] By 2005, Freedom Park promotional materials added yet another layer by attributing the idea for a wall of names to Thabo Mbeki who stated that "it was important for the nation to know who the heroes and heroines were who sacrificed their lives for humanity and freedom."[23] In this version, the creation of pantheons eclipses more somber remembrances of the gross human rights abuses committed during apartheid. TRC victims are still included in this formulation of Freedom Park, but they are certainly overshadowed by a more pressing need to present the nation with its heroes from all its epochs. Presently, the Freedom Park website describes the Wall of Names as a memorial to the "various conflicts that shaped present-day South Africa and remembers those who died during these struggles."[24] Given these expanding and contracting definitions and the complex logical matrices these shifts in definition entail, it comes as little surprise that the Wall of Names became a highly controversial conceptual muddle.

The liberation struggle section of the wall begs the most number of questions about the criteria for inclusion and organization. Who, precisely, is being commemorated on this wall? In some subsections, it is an honor roll of heroes, irrespective of the manner or timing of their death; in others, it is victims of state violence, presumably heroes and non-heroes alike; in still others, like the section devoted to Cuban casualties, it celebrates non–South Africans who fought in other African liberation struggles. Is one criterion for inclusion the manner of a person's death? Cenotaphs dedicated to earlier conflicts such as World War I separate out combat casualties in the trenches from noncombat casualties such as those who drowned when the SS *Mendi* sank after an accidental collision with another ship.[25]

The liberation struggle section equally does not impose a clear-cut spatial division between combat and noncombat casualties. There are places where combat deaths can be inferred, but in others, people who certainly died in combat appear next to those executed by the state, activists murdered in extrajudicial killings by state agents or their proxies, bystanders caught in cross-fire, as well as those who died of natural causes or old age decades after 1994. Instead, a minority of names are grouped here and there according to how they died, while others are grouped according to where they died and a select few by their stature and rank within the struggle.[26] The majority of names, however, appear in no discernable order. My tour guide indicated that this mass block of names were individuals who were involved in the "mass struggle" in some capacity, at some point in time. In this section, political affiliation is not visible although it can be inferred as in the case of certain events such as SADF cross-border raids that specifically targeted ANC facilities. The inclusion of these raids and not others suggests a privileging of ANC history, which lends credence to critics' claims that Freedom Park is really "ANC Park." However, there really is no MK "section" to speak of.[27] Certainly, there are hundreds of MK cadres on the wall, but for the most part, they are included under some other category of service or circumstance of death.

What explains this? "Mass struggle" appears to refer to "mass mobilization," which was part of the "Four Pillars of Struggle" that defined the ANC's strategic formulations in the 1980s.[28] Like all catch-all categories, mass struggle is perhaps best defined in the negative. The mass struggle includes all of those activities that were not part of other pillars such as the armed struggle, the underground, or international solidarity work or connected to any specific event or manner of death.[29] If defined in the positive, it might include efforts at mass mobilization of the kind practiced by the United Democratic Front, which could include, say, trade union work alongside cultural contributions such as writing a protest novel. What this vague definition does in practice is grant the management the ultimate discretion over who can and cannot be included in this subsection. However, it also simplifies our perception of what participation meant. Where do individuals who served in multiple capacities—both military and noncombat, aboveground and underground, as exiled activists and internal protesters—fit? Is there a subtle hierarchy among different forms of struggle that would automatically place these individuals in one section over another? Again, these dilemmas point to the forced fit of lists of names over archival complexities. Neat divisions of labor imposed by listing belie the messy and overlapping roles played by individuals in the liberation struggle.

Enormous attention has been paid to the exclusion of SADF veterans and the inclusion of Cuban veterans in a separate subsection.[30] In many ways, this controversy distracts from a more sensitive and as-yet-unaddressed issue: if Cuban casualties are included as a recognition of international actors who contributed to the liberation struggle, where are the Angolan casualties, either civilian or military? If the Wall of Names allows for the inclusion of nations who struggled in solidarity with the liberation struggle, then surely all casualties incurred in the frontline states throughout southern Africa should be included, given that these countries sacrificed more, by far, for the liberation of South Africa than any non-African power. Given that the Soviet Union was the most generous supporter of the ANC in exile, where are the names of Soviet casualties or their "very influential persons"? If conflicts that occurred during the Cold War are included, then where are the names of South Africans who died during the Korean War, a "police action" conducted under the authority of the United Nations? The answer points to another problem with the forced fitting of imported memorial technologies—the finite space available to memorialize the millions who were impacted in some fashion by the apartheid regime and the struggle against it.

But staying within the bounds of the liberation struggle itself, where are the names of MK cadres who died fighting UNITA in Angola?[31] Does fighting in a civil war in a host country count as a contribution in the same way dying in a pitched battle with police in a township does? At present, MK cadres who died in the Angolan Civil War do not have a subsection. Many may be listed in other subsections, most likely the "mass struggle" subsection, despite the fact that "mass struggle" seems geographically bound to activities within South Africa and by the ANC's own definition excludes combat. As a result of this exclusion, MK casualties in Angola comprise an unacknowledged "fifth pillar" of struggle—the part of the South African armed struggle that was entangled in the internal and external conflicts of other countries.

A straightforward explanation can be offered for their absence. Acknowledging the names of cadres who died in the Angolan Civil War might initiate an uncomfortable public conversation about why MK incurred so many casualties fighting for the liberation of a country other than South Africa.[32] Such a conversation would also raise the related problem of deployment. By the admission of its own leadership, the ANC never developed the internal structures necessary to fully deploy its army. This inability to deploy cadres led to widespread frustration that burst to the surface during the Mkatashinga, a mutiny that occurred in several MK camps in Angola in 1984/85. Opening that issue might raise another even more explosive one: Are the mutinous MK cadres who died in summary executions authorized by ANC military tribunals included anywhere on the Wall of Names? Further, are MK cadres and others labeled as spies and tortured to death before, during, and after mutiny included anywhere on the Wall of Names? Are their torturers and executioners included or excluded? This is the sort of flattening that turns a complicated and circuitous armed struggle into a linear armed struggle that marches forward, inexorably and heroically, from oppression to liberation.

The technology of the Wall of Names also bears the imprint of these uneven attempts to domesticate the armed struggle through listing of names. There is a subtle but telling difference between the liberation struggle wall with its modular tiles and the cenotaphs dedicated to earlier struggles. Individual names on the liberation struggle wall are inscribed on tiles that can be and are removed and rearranged, while the columns of names on the cenotaphs are inscribed on a single tablet that offers no such modification without significant expense or effort. This difference in design and material suggests that the liberation struggle section reflects a greater uncertainty about the stability of official narratives, is more sensitive to prevailing political sensibilities and more vulnerable to criticism from individuals' families than earlier conflicts that are literally and figuratively set in stone. The liberation struggle section of the Wall of Names was clearly designed to accommodate these changes, and changes were certainly made between my visits in 2008 and 2015 although, again, the lack of a publicly accessible database of names and wall coordinates prevents a thorough investigation of these changes.[33]

On that note, initial plans for the Wall of Names included touch-screen displays networked to a database where visitors could search for individual names and find their location on the wall. Those displays appear in the Gallery of Leaders and have been installed at least since my 2008 visit. They were nonfunctional then, and they were still nonfunctional in 2015.[34] Freedom Park management is reluctant or unwilling to make the full list of names public, either citing the fact that verification is a constant process or technical problems with the database files themselves. In 2015, the only way to locate a loved one or fallen comrade was to manually scan the wall which would take hours, if not days, given that seventy-five thousand names were already inscribed. Formal requests for confirmation of individual names are unanswered, deflected, or met with defensiveness.[35] In many ways, the modularity of tiles and the secrecy surrounding the addition and location of names is another attempt to reserve discretion and, perhaps more importantly, conceal changes should alterations need to be made. But these technologies also have more personal consequences: family members and comrades who want the recognition and permanence that they believe a memorial can deliver cannot locate their loved ones without enormous difficulty or the permission and guidance of the management.

Isivivane: The Surrogate Heroes Acre

The Isivivane was the first structure to be completed on Salvokop aside from roadways and earthworks. It is a circular outdoor terrace located down a long concrete path that branches off the main sidewalk that rings the koppie (see figure 8). Originally, the Isivivane was to be the center of the Garden of Remembrance, but at present, it stands alone. The terrace is fitted with eleven upright boulders, nine of which come from each province of South Africa and the remaining two represents the government of South Africa and the international community respectively. Within this circle of stones, several water spigots spray a fine mist that collects at ground level and is lit at night by recessed lighting that provides a spectral glow. Before walking down the path to the terrace, visitors are asked to remove their shoes. Once the tour guide has explained the features of the site, tour groups are instructed to hold hands in a circle around the stones and observe a moment of silent prayer or reflection. Upon their return up the path, tour guides instruct visitors that it is customary to wash their hands in a fountain.

In many ways, the Isivivane serves as a surrogate tomb or heroes acre, which are burial grounds generally reserved for military or political heroes.[36] Various parties made calls for a heroes acre to be built even before the ANC assumed power in 1994. These calls were mainly animated by desires to place South Africa's liberation struggle alongside their counterparts in southern Africa. Zimbabwe and Namibia boast prominent heroes acres, and the absence of one devoted to the South African liberation struggle was glaring to many and galling to some. This was compounded by the fact that previous regimes have built heroes acres throughout South Africa, the first being the reburial of the remains of celebrated Voortrekkers in the late nineteenth century.[37] But Freedom Park's planners did not make a heroes acre a priority despite local pressures and the influential models that planners drew inspiration from, foremost among them Yad Vashem.

In this regard, the Isivivane is a response to these calls for a South African liberation struggle heroes acre, despite the fact that there are no current plans to bury or rebury human remains at Freedom Park. Instead, it is a ritual space infused with generic African "traditions" unmoored from local specificity. What it shares with a heroes acre is a basic ceremonial function: both are places to make communion with the dead and put them to rest. Thus the Isivivane can be seen as a way to avoid contentious questions about the exhumation and reburial of remains of all MK cadres. Although the remains of individual leaders have been reburied elsewhere in South Africa with much official fanfare, the remains of the majority of ordinary cadres remain in place, many outside the country in unmarked graves.[38] Reburial and repatriation also raises another unacknowledged aspect of the armed struggle that does not easily yield to celebratory narratives; according to ANC statistics, an MK cadre stood a roughly equal chance of dying outside South Africa as he or she did of dying within its borders. A conspicuous minority of those deaths also occurred at the hands of the ANC itself, through military tribunals that handed out death sentences to mutineers labeled as informants or agents of the apartheid state.[39] Although officials most often cite the cost and logistical problems associated with repatriation and reburial of ordinary cadres, disinterring bodies also disinters narratives that trouble official accounts of the armed struggle. Official narratives portray an armed struggle that was more efficient and successful than it actually was by emphasizing only successful internal operations and presenting deployment as unproblematic. Disinterring remains within South Africa reinforces that narrative and has occurred several times with much fanfare and ceremony. However, the exhumations of remains buried outside South Africa are infrequent, met with much less publicity, and primarily limited to prominent ANC leaders. The Isivivane answers calls for a heroes acre without creating an actual burial ground that would force a more destabilizing question: how do you explain the many deaths of cadres who fought in conflicts outside of the country they intended to liberate?

The troweling of a generic African spiritualism into the Isivivane plasters over this unruly history.[40] If the bodies of some cadres could not be returned to South Africa, the official logic goes, at least their spirits could come to rest through the performance of culturally appropriate rituals. Significant resources have been poured into public ceremonies held at the Isivivane, with traditional healers hired on retainer. The Freedom Park Trust also funded seventeen ceremonies in seven different countries, including Angola, Zambia, and Tanzania, in an attempt to close the circuit of migration of spirits. Wherever they are held, this highly public ritualization highlights the present-day utility of inscribing African culture over the history of the armed struggle.

One example of this maneuver was the ritual performed in Morogoro, Tanzania, in 2007.[41] At that event, Stella Williams, the traditional healer performing the ritual, called "upon the spirits of Oliver Tambo, Bram Fischer, Moses Kotane, Adelaide Tambo, Mangaliso Sobukwe, Victoria Mxenge and Chris Hani to ensure the safe return of the freedom fighters who died in Tanzania."[42] Thus summoned, the spirits were "fetched" by four individuals who served as symbolic representatives of a mother, father, sister, and brother.

These official rituals inscribe African spiritualism over the cosmopolitanism, secularism, or atheism of many MK cadres and much of the leadership.[43] Although it is difficult to gauge the spiritual beliefs of MK cadres as a whole, training camp schedules did not allot time for worship services, there is scant evidence of rituals at burials in exile aside from the singing of freedom songs such as "Hamba Kahle Mkhonto," and there were no military parades and passing-out ceremonies prefaced by prayer. The closest one gets to spiritualism was the slaughter of an animal prior to the Wankie Campaign, which may have had more to do with boosting morale through a good meal than communication with ancestors. Given this official secularism in the training camps, would cadres recognize these religious rituals as an appropriate commemoration of their military service? What might atheist cadres make of their posthumous enlistment in this sort of pseudo-religious ritualized reburial? Although reactions to these rituals have been mixed, it is safe to say that they are primarily intended to inexpensively and quietly satisfy demands from families rather than to memorialize cadres in a manner that would be consistent with their politics and belief.

A Movable Pantheon: The Gallery of Leaders

The Gallery of Leaders is a crescent-shaped hall that partially shares a wall with the sanctuary located in the Sikhumbuto. During my last visit the gallery stood mostly empty. There are no permanent exhibits installed save for a bank of nonfunctional public computer terminals. The only features that indicate that this is a gallery of leaders are the printed banners emblazoned with the portraits of prominent figures hanging from the ceiling (see figure 9). Those portraits are accompanied by quotes by that individual. Banners have been added and removed at different points in the past, and all banners are removed when the Gallery of Leaders is hired out as an event venue. The only significant change I saw between 2008 and 2015 was the inclusion of a photo exhibit of forced removals hanging in a corner of the gallery on the wall and easels.[44]

The placard at the entrance to the Gallery of Leaders states that it "pays tribute to some of the many people whose leadership qualities and achievements have been pivotal in the struggle for humanity and freedom nationally, continentally and internationally." These individuals were chosen over others because their actions "influenced the course of history" and were "exemplary role models." The Gallery of Leaders has a clear didactic purpose as a place of beatification. Early explanations of the Gallery of Leaders state that visitors to the hall must be "inspired to emulate [these] sacrificial and heroic lives" and impressed with a space that gives a "sense of being unique and exceptional."[45] In 2006, their website included a form for submitting the names of heroes and heroines, but it is unclear how the public was consulted beyond this.[46] A 2009 press release announced the names of those to be included: Cetshwayo, Bram Fischer, Helen Joseph, Moses Kotane, Albert Luthuli, Manthatisi, J. B. Marks, Moshoeshoe, Lilian Ngoyi, Robert Sobukwe, Agostinho Neto, Kwame Nkrumah, Julius Nyerere, and Thomas Sankara.[47] Since then, the banners of individuals on display have been in flux. Currently, only six portraits hang in the gallery: Joseph, Ngoyi, Sobukwe, Neto, Steve Biko, and Che Guevara. Nyerere, Nkrumah, Oliver Tambo, and Christiaan de Wet have appeared and disappeared over the years.[48] My tour guide informed me that management was in the process of creating more permanent exhibits and that more names would be included such as Sekhukhune, John Garang, Amilcar Cabral, Marcus Garvey, Toussaint Louverture, and W. E. B. DuBois.[49]

The shifting nature of the Gallery of Leaders is another example of the modularity and ephemeral quality of many commemorative features at Freedom Park. In terms of the armed struggle, the significance of the Gallery of Leaders lies in who is not present—namely, any member of MK who participated in the armed struggle during exile. Fischer, who was on display in the past but not in 2015, was indeed involved in the sabotage campaign within South Africa in the early 1960s, but this phase of the armed struggle fits neatly within the official history of the armed struggle as purposeful and effective, unlike the troubling decade and a half MK spent in Angola. Fischer and sabotage aside, where are leaders such as Hani and Slovo who played key roles directing the armed struggle from the frontline states in the 1970s and 1980s? Where are cadres such as Barney Molokoane, Solomon Mahlangu, and Basil February who fought in notable operations orchestrated from exile? Why is Oliver Tambo only a temporary presence in the gallery? Tambo assumed the role of acting ANC president in exile, was by default the commander in chief of MK, and was intimately involved in military decision making during exile. However, his banner is on display less regularly than others. Surely, any of these individuals warrant permanent inclusion in a Gallery of Leaders?

The absence of MK figures, puzzling as it may seem, does point to the broader purpose of the Gallery of Leaders. The majority of individuals proposed for inclusion in the Gallery of Leaders suggest that this memorial is about a more recent political agenda that dates to Mbeki's African Renaissance and pursued, albeit with slightly different aims and means, by his successor, Jacob Zuma. In order to place South Africa at the helm of a continent-wide renaissance, its history must be woven back into struggles occurring elsewhere on the continent and into a generic and unified precolonial past. The conceptual frame that allows Garang, de Wet, and Nonqawuse to occupy the same heroic space has little to do with historical coherence or relevance to the South African liberation struggle.[50] Consequently, the Gallery of Leaders need not make reference to the armed struggle to achieve its political aims as a pan-African and transhistorical pantheon. Including the heroes who fought a contested and complicated armed struggle may prove to be more trouble than it is worth if the driving force behind the Gallery of Leaders is a contemporary political agenda that reaches out to Africa and the diaspora through trade deals, peacekeeping, and cultural preservation efforts.

The //hapo: Liberation on a Geologic Time Scale

The //hapo is the interpretive museum that opened at Freedom Park in 2013.[51] Interpretive displays in the foyer inform visitors that the name //*hapo* means "dream" and comes from an aphorism based in the "ancient wisdom of the Khoi and San people" that "A dream is not a dream until it is shared by the entire community."[52] The purpose of this dream made manifest in museum form is to "aim to give expression to a much distorted African voice; that affirms African cultural values and ways of understanding the world and promotes a positive African identity."[53] This expression is broken into seven exhibit spaces, each representing an individual epoch that collectively comprise a chronological narrative which spans 3.6 billion years. Those epochs are titled "Earth," which includes the African creation story that begins with the emergence of single-celled organisms; "Ancestors," which examines African spirituality and the significance of ancestors; "Peopling," which traces the development of early African civilization and highlights precolonial systems of leadership and introduces the slave trade; "Resistance and Colonization," which highlights the generosity of African peoples to European explorers, precolonial indigenous knowledge systems, and colonial conquest; "Industrialization and Urbanization," which highlights the mineral revolution, the exploitation of black labor by mining concerns, and ends with the disenfranchisement of blacks after the Act of Union: "Nationalism and Liberation Struggle," which highlights the difference between exclusive and inclusive nationalisms, spotlights early figures in the ANC, and details the composition of the Freedom Charter; and "Nation Building and Continent Building," which describes the circumstances that led to negotiations, government-sponsored violence, the TRC, the formation of the African Union, and ends with the 2010 World Cup celebrations.[54]

The conceptual frame that supposedly links these epochs together is a constant and evolving struggle for various freedoms, including freedom of consciousness, freedom from death, freedom from natural forces, freedom through technology, freedom for a group to define its own destiny, freedom from exploitation, and freedom of expression.[55] Along the way, visitors are shown short interviews with various experts presented on television displays, numerous placards introducing each epoch and bearing significant amounts of text, and dozens of display cases bearing various artifacts from each historical era that are mostly unaccompanied by an identifier or description (see figure 10). By any measure, this museum is an extraordinarily ambitious project.

Along the way, the narrative is stitched together with statements of national destiny. Accompanied by ancestor spirits, African people emerged from a hoary creation myth. "Their fiery spirit of resistance continued to burn" through the centuries, despite colonization and the disruption of their culture, which "further ignited their fight to be free and decide their own destiny." Despite the dislocations caused by industrialization, the people "never gave up the struggle to be free from the exploitation that governed their lives." When government silenced their calls for inclusive nationalism, "their desire for freedom grew even stronger." Then the 1976 uprising "marked the start of a tide of mass resistance and political energy that could not be stopped." The state of emergency that followed could not "blunt the resilience and determination of the masses to continue until they were victorious," even though state-sponsored violence threatened to derail the negotiations, "the will to succeed prevailed," and finally, "after years of isolation, a liberated South Africa was integrated with the other independent African states that had stood united in their resistance to colonialism." From the moment the primordial African man stepped forth from the reeds, he was set on a singular path of successive struggles against the elements, colonization, industrialization, segregation, and apartheid to take his rightful place as a South African among the African nations of the world.[56]

Cynthia Kros suggests the drive to trace the birth of the nation 3.6 billion years ago to the present is an attempt to evoke solemnity by creating an illusory history that overlooks the "multiple forms of heterogeneity, conflict, struggle to the death and unpredictable evolutionary paths that have been accomplished mostly through mutation and accident."[57] The nation is depicted as having a single genealogy, extending solely from an African taproot set in a harmonious communal precolonial cultural and social order presided over by benevolent kings and chiefs. The //hapo connects the past and the present by tracing a patrimonial heritage that resounds through every epoch to the present day. Before colonization, generous and friendly Africans worked the land held in common by a benevolent aristocracy of dikgosi and bound by a primordial cultural definition of leadership. As Africans urbanized during industrialization, they longed to return to this halcyon precolonial order. Exhibits on the liberation struggle reproduce this historical continuity. Wise and benevolent leaders of the liberation struggle led the undifferentiated and anonymous masses to freedom.

This imperative to present a parallel between patrimonial past and present has important consequences for the way the armed struggle is interpreted. Culturally inscribed politics is the thread that extends across generations. Consequently, culture, not close readings of history, best explains the history of the liberation struggle and the armed struggle within it. Culture is constantly emphasized as the weapon of the struggle, rather than actual weapons being the weapons of the struggle. Training camps become rehearsal venues for cultural groups such as Amandla. Military training and the lived experience of cadres in those camps are not examined in close detail. The armed struggle is reduced to a largely symbolic role, as the site of production of freedom songs, toyi-toyi, and legends that motivated internal protest and external solidarity. What is missing is any sustained account of the armed struggle being prosecuted as a war and its participants as soldiers rather than performers and artists.

Conclusion

Despite its overtly African architectural vocabulary and nods to precolonial culture, Freedom Park remains a fairly generic nationalist memorial modelled after those found in Europe and North America. Freedom Park's purpose is to uphold the nationalist narrative put forth by the ANC, and it fulfills this purpose above all else. Incorporating the armed struggle into exhibits and memorials threatens this function by introducing narratives that are too messy to fit within the confines of the history that Freedom Park is supposed to maintain. Where the armed struggle is permitted to make an appearance, it must be presented in tightly choreographed routines that must closely conform to the nationalist epic on display.

A good example of this choreography comes from a recent event held at Freedom Park. In July 2015, Michael Masutha, the Minister of Justice and Correctional Services, returned the newly discovered remains of 10 MK cadres to their families in a memorial service.[58] Aside from speeches by Masutha and Kebby Maphatsoe, the deputy director of the Department of Military Veterans and chairperson of the Umkhonto we Sizwe Veterans Association (MKMVA), the service featured soldiers in camouflage fatigues acting as pallbearers who later closed out the ceremony with freedom songs and toyi-toying.[59] Eight of the ten deceased were identified specifically as MK cadres who died in separate operations within South Africa or on its borders. However, two of the ten, Corlett Lolo Sono and Siboniso Shabalala, were not identified as MK cadres but as youth activists, or couriers, working with MK at the time of their deaths.[60] TRC testimony revealed that Sono and Shabalala had transported cached ammunition and munitions for MK cadres operating in the area and had collected valuable intelligence by keeping watch over their neighborhood. In addition, Sono came from a family deeply imbricated in the armed struggle; his father sheltered at least one MK cadre in the family home and his cousin was himself an MK commander.[61] Sono and Shabalala's deaths were categorically different from the deaths of the other cadres honored that day. Both were allegedly killed by members of the Mandela United Football Club, the bodyguard unit that was formed, ostensibly, to protect Winnie Madikizela-Mandela, but that was later implicated in a number of suspicious deaths in the late 1980s. Testimony to the TRC revealed that elements within the Mandela United Football Club accused Sono and Shabalala of being spies, and held them responsible for the ambush of two MK cadres. These accusations were levied before Sono and Shabalala disappeared in November 1988.[62] Their remains were only discovered when an overlooked mortuary report was discovered in 2013. Following this discovery the National Prosecuting Authority's (NPA) Missing Persons Unit conducted a much publicized exhumation in a pauper's grave in Avalon Cemetery in Soweto.[63]

Given the circumstances and nature of their deaths, why would organizers of the ceremony include Sono and Shabalala with the eight other MK cadres? After all, their deaths were at the hands of the liberation movement, not the apartheid government, and their murder raises all of the specters that continually haunt the sort of simplistic narratives on display at Freedom Park. Placing them side by side more easily as incorporated heroes of the struggle creates a jarring juxtaposition that threatens to upset the meanings that official reburial and repatriation ceremonies are intended to reinforce. Although we can only speculate about the reasons behind their inclusion, one strong possibility may be that their inclusion was a compromise intended to once again put to rest a very public controversy that had submerged and resurfaced at least three times over three decades and was covered by the domestic and international press.[64] When the bodies were discovered there was speculation that the NPA might charge Winnie Madikizela-Mandela with their murder. If the NPA charged Madikizela-Mandela others could also be implicated, which would have ultimately led to a series of embarrassing trials and more negative press coverage. The inclusion of Sono and Shabalala may best be interpreted as a preemptive maneuver that gave the two some sort of recognition, placated their long aggrieved families, and thwarted any public accusation of a government cover-up. That said, while inclusion in the ceremony may warrant a mention of their names, the barest quantum of recognition given at Freedom Park, it comes at the cost of a detailed account of their stories. In this case, the price of admission to the Gallery of Leaders was the naming of Sono and Shabalala without an honest reckoning of a more complicated history and their place within it.

To be sure, Masutha and Maphatsoe did not delve into the murky circumstances surrounding these deaths during their remarks, even while they recognized Sono and Shabalala's service.[65] Instead, Masutha chose to foreground the story of two other MK cadres who died more typical deaths at the hands of the SADF. These two stories were served up as emblematic examples of the entire group's collective sacrifice to the nation. This foregrounding creates a synecdoche that deliberately bypasses the circumstances that both differentiate Sono and Shabalala from the rest of the group and trouble the nationalist narrative both Masutha and Maphatsoe are charged with upholding. In doing so, all sorts of questions are removed from consideration. Did those who died at the hands of the liberation movement, however defined, make the same sort of sacrifice as those who were killed in combat with the apartheid state? If not, what is the status of their deaths and how should they be remembered? Further, are individuals who never "carried the gun" but died in service to the armed struggle due the same honor and respect as formally inducted MK cadres who died in combat?[66] Any complete appraisal of the 'struggles within the struggle' provides uncomfortable answers to these questions, because a more inclusive and complex history of the armed struggle would doubtlessly blur the boundaries between heroes and villains, victims and perpetrators, and veterans and civilians that are supposed to order the nationalist narrative on display at Freedom Park.

Masutha ended his homily that afternoon with a quote from Shakespeare's *Julius Caesar*. Specifically, he quoted Antony's reaction to viewing Caesar's body immediately after his murder: "O mighty Caesar! Dost thou lie so low? Are all thy conquests, glories, triumphs, spoils shrunk to this little measure? Fare thee well."[67]

How might we interpret the inclusion of this quote? Could it be that Masutha may have deployed it as the sort of learned window dressing that closes out many official speeches? He could have casually plucked it from *Bartlett's Familiar Quotations* or another compendium while searching for a convenient way to end his speech with a bit of profundity and a touch of class. But might this quote have been received as a deliberate and even subversive way to delicately acknowledge that what could not be said that day, as well as a nod to the reasons behind that enforced silence? The way African elites use Shakespeare in private conversation and public life has too broad a history to adequately describe here, but it is entirely plausible that someone listening to this speech, or more likely reading it later, would recognize the veiled message it was intended to send.[68] The quotation comes from act three where Antony, fearing for his life after the assassination, ingratiates himself to Brutus and his coconspirators by acknowledging that even though he was enormously loyal to Caesar when he was alive, he would cause them no trouble after his death. With this pledge of obedience, Brutus later allows Antony to speak at Caesar's funeral on the condition that he not arouse popular discontent by publicly castigating the conspirators or overly praising his deceased friend. Antony repays Brutus in bad faith by issuing his famed *recusatio* at the funeral, where he disingenuously states that he "[came] not to praise Caesar but to bury him" and then precedes to praise him anyway by listing his praiseworthy traits and accomplishments by saying he was not going to talk about this particular one or that particular one.[69]

Antony's sly acknowledgment of the limits placed on his speech and the brilliance of his rhetorical strategy of saying things without saying them could not go unnoticed by an audience member with knowledge of both the play and Sono and Shabalala's fate. Intentional or not, this quote signals to many what many in positions of power are unwilling or unable to acknowledge about Sono and Shabalala. The reference resonates with informed audiences who are aware that there is more to be said about this history by those who are willing, bold, and sympathetic. We are left with a supremely ironic scene at Freedom Park: the veneration of heroes whose exploits and fate cannot be recounted in the gallery built to honor them. This is the nationalist narrative of the armed struggle at work.

Notes

1. The final report of the TRC makes recommendations for symbolic reparations that include "national day of remembrance and reconciliation, erection of memorials and monuments, and the development of museums." Truth and Reconciliation Commission of South Africa, *Truth and Reconciliation of South Africa Report, Volume 2* (New York: Palgrave Macmillan, 2001). Department of Arts and Culture, Legacy Committee, "Portfolio of Legacy Projects: Discussion Document." Nelson Mandela, "Address by President Nelson Mandela at Freedom Day Celebrations, Umtata," accessed June 24, 2016 (http://www.mandela.gov.za/mandela_speeches/1999/990427_freedomday.htm). Education and Recreation Select Committee, "Joint Meeting, 12 November 2002,

Freedom Park: Briefing," accessed June 24, 2016 (https://pmg.org.za/committee-meeting/2007/). Sakhela Buhlungu et al., *State of the Nation: South Africa 2007* (Cape Town: HSRC Press, 2007), 279. I made extensive use of archived versions of Freedom Park's website archived on The Wayback Machine. The date of the archived version appears after the title, prior to the accessed date. Freedom Park. "About Us (4-3-2006)," accessed June 24, 2016 (https://web.archive.org/web/20050403223910/http://www.freedompark.co.za/aboutus.html).

2. Freedom Park, author's field notes, June 7, 2015.

3. Norma Krieger, *Guerrilla Veterans in Post-War Zimbabwe: Symbolic and Violent Politics, 1980–1987* (Cambridge: Cambridge University Press, 2003). Reinhart Kössler, "Facing a Fragmented Past: Memory, Culture and Politics in Namibia," *Journal of Southern African Studies* 33 (2007): 361–82. Reuben Makayiko Chirambo, "'A Monument to a Tyrant,' or Reconstructed Nationalist Memories of the Father and Founder of the Malawi Nation, Dr. H. K. Banda?" *Africa Today* 56 (2010): 2–21.

4. See Appendix B: ANC/MK Deaths in Angola by Category, Appendix C: ANC/MK Combat Deaths by Country, Appendix D: ANC/MK Combat Deaths by Country. These figures were compiled from two sources: the list of deaths provided at the ANC's website and a separate list provided at South African History Online. I combined the data and validated the list by eliminating duplicate entries. These figures are undoubtedly incomplete. The list of names included in the final report of the TRC is not categorized by political membership and/or the manner of death, making it difficult to extract further data on ANC/MK combat and/or noncombat deaths. I requested access to the database of names compiled by the research staff at Freedom Park but was informed that temporary technical problems have made the database inaccessible to outside researchers. Freedom Park research unit staff have not responded to two subsequent requests.

5. Sabine Marschall, "Landscape of Memory," accessed August 12, 2015 (https://openaccess.leidenuniv.nl/handle/1887/18536). Jonathan Alfred Noble, *African Identity in Post-Apartheid Public Architecture* (Burlington, VT: Ashgate, 2011), 213–39.

6. The irony of using a natural-cum-national history museum to tell the story of liberation from colonialism and apartheid is painfully apparent when one takes into account that such museums were colonial institutions par excellence and an important part of the repressive ideological apparatus that undergird colonialism. The presence of a quintessentially colonial institution in a park devoted to freedom accentuates the ambient irony of Freedom Park. This redeployment of a colonial classificatory grid is not unique to post-apartheid South African nationalism, but it impacts the reception of exhibits and artifacts related to anticolonial and anti-apartheid struggles. Benedict Anderson, *Imagined Communities: Reflections on the Origins and Spread of Nationalism* (London: Verso, 2003), 178–85.

7. Thula Simpson details the careful stage management of images of the armed struggle by the ANC leadership during the transition to negotiations. Thula Simpson, "Toyi-Toyi-ing to Freedom: The Endgame in the ANC's Armed Struggle, 1989–1990," *Journal of Southern African Studies* 35 (2009): 507–21.

8. Cynthia Kros, "A New Monumentalism?: From Public Art to Freedom Park," *Image and Text* 19 (2012): 34–51. Noble, *African Identity in Post-Apartheid Public Architecture*, 224, 232–37.

9. A growing literature discusses the conceptualization and construction of Freedom Park at length. Pieter Labuschagne, "Monument(al) Meaning Making in the 'New' South Africa: Freedom Park as a Symbol of a New Identity and Freedom?," *South African Journal of Art History* 25 (2010): 112–24. Heather Hughes, "Rainbow, Renaissance, Tribes and Townships: Tourism and Heritage in South Africa since 1994," in *State of the Nation: South Africa 2007*, ed. Sakhela Buhlungu et al (Cape Town: HSRC Press, 2007), 266–88. Noble, *African Identity in Post-Apartheid Public Architecture*. The critical literature on heritage in South Africa is too voluminous to list here. However, the following pieces provided much inspiration for the theoretical perspectives presented in this chapter. Veronique Rioufol, "Behind Telling: Post-Apartheid Representations of Robben Island's Past," *Kronos* 26 (2000): 22–41. Leslie Witz, *Apartheid's Festival: Contesting South Africa's National Pasts* (Bloomington: Indiana University Press, 2003). Julia Wells, "'Are We Nation-Building Yet?': The Role of Oral Historians in Documenting the Transition Out of Apartheid," in *Oral History in a Wounded Country: Interactive Interviewing in South Africa*, ed. Philippe Denis and Radikobo Ntsimane (Scottsville: University of KwaZulu-Natal Press, 2008), 22–42. Tim Nuttall and John Wright, "Probing the Predicaments of Academic History in Contemporary South Africa," *South African Historical Journal* 42 (2000): 26–48. Ciraj Rassool, "The Rise of Heritage and the Reconstitution of History in South Africa," *Kronos* 26 (2000): 1–21. Sifiso Ndlovu, "'He Did What Any Other Person in His Position Would Have Done to Fight the Forces of Invasion and Disruption': Africans, the Land and Contending Images of King Dingane ('the Patriot') in the Twentieth Century, 1916–1950s," *South African Historical Journal* 38 (1998): 99–143. Jennifer Robinson, "Apartheid Subjects and Postcolonialism: Native Administrators in Port Elizabeth, 1945–1970," unpublished conference paper, Wits History Workshop, July 13–15, 1994. Robyn Autry, "Doing Memory in Public: Post-Apartheid Memorial Space as an Activist Project," in *Memory and Post-War Memorials: Confronting the Violence of the Past*, ed. Marc Silberman and Florance Vatan (New York: Palgrave Macmillan, 2013), 137–54. Carolyn Hamilton, "Emerging Themes and Trends, Opportunities and Challenges," accessed August 3, 2015 (http://www.saha.org.za/resources/docs/PDF/Publications/MHPI.pdf).

10. Freedom Park, author's field notes, March 8, 2008.

11. Bruce Venter, "Park Honours Those Who 'Outsoared the Shadow," accessed June 24, 2016 (http://www.iol.co.za/news/south-africa/park-honours-those-who-outsoared-the-shadow-207986). Freedom Park Trust, "Press Release: Freedom Park Hands Over Site for Construction, 6-23-2003." Jacob Zuma, "Address by Deputy President Jacob Zuma at the Launch of the Freedom Park Trust, 6-1-2000," accessed June 24, 2016 (http://www.polity.org.za/polity/govdocs/speeches/2000/sp0601.html). Motlanthe,

Kgalema, "Address by Deputy President Kgalema Motlanthe on the Occasion of the Official Opening of the Freedom Park //hapo Museum, Pretoria, 4-22-2013," accessed June 24, 2016 (http://www.thepresidency.gov.za/pebble.asp?relid=15286&t=79).

12. Freedom Park, author's field notes, June 7, 2015.

13. Hundreds, if not thousands, of prehistoric, precolonial, colonial, and postapartheid artifacts appear in glass cases in the //hapo. The vast majority appear without individual placards providing identifiers, dates, and historical significance. In many ways, these artifacts presented without context are the empty modifiers that allow room for maneuver as the narrative of Freedom Park is no doubt adjusted in the future.

14. The Gallery of Leaders does not currently feature full life-size statues of leaders, although there are plans to install permanent statues after a design competition. How abstract or how representative those statues may be will be up to the artists who win the tender for individual figures. A multimillion-rand statue garden is currently under construction at a separate site a few miles from Freedom Park. This park, which is under separate management, will feature several hundred statues of prominent struggle heroes. The absence of representational statuary at Freedom Park is a curious departure from standard nationalist memorial conventions, despite the fact that the rest of the park follows closely the conventional playbook. Vusi Mahanjana, "Go Ahead, Honor Our Heroes," *Weekly Mail and Guardian*, October 9, 2003. Matthew Partridge, "Dali Tambo's R600m Struggle Theme Park," accessed June 24, 2016 (http://www.financialmail.co.za/features/2014/05/02/dali-tambo-s-r600m-struggle-theme-park).

15. In addition, a projection screen can be lowered behind the eternal flame for events such as a viewing party for the 2010 World Cup. The pool was, however, drained for a performance of traditional African dancing during a reception for the Miss World Contestants in 2009. It is unclear if the eternal flame is extinguished during these projections. Freedom Park, author's field notes, June 7, 2015. Lynley Donnelly and Lucky Sindane, "Jo'burg's Miss World Debacle," *Mail and Guardian*, December 11, 2009.

16. Freedom Park, author's field notes, June 7, 2015.

17. MK names were nom de guerres used by cadres in camps to conceal their identities and in theory protect their families from harassment, imprisonment, or worse, by the apartheid government. A separate set of names were used by cadres deployed in South Africa. These names were affixed to legends, long fictitious biographical narratives that were memorized by cadres to conceal their true identity and underground activities. It was possible for a cadre to have a number of MK names and a number of names when deployed.

18. Premesh Lalu, *The Deaths of Hintsa: Postapartheid South Africa and the Shape of Recurring Pasts* (Cape Town: HSRC Press, 2009), 10–15.

19. Truth and Reconciliation Commission of South Africa, *Truth and Reconciliation of South Africa Report, Volume 2*. Legacy Committee, Department of Arts and Culture, "Portfolio of Legacy Projects: Discussion Document, 11-1997." Mandela, "Address by President Nelson Mandela at Freedom Day Celebrations, Umtata."

20. Hillary Rodham Clinton stressed the value of the Vietnam War Memorial in Washington, DC, to the postwar healing process in the United States in conversations with Desmond Tutu prior to the TRC's formulation of symbolic reparations. SAPA, "Memorial to Victims Possible," accessed June 24, 2016 (http://www.justice.gov.za/trc/media%5C1997%5C9703/s970319e.htm). Yad Vashem was also offered in expert testimony to the TRC. Truth and Reconciliation Commission of South Africa, "R&R Workshop, Day 3, Johannesburg, 2-20-1998," accessed August 24, 2015 (http://www.justice.gov.za/trc/reparations/joburg3.htm). Freedom Park bears more than a passing resemblance to Ntabakandoda, the "Ciskei's Valhalla," both in terms of the modularity and sprawl of the site itself as well as in purpose—namely, to cement national identity during a time when it is called into question. Anonymous, "Ethnicity and Pseudo Ethnicity in the Ciskei," in *The Creation of Tribalism in Southern Africa*, ed. Leroy Vail (Berkeley, University of California Press, 1991), 395–413. Lennox Sebe reportedly took inspiration from Mount Masada in Israel during the planning of Ntabakandoda.

21. "Education and Recreation Select Committee, Freedom Park: Briefing," accessed June 25, 2016 (https://pmg.org.za/committeemeeting/2007/).

22. According to the National Heritage Resources Act (1999), "'victims of conflict' include *certain* persons who died in any area now included in the Republic as a direct consequence of any war or conflict specified in the regulations," excluding British World War I and World War II deaths covered by the Commonwealth War Graves Act (1992) but "including forces of Great Britain and the British Empire who died in active service in the Republic prior to 4 August 1914," including Anglo-Boer War prisoners of war who died in overseas prison camps, and *certain* categories of persons who died in the "liberation struggle." The same act stipulated that the South African Heritage Resources Agency provide a list of names of those who died during the liberation struggle within five years.

23. Mbeki was quoted as calling for a wall at the 2004 opening of the Isivivane. The quote provided in the 2008 annual report is from his earlier comments. Freedom Park Trust, "Annual Report 2008," 31.

24. Freedom Park, "Homepage," accessed June 25, 2016 (http://www.freedompark.co.za/36-galleries).

25. Freedom Park, author's field notes, June 7, 2015.

26. Status-based subsections include those exclusive to church leaders, well-known executed prisoners, and what my tour guide described as "VIPs." Prisoners who died on Robben Island also have their own subsection in recognition of the fact that they were imprisoned and/or died at that particular prison and not somewhere else. My guide pointed out Nelson Mandela could be included in this, despite the fact that he died twenty-five years after he left Robben Island. He also indicated that Mandela's name may also appear in another subsection for "very influential people" as well as honored in the Gallery of Leaders. There is precedent for double listing. Celebrated

cadre Vuyisile Mini is simultaneously in the subsection of the executed as well as in the "influential persons" section, which presently contains comparatively few names. The very fact that he, and presumably others, appear twice is another detail that seriously calls into question the conceptual basis of the wall.

27. Freedom Park Trust, "Freedom Park News 2007," 8.

28. Perhaps unsurprisingly, the temporal boundaries of this section are fuzzy. The "mass struggle" subsection also includes those who died prior to apartheid. African National Congress, "Statement to the Truth and Reconciliation Commission, August 1996," accessed June 17, 2016 (http://www.justice.gov.za/trc/hrvtrans/submit/anc truth.htm).

29. At present, the three other pillars of struggle do not have their own subsection.

30. Gary Baines, "Site of Struggle: The Freedom Park Fracas and the Divisive Legacy of South Africa's Border War/Liberation Struggle," *Social Dynamics* 35 (2009): 330–44.

31. Using figures provided by the ANC, I calculated that approximately one-fifth of all MK deaths occurred in Angola. Approximately one-third of all ANC deaths in Angola were the result of engagements with UNITA. Approximately 12 percent of ANC deaths in Angola were the result of executions conducted by the ANC of mutineers and spies, and an equal percentage of ANC deaths were attributed to suicide. These three categories of deaths are not represented at Freedom Park.

32. According to ANC statistics, ANC members had a roughly equal chance of dying outside South Africa as within the country during the liberation struggle. See Appendix C: ANC/MK Combat Deaths by Country. "List of ANC and MK Members Killed in Combat," accessed June 25, 2016 (http://www.sahistory.org.za/topic/list-anc-and-mk-members-killed-combat-1980s). African National Congress, "List of ANC Members Who Died in Exile," accessed June 25, 2016 (http://www.anc.org.za/show.php?id=100).

33. Tlou Makura, e-mail to author, July 21, 2015.

34. Freedom Park, author's field notes, March 8, 2008. Freedom Park, author's field notes, June 7, 2015.

35. Author, "Malixoli Hadi, Freedom Park Name Submission," July 13, 2009.

36. There have been long-standing calls for the creation of a central heroes acre in South Africa modeled on post-liberation heroes acres in other southern African countries and within South Africa itself. "Events Planned in Honour of Our Fallen Heroes." Although local heroes acres have sprung up in existing cemeteries throughout South Africa, grand plans to rebury fallen comrades in a single central burial ground have not yet materialized. The genealogy of heroes acres, which appear throughout southern Africa, has yet to be explored. "Events Planned in Honour of Fallen Heroes," *The Herald*, March 21, 2006, 3. "Border Clamp," *The Citizen*, January 15, 1986, 6. "SA Must Not Honour Colonial Wars," *The Sowetan*, October 13, 1999, 10. "AZAPO Calls for Heroes Acre in SA," *The Citizen*, June 7, 1995, 11. Mahanjana, "Go Ahead, Honour

Our Heroes." Bongani Fuzile, "Military Heroes Acre on the Cards," *Daily Dispatch*, February 5, 2013, 4. "Let Us Not Airbrush Our History for the Sake of Our Real Heroes," *Sunday World*, November 7, 1999, 2. "Plan to Rebury All ANC Freedom Fighters," *Daily Dispatch*, February 2, 2006, 6.

37. Leonard Thompson, *Political Mythology of Apartheid* (New Haven, CT: Yale University Press, 1986), 172.

38. Although the newly created Department of Military Veterans has discussed mass repatriation and the creation of an actual heroes acre, the cost of exhumation and reburial largely falls on individual families, which many cannot afford. One mother stated that it would cost R40,000 to return the remains of her son from Lusaka. "My Brother Is with Us Again," *City Press*, April 4, 2009.

39. Truth and Reconciliation Commission, "Chapter 4: The Liberation Movements from 1960–1990," in *The Report of the Truth and Reconciliation Commission, Volume 2*, accessed June 25, 2016 (http://www.justice.gov.za/trc/report/finalreport/Volume%202.pdf).

40. Noble, *African Identity in Post-Apartheid Public Architecture*, 233, 235, 240.

41. Patrick Hlahla, "Ritual Returns Spirits of Fallen Heroes Back Home," *Pretoria News*, September 25, 2007.

42. Ibid.

43. Stephen Clingman, *Bram Fischer: Afrikaner Revolutionary* (Cape Town: David Philip, 1998), 297. Joe Slovo, "Shared Values—Socialism and Religion," *The African Communist* 136 (1994): 20–25. Phyllis Naidoo, interview with Padraig O'Malley, October 26, 2003, accessed June 25, 2016 (https://www.nelsonmandela.org/omalley/index.php/site/q/03lv03445/04lv03833/05lv03891/06lv03909.htm).

44. Freedom Park, author's field notes, March 8, 2008. Freedom Park, author's field notes, June 7, 2015.

45. Freedom Park, author's field notes, June 7, 2015.

46. Freedom Park, "Public Participation Form, 9-27-2006," accessed June 25, 2016 (https://web.archive.org/web/20060927174103/http://www.freedompark.co.za/publicparticipationform.html).

47. South African Government News Agency, "Freedom Park Trust Honours 24 Heroes," accessed June 25, 2016 (http://www.sanews.gov.za/features/freedompark trusthonours24struggleheroes).

48. Freedom Park, author's field notes, June 7, 2015. Freedom Park, "Virtual Tour," accessed June 25, 2016 (http://www.freedompark.co.za/visit-us/virtual-tour/). "Remembering and Forgetting at Freedom Park," accessed June 25, 2016 (http://www.archivalplatform.org/news/entry/remembering_and_forgetting/). Education and Recreation Select Committee, "Freedom Park: Briefing," accessed June 24, 2016 (https://pmg.org.za/committee-meeting/2007/).

49. Freedom Park, author's field notes, June 7, 2015.

50. Education and Recreation Select Committee, "Freedom Park: Briefing," accessed June 24, 2016 (https://pmg.org.za/committee-meeting/2007/).

51. "Address by Deputy President Kgalema Motlanthe on the Occasion of the Official Opening of the Freedom Park //hapo Museum, Pretoria," accessed June 25, 2016 (http://www.thepresidency.gov.za/pebble.asp?relid=15286&t=79).

52. Freedom Park, author's field notes, June 7, 2015.

53. A passage from Mbeki's "I Am an African" speech appears in the foyer of the //hapo. Freedom Park, author's field notes, June 7, 2015.

54. Bongani Mkhize, "Taking Freedom Park to the People," accessed June 25, 2016 (sashtw.org.za/WP/wp-content/uploads/.../FREEDOM-PARK-PRESENTATION.ppt).

55. Freedom Park, author's field notes, June 7, 2015.

56. Ibid.

57. Kros, "A New Monumentalism?," 47.

58. Patricia Visagie, "Mortal Remains of 10 Anti-Apartheid Activists Returned to Their Families," accessed September 13, 2017 (https://www.youtube.com/watch?v=4e78boynAAk).

59. African National Congress, "ANC Missing Remains of MK Combatants Killed by Apartheid Regime Handed Over to Families 24 J," accessed September 13, 2017 (https://www.youtube.com/watch?v=HKH1bn5YjcQ).

60. Mthunzi Mhaga, "Handover Ceremony of the Exhumed Remains of 10 Former MK Members" accessed September 13, 2017 (http://www.freedompark.co.za/stay-informed/news-and-media-releases/148-handover-of-mk-cadres.html).

61. Truth and Reconciliation Commission, "Nicodemus Sono and Nomsa Shabalala, Human Rights Violation Hearing Testimony, 25-July-1996," accessed September 13, 2017 (http://www.justice.gov.za/trc/hrvtrans%5Csoweto/sono.htm).

62. Ibid.

63. Michelle Faul, "Mandela's Ex-Wife Shocked at Possible Prosecution," *Associated Press*, March 13, 2013.

64. A press report noted that ANC officials attempted to prevent Sono's family from speaking to the press at the public exhumation. Michelle Faul, "Mandela's Ex-Wife Shocked at Possible Prosecution," *Associated Press*, March 13, 2013.

65. Michael Masutha, "Speech by Minister of Justice and Correctional Services Michael Masutha, MP (Adv), on the Occasion of Handover of Remains of MK Soldiers at Freedom Park," accessed September 13, 2017 (http://www.justice.gov.za/m_speeches/2015/20150724_TRC.html).

66. The phrase "carrying the gun" was used by several of my interviewees to distinguish those who were engaged in active combat in MK operations, or at least possessed weapons delivered by the underground structures and were authorized to use them. What is indeterminate is whether or not those who carried the gun were or were not formal members of MK. This indeterminacy may be a deliberate attempt to broaden the category of "veteran."

67. William Shakespeare, *The Dramatic Works of William Shakespeare Volume IV* (Boston: Philips and Sampson, 1846), 48–55.

68. David William Cohen and E. S. Atieno Odhiambo, *Burying SM: The Politics of Knowledge and the Sociology of Power in Africa* (Portsmouth, NH: Heinemann, 1992), 1–2. Ashwin Desai, *Reading Revolution: Shakespeare on Robben Island* (Chicago, IL: Haymarket, 2014). Julius Nyerere, *Juliasi Kaisari* (Nairobi: Oxford University Press, 1963).

69. William Shakespeare, *The Dramatic Works of William Shakespeare Volume IV* (Boston: Philips and Sampson, 1846), 48–55. My sincerest thanks to Dan Gargola and Bruce Holle for pointing out the multiple layers of interpretation that encompass this history and the tales told about it. Any errors in interpretation are my own.

APPENDIX A: LISTS OF ANC MEMBERS KILLED IN THE MATOLA RAID (JANUARY 29-30, 1981)

TRC List of Victims	*TRC Final Report*	*TRC Notes Errata*	*Llhanguene Cemetary*	*Gifford (1981)*	*SADET (2010)*	*Order of Menli*
Thabang Moses Bookalane	Thabang Bookalane	Mduduzi Guma	Thabang Bookholane	Thabani Burulani	Thabani Burulani	Thabang Bookolane
Themba Francis Dimba	Mandla Daka	Thabang Moses Bookalane	Themba Dimba	Mduduzi Guma	Joseph Mduduzi Guma	Mandla Daka
Mduduzi Guma	Themba Dimba	Lancelot Mfanafuthi Hadebe	Mduduzi Eric Guma	Lancelot Hadebe	William Khanyile	Mduduzi Guma
William Khanyile	Mduduzi Gama (sic)	William Khanyile	Lancelot Hadebe	William Khanyile	Beki Magubane	Lancelot Hadebe
Bheki Magubane	William Khanyile	Bhekumuzi Lawrence Magubane	William Fano Khanyile	Beki Magubane	Nelson Manakaza	William Khanyile
Montso Mokgabudi	Vikeliswe Khumalo	Levinson Mandisi Manakaza	Bheki Felix Magubane	Nelson Manakaza	Selby Mavuso	Collin Khumalo
Daniel Molebatsi	Mankazana Levinson	Dumisani Matandela	Levson Solly Manakaza	Motso Mokgabudi	Motso Mokgabudi	Albert Mahutso
Stephen Ngcobo	Bhekumuzi Magubane	Motso Aubrey Mokgabundi	Vuyani Selby Mavuso	Daniel Molebatsi	Daniel Molebatsi	Levinson Mankankaza
Vusumuzi Patrick Ngwenya	Solomon Mahutso	Daniel Molebatsi	Motso Mokgabudi	Nelson Ndunamvula	Nelson Ndunamvula	Vuyani Mavuso
Krishna Rabilal	Motso Mokgabundi (Obadi)	Nelson Ndunamvula	Daniel Mokhosi Molebatsi	Stephen Ngcobo	Stephen Ngcobo	Motso Mokgabudi
Lancelot Mfanafuthi Hadebe	Daniel Molikisi	Stephen Ngcobo	Nelson Nduna Mvula	Krishna Rabillal	Thibe Nisekeng	Daniel Molekisi
Sinzinzo Skweyiya	Steven Ngcobo	Krishna Rabilal	Stephen Ngcobo	Richard Sibonyoni	Krish Rabillal	Vusunzi Ngwema
Nelson Ndunamvula	Vusumzi Ngwenya	Sizinzo Skweyiya	Khrisnha Godwin Rabilal	Sizinzo Sikweyiya	Lancelot Radebe	Krishna Rabilal
	Krishna Rabilall	Naledi Eugenia Dongwe	Mduduzeli Sibanyoni		Zizinzo Wilberforce Skweyiya	
	Mfanafuthi Radebe	Themba Dimba	Sizinzo Skweyiya		David Thobela	
	Sinzino Skweyiya					

Matola Monument	*ANC Website*	*DAC Matola Deceased Profiles*	*DMV "Unveiling Matola"*	*DAC Discussion Document*	*Matola Exhibit Film*
Thabang Henry Bookholane	Thabang Bookolane	Thabang Victor Bookholane	Thabang Bookolane	Thabang Bookholane	Thabang Bookholane
Mduduzi Eric Guma	Mandla Henson Daka	Mduduzi Eric Guma	Mandla Daka	Themba Dimba	Mduduzi Guma
Lancelot Mfanafuthi Hadebe	Themba Francis Dimba	Lancelot Mfanafuthi Hadebe	Themba Dimba	Mduzdi Guma	Mfanafuthi Hadebe
William Fano Khanyile	Mduduzi Guma	William Fano Khanyile	Lancelot Hadebe	Lancelot Hadebe	William Khanyile
Bhekimuzi Felix Magubane	William Khanyile	Bhekumuzi Magubane	William Khanyile	William Khanyile	Levison Manakaza
Albert Mahutso	Vikeliswe Colin Khumalo	Albert Mahutso	Collin Khumalo	Bheki Felix Magubane	Montso Mokgabudi
Levinson Solly Manakazi	Mankankaza Levinson	Levsen Mandisi Manakaza	Albert Mahutso	Levson Solly Manakaza	Daniel Molebatsi
Vuyani Mavuso	Bheki Magubane	Selby Vuyani Mavuso	Levinson Mankankaza	Levinson Mankankaza	Nduna Mvula
Montso Mokgabudi	Solomon Albert Mahutso	Montso Mokgabudi	Motso Mokgabudi	Daniel Mokhosi Molebatsi	Stephen Ngcobo
Daniel Molebatsi	Motso Mokgabudi	Daniel Molebatsi	Daniel Molebatsi	Nduna Mvula	Krishna Rabilal
Nduna Mvula	Daniel Molokisi	Nduna Mvula	Nduna Mvula	Stephen Ngcobo	Mduduzeli Sibanyoni
Steven Ngcobo	Steven Ngcobo	Stephen Ngcobo	Stephen Ngcobo	Khrisna Godwin Rabilal	Sizinzo Skweyiya
Ashwin Krishna Rabilal	Vusumuzi Justice Ngwema	Thiba Ntsekeng	Vusumzi Ngwema	Mduduzi Sibanyoni	
Mduduzeli Sibanyoni	Krishna Rabilall	Krishna Rabilal	Krishna Rabilal	Sinzinzo Sweyiya	
Sizinzo Wilberforce Skweyiya	Lancelot Manafuthu Radebe	Mduduzeli Sibanyoni			
	Sinzingo W. Skweyiya	Sizinzo Wilberforce Skweyiya			
		David Thobela			

Note: The many inconsistencies and omissions in lists of casualties drawn from a single discrete event that was amply documented indicates the broader problem of using lists to memorialize the entire anti-apartheid struggle.

229

APPENDIX B: ANC/MK DEATHS IN ANGOLA BY CATEGORY

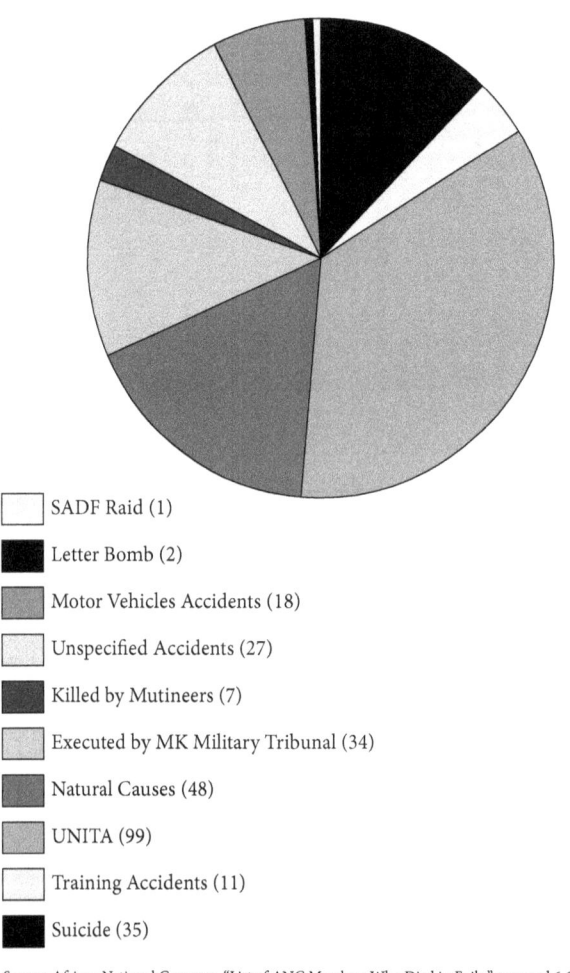

- SADF Raid (1)
- Letter Bomb (2)
- Motor Vehicles Accidents (18)
- Unspecified Accidents (27)
- Killed by Mutineers (7)
- Executed by MK Military Tribunal (34)
- Natural Causes (48)
- UNITA (99)
- Training Accidents (11)
- Suicide (35)

Source: African National Congress, "List of ANC Members Who Died in Exile," accessed 6-25-2016, http://www.anc.org.za/show.php?id=100. "List of ANC and MK Members Killed in Combat" accessed 6-25-2016. http://www.sahistory.org.za/topic/list-anc-and-mk-members-killed-combat-1980s

APPENDIX C: ANC/MK COMBAT DEATHS BY COUNTRY

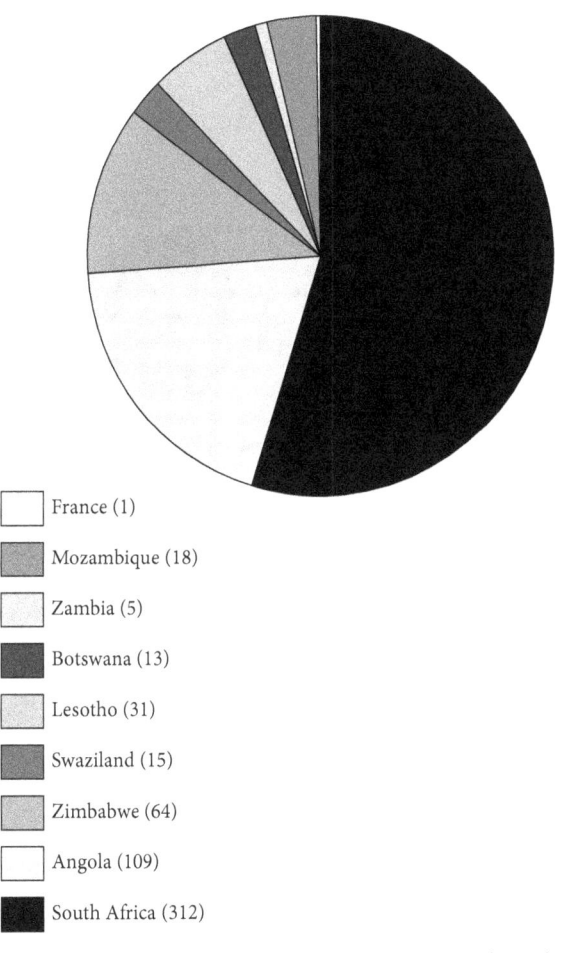

- France (1)
- Mozambique (18)
- Zambia (5)
- Botswana (13)
- Lesotho (31)
- Swaziland (15)
- Zimbabwe (64)
- Angola (109)
- South Africa (312)

Source: African National Congress, "List of ANC Members Who Died in Exile," accessed 6-25-2016, http://www.anc.org.za/show.php?id=100. "List of ANC and MK Members Killed in Combat" accessed 6-25-2016. http://www.sahistory.org.za/topic/list-anc-and-mk-members-killed-combat-1980s

APPENDIX D: ANC/MK COMBAT DEATHS BY COUNTRY

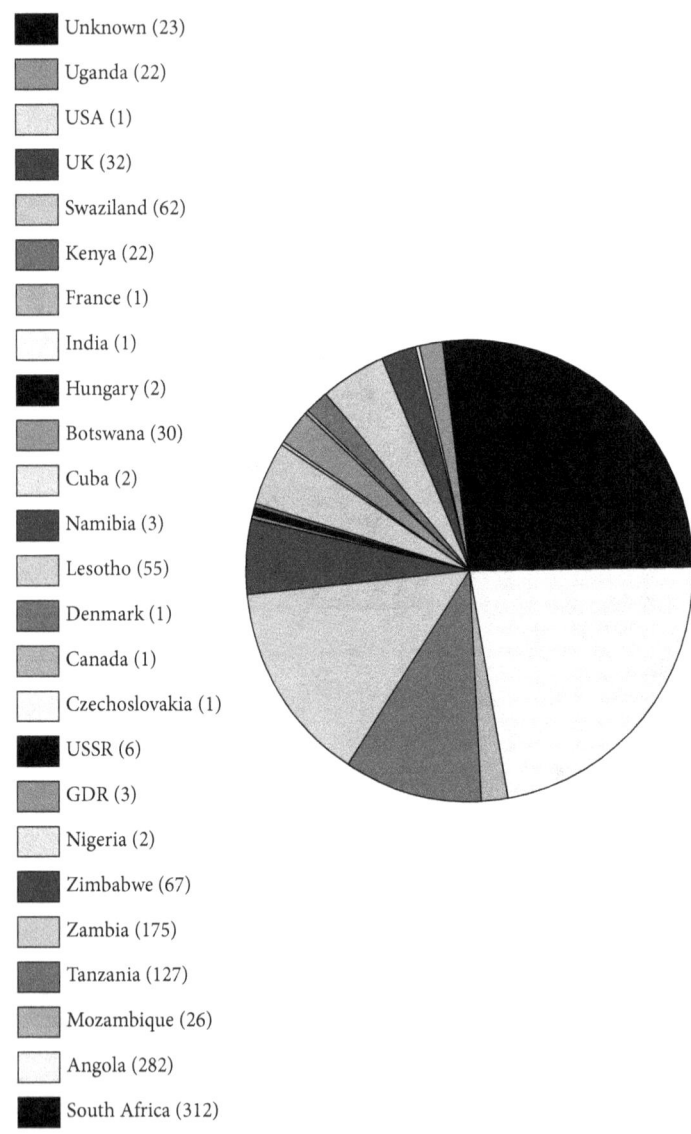

- Unknown (23)
- Uganda (22)
- USA (1)
- UK (32)
- Swaziland (62)
- Kenya (22)
- France (1)
- India (1)
- Hungary (2)
- Botswana (30)
- Cuba (2)
- Namibia (3)
- Lesotho (55)
- Denmark (1)
- Canada (1)
- Czechoslovakia (1)
- USSR (6)
- GDR (3)
- Nigeria (2)
- Zimbabwe (67)
- Zambia (175)
- Tanzania (127)
- Mozambique (26)
- Angola (282)
- South Africa (312)

Source: African National Congress, "List of ANC Members Who Died in Exile," accessed 6-25-2016, http://www.anc.org.za/show.php?id=100. "List of ANC and MK Members Killed in Combat" accessed 6-25-2016. http://www.sahistory.org.za/topic/list-anc-and-mk-members-killed-combat-1980s

BIBLIOGRAPHY

Primary Sources

Karis Gerhart Biographical Files

Ngqungwana, Lizo Bright. Karis Gerhart Biographical Files.

KwaZulu-Natal High Court, Pietermaritzburg

Nkosi, Leonard. "Testimony." *State vs. James April*. Pietermaritzburg: High Court of South Africa, 1971.

Department of Military Veterans, Pretoria

Department of Military Veterans. "DMV Strategic Plan 2011–2016." Department of Military Veterans.

African National Congress Archives, University of Fort Hare, Alice

"Military and Combat Work." ANC Archives, University of Fort Hare.

Western Cape High Court, Cape Town

Basil February MK Squad. "Letter to Reporter, July 23, 1987." *State vs. Yengeni and 13 Others*, Supreme Court of South Africa, Cape of Good Hope Provincial Division.

"Evidence." *State vs. Yengeni and 13 Others*, Supreme Court of South Africa, Cape of Good Hope Provincial Division.

Giffard, Chris. "Statement." *State vs. Yengeni and 13 Others*, Supreme Court of South Africa, Cape of Good Hope Provincial Division.

"List of Charges against Yengeni et al." *State vs. Yengeni and 13 Others*, Supreme Court of South Africa, Cape of Good Hope Provincial Division.

"Terrorisme in die RSA." *State vs. Yengeni and 13 Others*, Supreme Court of South Africa, Cape of Good Hope Provincial Division.

Karis Gerhart Collection, Historical Papers Research Archive, Cullen Library, University of the Witwatersrand

ANC Political Department. "Politics Department on Civil and Criminal Code of the People of South Africa, November 12, 1980." Karis Gerhart Collection, Historical Papers Research Archive, Cullen Library, University of the Witwatersrand.

"Extracts from the Confessions of an Enemy Agent Ralph Mgcina Alias Fear Who Died of Natural Causes Recently, September 3, 1988." Karis Gerhart Collection, Historical Papers Research Archive, Cullen Library, University of the Witwatersrand.

"Guidelines on Underground Construction, 1988." Karis Gerhart Collection, Historical Papers Research Archive, Cullen Library, University of the Witwatersrand.

"Minutes of the First Session of the Dar es Salaam Zonal C. C. Conference Held at the Zone II Cultural Club on Wednesday, April 17, 1985 at 10:25 AM." Karis Gerhart Collection, Historical Papers Research Archive, Cullen Library, University of the Witwatersrand.

"Planning for People's War Discussion Document, November 1983." Karis Gerhart Collection, Historical Papers Research Archive, Cullen Library, University of the Witwatersrand.

"Some Aspects of Enemy Counter-Guerrilla Tactics Compiled from Our Own Experience, May 1984." Karis Gerhart Collection, Historical Papers Research Archive, Cullen Library, University of the Witwatersrand.

"Typed Version of a Diary Recovered at Ingwavuma on December 14, 1984." Karis Gerhart Collection, Historical Papers Research Archive, Cullen Library, University of the Witwatersrand.

Commission of Inquiry. "Report: Commission of Inquiry into Recent Developments in the People's Republic of Angola, March 14, 1984." Karis Gerhart Collection, Historical Papers Research Archive, Cullen Library, University of the Witwatersrand.

Kasrils, Ronnie. "Report from Women's Day Meeting at Kaunda Square, August 9, 1989." Karis Gerhart Collection, Historical Papers Research Archive, Cullen Library, University of the Witwatersrand.

Miya, Nelson. "The ANC Code of Conduct, January 28, 1988." Karis Gerhart Collection, Historical Papers Research Archive, Cullen Library, University of the Witwatersrand.

Sachs, Albie. "Civil and Criminal Code of the People of South Africa, October 29, 1980." Karis Gerhart Collection, Historical Papers Research Archive, Cullen Library, University of the Witwatersrand.

Senior Organ, T/Q Area. "Rules of Security, Defence and Code of Conduct, March 1981." Karis Gerhart Collection, Historical Papers Research Archive, Cullen Library, University of the Witwatersrand.

Sparg, Marion, Jenny Schreiner, and Gwen Ansell. "The Angolan Diaries of Jack Simons." Karis Gerhart Collection, Historical Papers Research Archive, Cullen Library, University of the Witwatersrand.

Marquart Architecten B.V., Amsterdam, Netherlands

Freedom Park Trust. *Freedom Park News 2007.* Marquart Architecten B.V.

———. *Annual Report 2008.* Marquart Architecten B.V.

Legacy Committee, Department of Arts and Culture. "Portfolio of Legacy Projects: Discussion Document, November 1997." Marquart Architecten B.V.

Mayibuye Centre Archives, Robben Island Museum, University of the Western Cape, Bellville

"Commission Five—Theoretical Paper on the Armed Struggle = 1959, 1984." ANC Collection, Mayibuye Centre Archives.

"Political and Ideological Work in the Region." ANC Collection, Mayibuye Centre Archives.

"Repot [sic] of Commission on Military Training Improvement of Skills and Deployment." ANC Collection, Mayibuye Centre Archives.

"Report on Security and Intelligence, 1985." ANC Collection, Mayibuye Centre Archives.

"Report on Security and Intelligence." ANC Collection, Mayibuye Centre Archives.

"The Role and Place of the Youth in Society, the Struggle, and in the ANC, 1985." ANC Collection, Mayibuye Centre Archives.

Commission 3. "General Report of the ANC Vanguard Role since 1959." ANC Collection, Mayibuye Centre Archives.

Davids, Cyril. Rivonia Trial Testimony. ANC Collection, Mayibuye Centre Archives.

De Wet, Quartus. Rivonia Trial Judgment. ANC Collection, Mayibuye Centre Archives.

NAT. "A Report on Some Aspects of NAT Work, February 20, 1988." ANC Collection, Mayibuye Centre Archives.

National Executive Committee and Politico-Military Committee. "NEC and PMC Documents, Document B1(b)—Codes of Conduct." ANC Collection, Mayibuye Centre Archives.

Nboxele, Caswell. Rivonia Trial Record. ANC Collection, Mayibuye Centre Archives.

Karis Gerhart Collection (Microfilm), Center for Research Libraries, Chicago

"Documents and Draft Documents Relating to the ANC Disciplinary Code." Karis Gerhart Collection (microfilm), Center for Research Libraries.

Department of Legal and Constitutional Affairs. "Departmental Report for the NEC, September 25, 1986." Karis Gerhart Collection (microfilm), Center for Research Libraries.

Politico-Military Committee. "PMC Organizational Report." Karis Gerhart Collection (microfilm), Center for Research Libraries.

Andrew Masondo Library, South African National Museum of Military History, Randburg

"Danie Theron Combat School: Basic Tactics of the ANC." Andrew Masondo Library, South African National Museum of Military History.

Ray and Jack Simons Collection, Manuscripts and Archives, University of Cape Town, Cape Town

Jack Simons. "Novo Catengue Diaries, I and II." Ray and Jack Simons Collection, Manuscripts and Archives, University of Cape Town.

———. "Jack Simons to Ray Simons, Correspondence, September 30, 1977." Ray and Jack Simons Collection, Manuscripts and Archives, University of Cape Town.

———. "Jack Simons to Ray Simons, Correspondence, March 5, 1978." Ray and Jack Simons Collection, Manuscripts and Archives, University of Cape Town.

Special Collections Library, University of Cape Town, Cape Town

African National Congress. "Commission of Inquiry into Recent Events in the People's Republic of Angola, March 14, 1984." Special Collections Library, University of Cape Town.

Commission of Inquiry. "Report of a Commission of Inquiry Set Up in November 1989 by the National Working Committee of the National Executive Committee of the African National Congress to Investigate the

Circumstances Leading to the Death of Mzwakhe Ngwenya (Also Known as Thami Zulu or TZ)." Special Collections Library, University of Cape Town.

Independent Board. *Who Lied?: Discussion of the Findings of the Harms Commission of Inquiry Prepared by the Independent Board.* Special Collections Library, University of Cape Town.

Stephen Ellis, Personal Collection, Leiden, Netherlands

"Report on the Activities of the Natal Machinery during the Period 1983–1988 When It Was under the Command of Muzi Ngwenya Alias Thami Zulu."

"Report on the Subversive Activities of Police Agents in Our Movement, July 1, 1981."

Douglas Commission. "The Report of the Douglas Commission, 1990."

Truth and Reconciliation Commission

Moshoeu, Gordon. TRC Testimony. CT02913/OUT.

Ngudle, Beauty. TRC Testimony. CT/00504.

United States Library of Congress

Stepanchuk, John. "Summary of Commentary in Pravda on Sub-Saharan Africa, January 22–February 21 1981." Washington, DC: Federal Research Division of the Library of Congress, 1981.

SECONDARY SOURCES

Journal Articles

African National Congress. "Racist Atrocities in Matola." *Sechaba* 15 (1981): 19–20.

Baines, Gary. "Site of Struggle: The Freedom Park Fracas and the Divisive Legacy of South Africa's Border War/Liberation Struggle." *Social Dynamics* 35 (2009): 330–44.

Bickford-Smith, Vivian. "South African Urban History, Racial Segregation and the Unique Case of Cape Town?" *Journal of Southern African Studies* 21 (1995): 63–78.

Bonner, Phil. "Keynote Address to the 'Life after Thirty' Colloquium." *African Studies* 69 (2010): 13–27.

Bozzoli, Belinda. "Intellectuals, Audiences and Histories: South African Experiences, 1978–88." *Radical History Review* 46 (1990): 237–63.

Chirambo, Reuben Makayiko. "'A Monument to a Tyrant' or Reconstructed Nationalist Memories of the Father and Founder of the Malawi Nation, Dr. H. K. Banda." *Africa Today* 56 (2010): 2–21.
Chissano, Joaquim Alberto. "We Are Ready to Accept the Challenge." *Sechaba* 15 (1981): 21–23.
Cooper, Frederick. "Conflict and Connection: Rethinking Colonial African History." *The American Historical Review* 99 (1994): 1516–45.
Delzell, Charles. "The Italian Anti-Fascist Resistance in Retrospect: Three Decades of Historiography." *Journal of Modern History* 47 (1975): 66–96.
Ellis, Stephen. "Politics and Crime: Reviewing the ANC's Exile History." *South African Historical Journal* 64 (2012): 622–36.
Freund, Bill. "The Art of Writing History." *Southern African Review of Books* 7 (1994): 24.
Friedman, Steven. "From Classroom to Class Struggle: Radical Academics and the Rebirth of Trade Unionism in the 1970s." *Journal of Asian and African Studies* 49 (2014): 526–43.
———. "Whose Liberation?: A Partly-Forgotten Left Critique of ANC Strategy and Its Contemporary Implications." *Journal of Asian and African Studies* 47 (2012): 18–32.
———. "Before and After: Reflections on Regime Change and Its Aftermath." *Transformation: Critical Perspectives on Southern Africa* 75 (2011): 4–12.
Fullard, Madeleine, and Nicky Rousseau. "Uncertain Borders: The TRC and the (Un)Making of Public Myths." *Kronos* 34 (2008): 215–39.
Hamilton, Carolyn. "'The Future of the Past': New Trajectories." *South African History Journal* 35 (1996): 146–48.
Hani, Chris. "The Wankie Campaign." *Dawn* 10 (1986): 4–6.
Hirson, Baruch. "The Struggle for a Post-Apartheid Society in South Africa." *Third World Quarterly* 12 (1990): 159–65.
Hobsbawm, E. H. "Ethnicity and Nationalism in Europe Today." *Anthropology Today* 8 (1992): 3–8.
Hofmeyr, Isabel. "'Wailing for Purity': Oral Studies in Southern African Studies." *African Studies* 54 (1995): 16–31.
Hopkins, Raymond F., and Robert C. Mitchell. "The Validity of Survey Research in Africa: Some Propositions." *African Studies Review* 17 (1974): 565–74.
Hühn, Peter. "The Detective as Reader: Narrativity and Reading Concepts in Detective Fiction." *Modern Fiction Studies* 33 (1987): 451–66.
Johns, Sheridan. "The Comintern, South Africa and the Black Diaspora." *The Review of Politics* 37 (1975): 200–34.
Johnson, Michael P. "Denmark Vesey and His Co-Conspirators." *William and Mary Quarterly* 58 (2001): 915–76.

Kössler, Reinhart. "Facing a Fragmented Past: Memory, Culture and Politics in Namibia." *Journal of Southern African Studies* 33 (2007): 361–82.

Kros, Cynthia. "A New Monumentalism?: From Public Art to Freedom Park." *Image and Text* 19 (2012): 34–51.

Labuschagne, Pieter. "Monument(al) Meaning Making in the 'New' South Africa: Freedom Park as a Symbol of a New Identity and Freedom?" *South African Journal of Art History* 25 (2010): 112–24.

Landau, Paul. "The ANC, MK and 'The Turn to Violence' 1960–1962." *The South African Historical Journal* 64 (2012): 538–63.

Legassick, Martin. "Debating the Revival of the Workers' Movement in the 1970s: The South African Democracy Education Trust and Post-Apartheid Patriotic History." *Kronos* 34 (2008): 240–66.

———. "Armed Struggle in South Africa: Consequences of a Strategy Debate." *Journal of Contemporary African Studies* 21 (2003): 285–302.

Lodge, Tom. "Spectres from the Camps: The ANC's Commission of Enquiry." *Southern Africa Report* 8 (1993): 19–30.

MacMillan, Hugh. "The Hani Memorandum: Introduced and Annotated." *Transformation: Critical Perspectives on Southern Africa* 69 (2009): 106–29.

Mann, Gregg. "An Africanist's Apostasy: On Luise White's *Speaking with Vampires*." *International Journal of African Historical Studies* 41 (2008): 117–21.

Maylam, Paul. "Tensions within the Practice of History." *South African Historical Journal* 33 (1999): 3–12.

Minkley, Gary, and Martin Legassick. "Recent Trends in the Production of South African History." *Alternation* 5 (1998): 98–129.

Mkatashingo. "The ANC Conference: From Kabwe to Johannesburg." *Searchlight South Africa* 6 (1991): 91–94.

Mthethwa, Nathi. "Viewpoint: Nathi Mthethwa." *ANC Today* 15 (2015).

Nasson, Bill. "The Was, the Is and the What-Might-Have-Been: Political Leadership in Post-Apartheid South Africa." *Journal of African History* 49 (2008): 467–74.

Ndlovu, Sifiso. "'He Did What Any Other Person in His Position Would Have Done to Fight the Forces of Invasion and Disruption': Africans, the Land and Contending Images of King Dingane ('the Patriot') in the Twentieth Century, 1916–1950s." *South African Historical Journal* 38 (1998): 99–143.

Ngani, Jethro. "Voice of Freedom." *Sechaba* 10 (1976): 38–49.

Nuttall, Tim, and John Wright. "Probing the Predicaments of Academic History in Contemporary South Africa." *South African Historical Journal* 42 (2000): 26–48.

Peires, Jeff. "The Art of Writing History." *South African Review of Books* 6 (1994): 24.

Rassool, Ciraj. "Writing, Authorship and I. B. Tabata's Biography: From Collective Leadership to Presidentialism." *Kronos* 34 (2008): 181–214.

———. "The Rise of Heritage and the Reconstitution of History in South Africa." *Kronos* 26 (2000): 1–21.
Riesman, David. "Orbits of Tolerance, Interviewers, and Elites." *Public Opinion Quarterly* 20 (1956): 49–73.
Riouful, Veronique. "Behind Telling: Post-Apartheid Representations of Robben Island's Past." *Kronos* 26 (2000): 22–41.
Saul, John. "Cry for the Beloved Country: The Post-Apartheid Denouement." *Monthly Review* 52 (2001): 1–51.
Scott, Joan. "Evidence of Experience." *Critical Inquiry* 17 (1994): 773–97.
Sibeko, Alexander (Ronnie Kasrils). "Four Who Were Communists." *African Communist* 87 (1981): 41–49.
———. "The Underground Voice." *The African Communist* 68 (1977): 48–58.
Simpson, Thula. "Toyi-Toyi-ing to Freedom: The Endgame in the ANC's Armed Struggle, 1989–1990." *Journal of Southern African Studies* 35 (2009): 507–21.
Sithole, Jabulani. "Contestations over Knowledge Production or Ideological Bullying?: A Response to Legassick on the Workers' Movement." *Kronos* 35 (2009): 222–41.
Slovo, Joe. "Shared Values—Socialism and Religion." *The African Communist* 136 (1994): 20–25.
Steiner, Peter. "Making a Czech Hero: Julius Fučík through His Writings." *The Carl Beck Papers in Russian and East European Studies* 1501 (2000): 1–61.
Suttner, Raymond. "Culture(s) of the African National Congress of South Africa: Imprint of Exile Experiences." *Journal of Contemporary African Studies* 21 (2003): 302–20.
White, Luise. "Poisoned Food, Poisoned Uniforms, and Anthrax: Or, How Guerrillas Die in War." *Osiris* 19 (2004): 220–33.
———. "'Not Telling': Secrecy, Lies, and History." *History and Theory: Studies in the Philosophy of History* 39 (2001): 11–22.
Witz, Leslie. "The Write Your Own History Project." *Radical History Review* 46 (1990): 377–87.
Witz, Leslie, and Carolyn Hamilton. "Reaping the Whirlwind: *The Readers Digest Illustrated History of South Africa* and Changing Popular Perceptions of History." *South African Historical Journal* 24 (1991): 185–202.
Witz, Leslie, and Ciraj Rassool. "Making Histories." *Kronos* 34 (2008): 6–15.
Worger, William H. "Review: *South Africa Belongs to Us*." *African Studies Review* 34 (1991): 145–46.

Books

Anderson, Benedict. *Imagined Communities: Reflections on the Origin and Spread of Nationalism*. New York: Verso, 2006.

Bayo, Alberto. *Ciento cincuenta preguntas a un guerrillero.* Havana: International Publishers, 1961.
Bell, Terry. *Comrade Moss: A Political Journey.* Cape Town: Redworks, 2009.
Benson, Mary. *The African National Congress: The African Patriots.* London: Faber & Faber, 1963.
Berger, John. *Ways of Seeing.* New York: Penguin, 1990.
Bernstein, Lionel. *Memory against Forgetting: Memoirs from a Life in South African Politics, 1938–1964.* London: Viking, 1999.
Bickford Smith, Vivian. *Ethnic Pride and Racial Prejudice in Victorian Cape Town: Group Identity and Social Practice, 1875–1902.* New York: Cambridge University Press, 1995.
Binda, Alexandre. *Masodja: The History of the Rhodesian African Rifles and Its Forerunner the Rhodesian Native Regiment.* Johannesburg: 30 Degrees South, 2007.
Bond, Patrick. *Elite Transition: From Apartheid to Neo-Liberalism in South Africa.* London: Pluto, 2000.
Booysen, Susan. *The African National Congress and the Regeneration of Political Power.* Johannesburg: University of the Witwatersrand Press, 2011.
Bopela, Thula, and Daluxolo Luthuli. *Umkhonto we Sizwe: Fighting for a Divided People.* Alberton: Galago, 2005.
Boraine, Alex. *What's Gone Wrong: On the Brink of a Failed State.* Cape Town: Jonathan Ball, 2014.
Bottoman, Wonga Welile. *The Making of an MK Cadre.* Pretoria: LiNc Publishers, 2010.
Braam, Connie. *Operation Vula.* Bellevue: Jacana, 2004.
Buhlungu, Sakhela, John Daniel, Roger Southall, and Jessica Lutchman. *State of the Nation: South Africa 2007.* Cape Town: HSRC Press, 2007.
Bundy, Colin. *Short Changed?: South Africa since Apartheid.* Auckland Park: Jacana, 2014.
Bunting, Brian. *Moses Kotane: South African Revolutionary.* London: Inkululeko, 1975.
Butler, Anthony. *The Idea of the ANC.* Athens: Ohio University Press, 2013.
Butterfield, Herbert. *The Whig Interpretation of History.* London: G. Bell, 1931.
Carr, E. H. *What Is History?* New York: Vintage, 1961.
Catholic Institute for International Relations. *Now Everyone Is Afraid: The Changing Face of Policing in South Africa.* London: Catholic Institute for International Relations, 1988.
Chabris, Christopher, and Daniel Simons. *The Invisible Gorilla: How Our Intuitions Deceive Us.* New York: Harmony, 2007.
Cherry, Janet. *Umkhonto we Sizwe.* Johannesburg: Jacana, 2011.
Clingman, Stephen. *Bram Fischer: Afrikaner Revolutionary.* Cape Town: David Philip, 1998.

Cohen, David William, and E. S. Atieno Odhiambo. *Burying SM: The Politics of Knowledge and the Sociology of Power in Africa.* Portsmouth, NH: Heinemann, 1992.

Comaroff, Jean, and John Comaroff. *Modernity and Its Malcontents: Ritual and Power in Postcolonial Africa.* Chicago: University of Chicago Press, 1993.

Cooper, Frederick. *Colonialism in Question: Theory, Knowledge, History.* Berkeley: University of California Press, 2005.

Desai, Ashwin. *Reading Revolution: Shakespeare on Robben Island.* Chicago, IL: Haymarket, 2014.

De Villiers, Heinrich. *Rivonia: Operation Mayibuye: A Review of the Rivonia Trial.* Johannesburg: Afrikaanse Pers Boekhandel, 1966.

Dlamini, Jacob. *Native Nostalgia.* Auckland Park: Jacana, 2009.

Douglas, Mary. *Witchcraft Confessions and Accusations.* London: Tavistock, 1970.

Duka, Norman. *From Shantytown to Forest.* Vancouver, BC: LSM Publishers, 1974.

Edwards, Stephen. *Photography: A Very Short Introduction.* New York: Oxford University Press, 2006.

Ellis, Stephen. *External Mission: The ANC in Exile, 1960–1990.* Oxford: Oxford University Press, 2013.

Ellis, Stephen, and Tsepo Sechaba. *Comrades against Apartheid: The ANC and the South African Communist Party in Exile.* Bloomington: Indiana University Press, 1992.

Esterhuyse, Willie. *Endgame: Secret Talks and the End of Apartheid.* Cape Town: Tafelberg, 2012.

Feinstein, Andrew. *After the Party: A Personal and Political Journey inside the ANC.* Johannesburg: Jonathan Ball, 2007.

Feit, Edward. *Urban Revolt in South Africa, 1960–1964: A Case Study.* Evanston, IL: Northwestern University Press, 1971.

Feldman, Alan. *Formations of Violence: The Narrative of the Body and Political Terror in Northern Ireland.* Chicago: University of Chicago Press, 1991.

First, Ruth. *117 Days.* London: Bloomsbury, 1965.

Fischer, David Hackett. *The Historians' Fallacy: Toward a Logic of Historical Thought.* New York: Harper & Row, 1970.

Fitzpatrick, Sheila. *The Russian Revolution.* New York: Oxford University Press, 1994.

Flower, Ken. *Serving Secretly: An Intelligence Officer on Record, 1964 to 1981.* London: John Murray, 1987.

Foucault, Michel, et al. *I Pierre Rivière, Having Slaughtered My Mother, My Sister, My Brother: A Case of Parricide in the 19th Century.* New Haven, CT: Yale University Press, 1975.

Frankel, Philip. *An Ordinary Atrocity: Sharpeville and Its Massacre.* Johannesburg: Jonathan Ball, 2001.

Fučík, Julius. *Notes from the Gallows*. London: New Century, 1948.
Gellner, Ernest, and John Breuilly. *Nations and Nationalism*. Ithaca, NY: Cornell University Press, 2008.
Gerhart, Gail. *Black Consciousness: Evolution of an Ideology*. Berkeley: University of California Press, 1978.
Gerhart, Gail, and Clive Glaser. *From Protest to Challenge: Challenge and Victory, 1980–1990, Volume 6*. Bloomington: Indiana University Press, 2010.
Gevisser, Mark. *Thabo Mbeki: A Dream Deferred*. Johannesburg: Jonathan Ball, 2007.
Gifford, Tony. *South Africa's Record of International Terrorism*. London: Anti-Apartheid Movement, 1981.
Ginzburg, Carlo. *Clues, Myths and the Historical Method*. Baltimore: Johns Hopkins University Press, 1989.
———. *The Cheese and the Worms: The Cosmos of the 16th Century Miller*. Baltimore: Johns Hopkins University Press, 1980.
Glaser, Clive. *The ANC Youth League*. Auckland Park: Jacana, 2012.
Gleijeses, Piero. *Conflicting Missions: Havana, Washington and Africa*. Chapel Hill: University of North Carolina Press, 2002.
Gluckman, Max. *Custom and Conflict in Africa*. Oxford: Blackwell, 1956.
Gordin, Jeremy. *Zuma: A Biography*. Johannesburg: Jonathan Ball, 2008.
Govender, Pregs. *Love and Courage: A Story of Insubordination*. Johannesburg: Jacana, 2007.
Grosskopf, Hein. *Artistic Graves*. Johannesburg: Ravan, 1993.
Guevara, Ernesto *Guerrilla Warfare*. Lincoln: University of Nebraska Press, 1985.
———. *The African Dream: The Diaries of the Revolutionary War in Cuba*. London: Harvill, 2000.
Gunn, Shirley. *If Trees Could Speak: The Trojan Horse Story*. Cape Town: Human Rights Media Centre, 2007.
Hadfield, Leslie. *Liberation and Development: Black Consciousness Community Programs in South Africa*. East Lansing: Michigan State University Press, 2016.
Hirson, Baruch. *The Revolutions in My Life*. Johannesburg: University of the Witwatersrand Press, 1995.
———. *Year of Fire, Year of Ash: The Soweto Revolt, Roots of a Revolution?* London: Zed, 1979.
Hobsbawm, Eric. *Nations and Nationalism since 1780: Programme, Myth, Reality*. Cambridge, UK: Cambridge University Press, 2012.
Holden, Paul. *The Arms Deal in Your Pocket*. Johannesburg: Jonathan Ball, 2009.
Holland, Heidi. *The Struggle: A History of the African National Congress*. New York: George Braziller, 1990.
Hutchinson, Sharon. *Nuer Dilemmas: Coping with Money, War and the State*. Berkeley: University of California Press, 1996.

Hynes, Samuel. *The Soldiers' Tale: Bearing Witness to Modern War.* New York: A. Lane, 1997.
James, Wilmot G., and Mary Simons. *The Angry Divide: Social and Economic History of the Western Cape.* Cape Town: David Philip, 1989.
Jeffrey, Anthea. *A People's War: New Light on the Struggle for South Africa.* Johannesburg: Jonathan Ball, 2009.
———. *The Truth about the Truth Commission.* Johannesburg: SAIRR, 1999.
Joffe, Joel. *The State versus Nelson Mandela: The Trial That Changed South Africa.* Oxford: Oneworld, 2011.
Karis, Thomas G., and Gail M. Gerhart. *From Protest to Challenge: A Documentary History of African Politics in South Africa, 1882–1990.* Bloomington: Indiana University Press, 1997.
Kasrils, Ronald. *Armed and Dangerous: From Undercover Struggle to Freedom.* Auckland Park: Jacana, 2013.
Keitseng, Fish. *Comrade Fish: Memories of a Motswana in the ANC Underground.* Gaborone: Pula, 1999.
Kgosana, Philip Ata. *Lest We Forget.* Johannesburg: Skotaville, 1988.
Krieger, Norma. *Guerrilla Veterans in Post-War Zimbabwe: Symbolic and Violent Politics, 1980–1987.* Cambridge, UK: Cambridge University Press, 2003.
Lalu, Premesh. *The Deaths of Hintsa: Postapartheid South Africa and the Shape of Recurring Pasts.* Cape Town: HSRC Press, 2009.
Le Carré, John. *Tinker, Tailor, Soldier, Spy.* New York: Penguin, 2011.
Legassick, Martin. *Armed Struggle and Democracy: The Case of South Africa.* Uppsala, Sweden: Nordiska Afrikainstitutet, 2002.
Lejune, Philippe. *On Diary.* Manoa: University of Hawaii Press, 2009.
Lenin, Vladimir. *What Is to Be Done?* New York: International Publishers, 1902.
Lerumo, A. (Michael Harmel). *Fifty Fighting Years: The Communist Party of South Africa.* London: Inkululeko, 1971.
Lewin, Hugh. *Bandiet.* New York: Random House, 1974.
Limb, Peter. *The ANC's Early Years: Nation, Class and Place in South Africa before 1940.* Pretoria: University of South Africa Press, 2010.
Lodge, Tom. *Black Politics in South Africa since 1945.* New York: Longman, 1983.
Mabuyane, Oscar. *Umbutho Wesizwe: The African National Congress of the Eastern Cape.* London: Harry's Printers, 2012.
Macmillan, Hugh. *The Lusaka Years: The ANC in Exile in Zambia, 1963 to 1994.* Johannesburg: Jacana, 2013.
Magaziner, Dan. *The Law and the Prophets: Black Consciousness in South Africa, 1968–1977.* Athens: Ohio University Press, 2010.
Magubane, Bernard. *South Africa: From Soweto to Uitenhage: The Political Economy of the South African Revolution.* Trenton, NJ: Africa World Press, 1989.

———. *The Political Economy of Race and Class in South Africa.* New York: Monthly Review Press, 1979.
Majeke, Nosipho (Dora Taylor). *The Role of Missionaries in Conquest.* Johannesburg: Society of Young Africa, 1952.
Mali, T. *Chris Hani: The Sun That Set before Dawn.* Johannesburg: SACHED, 1993.
Mandela, Nelson, with Richard Stengel. *Long Walk to Freedom: The Autobiography of Nelson Mandela.* Boston: Little, Brown, 1994.
Manghezi, Nadja. *The Maputo Connection: The ANC in the World of Frelimo.* Auckland Park: Jacana, 2009.
Manong, Stanley. *If We Must Die: An Autobiography of a Former Commander of uMkhonto we Sizwe.* Johannesburg: Nkululeko, 2015.
Marx, Anthony W. *Making Race and Nation: A Comparison of South Africa, the United States, and Brazil.* Cambridge, UK: Cambridge University Press, 1998.
Marx, Karl. *18th Brumaire of Louis Napoleon.* New York: International Publishers, 1852.
Matakata, Jama. *Hills of Hope.* Pietermaritzburg: Nutrend, 2004.
Matthews, Z. K. *Freedom for My People: The Autobiography of Z. K. Matthews: Southern Africa 1901 to 1968.* Cape Town: David Philip, 1981.
Mbali, Fanele. *In Transit: Autobiography of a South African Freedom Fighter.* Observatory: South African History Online, 2012.
Mbeki, Govan. *The Peasants' Revolt.* Harmondsworth, UK: Penguin, 1965.
McCuen, John. *The Art of Counter-Revolutionary War: The Strategy of Counter-Insurgency.* Harrisburg, PA: Stackpole Books, 1966.
Meer, Fatima. *Higher Than Hope: The Authorized Biography of Nelson Mandela.* New York: Harper & Row, 1988.
Meli, Francis. *South Africa Belongs to Us: A History of the ANC.* Bloomington: Indiana University Press, 1988.
Mnguni (Hosea Jaffe). *Three Hundred Years.* Cape Town: New Era Fellowship, 1952.
Morris, Errol. *Believing Is Seeing: Observations on the Mysteries of Photography.* New York: Penguin, 2011.
Morrow, Sean, Brown Maaba, and Loyiso Pulumani. *Education in Exile: SOMAFCO: The ANC School in Tanzania, 1978 to 1992.* Cape Town: HSRC Press, 2004.
Morse, Eleanor. *White Dog Fell from the Sky.* London: Penguin, 2013.
Naidoo, Phyllis. *Le Rona Re Batho: An Account of the 1982 Maseru Massacre.* Johannesburg: Verulam, 1992.
Ngculu, James. *The Honour to Serve: Recollections of an Umkhonto Soldier.* Cape Town: David Philip, 2009.
Noble, Jonathan Alfred. *African Identity in Post-Apartheid Public Architecture.* Burlington, VT: Ashgate, 2011.

Nyerere, Julius. *Juliasi Kaisari*. Nairobi: Oxford University Press, 1963.
O'Malley, Padraig. *Shades of Difference: Mac Maharaj and the Struggle for South Africa*. New York: Viking, 2007.
Pampallis, John. *Foundations of the New South Africa*. Cape Town: Maskew Miller Longman, 1991.
Perrault, Gilles. *The Red Orchestra*. New York: Simon & Schuster, 1969.
Pike, Henry. *A History of Communism in South Africa*. Johannesburg: Christian Mission International of South Africa, 1988.
Portelli, Allesandro. *The Order Has Been Carried Out: History, Memory and Meaning of a Nazi Massacre in Rome*. New York: Palgrave Macmillan, 2003.
Pritchard, E. E. *Witchcraft, Oracles and Magic among the Azande*. Oxford: Clarendon, 1937.
Roux, Edward. *Time Longer Than Rope*. London: V. Gollancz, 1948.
———. *S. P. Bunting: A Political Biography*. Johannesburg: Self-published, 1944.
Sachs, Albie. *The Jail Diary of Albie Sachs*. London: Harvill, 1966.
Seekings, Jeremy. *The UDF: A History of the United Democratic Front in South Africa 1983–1991*. Cape Town: David Philip, 2000.
Sewell, Kenneth. *Herbert Butterfield and the Interpretation of History*. New York: Palgrave Macmillan, 2005.
Shakespeare, William. *The Dramatic Works of William Shakespeare Volume IV*. Boston: Philips and Sampson, 1846.
Schuster, Linda. *A Burning Hunger: One Family's Struggle against Apartheid*. Athens: Ohio University Press, 2004.
Shubin, Vladimir. *ANC: A View from Moscow*. Auckland Park: Jacana, 2012.
Sibeko, Archie. *Archie Sibeko's Roll of Honour: Western Cape ANC Comrades*. Bellville: University of the Western Cape, 2006.
Sibeko, Archie, with Joyce Leeson. *Freedom in Our Lifetime*. Durban: University of Natal Press, 1996.
Simons, H. J., and R. E. Simons. *Class and Colour in South Africa, 1850–1950*. Harmondsworth, UK: Penguin, 1969.
Slovo, Gillian. *Every Secret Thing*. New York: Brown, Little, 1997.
Smith, Anthony D. *Theories of Nationalism*. New York: Holmes & Meier, 1983.
Smith, Janet, and Beauregard Tromp. *Hani: A Life Too Short*. Johannesburg: Jonathan Ball, 2009.
Smith, Leonard. *Between Mutiny and Disobedience: The Case of the French Fifth Infantry Division during World War I*. Princeton, NJ: Princeton University Press, 1994.
Smythe, Hugh H., and Mabel M. Smythe. *The New Nigerian Elite*. Palo Alto, CA: Stanford University Press, 1960.

Sparg, Marion, Jenny Schreiner, and Gwen Ansell. *Comrade Jack: The Political Lecture and Diary of Jack Simons, Novo Catengue*. Johannesburg: STE Publishers, 2004.
Sparks, Allister. *Tomorrow Is Another Country: The Inside Story of South Africa's Road to Change*. Chicago: University of Chicago Press, 1996.
Stiff, Peter. *Silent War: South African Recce Operations, 1969–1994*. Johannesburg: Galago, 2007.
Suttner, Raymond. *The ANC Underground in South Africa, 1950–1976*. London: First Forum Press, 2009.
———. *ANC Underground in South Africa: A Social and Historical Study*. Johannesburg: Jacana, 2008.
Tabata, I. B. *The Awakening of a People*. Cape Town: All African Convention, 1950.
Taber, Robert. *The War of the Flea*. New York: L. Stuart, 1965.
Thomas, Scott. *The Diplomacy of Liberation: The Foreign Relations of the African National Congress since 1960*. London: Tauris Academic Studies, 1994.
Thompson, E. P. *The Making of the English Working Class*. New York: Vintage, 1963.
Thompson, Leonard. *Political Mythology of Apartheid*. New Haven, CT: Yale University Press, 1986.
Trewhela, Paul. *Inside Quatro: Uncovering the Exile History of the ANC and SWAPO*. Auckland Park: Jacana, 2009.
Truth and Reconciliation Commission of South Africa. *Truth and Reconciliation Commission of South Africa, Report, Volume 2*. Cape Town: Palgrave Macmillan, 2001.
Turok, Ben. *Nothing but the Truth: Behind the ANC's Struggle Politics*. Johannesburg: Jonathan Ball, 2003.
———. *The ANC and the Turn to Armed Struggle, 1950–1970*. Auckland Park: Jacana, 2011.
———. *With My Head above the Parapet: An Insider Account of the ANC in Power*. Auckland Park: Jacana, 2013.
Twala, Mwezi, and Ed Benard. *Mbokodo: Inside MK: A Soldier's Story*. Johannesburg: Jonathan Ball, 1994.
Van Onselen, Charles. *The Seed Is Mine: The Life of Kas Maine, a South African Sharecropper, 1894–1985*. Cape Town: David Philip, 1996.
Westad, Arne Odd. *The Global Cold War*. Cambridge, UK: Cambridge University Press, 2007.
White, Luise. *Speaking with Vampires*. Berkeley: University of California Press, 2001.
———. *The Assassination of Herbert Chitepo: Texts and Politics in Zimbabwe*. Bloomington: Indiana University Press, 2003.

Wilkinson, James. *The Intellectual Resistance in Europe*. Cambridge, MA: Harvard University Press, 1981.
Williams, Donovan. *A History of the University College of Fort Hare, South Africa: The 1950s: The Waiting Years*. Lewiston, NY: Edwin Mellen, 2001.
Witz, Leslie. *Apartheid's Festival: Contesting South Africa's National Pasts*. Bloomington: Indiana University Press, 2003.
Wolpe, Harold. *Race, Class and the Apartheid State*. Trenton, NJ: Africa World Press, 1990.

Chapters in Edited Volumes

Alexander, Neville. "Non-Collaboration in the Western Cape." In *The Angry Divide: Social and Economic History of the Western Cape*, edited by Wilmot G. James and Mary Simons., 180–92. Cape Town: David Philip, 1989.
Anonymous. "Ethnicity and Pseudo Ethnicity in the Ciskei." In *The Creation of Tribalism in Southern Africa*, edited by Leroy Vail, 395–413. Berkeley: University of California Press, 1991.
Autry, Robyn. "Doing Memory in Public: Post-Apartheid Memorial Space as an Activist Project." In *Memory and Post-War Memorials: Confronting the Violence of the Past*, edited by Marc Silberman and Florance Vatan, 137–54. New York: Palgrave Macmillan, 2013.
Berger, Michelle. "Chris Hani." In *They Fought for Freedom*, edited by John Pampallis, 19–24. Cape Town: Maskew Miller Longman, 1994.
Bonner, Phil. "Fragmentation and Cohesion in the ANC: The First 70 Years." In *One Hundred Years of the ANC: Debating Liberation Histories Today*, edited by Arianna Lissoni, Jon Soske, Natasha Erlank, Noor Nieftagodien, and Omar Badsha, 1–12. Johannesburg: University of the Witwatersrand Press, 2012.
Booysen, Susan. "Regeneration of ANC Political Power, from the 1994 Electoral Victory to the 2012 Centenary." In *One Hundred Years of the ANC: Debating Liberation Histories Today*, edited by Arianna Lissoni, Jon Soske, Natasha Erlank, Noor Nieftagodien, and Omar Badsha, 301–24. Johannesburg: University of the Witwatersrand Press, 2012.
Bozzoli, Belinda. "Experience, History and Culture." In *Town and Countryside in the Transvaal: Capitalist Penetration and Popular Response*, edited by Belinda Bozzoli, 1–47. Johannesburg: Ravan, 1983.
Bozzoli, Belinda, and Peter Delius. "Radical History and South African History." In *History from South Africa: Alternative Visions and Practices*, edited by Joshua Brown, 4–25. Philadelphia: Temple University Press, 1991.
Brecht, Bertolt. "The Carpet Weavers of Kuyan-Bulak Honour Lenin." In *The Collected Works of Bertolt Brecht*, edited by Erik Willet, 53–72. London: New World, 1929.

Bundy, Colin. "New Nation, New History?: Constructing the Past in Post-Apartheid South Africa." In *History Making and Present Day Politics*, edited by Hans Erik Stolten, 73–97. Uppsala, Sweden: Nordiska Afrikainstitutet, 2007.

Callinicos, Luli. "The 'People's Past': Toward Transforming the Present." In *Class, Community and Conflict*, edited by Belinda Bozzoli, 44–60. Johannesburg: Ravan, 1987.

Edgar, David. "The Jail Diary of Albie Sachs." In *Plays: One*, edited by David Edgar, 51–103. London: Methuen, 1987.

Hemson, David, Martin Legassick, and Nicole Ulrich. "White Activists and the Revival of the Workers' Movement." In *The Road to Democracy in South Africa: Volume 2, 1970–1980*, edited by Bernard Magubane, 243–316. Pretoria: University of South Africa Press, 2006.

Houston, Gregory, and Bernard Magubane. "The ANC Political Underground in the 1970s." In *The Road to Democracy in South Africa: Volume 2, 1970–1980*, edited by Bernard Magubane and Gregory Houston, 371–72. Pretoria: University of South Africa Press, 2006.

———. "The ANC's Armed Struggle in the 1970s." In *The Road to Democracy in South Africa: Volume 2, 1970–1980*, edited by Bernard Magubane and Gregory Houston, 453–530. Pretoria: University of South Africa Press, 2006.

Houston, Gregory. "The ANC's Armed Struggle in South Africa." In *The Road to Democracy in South Africa, Volume 4 (1980–1990)*, edited by Gregory Houston, 1037–1170. Pretoria: University of South Africa Press, 2010.

Hughes, Heather. "Rainbow, Renaissance, Tribes and Townships: Tourism and Heritage in South Africa since 1994." In *State of the Nation: South Africa 2007*, edited by Sakhela Buhlungu, John Daniel, Roger Southall, and Jessica Lutchman, 266–88. Cape Town: HSRC Press, 2007.

Hyslop, Jonathan. "Food Authority and Politics: Student Riots in South African Schools 1945–1976." In *Regions and Repertoires: Topics in South Africa Politics and Culture*, edited by Stephen Clingman, 84–116. Johannesburg: Ravan, 1991.

Lodge, Tom. "Resistance and Reform, 1973–1994." In *The Cambridge History of South Africa: Volume 2, 1885–1994*, edited by Robert Ross, Anne Kelk Mager, and Bill Nasson, 409–91. Cambridge, UK: Cambridge University Press, 2012.

———. "Rebellion: The Turning of the Tide." In *All, Here, and Now: Black Politics in South Africa in the 1980s*, edited by Tom Lodge and Bill Nasson. 58–64. New York: Ford Foundation, 1991.

Magubane, Bernard. "Whose Memory—Whose History?: The Illusion of Liberal and Radical Historical Debates." In *History Making and Present Day Politics: The Meaning of Collective Memory in South Africa*, edited by Hans Erik Stolten, 251–79. Uppsala, Sweden: Nordiska Afrikainstitutet, 2007.

———. "Preface." In *The Road to Democracy in South Africa: Volume 1, 1960–1970*, edited by Bernard Magubane, i–xix. Cape Town: Zebra Press, 2004.

Mbeki, Thabo. "Foreword." In *The Road to Democracy in South Africa: Volume 1, 1960–1970*, edited by Bernard Magubane, vii–xii. Cape Town: Zebra Press, 2004.

Minkley, Gary, and Ciraj Rassool. "Orality, Memory, and Social History in South Africa." In *Negotiating the Past: The Making of Memory in South Africa*, edited by Sarah Nuttall and Carli Coetzee, 9–99. Oxford: Oxford University Press, 1998.

Ndlovu, Sifiso, and Jabulani Sithole. "The Revival of the Labour Movement, 1970–1980." In *The Road to Democracy in South Africa: Volume 2, 1970–1980*, edited by Bernard Magubane, 187–242. Pretoria: University of South Africa Press, 2006.

Ndlovu, Sifiso Mxolisi. "The ANC's Diplomacy and International Relations." In *The Road to Democracy in South Africa: Volume 2, 1970–1980*, edited by Bernard Magubane, 658–60. Pretoria: University of South Africa Press, 2006.

Ralinala, Rendani, Jabulani Sithole, Gregory Houston, and Bernard Magubane. "The Wankie and Sipolilo Campaigns." In *The Road to Democracy in South Africa: Volume 1, 1960–1970*, edited by Bernard Magubane, 479–541. Cape Town: Zebra Press, 2004.

Reid-Daly, Ron. "War in Rhodesia: Cross-Border Operations." In *Challenge: Southern Africa within the African Revolutionary Context*, edited by Al Venter, 146–82. Johannesburg: Ashanti, 1989.

Riot, Philippe, "The Parallel Lives of Pierre Riviere." In *I Pierre Rivière, Having Slaughtered My Mother, My Sister, My Brother: A Case of Parricide in the 19th Century*, edited by Michel Foucault. New Haven, CT: Yale University Press, 1975.

Sapire, Hilary, and Chris Saunders. "Liberation Struggles in Southern Africa in Context." In *Southern African Liberation Struggles*, edited by Hilary Sapire and Chris Saunders, 1–31. Cape Town: University of Cape Town Press, 2013.

Soske, Jon, Arianna Lissoni, and Natasha Erlank. "One Hundred Years of the ANC: Debating Struggle History after Apartheid." In *One Hundred Years of the ANC: Debating Liberation Histories Today*, edited by Arianna Lissoni, Jon Soske, Natasha Erlank, Noor Nieftagodien, and Omar Badsha, 29–53. Johannesburg: University of the Witwatersrand Press, 2012.

Southall, Roger. "The ANC: Party Vanguard of the Black Middle Class?" In *One Hundred Years of the ANC: Debating Liberation Histories Today*, edited by Arianna Lissoni, Jon Soske, Natasha Erlank, Noor Nieftagodien, and Omar Badsha., Johannesburg: University of the Witwatersrand Press, 2012.

Wells, Julia. "'Are We Nation-Building Yet?': The Role of Oral Historians in Documenting the Transition Out of Apartheid." In *Oral History in a Wounded*

Country: Interactive Interviewing in South Africa, edited by Philippe Denis and Radikobo Ntsimane, 22–42. Scottsville: University of KwaZulu-Natal Press, 2008.

White, Luise. "True Stories: Narrative, Event, History, and Blood in the Lake Victoria Basin." In *African Words, African Voices: Critical Practices in Oral History*, edited by Luise White and Stephen Miescher, 281–304. Bloomington: Indiana University Press, 2001.

Conference Papers

Delius, Peter. "Thompson's Child or a Relative from the Colonies: A Footnote from a Foot Soldier in South Africa's History Wars, 1970–1990." Paper presented at the History after E. P. Thompson conference, University of Michigan, Ann Arbor, November 16, 2015.

Robinson, Jennifer. "Apartheid Subjects and Postcolonialism: Native Administrators in Port Elizabeth, 1945–1970." Paper presented at the Wits History Workshop, University of the Witwatersrand, Johannesburg, July 13, 1994.

Conversations and Correspondence with Author

Author to Freedom Park, "Malixoli Hadi, Name Submission." July 13, 2009.
Judith Van Allen, conversation with author, April 11, 2010.
Ineke Van Kessel, conversation with author, October 2007.
Tlou Makura, correspondence with author, July 21, 2015.

Field Notes

Freedom Park, field notes, March 8, 2008.
Freedom Park, field notes, June 7, 2015.

Films

Berlin: Symphony of a Great City. DVD. Directed by Walter Ruttman. USA, Fox Film Corporation. 1927.
First Blood. DVD. Directed by Ted Kotcheff. Hollywood, CA, Lion's Gate. 2004.
Nqose, Zolile. *The Luthuli Detachment*. DVD. Cape Town, Qoma Film Productions. 2007.
The Gugulethu Seven. VHS. Directed by Lindy Wilson. Cape Town, Wilson Films. 2007.

Interviews by Author

April, James, interview with author, April 30, 2008.
Barrell, Howard, interview with author, November 1, 2007.

Cronin, Jeremy, interview with author, June 2, 2008.
Esau, Cecyl, interview with author, November 14, 2007.
Fester, Gertrude, interview with author, January 29, 2008.
Giffard, Chris, interview with author, January 30, 2008.
Giffard, Chris, interview with author, June 14, 2016.
Goldberg, Denis, interview with author, May 20, 2008.
Gunn, Shirley, interview with author, November 20, 2007.
Gunn, Shirley, interview with author, December 19, 2007.
Gunn, Shirley, interview with author, January 18, 2008.
Hadi, Malixoli, interview with author, January 12, 2008.
Hodgson, Spencer, interview with author, December 13, 2007.
Jonas, Bongani, interview with author, July 12, 2006.
Mahlale, Captain, interview with author, January 25, 2008.
Matanjana, Patrick, interview with author, November 25, 2007.
Moss, Ish, interview with author, September 25, 2007.
Myrdal, Brett, interview with author, July 2, 2008.
Ozinsky, Max, interview with author, January 24, 2008.
Rabkin, Sue, interview with author, May 12, 2008.
Rampeng, Kennedy, interview with author, December 15, 2007.
Rampeng, Kennedy, interview with author, December 29, 2007.
Seremane, Joseph, interview with author, November 13, 2007.
Thornton, Amy, interview with author, June 3, 2008.
Willie, Alfred, and Sandile Sejake, interview with author, May 28, 2008.

Interviews by Others

Karis Gerhart Collection, Historical Papers Research Archive, Cullen Library, University of the Witwatersrand, Johannesburg

Anderson, Bill, interview with Howard Barrell, April 8, 1991. Karis Gerhart Collection, Historical Papers Research Archive, Cullen Library, University of the Witwatersrand.

Goldberg, Denis, interview with Howard Barrell, February 8, 1990. Karis Gerhart Collection, Historical Papers Research Archive, Cullen Library, University of the Witwatersrand.

Kasrils, Ronnie, interview with Howard Barrell, October 28, 1990. Karis Gerhart Collection, Historical Papers Research Archive, Cullen Library, University of the Witwatersrand.

Maharaj, Mac, interview with Howard Barrell, November 20, 1990. Karis Gerhart Collection, Historical Papers Research Archive, Cullen Library, University of the Witwatersrand.

Maharaj, Mac, interview with Howard Barrell, November 30, 1990. Karis Gerhart Collection, Historical Papers Research Archive, Cullen Library, University of the Witwatersrand.

Rabkin, Sue, interview with Howard Barrell, July 7, 1989. Karis Gerhart Collection, Historical Papers Research Archive, Cullen Library, University of the Witwatersrand.

Rabkin, Sue, interview with Howard Barrell, November 26, 1990. Karis Gerhart Collection, Historical Papers Research Archive, Cullen Library, University of the Witwatersrand.

Rabkin, Sue, interview with Howard Barrell, November 27, 1990. Karis Gerhart Collection, Historical Papers Research Archive, Cullen Library, University of the Witwatersrand.

Stadler, Herman, interview with Howard Barrell. Karis Gerhart Collection, Historical Papers Research Archive, Cullen Library, University of the Witwatersrand.

Strachan, Garth, interview with Howard Barrell, December 28, 1990. Karis Gerhart Collection, Historical Papers Research Archive, Cullen Library, University of the Witwatersrand.

Zuma, Jacob, interview with Howard Barrell, August 18, 1989. Karis Gerhart Collection, Historical Papers Research Archive, Cullen Library, University of the Witwatersrand.

Mayibuye Centre Archives, Robben Island Museum, University of the Western Cape, Bellville

Binda, Sipho, interview with Wolfie Kodesh, March 24, 1993. Wolfie Kodesh Collection, Mayibuye Centre Archives.

Goldberg, Denis, interview with John Pampallis, June 13, 1985. Mayibuye Centre Archives.

Goldberg, Denis, interview with Wolfie Kodesh, August 6, 1993. Wolfie Kodesh Collection, Mayibuye Centre Archives.

Hani, Chris, interview with Wolfie Kodesh. Wolfie Kodesh Collection, Mayibuye Centre Archives.

Masondo, Andrew, interview with Hilda Bernstein. Hilda Bernstein Collection, Mayibuye Centre Archives.

Matanjana, Patrick, interview with anonymous. Mayibuye Centre Archives.

Mfene, Peter (Teddington Nqaphayi), interview with Wolfie Kodesh, February 19, 1992. Wolfie Kodesh Collection, Mayibuye Centre Archives.

Mochele, Meshack, interview with Wolfie Kodesh, December 15, 1992. Wolfie Kodesh Collection, Mayibuye Centre Archives.

Morodi, Graham, interview with Wolfie Kodesh, March 23, 1993. Wolfie Kodesh Collection, Mayibuye Centre Archives.
Motaung, Peter, and Katleho Moloi, interviewed by Hilda Bernstein. Hilda Bernstein Collection, Mayibuye Centre Archives.
Mzimela, Cletus, interview with Jabulani Sithole, 2001. South African Democratic Education Trust.
Rabkin, Sue, interview with Howard Barrell, July 7, 1989. Mayibuye Centre Archives.
Rabkin, Sue, interview with Wolfie Kodesh, March 24, 1993. Wolfie Kodesh Collection, Mayibuye Centre Archives.
Shoke, Solly, interview with Wolfie Kodesh, July 4, 1993. Wolfie Kodesh Collection, Mayibuye Centre Archives.
Turok, Ben, interview with Wolfie Kodesh, March 8, 1993. Wolfie Kodesh Collection, Mayibuye Centre Archives.

South African Democratic Education Trust (SADET) Interviews

"James April, interview with Nhlanhla Ndebele and Moses Ralinala." In *The Road to Democracy: South Africans Telling Their Stories: Volume I, 1950–1970*, edited by Gregory Houston, 47–59. Johannesburg: South African Democracy Education Trust, 2008.
"Justice 'Gizenga' Mpanza, interview with Jabulani Sithole and Bernard Magubane." In *The Road to Democracy: South Africans Telling Their Stories: Volume I, 1950–1970*, edited by Gregory Houston, 337–49. Edenvale: Mutloatse Arts Heritage Trust, 2008.
"Lawrence Phokanoka (Peter Tladi), interview with Siphamandla Zondi." In *The Road to Democracy: South Africans Telling Their Stories: Volume I, 1950–1970*, edited by Gregory Houston, 409–23. Edenvale: Mutloatse Arts Heritage Trust, 2008.

Newspaper, Magazine, and Periodical Articles

"Abduction Plan in Matola Raid." *The Argus*, February 3, 1981.
Ali, Tariq. "Southern Africa: A Betrayal." *The Black Dwarf*, November 26, 1969.
"AZAPO Calls for Heroes Acre in SA." *The Citizen*, June 7, 1995, 11.
"Bandit Raid." *Pravda*, January 31, 1981.
"Border Clamp." *The Citizen*, January 15, 1986, 6.
Donnelly, Lynley, and Lucky Sindane. "Jo'burg's Miss World Debacle." *Mail and Guardian*, December 11, 2009.
"Events Planned in Honour of Fallen Heroes." *The Herald*, March 21, 2006, 3.
Faul, Michelle. "Mandela's Ex-Wife Shocked at Possible Prosecution." *Associated Press*, March 13, 2013.

Freedom Park Trust. "Press Release: Freedom Park Hands over Site for Construction." June 23, 2003.
Fuzile, Bongani. "Military Heroes Acre on the Cards." *Daily Dispatch*, February 15, 2013, 4.
Gibson, Nat. "South Africa Army Vows More Border Attacks on Blacks." *UPI*, February 1, 1981.
Harper, Paddy. "Tears in Memory of Matola Raid." *City Press*, February 27, 2011, 10.
Hlahla, Patrick. "Ritual Returns Spirits of Fallen Heroes Back Home." *Pretoria News*, September 25, 2007.
"I Joined ANC after Soldiers Shot My Wife." *Rand Daily Mail*, November 27, 1982, 2.
"Let Us Not Airbrush Our History for the Sake of Our Real Heroes." *Sunday World*, November 7, 1999, 2.
Mahanjana, Vusi. "Go Ahead, Honour Our Heroes." *Weekly Mail and Guardian*, October 9, 2003, 23.
"Maputo Raid Is Condemned." *The Sowetan*, February 2, 1981.
"Matola Raid." *The Sowetan*, February 13, 2004.
"Mozambique Pledge at ANC Funeral." *The Star*, February 9, 1981, 3.
"My Brother Is with Us Again." *City Press*, April 4, 2009.
Naran, Juggie. "Commemoration to Mark Death of Struggle Hero." *Sunday Tribune*, January 22, 2006, 3.
———. "Lesson from Activist." *Sunday Tribune*, April 15, 2007.
"Plan to Rebury All ANC Freedom Fighters." *Daily Dispatch*, February 2, 2006, 6.
"Raids by SA 'Act of War' Says Machel." *Rand Daily Mail*, February 16, 1981, 3.
"SA Must Not Honour Colonial Wars." *The Sowetan*, October 13, 1999, 10.
"SA-Mozambique Ties Are Key." *The Sowetan*, February 16, 2014.
"South Africa: The Black Pimpernel." *Time*, August 17, 1962.
"The Booze Brigade," *Sunday Tribune*, February 15, 1981, 1.

Internet Sources

African National Congress. "ANC Missing Remains of MK Combatants Killed by Apartheid Regime Handed Over to Families 24 J." Accessed September 13, 2017, https://www.youtube.com/watch?v=HKH1bn5YjcQ.
———. "ANC Submission to the TRC in Reply to the TRC's 'Findings on the ANC.'" Accessed June 17, 2016, http://www.anc.org.za/show.php?id=2667.
———. "Further Submissions and Responses by the ANC to Questions Raised by the Commission for Truth and Reconciliation, 12 May 1997." Accessed June 20, 2016, http://www.anc.org.za/show.php?id=2645.
———. "List of ANC Members Who Died in Exile." Accessed June 25, 2016, http://www.anc.org.za/show.php?id=100.

———. "Nation-Formation and Nation Building: The National Question in South Africa." Accessed June 18, 2016, http://www.anc.org.za/show.php?id=309.

———. "Statement to the Truth and Reconciliation Commission, August 1996." Accessed June 17, 2016, http://www.justice.gov.za/trc/hrvtrans/submit/anctruth.htm.

———. "Statement to the Truth and Reconciliation Commission, August 1996." Accessed June 20, 2016, http://www.anc.org.za/show.php?id=2639.

Alexander, Neville. "100 Years of the African National Congress." Accessed November 6, 2014, http://www.sahistory.org.za/archive/100-years-african-national-congress-neville-alexander.

Armchair General. "Operation Beanbag." Accessed June 25, 2016, http://www.armchairgeneral.com/forums/showthread.php?p=1846206.

Congress of the People. "The Freedom Charter." Accessed June 18, 2016, http://www.anc.org.za/show.php?id=72.

De Klerk, F. W. "Submission to the Truth and the Reconciliation Commission by Mr. FW De Klerk, Leader of the National Party." Accessed June 22, 2016, http://www.justice.gov.za/trc/hrvtrans/submit/np_truth.htm.

Department of Arts and Culture. "Education and Recreation Select Committee, Arts, Culture, Science and Technology Portfolio Committee: Joint Meeting. 12 November 2002. Freedom Park: Briefing." Accessed June 25, 2016, https://pmg.org.za/committeemeeting/2007/.

———. "Matola Deceased Profiles." Accessed June 25, 2016, https://artsculturesa.files.wordpress.com/2015/09/matola-deceased-profiles.docx.

———. "Matola Exhibition Film." Accessed June 25, 2016, https://youtu.be/3Jv1P987PnE.

———. "Matola Raid Memorial Project Unveiling Ceremony: 11 September 2015, Internal Discussion Document." Accessed June 25, 2016, https://artsculturesa.files.wordpress.com/2015/09/20150309_matola-unveiling-briefing-document.pdf.

Department of Military Veterans. "Unveiling of Matola Raid Monument and Intepretive [sic] Centre." Accessed June 25, 2016, http://www.dmv.gov.za/news/matola-raid.htm.

Dubula, Sol (Joe Slovo). "Strategy and Tactics." Accessed June 18, 2016, https://www.marxists.org/subject/africa/anc/1969/strategy-tactics.htm.

Education and Recreation Select Committee, Arts, Culture, Science and Technology Portfolio Committee. "Joint Meeting, 12 November 2002, Freedom Park: Briefing." Accessed June 24, 2016, https://pmg.org.za/committee-meeting/2007/.

Freedom Park. "About Us, April 3, 2006." Accessed June 24, 2016, https://web.archive.org/web/20050403223910/http://www.freedompark.co.za/aboutus.html.

———. "Homepage." Accessed June 25, 2016, http://www.freedompark.co.za/36-galleries.

———. "Public Participation Form." Archived website September 27, 2006. Accessed June 25, 2016, https://web.archive.org/web/20060927174103/http://www.freedompark.co.za/publicparticipationform.html.

———. "Remembering and Forgetting at Freedom Park." Accessed June 25, 2016, http://www.archivalplatform.org/news/entry/remembering_and_forgetting/.

———. "Virtual Tour." Accessed June 25, 2016, http://www.freedompark.co.za/visit-us/virtual-tour.

Gunn, Shirley. "Human Rights Violation Hearing Testimony, 7-August-1996." Accessed June 23, 2016, http://www.justice.gov.za/trc/hrvtrans%5Chelder/ct00792.htm.

Hamilton, Carolyn. "Emerging Themes and Trends, Opportunities and Challenges." Accessed August 3, 2015, http://www.saha.org.za/resources/docs/PDF/Publications/MHPI.pdf.

Harms Commission. "Harms Commission of Inquiry Evidence." Accessed June 22, 2016, http://www.historicalpapers.wits.ac.za/?inventory/U/collections&c=AK2300/R/.

Hyslop, Jonathan. "E. P. Thompson in South Africa." Accessed October 14, 2014, https://www.academia.edu/4690108/E.P._THOMPSON_IN_SOUTH_AFRICA_REVISED_.

Mandela, Nelson. "Address by President Nelson Mandela at Freedom Day Celebrations, Umtata." Accessed June 24, 2016, http://www.mandela.gov.za/mandela_speeches/1999/990427_freedomday.htm.

Marschall, Sabine. "Landscape of Memory." Accessed August 12, 2015, https://openaccess.leidenuniv.nl/handle/1887/18536.

Masondo, Andrew. "12 October 2001, Section 29 Hearing, March 26, 1998." Accessed June 21, 2016, https://cryptome.org/za-masondo.txt.

Masutha, Michael. "Speech by Minister of Justice and Correctional Services Michael Masutha, MP (Adv), on the Occasion of Handover of Remains of MK Soldiers at Freedom Park." Accessed September 13, 2017, http://www.justice.gov.za/m_speeches/2015/20150724_TRC.html.

Mazibuko, Joseph Titus. "Human Rights Violation Hearing Testimony, February 4, 1997." Accessed June 23, 2016, http://www.justice.gov.za/trc/hrvtrans%5Cduduza/mazibuko.htm.

Mhaga, Mthunzi. "Handover Ceremony of the Exhumed Remains of 10 Former MK Members." Accessed September 13, 2017, http://www.freedompark.co.za/stay-informed/news-and-media-releases/148-handover-of-mk-cadres.html.

Mkhize, Bongani. "Taking Freedom Park to the People." Accessed June 25, 2016, sashtw.org.za/WP/wp-content/uploads/…/FREEDOM-PARK-PRESENTATION.ppt.

Motlanthe, Kgalema. "Address by Deputy President Kgalema Motlanthe on the Occasion of the Official Opening of the Freedom Park //Hapo Museum, Pretoria, April 22, 2013." Accessed June 24, 2016, http://www.thepresidency.gov.za/pebble.asp?relid=15286&t=79.

Mthembu, Mtunzi Gabriel. "10 October 2001, Section 29 Hearing, April 3, 1998." Accessed June 21, 2016, https://cryptome.org/za-mthembu.txt.

Mthimkhulu, Joyce. "Human Rights Violations Hearing Testimony, June 26, 1996." Accessed June 22, 2016, http://www.justice.gov.za/trc/hrvtrans%5Chrvpe2/mtimkhul.htm.

O'Malley, Padraig. "Phyllis Naidoo, interview with Padraig O'Malley, October 26, 2003." Accessed June 25, 2016, https://www.nelsonmandela.org/omalley/index.php/site/q/03lv03445/04lv03833/05lv03891/06lv03909.htm.

Partridge, Matthew. "Dali Tambo's R600m Struggle Theme Park." Accessed June 24, 2016. http://www.financialmail.co.za/features/2014/05/02/dali-tambo-s-r600m-struggle-theme-park.

Rabilal, Raj. "My Slideshow." Accessed June 25, 2016, https://youtu.be/IuO_yMpNXTY.

Rassool, Ciraj. "Power, Knowledge and the Politics of Public Pasts." Accessed September 4, 2014, http://www.nelsonmandela.org/images/uploads/PAPER_-_RASSOOL.pdf.

SABC Digital News. "Elias Zwane on Matola Raid Massacre." Accessed June 25, 2016, https://youtu.be/gfQQ2tm1d4E.

SAPA. "Memorial to Victims Possible, March 19, 1997." Accessed June 24, 2016, http://www.justice.gov.za/trc/media%5C1997%5C9703/s970319e.htm.

Sejake, Sandile. "Inside the Wankie Campaign: ANC-ZAPU Armed Actions in Rhodesia during 1967–68." Accessed June 19, 2016, http://panafricannews.blogspot.com/2007/11/inside-wankie-campaign-anc-zapu-armed.html.

Seremane, Joseph. "Testimony, July 22, 1997." Accessed June 21, 2016, http://www.justice.gov.za/trc/special%5Cprison/seremane.htm.

South African Defense Force. "SADF Involvement in the Internal Security Situation in the Republic of South Africa." Accessed June 22, 2016, http://www.justice.gov.za/trc/hrvtrans/submit/sadf.htm.

South African Government News Agency. "Freedom Park Trust Honours 24 Heroes." Accessed June 25, 2016, http://www.sanews.gov.za/features/freedomparktrusthonours24struggleheroes.

South African History Online. "List of ANC and MK Members Killed in Combat." Accessed June 25, 2016, http://www.sahistory.org.za/topic/list-anc-and-mk-members-killed-combat-1980s.

———. "Umkhonto we Sizwe, the ANC and the Turn to Armed Struggle." Accessed June 25, 2016, http://www.sahistory.org.za/topic/umkhonto-wesizwe-mk-exile?page=7.

Tambo, Oliver. "Speech by Oliver Tambo at a Frelimo Mass Rally at Bairro de Liberdade." Accessed June 25, 2016, http://www.anc.org.za/show.php?id=4404.

The Presidency. "Matola Raid Martyrs, Order of Mendi." Accessed November 5, 2015, http://www.thepresidency.gov.za/pebble.asp?relid=7617.

Thobela, Sipho Matthews. "Amnesty Hearing Testimony, 08 May 1998." Accessed June 25, 2016, http://sabctrc.saha.org.za/documents/amntrans/pretoria/54884.htm?t=%2BSoweto+%2Buprising.

Trewhela, Paul. "Inside Quatro: End of an Era." Accessed June 21, 2016, https://www.marxists.org/history/etol/revhist/supplem/hirson/quadro.html.

Truth and Reconciliation Commission of South Africa. "Chapter 4: The Liberation Movements from 1960–1990." Accessed June 25, 2016, http://www.justice.gov.za/trc/report/finalreport/Volume%202.pdf.

———. "Errata to the Final Report of the Truth and Reconciliation Commission, October 1998." Accessed June 25, 2016, http://archive.niza.nl/docs/200510141507453724.pdf.

———. "List of Victims." Accessed June 25, 2016, http://www.justice.gov.za/trc/report/finalreport/victims_list_vol7.pdf.

———. "Questions from the TRC to ANC in Response to the ANC First Submission to the TRC, November 1996." Accessed June 20, 2016, http://www.anc.org.za/show.php?id=2644.

———. "Nicodemus Sono and Nomsa Shabalala, Human Rights Violation Hearing Testimony, 25-July-1996." Accessed September 13, 2017, http://www.justice.gov.za/trc/hrvtrans%5Csoweto/sono.htm.

———. "R&R Workshop, Day 3, Johannesburg, February 20, 1998." Accessed August 24, 2015, http://www.justice.gov.za/trc/reparations/joburg3.htm.

———. "The TRC Report." Accessed June 22, 2016, http://www.justice.gov.za/trc/report/.

———. "TRC Final Report, Volume 2, Chapter 2, Subsection 40, Cross-Border Military Operations/Raids." Accessed June 25, 2016, http://www.sabctrc.saha.org.za/reports/volume2/chapter2/subsection40.htm&tab=report.

van der Merwe, Johan. "Recall of Gen Johan Velde van der Merwe, July 20, 1998." Accessed June 23, 2016, http://www.justice.gov.za/trc/amntrans%5C1998/98072031_pre_cosatu7.htm.

Venter, Bruce. "Park Honours Those Who 'Outsoared the Shadow,' March 9, 2004." Accessed June 24, 2016, http://www.iol.co.za/news/south-africa/park-honours-those-who-outsoared-the-shadow-207986.
Visagie, Patricia. "Mortal Remains of 10 Anti-Apartheid Activists Returned to Their Families." Accessed September 13, 2017, https://www.youtube.com/watch?v=4e78boynAAk.
Zuma, Jacob. "Address by Deputy President Jacob Zuma at the Launch of the Freedom Park Trust, June 1, 2000." Accessed June 24, 2016, http://www.polity.org.za/polity/govdocs/speeches/2000/sp0601.html.

Dissertations and Theses

Barrell, Howard. "Conscripts to Their Age: African National Congress Operational Strategy, 1976–1986." PhD diss., University of Oxford, 1993.
Fullard, Madeleine. "The State and Political Struggle: Strategies of Repression and Resistance in the Greater Cape Town Area from 1985 to 1989." MA thesis, University of the Western Cape, 2000.
Molapo, Rachidi. "Aspects of the South African Youth Experiences in Exile, 1960–1994." PhD diss., University of the Western Cape, 2005.
Rantete, Johannes. "Facing the Challenges of Transition: A Critical Analysis of the African National Congress in the 1990s." MA thesis, University of the Witwatersrand, 1994.
Shandler, David. "'Nie Meer in die Nag Nie': Popular Struggles in Worcester 1950–1960." MA thesis, University of Cape Town, 1985.
Suttner, Raymond. "Rendering Visible: The Underground Organizational Experience of the ANC-Led Alliance until 1976." PhD diss., University of the Witwatersrand, 2007.
von den Steinen, Lynda. "Experiencing the Armed Struggle: The Soweto Generation and After." PhD diss., University of Cape Town. 2007.

Reference Works

"Detective Fiction." In *Oxford Dictionary of Literary Terms*, edited by C. Baldick, 332–37. Oxford: Oxford University Press, 2007.

INDEX

//hapo, 202, 203, 214–217

action heroes, 52
activism, xxxi, 178, 207
Africa, decolonization, 3, 5, 15
African Communist, 167
African National Congress, xvii, xxvii; Africanists, xix, 3, 12, 16; armed struggle, 6, 207; corruption, 10; culture of exile, xviii, xxi, xxii, 10, 11, 12, 16, 113; exile, xviii, 1, 7, 8, 9, 107; factionalism, xxiii, 3, 11, 16, 61, 113, 146, 201; heroism, 134, 136, 204, 205, 212–214, 219; international solidarity, 5, 6, 7, 9, 15, 44, 47, 61, 200, 207; Kabwe Conference (1985), 93, 98, 104; legitimacy, xvii, 130, 134, 139; Lobatse Conference (1962), 6; Marxist Workers' Tendency (MWT), xx; mass politics, xxi, xxxi, 2, 3, 6; Morogoro Conference (1969), 11–14, 16, 78; National Executive Committee, 10, 12, 13, 16, 20; negotiated settlement, xviii, xxi, xxix, 49, 52, 170, 199; nonracialism, 13; nonviolence, 3, 4; rank-and-file, xxi, xxii; as ruling party, xvi, xviii, xxvii, xxix, xxxviii, xlii, 198; Revolutionary Council, 13, 14, 17, 159, 160, 161, 163, 164; ruling party, xlii, xv, xvi, xvii, xxix, xxxii, xxxviii, 198; security department (Mbokodo or Nat), 20–21, 86, 87; underground, 164, 207; violence, 3, 4, 6
African National Congress Youth League, 29
African People's Liberation Army (APLA), 133, 135

African Renaissance, 214
Afrikaans universities, xxv
agency, 112
Alleg, Henri, 47
Anglo-Boer War, 205
Angola, xiii, 13, 15–17, 20–22, 33, 47, 55, 85, 96, 111, 146, 148–149, 153, 157, 198, 207, 208, 211, 213, 230; independence, 15
Anti-Apartheid Movement (Great Britain), 47
apartheid: Bantu Education Act, 15; Group Areas Act (1950), 28
April, James, 36, 38, 51, 74–78
archetypes, 52, 105
Area Politico-Military Committee (APC), 169
armed propaganda, 18
armed struggle, xiii, xiv, xv, xviii, xx, xxi, xxxii, xxxiii, xxxiv, xxxv, 1, 2, 4, 6–7, 10, 12–13, 14, 21–22, 26–27, 29, 30, 33, 36, 41, 44, 47–53, 63, 78, 80, 85, 87–88, 96, 101–102, 108, 110, 112, 114, 129–130, 132–135, 142, 149, 151, 157, 165, 173, 175, 180, 182, 197–202, 204, 207–208, 211, 213–214, 216–217, 219, 220; cultural authenticity, 216; historiography on, xv–xxiii, xxxiii; origins, 4; as unstable concept, xxxii, 2, 41, 88
askaris, 36, 76
assassination, 20, 45, 48, 86, 94, 97, 100, 101, 142–143, 170–171, 175, 220
authenticity, xxiii
autobiography and biography, xxxiii, 32, 45, 50–51, 73, 91, 99–100, 135, 153, 177
autochthony, xxxii

262 | Index

Baloyi, Robert, 71
Barrell, Howard, 18, 134
Basil February MK Squad, 151, 158, 169, 170–172, 174–175, 178
Battlefield Gothic, 59, 63, 76, 81
Bernstein, Lionel, 44, 47
Berrange, Vernon, 34–35, 43
Bickford-Smith, Vivian, 130
Biko, Steve, 213
Black Consciousness, 106
Black Consciousness Movement (BCM), xx, 15, 17, 97
Black September, xiii–xiv, xxxiii, 19, 92–93
Bond, James, 162
Bopela, Thula, 63, 71, 73, 75, 79
Boshielo, Flag, 12
Botswana, xvii, 7, 11, 62, 64–65, 75, 77–80, 155, 166–167, 178
Braam, Connie, 178–180
bricolage, 50, 140, 167
British South Africa Police (BSAP), 61
bucket bombs (leaflet bombs), 15, 157, 169–172, 213
Butterfield, Herbert, 135–136

Cabral, Amilcar, 213
Cape Flats, 158
Carr, Edward Hallett, 136
Castro, Fidel, 37–38
Central Intelligence Office (Rhodesia), 10
Cetshwayo, 213
China, 8–9, 74–75
civilians, 5, 102, 142–144, 174, 176, 207, 219
Cold War, xiv, xvi, xix, 74, 207
Coloured People's Congress, 51–52
Comaroff, Jean, 89
Comaroff, John, 89
communism, xxi, 74
comrades, definition, 39–40, 80, 89, 94, 142
Conan Doyle, Arthur, 105
Congress Alliance, xxxi, 2, 28, 39, 50, 52; liberals, 3; Marxists, 3
Congress of Democrats, 3, 37
Congress of South African Trade Unions (COSATU), xxi
conscientization, 147, 150, 168

contingency, xxxii, 87–88, 112, 130, 148, 150, 153
Cooper, Frederick, xix, 131
counterinsurgency: warfare, 141; welfare, 140–141; Winning Hearts and Minds (WHAM), 140
court testimony, 27, 31–32, 35–36, 76, 156
critical history, xx, xxviii
Cronin, Jeremy, 15, 157, 159, 163, 164
cross-border raids, 166, 170
Crossroads, 141–142
Cuba, 60, 92–93, 108–109, 114, 150, 153–154, 206, 207
cultural authenticity, 199–200, 211–212, 214, 216–217

Dadoo, Yusef, 13, 163
Danie Theron Combat School, 151
Davids, Cyril, 31, 33–37, 39–40
de Wet, Christiaan, 213, 214
De Wet, Quartus, 40
Defiance Campaign, 16, 29
delegitimization, xvi
Department of Arts and Culture, 205
desk novels, 43
detective novels, 90–93, 96, 100, 104–105
detention, 31, 36, 45, 103, 143, 145, 157
determinism, xxxi, 136
diaries, 88, 105–114
Dlamini, Jacob, xxix
Douglas, Mary, 89
Dube, John, 73–75, 77
DuBois, W.E.B., 213

Edgar, David, 42, 47–48
elites, xv, xxi, xxii, xxiii, 143, 180, 219
Ellis, Stephen, ix, 6, 9
episode(s), xiii, xiv, xix, xxxv, 197, 201–202
Esau, Cecyl, 155, 157–158, 165–168
ethnography, 88–90, 170
Evans-Pritchard, E. E., 88
everyday life, xvii, 95–97, 139, 144, 146, 151, 161
execution, xvii, 20–21, 94–96, 208
experience, xvii, xxv, 2, 8, 59, 127–129, 133–135, 137–139, 144, 154, 159

Index | 263

explosives, 5, 7, 15, 18, 19, 34, 71, 85, 86–88, 92–93, 97–100, 102–103, 106, 111–114, 157, 168, 170–175, 177, 201

fantasy, 163–164
fashion, 162–163
February, Basil, 213
Federation of South African Trade Unions (FOSATU), xx
Feldman, Alan, 170
fiction, 167, 180
firearms, 30, 34, 52, 67, 74, 76, 108, 142, 147, 161, 166, 170–171, 173, 174, 176, 177, 201, 219
Fischer, Bram, 43, 213
Fischer, David, xix
Fleming, Ian, 162
Flower, Ken, 10
forensic archive, 139–146
Freedom Charter, 2, 3, 13, 215
Freedom Park, xxxii, xxxv, 197–220
freedom songs, 200, 212, 216–217
Frye, Northrop, 42
Fučík, Julius, 42, 43
Fullard, Madeleine, 139–145

Gallery of Leaders, 202, 209, 212–214
Garang, John, 213–214
Garvey, Marcus, 213
Gerhart, Gail, 106
Ghana, 5
Giap, Vo Nguyen, 17–18
Giffard, Chris, 158, 171–173, 175, 178
Ginzburg, Carlo, 33, 44, 136–137, 153, 155
Goldberg, Denis, ix, 26, 31, 33–35, 37–40, 50–52, 122–123
guerrilla training camp, xiii, xiv, xxii, xxxii, xxxiii, 5, 8, 26, 31, 33–34, 40–41, 44, 64, 72, 73, 85, 115, 200, 212, 216
guerrilla warfare, xxxiii, 21, 27, 35–38, 49, 60–61, 68, 81, 88, 94, 96, 98, 155
guerrillas, xiii, xvii, xxxiii, 2, 7–11, 14, 17–21, 26–27, 31–41, 49–50, 60–62, 64–65, 67–81, 88, 94, 98, 108, 155
Guevara, Ernesto (Che), 36, 40, 213
Gunn, Shirley, 153–154

habituated eye, 153–156, 179
hagiography, 61
Hani, Chris, 12, 20–21, 66–67, 70–73, 77–78, 211, 213
Hani Memorandum, xvii, 11, 12, 78
hardmen, 170
Harms Commission, 139
heritage, xxviii, xxxii, xxxv, 51, 197
hermeneutics, 92, 104
heroes acre(s), 209, 210–211
Hirson, Baruch, 106
historicism, 149–151
historiography, xiv, xix, xxiii, xxxii, xxxiv, 86, 136, 155, 197
hitting back, 169–170, 174–177, 179
Hobsbawm, Eric, xv
Hodgson, Jack, 5
Hofmeyr, Isabel, xxvi
Hühn, Peter, 91, 93, 105
human rights abuses, xix
Hynes, Samuel, 59
Hyslop, Jonathan, xxix, 106

imagination, 33, 35, 44, 47, 59, 62, 74, 128, 132, 155, 167, 169, 180
International Defense and Aid (IDAF), 47
interrogation, 20, 33, 36, 45–47, 66, 75–76, 87, 91, 98, 103–104, 165
investigative reports, 85–86, 88, 90, 92, 95–96, 98, 106, 111
Isivivane, 124, 202, 209–212

Jaffe, Hosea, xxxi
Joffe, Joel, 34–35, 42–44, 47
Joseph, Helen, 213
Julius Caesar, 219–220

Kambona, Oscar, 9
Kasrils, Eleanor, 163
Kasrils, Ronnie, 5, 7–8
Kasrils, Ronnie (aka Frank), 157, 163
Keitseng, Fish, 7
kitkonstabels, 145
Kodesh, Wolfie, 64, 159
Korean War, 207

Kotane, Moses, 6, 13, 213
Kros, Cynthia, 216

Le Carre, John, 155, 164, 167, 168
leaflets, 5, 15, 59, 168–173, 176, 178
Leballo, Potlako, 9
Lesotho, 166
life history, xxvi, 165
Liliesleaf Farm, 31, 121
literacy, 137
literary criticism, 90, 146
logistics, 170
Louverture, Toussaint, 213
Luthuli, Albert, 213
Luthuli, Daluxolo, 63, 71, 73, 79

Madikizela-Mandela, Winnie, 218
Mahamba, Kenneth, 103–104
Maharaj, Mac, 150
Mahlale, Captain, 164–166
Mahlangu, Solomon, 213
Maine, Kas, xxvi
Makiwane, Tennyson, 16
Malaya, 140
Maliba, Julius (aka Manchecker), 71
Mampe, Absalom, 110
Mampuru, Christopher, 67
Mandela, Nelson, xiii, 4–6, 22, 43, 90, 203
Mandela Plan (M-Plan), 164
Mandela United Football Club, 218
Mandelstam, Nadezhda, 43
Manthatisi, 213
Maphatsoe, Kebby, 217, 219
mapping, 62, 64
Marks, J. B., 213
Marwick, Max, 89
Marxism, 106, 149–150, 167, 180
Marxist historiography, xxiv
Masipa, Barry, 71
Masondo, Andrew, 93
mass politics, 18
mass protest, 141, 150, 152, 200
mass struggle, 206–208
Masutha, Michael, 217, 219
Matanjana, Patrick, 74
Matola Raid, xxxv
Matthews, Joe, 5, 10

Mbeki, Govan, xxxi
Mbeki, Thabo, xxix, 58, 105, 205, 214
Mbokodo (Nat), 20, 21, 86, 87
McCuen, John, 140
memorial technologies, 201, 207
memorials and monuments, 197–220
memory, xxvi, 2, 156
Mhlongo, Peter, 70–71
microhistory, 129, 136, 137
Military and Combat Work (MCW), 145, 146–153, 156, 158, 160, 166, 170, 171, 175–176, 180
mise-en-scene, 132
Mitchell, Clyde, 89
Mkatashinga, 21, 96, 208
Modern Youth Society, 28–29, 31, 33, 38; political education, 29, 31
Modise, Joe, 10, 17, 63
Modulo, Ernest, 67
Molapo, Rachidi, 133, 135, 137
Moloi, Sparks, 71
Molokoane, Barney, 213
monuments, 51
Morodi, Graham, 64, 67–68, 77, 80
Moshoeshoe, 213
Motlanthe, Kgalema, 113
Mozambique, 157, 159, 166; independence, 15
Mozambique Liberation Front (FRELIMO), 9, 15, 94
Mrabalala, Christopher, 52
Mtolo, Bruno, 7, 44
museums, 198
mutiny, 208, 211
Mzimela, Cletus, 67, 78

Namibia, 22, 140, 210, 232
naming, 139, 204–207
narrative history, xiv
National Democratic Revolution, xviii
national idea, xv
National Party, xxv, xxviii
National Prosecuting Authority (NPA), 218
National Security Management System (NSMS), 141
nationalism, xv, xx, xxix, xxx, 197, 199, 205, 217, 215–216

Index | 265

nationalist historiography, xiv–xv, xxix, xxviii, xxx, xxxi, xxxii, xxxv
natural history, 198–199, 214
Nboxele, Caswell, 31, 33–34, 36–40
Neto, Agostinho, 213
Ngoyi, Lilian, 213
Ngqungwana, Lizo, 158
Ngudle, Looksmart, 31, 34, 37
Nkosi, Leonard, 76
Nkrumah, Kwame, 5, 213
Nokwe, Duma, 6, 11
Non-European Unity Movement (NEUM), xx, 51
Nongqawuse, 214
nonracialism, 2–3, 12–13, 16, 37
Northern Ireland, 170
Nqaphayi, Teddington, 30, 64
Nqose, Zolile, 63–64, 70, 72, 75, 80
Nyanga Cultural and Social Organization, 28, 30–31, 38
Nyerere, Julius, 9, 213

oathing, 133, 165
official narratives, xxix, xxxv, 58, 209, 211
Operation Vula, 178, 180
oppositional histories, xxx, xxxi
oral history, 58, 134, xxii, xxix, xxvi
oral sources, 59, 87, xxiv, xxvi
oral testimony, xvii, xxiii, xxix, xxvi, xxvii, xxxiv, 49, 50, 52, 128–129, 131, 133–134, 137–138, 146, 154, 156, 159, 166; eyewitnesses, 49, 60, 70, 76, 80; life histories, xxiv; voice, 49
orality, xxiii, xxvi
organization, as historical actor, xxiii
Organization of African Unity (OAU), 6, 9
organizational history, xvi, xxiii, 134–135
Ozinsky, Max, 145, 149, 150, 158, 178, 179

Pan-African Freedom Movement for Eastern, Central, and Southern Africa (PAFMESCA), 5
Pan-Africanist Congress (PAC), xx, 3, 9–10
People's Movement for the Liberation of Angola (MPLA), 9, 15, 20
performance, 155
periodization, 132

Perrault, Gilles, 127–130, 153, 165, 167, 178
photography, 152–154
Piliso, Mzwai, 12, 16
plausible deniability, 141
poisoning, xiii, xxxiii, 19, 85–88, 92, 97–98, 100–101, 103, 105, 108–109, 112, 114, 116, 119, 120
polarization, xix, xvi, 59, 60
political violence, 132, 139, 141, 147, 170
positivism, xxxiv, 27, 134
post-apartheid, pessimism, xxix
postcolonialism, xxiv, xxix, xxv, xxvii, xxviii
poststructuralism, xxiv, xxix, xxv, xxvii
precolonial history, 199, 214–216
presentism, xix, xvi
prison diaries, 41–49; factography, 41–42, 48; romantic conventions, 42
professional historians, xxvii, xxviii, xxx, 49
propaganda, 59, 140, 160, 162, 163, 167–168, 170
Prussian blue, 109

Rabkin, David, 15, 157, 161–162, 164
Rabkin, Sue, 15, 147, 157, 159–164, 172
Radio Freedom, 21, 167
Rambo, John, 53
Rassool, Ciraj, xxvi
rationality, 112
Red Orchestra, The, 127–129, 155, 165, 167, 178
Reid-Daly, Ron, 75, 79
remains, reburial and repatriation, 210–212
representivity, 131, 136, 138, 156
repression, xvii, 4, 30, 132, 138–139, 141–142, 145, 148, 164
Resha, Robert, 16
resistance, xxxi, 127–129, 131–132, 139–140, 143, 145, 153; heroism, 128
Revolutionary Council (RC), 159, 160, 164
revolutionary theory, 148–150, 160
Rhodesia, xvii, 7, 140
Rhodesian African Rifles (RAR), 61, 68, 73–75, 79, 80
Rhodesian Army, 59
Rhodesian Bush War, xvii, xxxiii, 10, 12
ritual, 203, 210–212, 215
Riviere, Pierre, 31
Rivonia Trial (1963), 31, 32, 41
Robben Island, 107, 151, 158

rooi gevaar, 32
Roux, Eddie, xxx
rules of conspiracy, 40
rumor, 79

Sachs, Albie, 26, 40, 42, 44–48, 52, 94–95
sacred texts, 47–48
Sankara, Thomas, 213
Savimbi, Jonas, 20
school riots, 106–107
Schreiner, Jenny, 178
secularism, 212
Seekings, Jeremy, 134
Sekhukhune, 213
Selous Scouts, 75
Shabalala, Siboniso, 217–220
Shakespeare, William, 219–220
Sharpeville Massacre (1960), 3, 30
Shishita Report, 104
Shubin, Vladimir, 11, 146
Sikhumbuto (Wall of Names), 202–209
Simons, Jack, xxx, xxxiii, 88, 105–114
Simons, Ray, xxx
Simpson, Thula, 22
Sino-Soviet split, 8
Sishuba, Charles, 71
Sisulu, Walter, 43
sites of struggle, 141–143
Slovo, Joe, 13, 14, 43, 213
Sobukwe, Robert, 213
social history, xix, xxiv, xxix, xxv, xxvi, xxvii, xxviii, xxxiv, 131, 134–138, 179
soldiers' narratives, 59
Sono, Corlett Lolo, 217–220
South Africa: apartheid, 12; counterinsurgency, 140, 151, 152; destabilization, 20, 102; post-apartheid, 53; resistance, regionalism, 130; security state, 139–143, 145, 149, 152–153, 201; total strategy, 140, 143; transition to democracy, xxii, xxv, xxvii, xxxi, xxxii, 49
South African Air Force (SAAF), 19, 85, 93
South African Communist Party (SACP), xvii, xx, xxi, xxx, 3, 4, 8, 6, 12–15, 17, 44, 105, 113, 160, 161, 200
South African Defense Force (SADF), xxxv, 151, 166, 219

South African Democracy Education Trust (SADET), 58, 67, 70–72
South African National Defense Force (SANDF), 63, 113
South West Africa People's Organization (SWAPO), 9
Soviet Union, 6–8, 10–11, 13, 43, 51, 64, 68, 95, 107, 128, 140, 146–148, 150, 152, 180, 207
Soweto Generation, 85, 87, 96–97, 99, 107, 133, 146
Soweto Uprising (1976), xxiv, 15–17, 47–48, 106, 140–142, 146, 150, 164
Sparg, Marion, 112–113
Springbok Legion, 4
spy fiction, 155, 167
spying, xxi, xxxiii, 19, 20, 51, 85, 89, 94–99, 102–103, 108, 111, 128, 145, 201, 211, 218
SS Mendi, 206
State of Emergency (1985), 142, 145
state witnesses, 31, 33, 36, 163
statutory armies, 201, 205
Steiner, Peter, 42
strikes (1973), xxiv
structuralism, xxiv
struggle autobiographies, xviii
struggle history, x, xxix, xxxv, 72, 113, 129, 131, 133, 135, 137, 139, 143, 145, 153, 156, 179–180, 197, 202
Stuart Commission Report, 96
student activism, 158, 164
Suttner, Raymond, 15, 133, 135, 137, 179
Swanepoel, Theunis, 43, 48
swart gevaar, 32

Tabata, I. B., xxxi
Tambo, Oliver, 5, 6, 21, 80, 113, 167, 213
Tanganyika African National Union (TANU), 9
Tanzania, 9–11, 14, 17, 22, 78, 211–212
Tanzania, Dar es Salaam, 7, 9
Taylor, Dora, xxxi
Terrorism Act (1967), 76
thallium, 109
Thompson, Edward Palmer, xv, xxiii, xxv, xxvi, xxviii, xx, 134
Tladi, Peter (Lawrence Phokanoka), 79–80
Toivo ja Toivo, Herman Andimba, 29

torture, 31, 45, 91, 94, 100
trade unions, xx, 18, 160, 207
tradecraft (spycraft), 152, 148, 155, 163
Treason Trial (1956), 29, 32, 41
Trepper, Leopold, 167
Tricameral Parliament, 141–142
Trotskyism, xxxi, 50, 106
Truth and Reconciliation Commission (TRC), 86–87, 90–91, 101, 103–105, 139, 156, 197, 199, 205, 215, 217
Turok, Ben, 62
Twala, Mwezi, 1

Umkhonto we Sizwe: Angola, 17, 20, 85–114, 146, 153, 157; casualties, 62, 86, 99; code of conduct, 93–94, 98, 104; conventional war, 8; deaths, 206; deployment, 7, 14, 16, 61, 107, 108, 110–111, 149, 152, 166, 208; discipline, 88, 95, 107–108, 110–111; expulsion from Tanzania, 10; food poisoning, 109; formation, 4, 6; Funda Camp, 17; guerrilla war, 8, 10–11, 14, 18–19, 27, 32, 108; heroism and antiheroism, 43, 45, 51, 52, 65, 92, 113, 134, 179; Liliesleaf Farm, 7; Mamre, 26–53; Marxism, 5, 17, 107, 110; mutiny, 19, 21, 61, 86, 96–99, 208; Novo Catengue Camp, xxxiii, 17, 85–114, 123; Operation J, 14; Operation Mayibuye, 7; operations, 18, 143, 169; political education, xxxiii, 17, 39, 88, 106, 110, 142, 165–166; Quibaxe Camp, 20–21; rank-and-file, 61, 97, 108, 110, 135, 138, 146; recruitment, 166; Rivonia Trial (1963), 7; sabotage campaign, 4–5, 7, 30, 32; special operations, 108; training, 52, 68–71, 85, 88, 146, 149, 152–153, 166; training camps, 7–8, 10, 12, 16–17, 19–20, 26–53, 85–114, 146; tribunals, 90, 93–95, 98, 100, 103–104, 208, 211, 230
Umkhonto we Sizwe (MK), violence, 2
Umkhonto we Sizwe Military Veterans Association (MKMVA), xxxiv, 217
Umsebenzi, 160, 167
underground: Area Political-Military Committee (APC), 158; Cape Town, xxxiv, 15, 127–180; cellular structure, 164–165, 169; legends, 159–164, 178; organization, 164–165; recruitment, 165–168; training, 166
underground work, 153, 160–162, 164, 167

Uniao Nacional para a Independencia Total de Angola (UNITA), 20, 207
United Democratic Front (UDF), 134, 141–142, 144, 158, 165, 207
United Nations, 207
University of Cape Town, 158
University of the Western Cape, 157, 165–166
University of the Witwatersrand (Wits), History Workshop, xxiv, xxv, xxvii, xxviii, xxx
useful history, 16, 114, 202

Vaal Triangle Uprising (1984), 142, 150–151, 164
van Allen, Judith, 155
van Onselen, Charles, xxvi
Vena, Mzwandile, 178
Vesey, Denmark, 31–32
veterans, xxiii, xxxiii, xxxiv, 52–53, 64, 78, 203, 217
Victor Verster Prison, 166
Vietnam, 17, 60, 64, 140
vigilantes, 144–145
vignettes, 156–177
visuality, 59–60, 65, 67, 69, 71, 80, 163
Vlakplaas, 143
Volunteers (Amavoluntiya), 28–29, 31, 40
von den Steinen, Lynda, 133, 135, 137
von Ranke, Leopold, 136

Wankie Campaign, xiii–xiv, xvii, xxxiii, 10–12, 155, 58–80
war-in-the-head, 59–60, 76
weapons, 170
Whiggish history, xix, xx, 135–136
White, Luise, 101
whites, 151–152
Willie, Alfred, 67, 70
Wilson, Monica, 89
witchcraft, 88–90, 112
World War I, 205–206
World War II, 4, 8, 68, 127, 150, 179–180, 205
written sources, xxix, xxvi, xxvii, xxxiv, 27, 33, 49–50, 52, 59–60, 87, 90, 129–131, 133–134, 137–138, 148, 150, 156, 178

Yengeni, Tony, 178
Yutar, Percy, 32

Zambia, 10–11, 14, 17, 22, 64, 79–80, 98, 111, 211
Zimbabwe African National Union (ZANU), 95
Zimbabwe African People's Union (ZAPU), 9, 61
Zimbabwean People's Revolutionary Army (ZIPRA), xvii, 8, 10, 61, 63, 66, 77
Zulu, Thami, 99, 110
Zuma, Jacob, 214

STEPHEN R. DAVIS is Associate Professor of History at the University of Kentucky.

www.ingramcontent.com/pod-product-compliance
Lightning Source LLC
Chambersburg PA
CBHW070301240426
43661CB00057B/2609